A HISTORY OF CUBA

and its relations with **THE UNITED STATES**

Volume II

Leaders of the Cuban war of independence; Carlos de Céspedes, Máximo Gómez, Antonio Maceo and José Martí

A HISTORY OF CUBA

and its relations with THE UNITED STATES

by PHILIP S. FONER

Volume II   1845-1895

From the Era of Annexationism to the Outbreak of the Second War for Independence

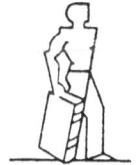

International Publishers · New York

This Printing 2020

Copyright © 1963 by International Publishers Co., Inc.
All rights reserved
Printed in the United States of America
ISBN 10: 0-7178-0861-0   ISBN 13: 978-0-7178-0861-8

PREFACE

In the first volume of *A History of Cuba and its Relations with the United States,* we traced the history of Cuba and of Cuban American relations from the discovery of Cuba and the conquest of the island by the Spanish *Conquistadores* to the mid-1840's. In the present volume, we pick up the story in 1845 and carry it forward another half century. We begin with an analysis of Cuban annexationism, discuss the efforts by the United States to annex Cuba, and trace the filibustering movements of the 1850's in which Southern slaveholding elements, determined to expand slavery, played a major role. After describing the failure of annexationism and discussing the reasons for its decline, we turn to the reform movement in Cuba and the outbreak of the War for Independence in 1868. In the chapters devoted to this long, heroic struggle, the reader will meet the *mambises,* those early guerrillas, white and Negro, ragged and half starving, many armed only with machetes, who roamed for ten years over mountains and plains, wearing down Spain's impressive military might. Their struggle for independence was seriously retarded by internal dissensions and by the anti-Cuban independence role played by the government of the United States, in opposition to the will of the American people.

Though the Cubans lost their first War for Independence, they had laid the groundwork for final victory. Revolutionary activity did not cease after 1878. The final chapters trace this story up to the beginning of the Second War for Independence in 1895.

Out of all these struggles three individuals especially emerge as significant figures not only in the history of Cuba and Latin America, but in world history: José Martí, "the Apostle," Máximo Gómez, the Dominican leader of the Cuban Liberating Army, and Antonio Maceo, the Negro independence fighter. Martí is known to students in the United States, though insufficiently so, and there are occasional references to Gómez in American history books. But Maceo is practically an unknown figure. Even in Cuba, where there is a large body of writings published on Maceo, including his correspondence, he is too often, as a Cuban scholar recently noted, regarded "solely as a great warrior, a man of action but not of ideas." (José Antonio Portuondo, editor, *El Pensamiento Vivo de*

Maceo, La Habana, 1962, p. 7.) The reader will quickly learn that the "Bronze Titan" (as Maceo is known) made a vast contribution to Cuba's heritage of social and political ideas as well as to her revolutionary military tradition.

In the first volume, we pointed out that contemporary Cuban development cannot be clearly understood unless the past is kept firmly in mind. This is especially true of contemporary Cuban-American relations. Therefore we have placed considerable emphasis on the role of the United States in the island's affairs.

In the preparation of this volume I have consulted a wide variety of sources in English and Spanish. They are so numerous that lack of space forbids a full list of references, while a selected one would have a doubtful value. I have, therefore, cited only sources for quoted material. I will be happy to furnish, upon request, specific sources for statements not indicated in the reference notes.

In writing this book I have received most generous help. I wish to acknowledge my indebtedness for facilities placed at my disposal by the Archivo Nacional, Havana, the National Archives, Washington, D.C., the Library of Congress, the Mississippi Department of Archives and History, and the libraries of Harvard University, Columbia University, Duke University, Northwestern University, University of North Carolina, University of Texas, University of Chicago, University of California, University of Virginia, and Yale University. Mrs. Louise Heinze, librarian of the Tamiment Institute Library, and the staff of the Library, were again especially helpful in obtaining material through interlibrary loans. Dr. Julio Girona of Havana was again extremely helpful in obtaining important documents, articles, and books from libraries, public and private, in Cuba. And my wife, Roslyn Held Foner, was again of tremendous assistance in translating sources from the Spanish, preparing the manuscript for publication, and reading the proofs.

PHILIP S. FONER

Croton-on-Hudson, New York
April, 1963

CONTENTS

	PREFACE	5
CHAPTER 1	The Cuban Annexationists	9
CHAPTER 2	The Inglorious Attempt to Purchase Cuba	20
CHAPTER 3	The Debate Over Cuba	30
CHAPTFR 4	The Filibusters: Narciso López	41
CHAPTER 5	Filibusters and Capitalists	66
CHAPTER 6	The "Africanization of Cuba" Scare	75
CHAPTER 7	The Quitman Expedition	86
CHAPTER 8	"Manifesto of the Brigands"	96
CHAPTER 9	Last of the Filibusters	106
CHAPTER 10	End of the Annexationist Era	116
CHAPTER 11	Cuba During the American Civil War	125
CHAPTER 12	Birth of Cuban Working-Class Consciousness	136
CHAPTER 13	High Hopes for Reform	149
CHAPTER 14	Failure of Reform and Outbreak of the War for Independence	162
CHAPTER 15	The Ten Years' War: The Early Phase, 1868–1869	174
CHAPTER 16	The Ten Years' War: The War Unfolds, 1869–1870	184
CHAPTER 17	The United States and the Independence of Cuba, 1868–1869	198
CHAPTER 18	The United States and the Independence of Cuba, 1869–1870	212
CHAPTER 19	The Ten Years' War: The Middle Phase, 1871–1875	224
CHAPTER 20	The United States and the Independence of Cuba, 1871–1875	240

8 · *Contents*

CHAPTER 21	*The Ten Years' War: The Final Phase, 1875–1878*	253
CHAPTER 22	*The Little War*	276
CHAPTER 23	*Political, Economic and Social Developments in Cuba, 1878–1895*	289
CHAPTER 24	*Revolutionary Activity, 1884–1890*	305
CHAPTER 25	*The Cuban Revolutionary Party*	318
CHAPTER 26	*The Menace of American Imperialism*	332
CHAPTER 27	*The Second War for Independence Begins*	347
	REFERENCE NOTES	360
	INDEX	379

chapter 1

THE CUBAN ANNEXATIONISTS

The movement in Cuba for annexation to the United States began as early as 1810, when representatives of the wealthy planters entered secret negotiations with the U.S. Consul in Havana. In the interests of preserving the slave system, they were ready, they informed him, to organize an annexationist conspiracy, provided the United States guaranteed support against British intervention, as well as against Spain. No such guarantee being forthcoming, the movement collapsed; but it revived in 1821 when, again, to preserve slavery against abolitionist proposals in the Spanish Cortes, the Cuban planters sent an agent to Washington to propose annexation to the United States. Nothing came of this project either. The government of the United States, considering the project premature, preferred to wait until conditions grew more promising. Meanwhile, its policy was to let Cuba remain in the possession of Spain, to block independence movements in the island and plans to transfer it to a foreign power, while refusing to commit the United States to any future self-denial. Its policy was thus characterized by the Congress of Cuban Historians in 1947: "To be for Spain until Cuba could belong to the United States, but never for the Cubans."[1]

With the exclusion of Cuba from the liberal Cortes of 1834–37, dashing the hopes of the Cuban reformers, and under the iron-handed rule of Tacón, a revival of annexationist sentiment developed. This was further stimulated by the publication, in 1837, of José Antonio Saco's powerful essay, *Paralelo entre la isla de Cuba y algunas colonias inglesas* (Parallel between the Island of Cuba and Some English Colonies), in which the exiled spiritual and intellectual leader of Cuban liberalism unfavorably compared the administration of Cuba with that of Canada, and debunked the Spanish

9

myth, propagated by the *Peninsulares*, that the island was the most happily governed of colonies. But there was one statement in the essay that seemed to point the way for Cuba: "If Cuba, degraded by circumstances, should have to throw herself into foreign arms, in none could she fall with more honor or glory than in those of the great North American Confederation [the United States]. In them she would find peace and consolation, strength and protection, justice and liberty."[2]

Nevertheless, in 1837 the Creole planters were not united behind the movement to annex the island to the United States. It took the slave uprisings of 1842-44 to frighten enough planters to make the annexation movement a significant force. The fear that the Spanish government would continue weak under British abolitionist pressure roused such alarm in Cuba, that a large percentage of the slaveowners looked toward junction with the slaveholding power in the United States as the only safeguard for the continuance of the institution.

Annexationist agitation was carried on both in Cuba and the United States. In Cuba, the movement was promoted by the formation of the *Club de la Habana* (Havana Club), largely composed of wealthy sugar planters. Among its members were Miguel Aldama, in whose palace the club held its meetings; José Antonio Echeverría; Cristóbal Madan y Madan, planter, merchant, and shipowner; and the American, John S. Thrasher, a resident of Havana and editor of *El Faro Industrial*, a Cuban trade journal. There was also a scattering of writers, professionals and other intellectuals, among them the novelist, Cirilo Villaverde; but the organization was dominated by the slaveholders.

Two other centers of annexationist activity existed: In Puerto Príncipe, led by Gaspar Betancourt Cisneros, generally known as *El Lugareño* (the Hick), and the "Conspiracy of the Cuban Rose Mines" in Matanzas and Las Villas, dominated by General Narciso López, one of the most controversial figures in Cuban history. There have been those who, like the Cuban historian, Herminio Portell Vilá, have insisted that the group led by López sought independence, but the evidence produced at the hearings of the arrested conspirators demonstrates that annexation to the United States was its aim.

Under the tyrannical rule of Tacón in 1837, many Cuban patriots, proscribed for their liberal views and their opposition to his despotism, fled to the United States. By the mid-forties, groups had established themselves in New York, New Orleans, and the ports of Florida. The New York group, led by Gaspar Betancourt Cisneros, José Aniceto Iznaga, and Cristóbal Madan, became, during the 1840's, the most active in promoting the annexationist cause. In 1847, the *Consejo Cubano* or Cuban Council was organized in New York with Madan, representing the Havana Club, as president. On January 1, 1848, its organ, *La Verdad* (The Truth) began publication. Subsidized partly by wealthy Cubans and partly by Moses Yale Beach, pro-annexationist editor of the New York *Sun* who arranged to have it printed without cost on the press of the *Sun*, it was circulated free of charge. Published in English and partly in Spanish, *La Verdad* spread the views and news of Cuban annexationists both in the United States and Cuba. It was banned in Cuba by the Captain General, but was smuggled into the island on trading vessels, and had a wide circulation there.

What influenced these Cuban exiles to fix their hopes on annexation to the United States?

Some were undoubtedly swayed by their personal experience of life in the United States, where they were infected by the "go-ahead spirit" and "get-rich doctrines" of American merchants and politicians. Due to the poor educational facilities in the island, most wealthy Cuban families sent their sons to be educated in the United States, where the young men were impressed by its institutions and prosperity. They returned to Cuba to make unfavorable comparisons of Havana with New York, imbued with new ideas which, as Captain General Concha observed in his *Memoria* of 1851, "naturally . . . must be unfavorable to Peninsular interests." Many, on their return to the island, worked actively for incorporation of Cuba into the United States. The custom of educating wealthy Cuban sons in the United States proved so great an influence toward Cuban annexation that it was banned in 1849. General Concha explained, "the young men . . . return to their country with revolutionary ideas, which they spread among relatives, friends and acquaintances."[3] Thereafter a Cuban youth could receive an education in North America only by subterfuge.

The desire for the removal of Spanish restrictions on commerce and industry and increased economic relations with the United States, played an important part in the annexationist drive. The rapid decline of the coffee industry, the poor sugar harvests of the mid-forties, and resentment over the exclusion by Spain of Cuban products from the American market, produced widespread discontent and stimulated annexationist sentiment. The Cuban sugar planters wanted duty-free sugar imports into the United States in return for essential goods, rid of burdensome tariffs. The United States was Cuba's principal market and her main source of imports. Spain hampered the normal process of this trade, and the best solution seemed to be annexation. It is significant that important members of the Havana Club were engaged in the trade between Cuba and the United States. "They expected great commercial and industrial advantages when Cuba became a member of the Union."[4]

Included in this group were foreign owners of property and businessmen in Cuba, primarily Americans. In the absence of banks in Cuba, American entrepreneurs made cash advances to sugar planters, and thus gained a huge stake in the prosperity of that key sector of the economy. In the early 'forties, the only sugar refinery on the island was owned by an American. As sugar plantations replaced horse power with steam power, American factories supplied much of the machinery, and American technicians swarmed throughout the island. Many plantations were already American-owned.

The city of Havana was lighted with gas by a New Orleans capitalist in 1844, and in 1849 Americans obtained the telegraph concessions. The first Cuban railroad was completed in 1838 by an American engineer with English funds. By the 1840's, American capitalists were associated with members of the Havana Club, such as Aldama and Echeverría, in the expansion of Cuban railroads. And, like these Cuban leaders, the American capitalists in Cuba had a dazzling vision of the enhanced opportunities for economic development of the island once it was annexed to the United States and freed from the restrictions and tyranny of Spanish rule.

Distinguished from the "annexationists for economic reasons," were those whom Herminio Portell Vilá calls "annexationists for patriotic reasons." These, he says, were Cubans who wished to escape Spanish rule but did not believe this possible without the assistance of the United States. Feeling that independence was unobtainable, they considered union with the neighbor to the north the next best thing. But this union would only be temporary, for "with the end of colonial despotism, and, as soon as the admission of the new state caused internal difficulties in the North American Union, they would be able to devote themselves with facility to the creation of the republic of which they dreamed."[5]

It is true that the motives of the Cuban annexationists were not all the same. But to attribute "patriotic motives" to the annexationists is to draw a veil over more sordid motives. There is no evidence that the annexationists thought of union with the United States as a temporary alliance. On the contrary, their literature abounds in statements pointing to the blessings Cuba would enjoy as a permanent member of the American Union. To be sure, the literature also contains many references to their struggle for the "independence" of Cuba. But, as Ramiro Guerra points out: "The word independence did not mean anything in the 1840's except separation from Spain and incorporation in the United States."[6] José María Sánchez Iznaga, writing of the "Conspiracy of the Cuban Rose Mines" with which he was associated, said: "Once the provisional government is installed and independence is recognized by the great American Republic, our next step will be to ask for annexation."[7]

The Cuban annexationists wanted to follow the example of Texas. The anti-slavery policy of the Mexican government, they thought, was a primary cause of the American slaveholder residents in Texas revolting against Mexico, and establishing Texan independence with ultimate annexation to the United States. The Cuban annexationists planned to pursue the same course, and one group, led by the Count of Pozos Dulces, brother-in-law of Narciso López, organized the "Order of the Lone Star" with that intent. They felt that they had the same reasons to act as did the Texans, chiefly the preservation of slavery.

It was this desire which united Cuban annexationists regardless of other motives, and that brought Creole planters and Spanish businessmen together. The Creole sugar mill operators and the *Peninsulares* in their counting houses had a common stake in preserving the slave system, whatever their differences might be on other issues. Saco, noting this phenomenon, observed that "there is nothing which unites opinions more than identity of interests."[8]

The influence of the Revolution of 1848 in Europe further intensified the annexationist feeling. At first, there was enthusiasm among the annexationists over the initial success of republicanism against tyranny. But when the new regime in France liberated all slaves in overseas possessions, including the West Indies islands, Martinique and Guadaloupe, the cry changed to one of alarm. The republican cause in Spain was even then gaining momentum, and it appeared that Spain might follow the French example and free the slaves.

These events brought the Cuban planters and the Spanish merchants still closer together on the issue of annexation. They were convinced that the British government would use the occasion to increase pressure on Spain to abolish slavery in the island. Relations between the two countries had been ruptured and war seemed imminent. Since Spain's defeat by England was regarded as inevitable, the Cuban slave interests feared that the first step the victor would take would be to abolish slavery in Cuba. Only annexation to the United States promised a way out. Thus Gaspar Betancourt Cisneros wrote in 1848: "The English cabinet asked several years ago that liberty be given to all the slaves introduced into Cuba since 1820; and as it is very much to be feared that she will renew her request and that Spain will consent to it, the annexationist revolution is indispensable for saving us."[9]

Clearly, Cuban annexationism had, as its chief objective, to save slavery through incorporation of Cuba into the United States. Other motives were secondary. It was the fear of losing their slaves and the profits from slavery that united *hacendados* and Spaniards behind the annexationist movement. *La Verdad* frankly admitted as much. In an editorial, probably written by Cisneros, it declared on March 1, 1849: "The annexationist party is united in its essential point— that of annexationism to the United States. Some expect more; others less, in favor of their particular interests, but the majority of the annexationists are for the political change to assure the property of their slaves."[10] Once the island was part of the North American union, the danger of British abolitionist pressure would end since the government of the United States, dominated by the slaveowners and their northern allies, would certainly rebuff British diplomatic suggestions to end slavery in Cuba. Nor was there any doubt in the minds of the Cuban annexationists that the United States would leap to defend their slave property. Was not the United States refusing effective co-operation with Great Britain in the closing of the slave trade?* Had not the American minister to France, Lewis Cass, been instrumental in causing that country to repudiate, in 1845, an earlier agreement giving Britain the right to search French vessels? Had not the British abolitionist, McCauley, denounced the United States in Parliament on February 26, 1845, as the "patron and champion of Negro slavery all over the world?"[11] Was it not wise, then, to ally Cuba with such a powerful defender of slavery? Then American military strength would be available to crush any mass uprising of the slaves, since a successful insurrection in Cuba would have profound repercussions on the slave system in the United States.

The anti-annexationist Cuban slave interests conceded that annexation offered such possibilities. But they considered the risks too great. Revolutionary action accompanying annexation could start formidable slave uprisings, or induce Spain to seek the Negroes as allies by liberating them. Under the circumstances, the best way to preserve slavery was to prevent the annexation movement from making headway.

Saco conceded that he had supported annexation as long as it could be accomplished peacefully and with Spain's consent, for this would guarantee that tranquillity would prevail on the plantations. (This approach reveals that Saco, like the annexationists, was dominated by the interests and values of slavocracy.) But he had become doubtful that annexation could be accomplished peacefully. "How can we be assured," he asked the annexationists, "that a war for annexation would not be the one certain way of losing our slaves?" In a letter from his exile home in Paris, March 10, 1848, Saco appealed to Cisneros to abandon his annexationist activities lest he produce precisely what he was seeking to avoid—the liberation of the slaves. "Would not [the Spanish government] if it felt itself weak call to its aid the Negroes, arming them and giving them liberty? . . . Would not England give her provisions and those black

---

* By the Webster-Ashburton Treaty of 1842, the United States promised only to station a force of 88 guns on the African coast, but it did not concede the right of search to Great Britain.

soldiers [from Jamaica] who would fully sympathize with our own Negroes? She could count on the Spaniards because she would be defending the interests of their government, and on the Negroes, for they know that she has given them liberty while the United States holds them in hard captivity. No, Gaspar, no, in the name of heaven! Let us put away such destructive thoughts." Rather let the Cubans endure "the yoke of Spain" heroically, meanwhile work to end the slave trade; "diminish without violence or injustice" the number of slaves in the island, increase white immigration, all in the hope that "Cuba, our beloved Cuba, shall some day be Cuba indeed."[12]

Cisneros refused to heed Saco, but he recognized that the argument the exiled leader raised reflected widespread fear among the Cuban *hacendados*. Hence he issued a proclamation on April 20, 1848, signed *"unos cubanos,"* which had a wide circulation in Cuba. It acknowledge that the Cuban slaveowners feared either that Spain, threatened by annexation, would liberate the slaves and use the Negroes as allies, or that the slaves, in the confusion of the conflict, would make a break for liberty. But the proclamation pointed reassuringly to Jamaica where, in 1832, a slave insurrection was easily crushed although the proportion was nearly eight Negroes to one white inhabitant. In Cuba in 1848 there were 418,291 whites and 619,333 Negroes. Such a number of white inhabitants could easily keep in subjection the unarmed and unorganized slaves. Having dismissed this major objection to annexationism, the proclamation asked: "What is a Cuban today?" It answered: "A slave, politically, morally, physically." On the other hand, what would Cuba be if annexed to the United States?

> Cuba united to this strong and respected nation, whose Southern interests would be identified with hers, would be assured quiet and future success; her wealth would increase, doubling the value of her farms and slaves, trebling that of her whole territory; liberty would be given to individual action, and the system of hateful and harmful restrictions which paralyzed commerce and agriculture would be destroyed.

The proclamation concluded with an appeal to Cubans to join the annexationist cause, and for Cuban leaders to "guide public opinion on the path which an imperious necessity advises and which philanthropy and reason demand to save the country."[13]

The last appeal was directed especially to Saco, who remained unmoved. Instead, he decided to make his views public. His famous pamphlet, *Ideas sobre la incorporación de Cuba en los Estados Unidos* (Ideas on the Incorporation of Cuba into the United States) was published in Paris on November 1, 1848, and immediately gained a wide circulation in Cuba. Saco elaborated the view that he desired political liberty for Cuba, but annexationism was not the way to attain it. The triumph of annexationism would not result in a Cuba for the Cubans but one dominated by foreigners. For, in a few years, an immigration of North Americans would inundate the island—men with a different language, different customs, and a different national outlook. Since it would be impossible for two cultures so opposed to fuse, one must prevail over the other. Inevitably the North Americans, by reason of their swelling population, their surging expansionism and their greater political experience, would impose their will over Cuba. In that event, Cubans would be permanently converted into an oppressed minority within their own country.

This, Saco said, he could not tolerate. He wanted the island to be "Cuban and not *Anglo-Saxon*." Hence he pleaded with his countrymen not to sell their birthright for the chimera of American incorporation. Referring to the hopes that had sustained him through 15 years of exile, Saco protested that he would find it a greater unhappiness to live as a foreigner in his own country under the American flag. "The day that I throw myself into a revolution . . . it will be for my own country."*

Secondly, Saco again raised the danger that the struggle for annexation would end in the liberation of the slaves who would either take advantage of the conflict between the whites to gain their own freedom, or gain it through their liberation by Spain as the price of their aid against the secessionists, a move which would have the support of England. Moreover, if the annexationists faced defeat, they might themselves have to call for the help of Negro slaves. Hence Saco warned his slaveholding friends in Cuba, who were sup-

---

* For his epitaph Saco wrote: "Here lies José Antonio Saco who was not an annexationist because he was more Cuban than all the annexationists." (José Antonio Saco, *Contra la Anexión: Colección de Libros Cubanos*, compiled by Fernando Ortiz, Havana, 1928, vol. II, p. cxliii.)

porting the annexationist cause, that they were digging their own graves, since the sole result of an annexationist insurrection would be the abolition of slavery.[14]

Saco's pamphlet fell upon the annexationists like a "thunderbolt burst on a picnic."[15] They knew that, commanding as he did the confidence and respect of his countrymen, his pamphlet would be widely read, and would dampen the enthusiasm for annexation in many *hacendados*. Hence they made haste to rebut Saco's arguments. Through the years 1848–52, Saco was engaged in a polemical war of pamphlets and letters with Betancourt, Madan, Ramón de Palma, and other annexationists.

The latter concentrated their main fire on Saco's arguments that annexation would threaten slavery in Cuba. In a lengthy article in *La Verdad*, Cisneros cited a number of arguments against Saco's position that the annexation struggle would provoke a successful uprising of the Negroes and end slavery. Cisneros concluded his refutation:

> Do not desire, then, fellow patriot, to intimidate us by mere phantoms. . . . The Negroes, the Negroes! Here is the bugbear with which the government [of Spain] intimidates us, and holds us in check. Like as to children they call out to us: *"Be quiet, for if you do not, I'll set the Negroes on to you!"* Cowardly threat! which at once reveals their own baseness, and the real fears on their part. If the government felt strong, it would not make use of artifice, of vain and foolish threats. If the government of Cuba should be capable of employing in Cuba the means it has employed in other parts of America, *an army* of fifty thousand Americans would immediately land in Cuba to the assistance of the white population.

But these pleas of the annexationists could not overcome Saco's arguments. Too many Cuban slaveowners knew that Saco was not raising "phantoms." Dionisio Alcalá Galiano, Director of the pro-Spanish *Diario de la Marina*, published in Havana, pointed out in 1858 that the wealthy planters had learned, during the annexationist fervor of the late 'forties, that Spain had decided to abolish slavery the moment an insurrection to join Cuba to the United States erupted, that this had convinced them of the soundness of Saco's arguments, and had converted many adherents of annexationism into its opponents.

Galiano was referring to a communication from the Count of Alcoy, Captain General of Cuba, to the Secretary of State in Spain, dated September 29, 1849, knowledge of which came to the attention of the *hacendados*. This letter pointed out the policy Spain should follow in Cuba to frustrate and smash the annexationist drive:

> Emancipation would be the ruin of the proprietors and merchants of the island. It would put an end to the only means of preventing the island's falling to the annexationists. What should then be the conduct of the Captain General in respect to slavery? As for myself, Your Excellency, I maintain the conviction that the terrible weapon [a decree of emancipation] could, in the last extreme, prevent the loss of the island, and if the inhabitants convince themselves that it will be used, they will tremble and renounce every illusion before bringing upon themselves such an anathema.[16]

By leaking the contents of the communication to men like Galiano, Alcoy made sure that the *hacendados* would "convince themselves" that the ultimate weapon would be used by Spanish authorities in Cuba. At the same time, they were made aware that if they remained loyal subjects, these authorities would sustain and protect slavery. All this lent weight to Saco's arguments, and he was to see his appeal against annexation gain more and more followers. By the end of the decade of the 'forties, many enthusiastic supporters of annexationism among the Cuban slaveowners had joined Saco's camp, agreeing with the exiled leader that continued alliance with Spain would serve their interests better than annexation to the United States, and that a move toward annexation would threaten the very existence of the slave system.

The remaining Cuban annexationists continued their polemics against Saco. But their hopes of convincing the *hacendados* and businessmen in the island were waning. More and more they looked to the slaveholding interests in the United States for aid in achieving their goal. Thus, by 1850, annexationism became less and less a Cuban movement and more and more a drive of interests in the United States.

chapter 2

THE INGLORIOUS ATTEMPT TO PURCHASE CUBA

In 1848, the United States signed the Treaty of Guadalupe Hidalgo with Mexico, which ended the two years' Mexican War. According to President Polk, it had been fought to protect Texas and "to vindicate with decision the honor, the rights, and the interests of our country," but the New England Workingmen's Association characterized it, in 1846, as a war to "plunder Mexican soil for the United States officers, slaveholders and speculators to convert into a mart for traffic in human blood and human rights."[1] In the treaty, the United States acquired, in addition to Texas and California, the huge area then called New Mexico, which included the present Nevada and Utah. Altogether, the United States came out of the Mexican War with a gain of about 918,000 square miles, including the treasure house of gold discovered in California just as the treaty was ratified.

Nevertheless, the appetite of the slaveowner-dominated, land-hungry Polk administration was only whetted by the feast. Its adherents began to look for other territory to acquire. For a while their hungry eyes were attracted to Yucatan and Jamaica, but their real interest lay in the "Pearl of the Antilles." In the Senate, the aged John C. Calhoun, dismissing any venture in Yucatan, a land unsuited for the crops which depended on slaves for their cultivation, went on to the subject dear to his slaveholder's heart. "There are cases of interposition," he declared, "when I would resort to the hazard of war with all its calamities. Am I asked for one? I will answer. I designate the case of Cuba." Two contingencies, said Calhoun, would justify such a step. One, a transfer of the island from Spain to some country other than the United States; second, if Spain, under English pressure, were to liberate the slaves and thus create a terrible hazard for the Southern states.[2]

The acquisition of Cuba would eliminate both dangers. It would also provide the slaveholders with a source of slaves, and an area into which they might expand their plantation, staple-crop agricultural system. Further, by adding one or two more slave states to the Union, it would strengthen the political power of the South in the government.

But how was Cuba to be acquired? There were three possible ways: by purchase; by seizing the island in an invasion, or by war with Spain. (An anti-annexationist American reduced it to two ways. He wrote: "There are two modes of getting it [Cuba]. One is by purchase. . . . The other is by robbery."[3])

The first method, that of buying Cuba, was logical. For one thing, the peaceful transfer of Cuba to the United States by purchase would avoid the danger either of a slave insurrection or a declaration of emancipation by Spain, which were the risks in the other two methods. For another, it would give the United States immediate control over the island, and reduce the bargaining power of the Cuban annexationists to impose limiting conditions on the joining of Cuba with the Union.

The first proposal to purchase Cuba was made by Senator Yulee of Florida in 1845. This was in the form of a resolution in the U.S. Senate. It was generally agreed, however, in 1845, that the time was not appropriate to pursue the matter, and Yulee withdrew his resolution before it came up for debate. In 1847, a plan for buying Cuba was advanced by a New Yorker who proudly called himself a pro-slavery man," John L. O'Sullivan, editor of the *Democratic Review*, coiner of the phrase "Manifest Destiny," and brother-in-law of Cristóbal Madan, the wealthy Cuban annexationist. Working closely with O'Sullivan was Moses Yale Beach of the New York *Sun*. Both men visited Cuba early in 1847, and attended meetings of the Havana Club, whose members urged President Polk to buy Cuba from Spain and thereby "liberate the island without danger of internal disorder and secure their property rights, especially in slaves, as firmly as they were guaranteed in the South."[4] The wealthy Cubans were ready to back up their words with money, pledging as much as $100,000,000 to a fund which the United States could use to pay Spain for the island.

On their return to the United States, O'Sullivan and Beach began separate campaigns to promote the purchase plan. On July 6, 1847, O'Sullivan sent a memorandum to Secretary of State James Buchanan reporting his meetings at the Havana Club, assuring him that wealthy Cubans, fearing a slave insurrection, did not want to be independent, and were prepared to contribute a huge sum toward purchase by the United States. O'Sullivan urged Buchanan to recommend the plan to President Polk, and offered to go to Madrid as an unpaid agent, to sound out the Spanish government.

Meanwhile, Beach's New York *Sun* was beating the drums for the purchase plan. Under the headline, "Cuba Under the Flag of the United States," the *Sun's* editorial (July 23, 1847) cried: "Cuba must be ours. . . . Give us Cuba and our possessions are complete." The Southern press took up the cry, and once the Mexican War was over and the treaty of peace signed, voiced it ever more loudly. "We have New Mexico and California! We will have old Mexico and Cuba," triumphantly cried J. B. De Bow, the pro-slavery proprietor of *De Bow's Review*. He complained that Cuba, a favorable area for the expansion of slavery, was being "unnaturally and arbitrarily separated from the South."[5]

Early in 1848, the organ of the Cuban émigrés, *La Verdad*, also urged immediate negotiations for purchase with Spain. On April 27, 1848, it advised Cubans to be ready to cast themselves into "the strong, friendly and protecting arms of the Union."

In Congress, too, the cry "Cuba must be ours" was heard. Southern Senators and Congressmen insisted that increased British pressure on Spain to abolish slavery in the island required immediate action. To prevent emancipation in Cuba, "the island must be ours," said Senator Jefferson Davis of Mississippi. Senator Westcott of Florida agreed. Britain, he said,

> . . . seeks to emancipate the slaves in Cuba, and to strike the southern portion of this Confederacy through its domestic institutions. . . . Are the southern States of this Confederacy prepared to see the slaves in Cuba emancipated by the efforts of Great Britain? . . . My State will not assent to such a state of things. . . . Why, sir, Florida would

be surrounded by the cordon of foreign colonial governments, the population of which would be emancipated slaves, under the control of the worst enemy of the United States.[6]

On May 10, 1848, Senator Lewis Cass of Michigan, a Northern "doughface"—i.e., a Northerner anxious to please and appease the Southern slaveholders—proposed the purchase of Cuba. On that same day, O'Sullivan and Stephen A. Douglas, Senator from Illinois, met with President Polk on the same subject. (Buchanan had not responded to O'Sullivan's memorandum, so the New Yorker went directly to Polk with his grand scheme.) Polk listened attentively but promised nothing, confiding to his diary that he favored purchase.

On May 30, Polk proposed the purchase of Cuba to his cabinet—on terms outlined by O'Sullivan and Beach who, in turn, were following the plan of the wealthy planters of the Havana Club. Robert J. Walker, Secretary of the Treasury and John Y. Mason, Secretary of the Navy, both Southerners, favored the move, and expressed willingness to pay a huge sum for the island. But Cave Johnson, Attorney General from Tennessee, opposed the venture, and Secretary of State Buchanan from Pennsylvania pretended to be in favor, but urged caution lest the proposal to acquire more territory hurt Democratic chances in the November elections. Polk was undismayed, and he pressed the subject at subsequent Cabinet meetings. Each time Buchanan voiced his antagonism, arguing that annexation would involve the United States in a war with England or France.

Polk kept up the pressure. He did not believe Buchanan was sincere; indeed, he told O'Sullivan he thought Buchanan was opposing the purchase of Cuba only as long as he, Polk, was President. This was a shrewd observation, for the acquisition of Cuba had already become an ambition of Buchanan's; but he wanted it to count as the achievement of *his* administration when he became President.

Little by little Buchanan yielded to Presidential pressure. Finally, on July 17, 1848, he agreed, without taking any responsibility himself, to accord full power to the American Minister to Madrid, Romulus M. Saunders, to negotiate the purchase of Cuba for a sum of up to $100,000,000.

What had finally produced the decision in Washington? To

understand this, we must turn our attention to developments in Cuba.

While the Cabinet in Washington had been debating whether or not to make the purchase offer, the Cubans had been acting on their own to accelerate annexation. On May 18, 1848, General Robert B. Campbell, U.S. Consul at Havana, informed Buchanan that a revolt led by a Spanish general would soon break out in the island, and if successful, "immediate application would be made to the United States for annexation."[7] Campbell did not name the general, but it was evidently Narciso López, who had been intriguing since 1843 for Cuba's separation from Spain and its annexation to the United States. Campbell had close contact with López, and, although the American Consul stressed U.S. neutrality laws and treaty obligations, the general was convinced that he could count on assistance from Washington in his conspiracy.

López had timed his uprising for June 29, 1848, when the festival of Saints Peter and Paul would permit public gatherings. It was to begin at Cienfuegos, and be spread by his supporters in provincial towns throughout the island. In the meanwhile, the wealthy Havana Club was not idle. Despairing of action by Washington to purchase the island, the Club sent an agent, Rafael de Castro, to Jalapa, Mexico, to offer General William Jenkins Worth and 5,000 of his men, veterans of the Mexican War, $3,000,000 to invade Cuba and drive out the Spanish garrison, to prepare the way for annexation to the United States. According to available evidence, Worth accepted the offer, contingent upon the resignation of his commission in the U.S. Army.

While negotiations were being conducted with Worth, the Havana Club asked López to postpone the date of his uprising until the American expeditionary force arrived. López fretted over being subordinated to Worth and the Havana Club, but on assurances by General Campbell, he acquiesced. Since López agreed with the Club on annexation once the Spanish authorities were overthrown, he had no reason not to co-operate. The date of his uprising was postponed to the middle of July, and he returned to the provinces to await instructions from the Havana Club.

Not all aspects of the maneuverings in Cuba were reported to Washington, but from Campbell, O'Sullivan, and others the administration learned enough of the plans for an uprising and of the agreement with Worth, to become alarmed. An uprising in Cuba, coupled with an invasion by an American expeditionary force, might precipitate what the Southern annexationists were anxious to prevent—either a slave insurrection or a decree from Spanish authorities liberating the slaves and arming the Negroes. Moreover, it was bound to disrupt the administration's efforts to purchase the island.

From its discussion, Polk's Cabinet came up with a strategy that would block the plans of the Cubans while demonstrating good faith to Madrid, which would be assured that the United States had Spain's best interests in mind in the proposal to purchase the island. General Butler in Mexico was ordered by Secretary of War Walker to prevent any Cuban expedition; strict orders were issued that no vessel with troops from Mexico should touch at Cuba, and Worth was recalled from Mexico. Campbell was instructed by Secretary of State Buchanan to warn the Cubans that "an unsuccessful uprising would delay, if it should not defeat, the annexation of the island to the United States," and that since the aid of American volunteer troops could not be obtained, the revolt had little chance of success. The Consul himself should do nothing to encourage such a movement but should remain strictly neutral. Copies of these documents were transmitted to Minister Saunders in Madrid to show the Spanish government.[8]

Nor was this all. Buchanan, whose earlier reluctance to approve the purchase of Cuba had disappeared with the realization that speed was essential, decided to earn Spain's everlasting gratitude by betraying the López conspiracy to Calderón de la Barca, Spanish Minister at Washington, and to Captain General Roncali through Campbell, the American Consul at Havana. Thus alerted, the Spanish authorities moved against López and his fellow conspirators. López, warned through a friend of Campbell, escaped on a small sailing vessel, the *Neptune*, bound for Providence, Rhode Island, where we will pick up his story later. A number of López's leading supporters were not so fortunate. They were captured and imprisoned. López himself was condemned *in absentia* to be shot. At the trial of López and his colleagues, it was brought out by witness after witness that "the object of the project [the 'Conspiracy of the Cuban Rose Mines'] was annexation to the United States."[9]

On August 15, Calderón revealed to Pedro J. Pidal, the Spanish Minister of State, that it was Buchanan who had informed him of the conspiracy. A month later, Pidal sent a letter to Calderón with instructions that a copy be given to Buchanan as a mark of Spain's gratitude. Buchanan must have been pleased with the reference in the letter to the fact that in gratitude for his information "concerning the plans of insurrection that are formed with respect to the island of Cuba," Her Majesty wished "to manifest how well disposed is the Government of Spain to do everything in its power to strengthen the friendly relations which have long united both nations." But Buchanan, who must have thought that "everything in its power," would include the sale of Cuba to the United States, was disillusioned to read:

> Your Excy must make it public that in Spain no Government could exist that should be capable of taking into consideration the transfer of the island of Cuba. Such an idea cannot be entertained by any patriotic Government nor would it be tolerated by the nation. . . . It is therefore expedient that everybody should know that Spain will neither now nor ever enter into any transaction having as an object the abandonment of her rights in the island of Cuba and Puerto Rico.[10]

Thus was foreshadowed the coming diplomatic fiasco in Madrid when the Polk administration pursued its designs for the purchase of Cuba.

In his instructions to Minister Saunders of June 17, 1848, Buchanan cited the familiar reasons why the United States could permit no other country to occupy Cuba, and the danger to the island in the strained relations between Spain and England. Perhaps Spain would be willing to have the United States take Cuba off her hands. The Cubans desired annexation and if Spain refused to sell, she might lose the island anyway. As for the United States, its benefits from the acquisition of Cuba would be well nigh incalculable. Yet, however desirable the island might be, "we would not acquire it except by the free consent of Spain. Any acquisition not sanctioned by justice and honor, would be too dearly purchased." No countenance, therefore, would be given those who wished to stir an insurrection in Cuba. But "the President has arrived at the conclusion that Spain might be willing to transfer the island to the

United States for a fair and full consideration." This offer was to be oral and informal so that a refusal would not embarrass future attempts to acquire the island. Finally Saunders, in his "confidential conversations" with the Spanish government, should make it known that the United States would forcefully resist the acquisition of the island by any other nation.[11]

Saunders caught this blunder immediately. He was well satisfied, he wrote, that nothing would induce Spain to part with her colony, but the "apprehension of a successful revolution in the island, or the fear of its seizure by England." He therefore suggested that it would be wise for him to omit promising aid to Spain if she became involved in a war with Britain. Otherwise, Spain would "rest confident" in her ability to maintain her sovereignty over Cuba and be more loath than ever to give up the island. To this Polk and Buchanan granted their consent.[12]

Once the procedure had been agreed upon, Saunders arranged a meeting with Narváez, the President of the Council, and led up to the subject through generalities about threatened insurrection in Cuba, the American policy of refusing encouragement to insurgents, and the fear of British designs on the island. Getting nowhere, the American Minister, on August 15, again sounded out the Spanish government. This time he approached Pidal, the new Minister of State. The President was afraid, Saunders intimated, that trouble between Spain and England might affect Cuba. Rather than become embroiled with England, the United States would prefer to purchase the Spanish possession. Pidal saw no immediate prospect for cession to the United States, but did not commit himself, leaving the impression that the subject might be reopened.

Meanwhile, something the administration had least expected happened. "The whole matter," Polk wrote in his diary, "was profoundly confidential, and the knowledge of it was confided to the Cabinet alone."[13] However, rumors of the conversations in Spain leaked out to the press. On October 20, the annexationist New York *Herald* published a letter from its Madrid correspondent reporting that negotiations were going on to transfer Cuba to the United States. This letter, reprinted in French, English, and Spanish papers, created an uproar in Spain.

Saunders at once assured Pidal that the leak had not come from his office and that matters would be set right at home. The Spanish Foreign Minister hastened to assure the public that there had been no negotiations; nevertheless, he was displeased by the turn of events. The Spanish people, scenting the truth in the *Herald* report, were aroused. Saunders wrote to Buchanan that "it is certain they regard Cuba as their most precious gem and nothing short of extreme necessity will ever induce them to part with it." He continued: "I have had no encouragement to renew the subject in regard to *Cuba*. So far as I have been able to collect the opinion of the publick [sic] it is against a cession, and I do not think the present ministry could or would venture on such a step."

Buchanan, however, dismissed this tactful suggestion that negotiations be abandoned, and instructed Saunders to return to the question in December. But Pidal was now cold to any proposal. He wanted to make it known publicly that there had been no direct offer from the United States, and intimated that it would be better if none were made. Saunders then stated that he merely wanted to know "whether any terms however liberal would induce Her Majesty to make the cession." Pidal answered that he understood Saunders' motive, but he could say most decidedly "that it was more than any Minister dare, to entertain any such proposition; that he believed such to be the feeling of the country, that sooner than see the Island transferred to *any power,* they would prefer seeing it sunk in the Ocean."

This celebrated answer ended the negotiations. Saunders recommended to Buchanan that after Pidal's "positive and candid avowal, I certainly should not renew the subject unless I should be specifically invited to do so." Since there was no prospect of this, it would be best to consider the affair ended, and he asked to be relieved of his post.[14]

Still Buchanan was not satisfied. He was inclined to attribute the failure to Saunders' blundering and his inability to speak Spanish, and thought a more skillful approach might yet succeed. "We must have Cuba," he wrote. "We can't do without Cuba, & above all we must not suffer its transfer to Great Britain. We shall acquire it by coup d'état at some propitious moment, which from the present state of Europe may not be far distant. . . . Cuba is already ours, I feel it in my finger ends."

Buchanan's estimate of Saunders' conduct was unjustified. Perhaps Robert Campbell gave the most intelligent explanation of the failure when he wrote from Havana that Spain's vested interests in Cuba would never permit a cession of the island:

> All the offices here are filled from Spain—all prominent officers of the household of her Majesty, of the army & navy, lawyers & doctors look to this Island as the place to obtain station & wealth—here their agricultural interests find their market—the manufacturing interests of Barcelona partially the same—from discriminating duties in favor of Spanish vessels, almost all European cargoes are imported under the Spanish flag, and the Island in this way sustains more than three-fourths of the whole mercantile marine of Spain—large capitals in Spain in the hands of unprincipled men are invested in the slave trade, causing an annual sale of slaves in this Island from three to four millions of dollars.[15]

Thus the diplomatic fiasco came to an end. All for naught the double-cross and betrayal of the Cuban annexationists. Spain was duly grateful, but that was where it ended.

This debacle was a serious setback to the annexationists in Cuba and the United States, especially since it was soon followed in November, 1848, by the election of the Whig candidate, Zachary Taylor, to the presidency. Although Taylor was a slaveowner of Mississippi and an old sympathizer of Cuban annexation, the Taylor administration, after the rebuff Polk had received, made it understood that it could not consider the purchase of Cuba without overtures from Spain. The administration policy was to leave Cuba in the possession of Spain, without, however, giving any guarantees; to oppose adamantly the transfer of the island to a foreign power, but not to commit the United States to any self-denial of Cuba for the future. But Spain was told, in no uncertain terms, that the only power to whom it could transfer Cuba was the United States. "The news of the cession of Cuba to any foreign power would, in the United States, be the instant signal for war."[16]

The failure to purchase Cuba ended, for a short time, American efforts to acquire the island through diplomacy. This, however, did not mean the end of annexation. On the contrary, the campaign to annex Cuba was now to begin in earnest.

chapter 3

THE DEBATE OVER CUBA

Spain's refusal to sell Cuba to the United States at any price, only accelerated the movement for the annexation of the island by other means. A massive propaganda campaign was launched in the United States to gain nationwide support for annexation. This was met by a counter-campaign by those who considered annexation to be against the best interests of the nation. The debate over Cuba became a major political issue up to the outbreak of the Civil War. "The Cuban question is now the leading one of the time," declared the *New York Times* on October 22, 1852.

The case for the annexation of Cuba began with the loud trumpeting of the "Spread Eagle doctrine" of "Manifest Destiny." The annexationists claimed that a vigorous young nation like the United States could have no limits fixed on its expansion. "There is vigor and power in this blooded Anglo-American race," cried the New Orleans *Creole*. "It is destined to sweep over the world with the might of a tornado. The Hispano-Morescan race will quail and disappear before our victorious march. The inferior must yield to the superior; it is the irrevocable law of God." "Providence," asserted Judge J. C. Larue of Louisiana, "had carved out a destiny for this country. There was to be but one language, with homogeneous laws and institutions, from the frozen regions to the Isthmus. Cuba, by Providence's decree, belongs to the United States and must be Americanized." The New Orleans *Delta* added that in the process of "Americanization":

> Their [the Cubans'] language is the first thing which disappears, for the bastard Latin of their nation cannot stand for any time against the conquering power of the robust and hardy English. . . . Their political sentimentalism and anarchical tendencies follow rapidly after

the language, and, by degree, the absorption of the people becomes complete—all due to the inevitable dominance of the American mind over an inferior race.

Thus, according to the annexationists, Cuba lay in the path of America's destiny, and belonged "naturally" to the United States, which should immediately take it.[1]

Prominent Northerners were exponents of "Manifest Destiny," among them James Buchanan, Stephen A. Douglas, William H. Seward, and Lewis Cass. But primarily, and especially after 1847, the movement was part of the drive to preserve and extend slavery. As Garvin B. Henderson points out in the *Journal of Southern History*: "Cuba . . . was of very special importance to Southern expansionists, who thought its acquisition would greatly strengthen the slave economy which they were determined to preserve at all costs."[2] They sought to annex Cuba for three reasons: (1) to prevent abolition of slavery in the island; (2) to acquire new land suited to the slave-plantation system; and (3) to increase the South's political power in the Union.

Let us consider each of these factors.

Since the early 'forties,* the Southern slaveowners had been increasingly concerned over English pressure against the Cuban slave-labor system. They believed that the stability and prosperity of slavery in the United States was linked to its preservation in Cuba. "All our strength should be reserved for Cuba which belongs to us by nature, and [which] is becoming more and more necessary to enable the holders of slave property in the U[nited] States to preserve it," a leading Southerner wrote to Calhoun in 1848.[3] Southern spokesmen charged that England, having ruined its own West India colonies by emancipation, sought to derange the economy of Cuba by the same means, and simultaneously threaten the existence of slavery in the United States.

If England succeeded in forcing Spain to abolish slavery in Cuba, this would constitute "a war on institutions of the South." "Free negroism," so close to America's shores, would render it physically impossible to hold the Negro slaves under subjection in the Gulf States. "From Cuba there will shoot out sparks which will kindle a great conflagration throughout the South." It would then be impos-

* *See* Volume I, pp. 224-228.

sible to prevent slave insurrections within the South itself. All this pointed up the "importance of placing the destiny of Cuba into hands firmer than those of the degenerate Spaniards, who cannot be counted upon to resist the British conspiracy to abolitionize the island."[4]

But Cuban annexation would sustain the South's "peculiar institutions" as well. At the end of the Mexican War, the South still had equal representation with the North in the Senate, and could block legislation hostile to the slave interests. It was determined to maintain this power in the Senate since, because of its greater free voting population, the North now controlled the House of Representatives. Should the North gain ascendancy in the Senate, too, it might pass protective tariff legislation for its rising industrial capitalism, more subsidies for internal improvements, more charters for national banks, more bounties for Northern shipping, and a Homestead Act to fill the federal public lands with free farmers and workers. As it gained an overwhelming numerical superiority, the North could effectively limit slavery to the states where it already existed, on the theory that in this way, it could doom the system. Finally, the day might come when the abolitionists, in alliance with the industrial capitalists, would end slavery and open the South to the penetration of an industrial society based on wage labor.

During the Mexican War, the Southerners and their Northern "doughface" allies had defeated the Northern attempt to push the Wilmot Proviso through Congress, a measure to prohibit slavery in any territory acquired from Mexico. But, in the Compromise of 1850, the South lost California as a slave state and, with it, its parity in the Senate. The stringent fugitive-slave law, which was part of the Compromise, could not offset this loss. The Southerners began, therefore, to look for new slave states by which the South could regain its power in the Senate.

The annexation of Cuba appeared to be the solution. Cuba could be converted into "at least three powerful slave states." With the annexation of Cuba consummated, wrote one slaveholder, "the rights of the South are no longer at the mercy of piratical Northern demagogues, or entrusted to the feeble hands of our compromising vacillating brethren." Cuba was far more valuable to the South than "all the fugitive-slave laws that ever were passed, or all the Supreme

Court decisions that ever were rendered."[5] The Richmond *Enquirer* conceded, in an editorial of March 17, 1854, entitled "Cuba and Slavery," that, under ordinary circumstances, it would not favor antagonizing a friendly nation like Spain. But these were not ordinary times:

> Our view of the policy of this measure, as of every other, is determined by the paramount and controlling consideration of Southern interests. It is because we regard the acquisition of Cuba as essential to the stability of the system of slavery and to the just ascendancy of the South, that we consent to forego our habitual repugnance to political change, and to advocate a measure of such vast, and, in some respects, uncertain consequences. . . .
> The only possible way by which the South can indemnify itself for the concessions to the anti-slavery fanaticism is by the acquisition of additional slave territory. . . . If we would restore to the South its proper position in the Confederacy, and the means of protecting its constitutional rights, we must re-enforce the power of slavery as an element of political control. And this can only be done by the annexation of Cuba. In no other direction is there a chance for the aggrandizement of slavery.

Thus far we have considered Cuban annexation as an expression of the slaveholders' determination to preserve their slave property. But annexation would do still more for the slave interests. It would satisfy the land-hunger of Southern planters who needed new soil to exploit with slave labor. Expansion north and west of the Rio Grande was blocked not only by the Missouri Compromise and the Compromise of 1850, but by a soil and climate unsuited to the slave-plantation system. This situation became more evident after the war with Mexico, because the conquered territory proved unsuitable for the slave-plantation system, though much of it was in Southern latitudes. Yet slavery had to expand or die. The one-crop plantation system exhausted the soil and led the slaveholders on a never-ending quest for virgin land. Moreover, the confinement of the slaves to a restricted area intensified police problems. There were already more than enough slave uprisings in the South to keep slaveowners in a state of chronic alarm; if they did not acquire new land into which the slave population could be spread, the South might be faced with an upheaval of Santo Domingo proportions.

Southerners, as a consequence, looked with covetous eyes at the ideal tropical area, Cuba, situated less than a hundred miles off the coast of Florida, where Americans were already prospering as plantation owners and helping develop a social pattern similar to that of the South. Hence the New Orleans *Bee* declared on August 14, 1858:

> There is no earthly use in seeking to plant slavery in Northern territory; climatic influences are against us there, and slavery will not flourish where white labor can compete with it successfully. But southward we have almost a boundless field of enterprise lying before us. There is Cuba. . . . Slave labor there already gives rich returns, and annexation to the Union would introduce superior American management in that island and raise the productivity of the individual slave laborers. . . . Let the people of the South cease an unavailing effort to force slavery into ungenial climes, and strive to plant it where it would naturally tend.

What more natural than to believe that Providence had destined Cuba for the South? Moreover, that same Providence had decreed that Cuba, annexed to the Union, should be the cornerstone of a slave empire in the tropics. Unlike Cuba, however, most of the tropical regions out of which the slave empire could be carved had abolished slavery. But this did not bother the Southern expansionists, for they had a simple solution to this problem: annex these regions and re-establish slavery. And this, too, was the will of Providence. For these countries had violated Natural Law when they had abolished slavery and given Negroes equal rights with the whites. It was America's mission to reclaim Haiti, Jamaica, and Mexico; "wresting that whole region from the mongrelism which now blights and blackens it, and making it yield its riches up to the hands of organized and stable industry and intelligent enterprise, this idea is firmly fixed in the American mind, and, sooner or later, its development must become a great fact—a historical reality—manifest destiny accomplished."[6]

Thus there spread before the land-hungry slaveowners the glowing prospect of a slave empire, beginning with the addition to the Union of "the boundless fertility of Cuba, and then renovating the West India Islands with the labor of the blacks."[7]

The chief device of the annexationists to divert attention from the slave-expansionist character of the movement was to emphasize Spanish despotism in Cuba. The Cubans were "persecuted, imprisoned, buried in dungeons, banished, sentenced to fortresses, and condemned to death for calumnies, for imaginary crimes and disloyalty, on no better foundation than flimsy suspicion, or false denunciations by infamous spies." Spanish rule in Cuba was "one of the veriest despotisms Christendom ever knew," and by this rule Spain had forfeited her right to the island.[8]

Most of what was said about Spanish rule in Cuba was, of course, the plain truth, but it was used to justify a minority of American slaveowners keeping millions of human beings in a worse bondage than Spain held the white Cubans, and extending that bondage to other millions who had just gained their liberty!

The annexationists, who were mainly from the South, tried to prove to the farmers of the Northeast, the manufacturers of New England and Pennsylvania, that they would be the greatest beneficiaries from the acquisition of Cuba. "It will be of more value to the northern people than to the South," went the refrain. In Cuba the duty paid on American flour was $10.81 a barrel and for Spanish flour $2.52. Annexation would be followed by the removal of the Spanish duties on flour which were so obnoxious to American producers, and the opening of a vast market for their flour, lard, beef, pork and other foodstuffs. If the discriminatory duties on jerked beef were removed, American producers could sell yearly in Cuba $1,500,000 of this item alone. And this was nothing compared with the growth of the flour trade. "Just think, when the duty of ten dollars on each barrel of flour is taken off, how much greater will be the consumption [in Cuba]." The presence of Cuba in the Union "will be felt on the thrashing floors of Minnesota."

But the grain and flour merchants of the Northwest, though interested in annexation, refused to be dazzled by such prospects. Rather it was the South, especially New Orleans, whose traffic with the states of the old Northwest had been cut by the Northern railroads, which thrilled over the economic promise of annexation. (The railroads were diverting western produce from its old outlet, the Mississippi River system, to New York and the Atlantic seaboard.) The Gulf of Mexico would become "the center of a richer commerce than the Mediterranean could ever boast," and New Orleans would regain control of the vital Northwest traffic. The lure of a cheap all-water route to the island would again bring the foodstuffs of the Northwest to the gates of New Orleans, and it would soon be "the Alexandria, as Havana would be the Constantinople, of our empire—far mightier and more extensive than the Roman." "It is not saying too much," declared *De Bow's Review*, "that if we hold Cuba, we will hold the destiny of the richest and most increased commerce that ever dazzled the cupidity of man. And with that commerce we can control the power of the world."[9]

Economic considerations at times united Southern slaveowners, Northern shipowners, the grain and flour interests of the upper Mississippi and Ohio valleys behind annexation. But the power behind the annexationist drive came chiefly from the South, and was aimed, first and foremost, at preserving and extending slavery. Such masking phrases as "Manifest Destiny," "the natural right of a superior people to dominate inferior peoples," "the will of Providence," and "Freedom, Democracy and Progress," were the propaganda rhetoric of the rapacious American Slave Power, as they were to become, several decades later, the propaganda rhetoric of a rapacious American Imperialism. Annexation of Cuba was of such paramount importance to the slaveowners that they classed anyone opposing it "among the groveling enemies of Southern institutions," who saw in the acquisition of Cuba, "a formidable obstacle to the progress of their desire to rule the South; to destroy slavery, and to make everything and everybody bend to their ethical principles."[10]

Fortunately, there were many Americans who were not intimidated by such charges, and they met the campaign to annex Cuba with a spirited counter-campaign.

The anti-annexationists hit back at the "Manifest Destiny" adherents. They believed in a destiny for the United States that did not include wars of conquest and territorial grabs. Horace Greeley, the distinguished editor of the New York *Tribune* wrote angrily in the issue of May 27, 1850, in opposing the annexation of Cuba:

> There is wrong enough to redress here without risking our necks and the peace of the world for those who do not ask and will not thank us for our intermeddling in their affairs. . . . A nation cannot simultaneously devote its energies to the absorption of others' territories and the improvement of its own. . . . Vainly should we hope

to clear, and drain, and fence and fertilize our useless millions of acres, at the same time that we are intent on bringing the whole vast continent under our exclusive dominion.

The United States had land enough "to satisfy the most grasping ambition" so that there was "really no overruling necessity for our acquiring Cuba." Here in this rich, bountiful land, Americans should build a civilization so based on freedom, and so dedicated to raising up the downtrodden, that the other countries would follow us as an example. This would do more to extend American ideals and democratic institutions than conquering other people's territories. "Our people," said the Boston *Atlas*, "are patriotic, but they love their country for what she is, and not for what unrighteous conquest would make of her. They believe her mission to be one of peace, rather than of war; and they wish to have her extend freedom by her example, rather than slavery in her own by war." "To indulge a desire for territorial aggrandizement . . . is to imitate the vulgar ambition of kings, and is unworthy of a free and enlightened people." Opposing the annexation of Cuba, Senator John P. Hale of New Hampshire envisioned a better destiny for America than the acquisition of the island, and warned that ". . . if we are led away and dazzled by the halo of military renown; if our judgments are warped by the graspings of a covetousness which will never be satisfied so long as anybody else owns lands contiguous to us;—then . . . it needs no other prophecy than that which the light of experience gives us—to foretell to us that we shall fail, and that we shall go the way of republics that have preceded us."[11]

The anti-annexationists saw no validity in the economic arguments of the annexationists. "Our trade with Cuba is large and profitable now," they said, and "it is generally a safe rule to let very well alone." Americans, after all, already dominated the Cuban market in practically every important item (except flour) which the United States could furnish the island. Any increase would come naturally, as it had in the past, and needed no stimulation from "Manifest Destiny" exponents. As to the discriminatory Spanish tariffs, an independent power had a right to impose any duties it might think fit, and Spanish rates were no more oppressive than those levied by Great Britain on American commerce with her West Indian provinces. They advised negotiating a new commercial treaty with Spain, for trade concessions in Cuba would be just as advantageous as annexation, besides avoiding the expense and problems that would be incurred by annexation. If a new treaty could not be arranged, then it was always possible to end American tariff reprisals on Spanish shipping. Then Spanish ships, laden with Cuban products, would crowd American ports, and American commerce would increase almost immediately by ten million dollars. Why risk, through annexation, a war with Spain (and perhaps also with Britain and France) for what could, at best, only produce a slight gain in trade? The New York *Journal of Commerce,* voice of the Northern merchants, summarized the commercial case against Cuban annexation: "It would involve us in disputes, if not in war, with the leading powers of Europe. Already we have a large share in the commerce of Cuba, without the necessity of defending the Island by fleets and armies. What more can we desire?"[12]

Of course, the anti-annexationists were aware that the slaveholders desired more than this. They understood and emphasized that the main drive for annexation came from the slaveowning interests in the South and that the glittering picture of expanding trade was a screen for the real aim, which was to preserve and extend slavery. Many anti-annexationists condemned the agitation for the acquisition of Cuba as a "plot" of the Slavocracy to perpetuate slavery in the United States. They believed that the "peculiar institution" would die out in this country unless it were given a transfusion through the acquisition of new territory suited to a slave-plantation system. "Slavery is like a poor system of farming; it must have successively new soils to work upon, or it will die of inanition." Cuban annexation was thus a "pledge of its continued existence, for while it opens a new field for slave labor, it converts the old and worn-out regions into slave grounds, for raising the necessary slave laborers." Many anti-annexationists who took this position were not abolitionists. They assured the slaveowners that they had no intention of interfering with slavery where it already existed. They would even defend it there, not because they esteemed it a good, but because they recognized the danger to the Union if the right of the South to maintain slavery within its borders were challenged. Beyond this they would not go. They were determined to protect free labor from further "disgrace" and "degradation," and refused categorically to annex "a million of half-naked negroes" to perpetuate slavery and give the South power to dominate the Federal Government. "No amount of sugar and molasses could sweeten such a black dose."[13]

What do we get if we annex Cuba? asked the Ohio *Statesman* in 1851. It answered: "We get a vast territory filled with slaves, and a population alien to us in religion, habits, language, and government. We get another chance to quarrel and wrangle about slavery, to the neglect of all the legitimate and pressing business of Congress."[14]

The last point was a telling one. Perhaps the most effective argument of the anti-annexationists was that it would upset the hard-won sectional compromises. After the passage of the Compromise of 1850, many Northerners believed that "these horrible questions . . . are settled." To be sure, decent Americans abhorred the incorporation of a stronger fugitive-slave act in the Compromise, demanded its repeal, and pledged themselves to resist its enforcement. But conservative elements insisted that the Compromise be accepted as a whole in order to save the Union. In this situation, any attempt to annex Cuba would definitely check "the healing of the deep and grievous wounds" already inflicted upon the Union and practically guarantee that it would be split apart. "If we annex it without slavery," declared the New York *Journal of Commerce* on August 4, 1851, "it will break up the Union; and, if with slavery, the Union would not last an hour." In short, it concluded: "The possession of Cuba at this time would open anew the dangerous questions relating to slavery and slave power."

Nor could Cuba restore the equilibrium between the sections. To hope so was "vain and delusive." For if the South acquired Cuba, the North would go about grabbing Canada. "First Cuba; then Canada! When shall we end?" Some astute Southerners saw that Cuban annexation could not guarantee that the South's position in the Union would be secure. W. J. Sykes of Tennessee pointed out: "If Cuba is annexed, it being a slaveholding state, the North will insist upon the annexation of Canada. . . . Are we of the South willing to take Canada for the sake of getting Cuba? . . . . With what grace can those in the South, who advocate the annexation of Cuba, oppose the proposition which will certainly be made to annex Canada?" In a resigned voice, Jeremiah Clemens of Alabama advised other Southern Senators on February 7, 1853, not to press for annexation, for the history of the last few decades proved that the South, politically speaking, could never regain equality with the North:

> If Cuba came in as a slave State, it would give us no additional political advantage, no additional political power. The once-cherished dream of southern statesmen of maintaining a balance of power in the Senate of the United States has been completely exploded. The North has already obtained a preponderance, and that preponderance will be increased from year to year. What we have lost can never be regained.[15]

But those who were intent upon adding slave territory to the Union and building a slave empire inside or outside of the Union, gave no heed. Joining forces with a small group interested in enlarging the commercial advantages of the United States in Cuba, they continued the campaign for annexation with speeches, pamphlets, editorials in the annexationist press, and letters to the editors. But the anti-annexationists also acted. At mass meetings in state after state, in speeches, editorials, pamphlets, and letters to editors and to their Congressmen, they continued the struggle against annexation.

The following pages will show which of the two causes triumphed.

chapter 4

THE FILIBUSTERS: NARCISO LÓPEZ

During the debate over Cuban annexation, the pro-slavery Southern expansionists were not satisfied to wait for the American people to decide. They were determined to force the decision by a *fait accompli*. Not trusting the federal government to act effectively, the pro-slavery Southern expansionists organized filibustering into Cuba. The sequence of revolution, independence, annexation, by which Texas had been won, was considered the example to follow in acquiring Cuba.

Into this situation stepped General Narciso López.

We have said before that Narciso López is one of the most controversial figures in Cuban history. The issue can be stated simply: Was Narciso López actually a martyr in the struggle for Cuban independence, or did he dedicate himself to the annexation of Cuba as a slave state to the United States?

The case for López has been stated in great detail and with considerable passion by Professor Herminio Portell Vilá in a three-volume work, *Narciso López y Su Epoca* (Narciso López and His Epoch), published successively in Havana in 1930, 1952, and 1958. In Professor Portell Vilá's judgment, Narciso López was the precursor of Cuban independence, pointing the way for the liberating wars of 1868–1878 and 1895–1898; he did not favor annexation to the United States. Those who have charged López with being an annexationist are dismissed by the author as "pseudo-historians."

But many Cuban historians remain unconvinced, and adhere to the judgment of José Martí, Cuba's great liberator, who charged that López was no precursor of Cuban independence, but "an active promoter of annexation to the United States."[1] Let us then turn to the Narciso López story and see to what conclusion the evidence leads.

Born in Venezuela in 1797, López, at an early age, joined the Spanish army operating against General Simón Bolívar, and rose rapidly in the ranks of the oppressors of his fellow countrymen. Upon the withdrawal of the Spanish forces from Venezuela in 1823, López accompanied them to Cuba, where he was welcomed by the Spanish authorities. From Cuba, López went to Spain, where he served the court against the Carlist rebels, and was rewarded with many honors. He returned to Cuba in 1841 with his personal friend Gerónimo Valdés, who had been named Captain General of the island, and who gave him important posts in the Spanish administration. As President of the Military Commission, López made himself notorious by the severity of the sentences imposed upon political dissenters, particularly free Negroes. When Valdés was replaced by Leopoldo O'Donnell as Captain General, López lost his posts. Refusing a subordinate position offered him by O'Donnell, he retired from the army, keeping his title as General without pay, and entered business. One after another, his business ventures failed, among them the iron and coal mine, "*La Rosa Cubana*," which was to give its name to López's first-known conspiracy—the "Conspiracy of the Cuban Rose Mines."

We last left the General in Providence, Rhode Island, where he had landed after his flight from Cuba, following the discovery and suppression of the "Conspiracy," a movement which, as we have seen, had annexation to the United States as its objective. Informing Secretary of State Buchanan of López's "escape to the United States," Robert McLean, U.S. Consul in Havana, expressed the opinion that the Cuban conspirators knew now that nothing could be achieved against Spain in Cuba "without assistance *from abroad*," and that the General would seek such assistance in the United States.[2]

This was an accurate forecast. The fiasco in Cuba did not dampen the ardor of the Cuban annexationists. Ambrosio J. González was commissioned by the Havana Club to see General Worth in New Orleans and again offer him $3,000,000 to land in Cuba with an army of 5,000 men. If Worth accepted, he was to put him in contact with López. Worth agreed, and undertook to have his expeditionary force "act in support of a small force headed in advance by General

López." González, López and Gaspar Betancourt Cisneros met with Worth in New York City, to plan the expedition. But Worth was suddenly separated from the enterprise by being ordered to Texas. The administration was seeking to annex Cuba through purchase and feared that the expedition would upset its plans. On May 7, 1849, Worth died at his new post, and the Cubans had to start afresh.

After a futile attempt to interest some Northern politicians, González and López concentrated on Southern leaders. López offered the command of the expedition to Jefferson Davis and subsequently to Robert E. Lee. Both declined. Despite these rebuffs, López remained convinced that once an expedition landed in Cuba, the United States would use the excuse of a revolution in the island to intervene on the side of the Cuban conspirators. López seems to have been assured of Southern support along these lines from Calhoun himself, who informed the General that the American people could lawfully aid an insurrection which had annexation as its objective. John L. O'Sullivan wrote to Calhoun in August, 1849: "The South ought (according to an expression which Gen. López has quoted to me from you) to flock down there in 'open boats,' the moment they hear the tocsin."[3]

Assured of Southern support, López decided to head the expedition himself with González as second-in-command. A number of American army officers accepted service in the expedition, among them Colonel Robert M. White. The latter had commanded a Louisiana company in the Mexican War and had participated in the suppression of the Indian rebellion in Yucatan. Nor were the other recruits of a higher caliber. Most were Southern veterans of the Mexican War, preference being given to men with previous military experience. A contemporary observer described them as the "most desperate creatures as ever were seen would murder a man for ten dollars." Undoubtedly they were attracted by López's promise of "plunder, women, drink, and tobacco." The men were to receive U.S. Army pay (about $8 a month) and rations, and if the expedition were successful, each would get a bonus of $1,000 and 160 acres of land in Cuba.[4]

The steamships *Fanny* and *Sea Gull* were purchased, and the *New*

Orleans was chartered to carry the recruits and arms and munitions to Cuba from New York, and from Cat and Round Islands off the coast of Mississippi. Recruits gathered at the two islands in July, 1849, and, while awaiting transportation, were organized into companies and drilled daily.

While some funds for the enterprise came from American sources, the major part of the $80,000 raised for the expedition was contributed by Cubans. Although the Havana Club and its agents in the Cuban Council of New York at first refused to support López, fearing that the expedition might incite a slave revolt or drive the Spanish authorities to decree emancipation,* these Cuban annexationists eventually decided to join in. The Havana Club offered to contribute $60,000 if the expedition would be increased to 1,500 men. López accepted this condition, and received $30,000 from Cisneros and Madan as a first installment. López welcomed this support, and in a letter to Miguel Teurbe Tolón of *La Verdad*, assured the wealthy Cuban annexationists that everything pointed to the "triumph of the common cause, *and the adding of the Star of Cuba to those which shine in the glorious flag of the American Union.*"[5]

At the end of July, 1849, the expedition was about ready. The main body, under the command of López, was in New York. The Southern wing, composed of about 800 American mercenaries, recruited by promises of bonuses and land grants, was gathering at Round Island, off the Louisiana coast, with instructions to sail about August 20–25. Simultaneous attacks on Cuba from New York and New Orleans were planned. Not all recruits knew exactly where they were bound; some were told by López that they were going to a foreign country; others that they were heading for California.

López hoped that, by covering up the expedition's exact destination, he could evade the Neutrality law of 1818, which forbade military expeditions against powers at peace with the United States from being launched in this country. But López was exceedingly naive. The operations at Round Island were conducted so openly that they practically advertised themselves to the spy service employed by Angel Calderón de la Barca, the Spanish Minister at

---

* Late in 1848, López, annoyed by the timidity of the wealthy Cuban *hacendados*, founded his own *Junta Cubana* in New York. But the two groups cooperated with each other.

Washington. Calderón presented the information gathered by his spies to the Taylor administration along with the request that the expedition be dispersed under the terms of the neutrality laws of the United States.

Secretary of State Clayton took prompt action. Three agents were dispatched to ferret out the exact designs of the filibusters, and to take legal steps to halt the enterprise. U.S. District Attorneys were instructed to crush the "nefarious undertaking." On his part, President Taylor issued a proclamation, warning that an expedition against Cuba would "grossly" violate the American neutrality laws, and that all persons associating themselves with such an expedition were liable to a prison term of up to three years and a $3,000-fine. Taylor also had the Navy dispatch vessels to blockade Round Island and prevent those who eluded the patrol from landing in Cuba.

By September 4, Round Island was blockaded and the recruits were deserting; and on September 7, the two ships acquired in New York were seized. On October 20, 1849, the Taylor administration learned that the expedition was "entirely abandoned."[6] Thus ended the first "invasion" of Cuba by Narciso López.

Why did the Taylor administration act with such dispatch? Portell Vilá gives this reason: The Taylor administration was determined to annex Cuba through purchase from Spain, and was convinced that López's objective was the independence of Cuba and not annexation. It acted, therefore, to prevent the establishment of a truly independent nation which would have ruled out annexation.

All the evidence, however, casts doubt on the validity of this conclusion. As we have seen, the Taylor administration made it clear that after the rejection of Polk's offer, it would only consider purchase if Spain offered to sell the island. This meant that this particular route to annexation was closed for the time being. For another, there is no evidence that the administration believed that López sought the independence of Cuba rather than its annexation to the United States. On the contrary, O'Sullivan, who served as López's business agent, was letting it be generally known in Washington that the advocates of Cuban annexation in the United States had the most to gain from the expedition, and that this consideration "ought to rouse all the youth and manhood of the Southern States in particular to rush down and help the Cuban Revolution." If he, a New Yorker, was "so deeply interested in behalf of this movement, what ought to be the enthusiasm of Southern gentlemen?"[7] So much, then, for Portell Vilá's contention that halting López's expedition ruined a chance for Cuban independence.

The reason for the action taken by the Taylor administration is quite simple. It was then involved in the Congressional measures soon to be incorporated into the Compromise of 1850. Support for the López expedition would promptly be understood by the North as a move to annex Cuba as a slave state, and the chance of a peaceful adjustment of the raging sectional dispute would be lost. The Taylor administration, therefore, chose to maintain strict neutrality in Cuban affairs primarily because a greater issue was then at stake—the continued existence of the Union. The lenient treatment of the filibusters—none were arrested—was attributed by González to "protection from high places,"[8] and indicates that the administration was secretly sympathetic to their annexationist goal.

Although the Round Island expedition was finished, the movement for the conquest of Cuba and subsequent annexation to the United States was not. Undaunted, López was preparing another attempt. But now he was confronted by a new and unexpected difficulty—defection in the Cuban annexationist ranks. While personality differences helped to precipitate this split, there were more deep-rooted causes.

The fundamental cause was the decline of the annexationist movement in Cuba. In part, this was due to the influence of José Antonio Saco's effective pamphleteering. But in a larger measure, it was the result of a stiffening of Spain's resistance to British pressure for the punishment of slave traders as pirates, and for the emancipation of slaves imported illegally. The Spanish government flatly refused the British demands that it declare the slave trade piracy, arguing that this would lead to British interference in Cuba, and it rejected the British proposal for a census of illegally acquired slaves. Madrid's taking this stand removed the chief source of annexationist sentiment in Cuba—fear of Spanish capitulation to British antislavery pressure. A few leaders of the Havana Club, heaving a sigh of relief, gravitated toward reformism, hoping for redress of their grievances from Spain.

A minority still clung to their belief in the necessity of annexationism, but even they began to doubt the success of López's expeditions. The cautious slaveowners of the Havana Club who still favored annexation now came out strongly in favor of a peaceful road to achieve this goal, through the cession of the island to the United States in return for a large indemnity to be paid by the wealthy Cubans. To this end, they planned to send a mission to Spain to negotiate the cession with the Cortes.

These developments in Cuba had repercussions among the Cuban émigrés in the United States. The Cuban Council, reflecting the view of its parent organization, the Havana Club, advised caution and delay while the negotiations for annexation through purchase were being conducted by the Club. Failing to impress their views upon the López group, the more cautious émigrés dissolved the Cuban Council and organized *"El Consejo del Gobierno Cubano."* Made up of a majority of the old Council, the new organization was headed by José Aniceto Iznaga, Gaspar Betancourt Cisneros, Victoriano Arrieta, and Cristóbal Madan. It established headquarters in New York, where it continued the publication of *La Verdad*, and maintained its close relations with the Havana Club.

In December, 1849, the López group, consisting of a scant half-dozen members—López, Juan Manuel Macías, José María Sánchez Iznaga, Ambrosio José González, José Manuel Hernández, and Cirilo Villaverde—announced the establishment in New York City of the *"Junta Pública Promovedora de los Intereses Políticos de Cuba"* (Public Council for the Promotion of the Political Interests of Cuba) which would act openly "without infringing on the laws of this country." The thousands of "noble spirits" in the United States who were friends of Cuban liberty were invited "to contribute any aid, honorably and legitimately in their power" to the cause. Communications were to be directed to a Post Office box in Washington.[9]

During the winter months of 1849, González operated in Washington, where he concentrated on gaining the backing of Southern politicians. Here he met John Henderson, Mississippi cotton planter and former Senator from that State. Henderson had been a leading supporter of the annexation of Texas and the acquisition of Mexican territory after the Mexican War, and was now ardently for the annexation of Cuba, which he regarded as the first step in the creation of a slave empire. He suggested that the López group move to New Orleans where money, supplies and men would be plentiful. González met other Southerners, all former officers in the Mexican War, who offered to raise, at their own expense, a regiment of Kentuckians and bring it to New Orleans for the expedition.

The López group then transferred its headquarters to New Orleans. On their way to New Orleans, López and González stopped at Jackson, Mississippi, where, on March 17, 1850, they met with General John A. Quitman, Governor of that state. A cotton and sugar planter with extensive holdings in Mississippi and Louisiana, Quitman was leader of the most rabid pro-slavery expansionists in the South. He had migrated to Mississippi from the North, had led filibusters into the Texas Republic, served as major-general in the Mexican War, and as a military governor of Mexico City after its surrender to the American forces. He favored acquisition of all of Mexico, the annexation of Cuba, and the creation of an empire to the south of the United States, based on slavery as the best of all possible labor systems. Elected Governor of Mississippi in 1849, he quickly placed that state against the proposed Compromise of 1850, which he denounced as treason to the South and to its institutions, and threatened that, if the slaveowners' interests were not fully protected by Congress, Mississippi would secede from the Union.

It was to this member of, and spokesman for, the most reactionary interests in the United States, that López offered military command of his expedition to Cuba, with "ever in view the ultimate triumph and establishment of free democratic republican government, *and ultimate annexation to the great confederation of the United States of the North.*" The proposal appealed to Quitman's hope of annexing Cuba and introducing there "American civilization and Southern institutions." But he could not see his way clear to quit the governorship of his state at this critical period, and could only "put his heart in the enterprise and contribute some pecuniary aid." He then outlined the strategy the López group should follow. Let the Cubans themselves first strike a blow for independence, which would entitle them to U.S. aid (as with the Texans in 1836), and annexation would follow. He cautioned López against the use of less than 2,000 men to maintain a foothold until United States reinforcements arrived. Once he had evidence that the Cubans had risen against

Spain, he himself would lead a military expedition to their aid. This López and González agreed to.

Quitman's strategy was essentially the same as López's. Cirilo Villaverde, one of the general's closest associates, wrote that López's plan had always been "independence and annexation to the American Union." Quitman had seen this strategy succeed in Texas and he and López imitated it. Spain would be thrown out of Cuba as Mexico had been ejected from Texas, and then, as an independent nation, Cuba would ask to be admitted to the American Union.[10]

Before leaving Mississippi, López received the active backing not only of Quitman, but also of Cotesworth Pinckney Smith, Judge of the State's Supreme Court, Henry S. Foote, John Henderson, and other leading slaveowners. Moving on to New Orleans, he obtained the support of other influential Southerners. Among them was Laurence J. Sigur, editor of the most ardent Cuban annexationist paper in the country, the New Orleans *Delta*, who backed the expedition editorially, contributed funds and let López use his home.

With Sigur's home as his headquarters, and with the constant advice and aid of influential Southerners, López set to work. Regiments were formed, composed mostly of Mexican War veterans from Kentucky, Mississippi, and Louisiana. Thousands of these men were stranded in New Orleans, searching for a livelihood; it was not difficut to enroll what even a leader of the expedition called "riffraff," for $7 a month, the promise of a $4,000 victory bonus and a grant of land in Cuba at the end of a year. The offers to officers were much higher: bonuses up to $10,000 and large estates in Cuba.

To finance the expedition, López issued six-percent bonds pledged on the "public lands and property" of Cuba. One or two million dollars' worth of these bonds was turned over to Henderson, who sold four or five hundred thousand dollars' worth at ten cents on the dollar. Henderson himself bought ten or fifteen thousand dollars' worth of bonds, and the rest were sold to speculators. In this manner, forty or fifty thousand dollars was raised to equip the expedition with arms and ammunition, to purchase the steamer *Creole,* and to charter the bark *Georgiana.* The Louisiana contingent also chartered the *Susan Loud* and, through connections with high State officials, obtained arms from the State arsenal of Louisiana.

López now sought to evade the Neutrality Act by having the

filibusters masquerade as emigrants to the gold fields of California via Panama in unarmed vessels. They were to be armed at an island rendezvous off Mexico. On April 25, 1850, the *Georgiana* cleared New Orleans for Chagres, Panama, with about 200 Kentucky filibusters on board, cheered on by a large crowd at the dock. On May 2, Colonel Wheat and 150 Louisianans followed in the *Susan Loud*; and on May 7, the *Creole* with López, González, and about 650 men, presumably bound for California by way of Chagres, left New Orleans. The port authorities of New Orleans, accepting the claims that the men were emigrants to California, despite common knowledge that they were bound for Cuba, cleared the filibusters' three vessels for Chagres.

The U.S. government had been kept informed of López's plans by the Spanish Minister in Washington, whose agents in New Orleans had had no difficulty in learning all there was to know about the expedition. But the officials in New Orleans who could have suppressed the expedition claimed that they had no proof of an overt violation of the Neutrality Act. The Spanish government charged that they did not act because they were part of the conspiracy, and there can be little doubt of the truth of this charge. Secretary of State Clayton, at the insistence of the Spanish Minister, did finally send three war vessels to intercept the filibusters, but they arrived too late.

The successful launching of the expedition was hailed with joy in the annexationist press. Both the New York *Sun* and the New Orleans *Delta* displayed the Cuban flag, designed by Miguel Teurbe Tolón, atop their office buildings. (This is the same flag used by the Cuban Republic since its formation in 1901.) They urged Americans to rush to assist an expedition destined to overthrow Spanish rule in Cuba and add another state to the United States. The New Orleans *Bulletin* predicted on May 20, 1850 that as soon as the filibusters dug in, in Cuba, they would be joined by thousands of others from the United States, and "after a nominal independence, Cuba would be annexed to the Union."

In New Orleans several newspapers printed a number of López's addresses and proclamations, which he left behind to be published after his departure. They gladdened the heart of every slaveholding annexationist in the United States. Referring to the flag that the filibusters were to raise on the soil of Cuba, López wrote: "The Flag on which you behold the Tri-color of Liberty, the Triangle of Strength and Order, the *Star of the future State*." In his proclamation to the inhabitants of Cuba, López again asserted his annexationist aim. It closed with the words: "And the Star of Cuba, today dark and obscured by the fog of despotism, will emerge beautiful and shining, on *being admitted with glory into the splendid North American constellation, where destiny leads it.*"[11]

On May 16, the *Creole* joined the other vessels at Contoy, an island off the coast of Yucatan, where arms were distributed and a military organization set up. About fifty of the recruits lost interest and returned to New Orleans on the *Georgiana* and *Susan Loud*. The remainder headed for Cuba on the *Creole*. López's objective was the town of Matanzas, about 100 miles east of Havana, but because the town was fortified and the filibusters had no artillery, they headed for Cárdenas, from which the expedition thereafter took its name. Cárdenas was 50 miles to the east, and the regiments could proceed to Matanzas by rail.

Before taking the Cárdenas expedition to Cuba, it is worth noting several significant aspects of the enterprise. Chester Stanley Urban says that "the dominant characteristic about the preparation for and participation in the Cárdenas expedition was its American stamp and cast." And, as L. M. Pérez put it: "The López expeditions were due in a very slight degree to Cuban enterprise; they were in essence —and in their execution—a Southern movement for the annexation of the island, and would probably have occurred had López never existed."[12] Of the entire force, only five men were Cubans; the rest came mainly from the Southern states. It is likely, moreover, that Cubans had not contributed a dollar toward outfitting the Cárdenas expedition, but that the money came entirely from Southern annexationists like Henderson.

Yet Portell Vilá would have us believe that the sole objective of an expedition organized completely in the South was for the independence of Cuba; that the Southern slaveowning expansionists backed López with men and money without the slightest guarantee or even assurance that he would incorporate Cuba into the Union. What more they needed from López than he had already told Quitman and O'Sullivan personally and stated publicly in his proclamations is difficult to understand. But all of this, according to Portell Vilá, was a camouflage behind which López hid his real objective—the establishment of an independent Cuba. He even asserts that in this free Cuba, López and his followers planned to emancipate the slaves, and it was this that led the conservative members of the Havana Club to break with him. He argues that O'Sullivan was an ardent "free soiler" who strove for Cuban freedom in the hope that independence would lead to the abolition of slavery in the island, and that once the free territory was annexed to the United States, it would accelerate the abolition of slavery in the Southern states.[13]

The truth is that O'Sullivan was a strong supporter of slavery and one of the staunchest Northern defenders of expanding the slave system throughout the United States. It is true that O'Sullivan was a "free soiler," belonging at one time to the political movement which stood for "No more slave states, no more slave territory, no more compromises with slavery." But he joined the Free Soil Party only because it opposed Lewis Cass, Democratic candidate for President in 1848, upon a platform framed to suit the South. O'Sullivan hated the Michigan Democrat and temporarily joined forces with his political opponents. It was nothing more than a political maneuver, and at no time did O'Sullivan indicate anything but bitter opposition to the anti-slavery principles of the Free Soil Party. In June, 1850, O'Sullivan, in a letter to Quitman, called for a sufficient number of Southern volunteers to assist López to make sure that the invasion would not free the Negroes held in bondage. During the Civil War, O'Sullivan wrote from London to Jefferson Davis, President of the Southern Confederacy: "I can only say that the darker may [be] the gloom of the clouds resting on the Southern Cause, the brighter and warmer burns the flame of my attachment to it. . . . Stand or fall, sink or swim, I am with you."[14]

It certainly requires the wildest imagination to conceive of rabid pro-slavery men like Quitman, Henderson, O'Sullivan and other supporters of López having anything to do with a man who might so much as dream of establishing a free Cuba in which slavery would be abolished. Not only did López never hint at such objectives, but all his utterances about slavery were the sort to endear him to his Southern slaveholding backers. López declared that slavery was not incompatible with the liberty of Cuba's citizens. History had demonstrated this again and again, and the world had "the excellent example of the United States where three million slaves did not impair the flowering of the world's most liberal institutions. In the future Cuba would emulate its great continental neighbor in this respect." Furthermore, in his proclamation to his soldiers, López gave as one of their objectives the prevention of Spain from liberating the slaves in Cuba, and "converting into worse than San Domingo, the richest and loveliest of the islands."[15] This was language out of the book of the wealthy slaveowners in both Cuba and the United States.

Let us follow the 600 American and five Cuban filibusters as they landed at Cárdenas during the night of May 19, 1850. They immediately marched to the plaza, and, in brief but vigorous fighting, overwhelmed the small Spanish garrison, and captured the Spanish governor.

This was their sole achievement. Only two Spanish soldiers joined López's forces, while most of the town's population fled to the hills. Soon a group of Spanish lancers made their appearance on the outskirts, and it was rumored that a large force was en route from Matanzas. Threatened with being surrounded and cut down in Cárdenas, and with many of his men demoralized by the failure of the Cubans to rally behind the expedition, López ordered his men back aboard the *Creole*. Before the retreat could be carried out, about six companies of Spanish infantry entered Cárdenas; and the filibusters re-embarked in the *Creole* only after much loss of life. With Key West as the objective, and the Spanish man-of-war *Pizarro* in hot pursuit, the filibusters raced for the haven of American sovereignty. After anxious hours, and by the sheerest luck, the *Creole*, its boilers leaking and wheezing, steamed into Key West a few hundred yards ahead of the *Pizarro*. The federal authorities in Key West seized the *Creole*, but allowed López and his men to disperse. Later, López and González surrendered to the United States government and were sent to New Orleans to stand trial for violating the neutrality laws.

The New Orleans grand jury returned true bills against 16 men, including López and González, and such outstanding supporters of the expedition as Quitman, Henderson, Judge Smith, Sigur and O'Sullivan. (Quitman resigned the governorship of Mississippi in order to submit to arrest as a private citizen.) Tried first as a test case, Henderson underwent three trials, the first and second ending in a mistrial. On March 6, 1851, the government gave up after a third jury voted 11–1 for acquittal. The government dismissed all suits.

Annexationists excused the failure of the López expedition on the ground that Cárdenas was inhabited chiefly by "Spaniards, foreigners, and a class of population from which but faint hopes could be entertained of any co-operation in a revolutionary movement." Had López made his attack anywhere else in Cuba, it was probable that Congress would now be discussing just when to add the island to the United States. The result of the expedition was, therefore, no indication that the Cubans were not "anxious for assistance, and ready to assist, with all their means, any expedition adequate to make a successful stand."[16]

This rationalization did not go down in 1850, nor have later versions been any more convincing. Dr. Portell Vilá explains that two factors operated against popular support for López: (1) that the filibusters were almost entirely American, and (2) that they spoke only English. But he refuses to draw the logical conclusion from these facts—namely, that on May 19, 1850, the Cubans were faced, in one corner of their island, with an expedition made up almost exclusively of North Americans seeking the establishment of a temporarily "independent" Cuba which would soon be annexed to the United States. That there was widespread dissatisfaction with Spanish rule in Cuba is true. But by this time, the dissatisfaction no longer reflected a desire for annexation to the United States. Judging correctly that the Cárdenas expedition, made up almost entirely of Americans, was essentially an annexationist movement and that López, its leader, was an annexationist agent of the slaveholding interests of the South, the Cubans refused to ally themselves with it.

Even while the filibusters and their accomplices were awaiting trial in New Orleans, and during the trials themselves, plans were hatched for a new expedition. Following the dismissal of the indictment against them, the filibusters stepped up their activity. The entire South from Charleston to Texas now hummed with filibustering activity, with New Orleans and Mobile as the centers. Men were recruited, and arms and ammunition were secured from Southerners in high places. In New York, John O'Sullivan and Louis Schlessinger, a Hungarian refugee, were also recruiting men, many of them exiles from Hungary and Italy.

López, however, was little interested in the Northern activity. He planned to make the expedition almost exclusively a Southern movement. López now conceived of his expedition as the starting-point for the creation of a vast new slave empire annexed to the United States. From all the available evidence, the Southern political leaders saw López as their instrument for annexing Cuba, and felt that the General not only was a willing instrument, but sympathized with their larger objective of using Cuba as the starting-point for a slave empire in which emancipated Negroes (for example, those in Haiti) would be re-enslaved. John Claiborne, a close associate of Quitman, wrote from New Orleans shortly after the Cárdenas expedition:

> The truth is that our people want Cuba free not only because they detest the Despotism of its government, but for reasons of the strongest political necessity. If the Cubans wish to become free and to be admitted to share our civil rights, very well. *If not, they must go away from Cuba which must be ours whether its present inhabitants desire it or not. Such is the reasoning of the great mass of our Southern and Western men.*[17]

These men were willing to support López because they knew he planned to fulfill their fondest hopes. Assured that the slave interests of Cuba would be protected, and that the General was even thinking of assisting the Southern slaveowners in their slave-empire dream, they threw their support behind López's new expedition.

This Southern support became all the more crucial on the collapse, in April, 1851, of the Northern wing of the project. The steamer *Cleopatra* was scheduled to leave New York with a contingent of about 400 men, join groups in Florida, and then proceed as one army to Cuba. But, in return for "a fair remuneration" from the Spanish Consul, one of the conspirators exposed the filibusters to the District Attorney, who seized the *Cleopatra*, and had O'Sullivan, Schlessinger and others brought to trial. The trial was delayed for almost a year and ended with the jury unable to reach a verdict.

The *Cleopatra* fiasco did not slow up López's activities in the South. Southerners eagerly joined the venture. A large group was already training in Mississippi; another paraded through the streets of Mobile; and Arkansas boasted a special school for filibustering military tactics. It was reported that the Governor of Georgia had equipped a contingent with arms from the state arsenal.

This Southern activity evoked complaints by exiled Cubans that López was showing favoritism toward Americans. They predicted that the expedition would receive the same cold reception from the people of the island as the Cárdenas venture. They proposed that the expedition be composed solely of Cubans. López, assured of Southern men and money, rejected the proposal. The exiled Cubans then broke off relations with López, and refused to have anything to do with the expedition, which became almost exclusively a Southern enterprise. The Southern annexationist press openly predicted that Cuba would soon become "a bright star in our galaxy."[18]

With proceeds of bond sales, again sold at ten cents on the dollar, arms and ammunition were purchased for the volunteers, thousands of whom were pouring into New Orleans from Louisiana, Mississippi, Georgia, and Arkansas. L. J. Sigur sold his share in the New Orleans *Delta*, purchased the 500-ton steamer, *Pampero*, for $40,000, and turned it over to the filibusters.

Meanwhile, the Spanish authorities in the United States, whose spies reported what was being prepared in the South, urged Washington to take action. But Millard Fillmore, who had succeeded Taylor as President after the latter's death, was, as one student notes, "inclined to appease the extremists in the South among whom López found his chief support, and [was] unwilling to use the stringent methods required to enforce the Neutrality Act."[19] To be sure, the President infuriated the Southern annexationists by denouncing the project, warning that its members rendered themselves liable to legal penalties and forfeited their claim to the protection of the government. But the administration took no steps to replace the indulgent customs authorities at New Orleans with men who could be trusted to fulfill their duty to prevent López from sailing for Cuba.

When it was understood that the *Pampero*, with López and over 500 on board, was ready to sail, all but one of the responsible Federal officials left New Orleans. And when, on the morning of August 3, 1851, the ship sailed, William Freret, Collector of Customs, who had remained in the city, refused to do anything to stop the expedition, asserting "that he was powerless to intervene against a venture which had such enthusiastic public support."[20] *

This time the expedition sailed with real hopes of success. On July 22, 1851, news had reached the United States of a revolution in Cuba. The New Orleans *Delta*, leading supporter of López, carried banner headlines on July 28 proclaiming:

> GLORIOUS NEWS FROM CUBA.
> THE REVOLUTION COMMENCED.
> FIRST BATTLE ON THE FOURTH OF JULY!
> THE PATRIOTS TRIUMPHANT! . . .
> THE GOVERNMENT PANIC STRICKEN!

But the Cuban uprising was considerably less extensive than pictured in the American annexationist press. Actually, there were two uprisings: one in Puerto Príncipe, a town in central Cuba, led by Joaquín de Agüero; and the other, soon afterwards, near Trinidad on the southern coast, led by Isidoro Armenteros, a friend of López. Agüero, a Cuban lawyer, was head of the *Sociedad Libertadora* (Liberating Society) which had printed proclamations and distributed them clandestinely throughout the island, calling for uprisings co-ordinated with López's expedition. When Agüero learned of the seizure of the *Cleopatra* in New York and the postponement of López's departure, he decided to precipitate action by an immediate revolt in Cuba.

The day set for the general uprising was an auspicious one—the Fourth of July—and the conspirators had prepared a declaration of independence and flags, copied after the one flown by López in Cárdenas. The declaration of independence listed "the calamities and hard oppression which all the natives of the country are suffering . . . besides other considerations of much weight," and announced that: "The Island of Cuba is unanimously declared to be independent of the government and Peninsula of Spain, in order that she may be recognized in the face of the world as an independent nation, which has spontaneously placed itself under the protection and auspices of the Republic of the United States, whose form of government we have adopted."[21]

---

* President Fillmore removed Freret from his position, but this was the usual case of locking the stable after the horse was gone.

The reference to protection by the United States indicates that Agüero and his followers were following the Texas route to annexation. It is interesting, also, that two different versions of this declaration were published in the United States—one in the North, which made no reference to the protection of slavery, and another in the South, specifically promising such protection. The Agüero group was linked with the slaveholding interests in Cuba (though Agüero himself had manumitted his slaves), and shared López's determination to leave slavery in the island untouched. The same can be said for the uprising led by Armenteros in Trinidad.

Neither uprising got very far. By July 4, Agüero had mustered only 44 followers. And the plot had been betrayed to Captain General José de la Concha by a priest, confessor to Agüero's wife. Before the rebels of Puerto Príncipe could act, Concha arrested 16 leaders, and captured Agüero after a brief battle in the mountains. He then squelched the uprising near Trinidad. By mid-August, all the rebels had been captured and executed.

López, however, knew only that an uprising had taken place. He had frequently urged his Cuban supporters to take up arms and then retreat to the mountains and await him and the relief force from the United States. Agüero had followed his advice, and had established a camp in the mountains, *El Buen Refugio*. But they won little support from the Cuban people, and the Spanish forces tracked them down and annihilated them.

In his haste to join Agüero, López had left New Orleans with only a fraction of the volunteers available, for the *Pampero* was too heavily loaded to take on any more. And he had to unload nearly a hundred men at Belize to make the vessel seaworthy. These, and the others who had been left behind, were assured that they would get their chance in the next landing, which would be under the command of Quitman.

The men López brought to Cuba numbered 435. Most of them were Southerners, but there were groups of Hungarians and Germans, and nine to 15 Cubans. William L. S. Crittenden, a nephew of the U.S. Attorney General John J. Crittenden, and a veteran of the Mexican War, who since that conflict had served in the New Orleans Customs House, was a Colonel in the expeditionary force, and second-in-command to López.

López intended to pick up arms and ammunition in Jacksonville and then proceed to the central part of Cuba, where Agüero had staged his revolt and where he would be far from the Spanish center of strength at Havana. At Key West he received word that the whole of western Cuba was in revolt. This information was probably planted by Captain General Concha's agents to divert the expedition to a point near Havana. López, taken in, sailed confidently for Bahía Honda, on the deserted shore of which he landed on August 11. On that very day, Agüero died in Puerto Príncipe!

López brought with him two proclamations to the people of Cuba. One offered a provisional government in which protection for slavery was guaranteed. The provisional government was to retain power until the election of a constituent assembly which would then —"if thus the sovereign people decide"—annex Cuba to the United States. The second proclamation made it clear what López intended the decision to be: "The star of Cuba, today hidden and closed in by the mists of despotism, will rise beautiful and shining perchance to be admitted gloriously into the spendid North American constellation according to its inevitable destiny."[22]

As the Cuban historian, Manuel Sanguily, points out, López was advancing the annexationist program of his American slaveholding supporters in 1851 just as he had done in 1850—with one slight difference: "In 1850 it appeared that the island was being disposed of [to the United States] without consulting its inhabitants. In 1851, it is declared that it is they—the Cubans—who will have to dispose of it in a sovereign way. But on both occasions, the opinion of López is that sooner or later, in one way or another, its destiny will force her to incorporate into the North American Confederation."[23]

Bahía Honda, less than 40 miles from Havana, proved a trap, being accessible to Captain General Concha's superior forces by sea and by rail. Concha lost no time springing the trap.

López sent the *Pampero* back to Florida to pick up a second shipload of filibusters. Then he split his forces into two groups: he led 300 men to Las Pozas, a small village some 10 miles inland, while Colonel W. H. Crittenden stayed behind with 120 men to guard the supplies and arms intended for the expected Cuban recruits. But no more Cubans rallied at Bahía Honda than at Cárdenas. The next morning López was attacked, and although he held the field, his losses were heavy. It was now imperative to rejoin Crittenden. Nearly 100 men were sent in his direction, but were recalled when it was learned that strong Spanish forces were now deployed between the two parties. Joined by some of Crittenden's men, López gave up hope of uniting the two groups, and set out for the interior of the island.

Crittenden, attacked by a superior force of Spaniards, failed to cut his way through to López at Las Pozas, and took to the woods with about 50 of his men. After great suffering, they made their way to the coast and set out for Key West in some small boats. On the second day, they were overtaken and captured by the Spanish steamer *Habanero*, and carried back to Havana. On the next day, August 6, 1851, after a summary trial, every man in the captured party was shot in the public square by order of Concha. It was reported that a mob committed atrocities on the dead and dying.

López and his men held out a few days longer, making hopeless and exhausting marches, fighting almost continuous bloody skirmishes, sometimes in scorching sunshine, sometimes in torrents of rain, sometimes without food. López and 160 wounded and starving survivors were captured and taken to Havana.

Concha had meanwhile rescinded his order that all captives be shot, but he excepted López, who was publicly garroted in Havana on the morning of September 1, 1851. Before he died, López bravely shouted, "My death will not change the destiny of Cuba!"

Four of the surviving 160 were released and the rest sent to Spain to serve lengthy terms in the quicksilver mines. After prolonged and touchy negotiations on the part of the United States, the prisoners were pardoned by Queen Isabella of Spain.

On August 20, the news reached the United States that the *Pampero* had landed in Cuba. The annexationist press, beside itself with joy, spread reports that "the Cuban people had risen *en masse* and joined the patriots"; that 4,000 Spanish soldiers had deserted to López; that López was marching on Havana at the head of a huge army, composed of Cubans and Spaniards as well as the filibusters, and in a few months a new star would be added to the American flag.

But within a few days came the sobering news of López's disaster.

Exaggerated reports of the manner in which Crittenden and his men were executed were played up by what President Fillmore correctly labelled "a mercenary and prostituted press." In the South, generally, and in New Orleans, particularly, journalists demanded vengeance. Americans were exhorted to rush to Cuba to wreak "a quick revenge upon the miserable government that [had] so outraged humanity." The precedent was clear, the annexationists cried. The massacre at Alamo had opened the campaign that gave Texas to the United States; the massacre at Havana should be followed by a war for the annexation of Cuba. "American blood has been shed," shrieked the Louisiana *Courier*. "It cries aloud for vengeance— vengeance on the tyrant! . . . blood for blood! Our brethren must be avenged! Cuba must be seized!"[24]

In New Orleans, a movement was actually formed to finance and equip an expedition to seize Cuba. A committee of leading annexationists was set up to receive donations; Cuban benefit performances were given; coffee-houses and barrooms contributed a day's receipts to the cause, and business establishments and private citizens donated funds. Nothing, however, came of the venture. Most of the money raised was used to provide for the filibusters who had been left behind.

The city then became the scene of a disgraceful riot. Mobs, partly drawn from the idle and restless filibusters who had been waiting to embark for Cuba, vented their fury on Spanish inhabitants and establishments. After eight hours of vandalism, during which the police did not interfere, the authorities finally quelled the disorders.

In his charge to the grand jury in the Federal Circuit court, 7th Circuit, Ohio, during the October term of 1851, condemning the violations of the neutrality laws of the United States by the López expeditionaries, Justice John McLean accurately summed up the whole nature of the movement:

> That expedition was organized in this country, and was composed, principally, of our own citizens. . . . They were induced to believe that a considerable portion of the people of Cuba were in arms, with the determination to overthrow their government. Those who were instrumental in creating this delusion have an awful account to render to their country and their God. The invading force, instead of meeting friends, met determined enemies with arms in their hands. At

every step the invaders were opposed, and it is not known that a single Cuban joined them. As might have been anticipated, the career of the invaders was short and extremely disastrous.

To Justice McLean the worst feature of the enterprise was the effect it had upon the American nation as a whole: "These unlawful enterprises cast a shade upon our national character, in the opinion of the civilized world. They unjustly, more or less, connect our government with the outrage, and they ascribe to it a lust for power and national aggrandizement." Concluding, Justice McLean declared tersely: "There never was an invasion among civilized nations, more atrocious and less excusable."[25]

The question still remained: Why had the López expedition failed? Almost universally, the annexationist press attributed the failure to the "degraded and imbecile" people of Cuba. But the real causes for López's failure are quite evident. Conditions both in Cuba and in the United States doomed the enterprise. The wealthy Cuban planters who formerly had favored annexation, no longer felt impelled to cast off Spanish domination and link the island to the United States, for Spain had stiffened against British pressure to end the slave trade and emancipate the new slaves. On the other hand, the danger did exist that if the invasion led by López developed into a major threat, the Spanish authorities would free the slaves and arm them against the invaders, in their determination to keep the colony.

In the United States, the intensifying sectional conflict witheld from López the massive support necessary for the conquest of Cuba. To be sure, López could go into action despite presidential proclamations, but a really huge and continuing invasion was out of the question. Not that the Whig administrations of Taylor or Fillmore would have hesitated to acquire Cuba. On the contrary, they let it be known that the United States had not abandoned this ambition. In the summer of 1851, Henry Clay, Whig party leader, visited Havana and was entertained by Captain General Concha. Clay assured Concha that he was a "faithful interpreter" of President Fillmore's sentiments. After complimentary comments on the administration of Cuba, and after expressing his and the President's "profound horror" at the filibustering expeditions, he noted that the economic and strategic interests of the United States would some day require the acquisition of the island; but only by means of an honorable treaty with Spain.

Edward Everett, Webster's successor as Secretary of State under President Fillmore, was even more emphatic. Upon the "anxious desire" of Spain, in 1852 England and France suggested to the United States that they make a joint disclaimer to Cuba, binding themselves to oppose any attempt on the part of any nation other than Spain, or any individuals, to obtain or maintain control of the island. Everett rejected the proposal outright. In his long and rambling reply, one point was clear—namely, that under no circumstances would the United States "impose a permanent disability" on itself as far as the annexation of Cuba was concerned.

> No administration of this Government, however strong in the public confidence in other respects, could stand a day under the odium of having stipulated with the great powers of Europe, that in no future time, under no change of circumstances, by no amicable arrangement with Spain, by no act of lawful war (should that calamity unfortunately occur), by no consent of the inhabitants of the island, should they, like the possessions of Spain on the American continent, succeed in rendering themselves independent, in fine, by no overruling necessity of self-preservation should the United States ever make the acquisition of Cuba.

Thus the United States haughtily and piously refused a proposal that would limit its "Manifest Destiny." Significantly, the annexationist press hailed Everett's reply as proof that the mishaps of López's expeditions should not discourage future attempts. Had not the administration refused to disavow the nation's aim to possess Cuba?[26]

Thus the failure of the Taylor and Fillmore administrations to support López's expeditions was not due to any unwillingness on their part to associate themselves with annexationist movements. What restrained them was the fear that annexation would pour oil on the flames that were threatening to consume the Union. Fillmore himself declared that the Cuban question was "a cause of division between the North and South," and threatened to destroy the Compromise of 1850 by reviving "all those dangerous discussions, which had menaced the existence of the Union, concerning Texas, California, and the other territories acquired or annexed."[27]

The Texas route was not possible in 1850–51, though everything about the López expeditions resembled the situation as it had been on the eve of the annexation of Texas. As Frederick Douglass, the Negro abolitionist, observed:

> The whole scene presents an aspect similar to that which existed just prior to the revolution in Texas, which finally resulted in the severance of that State from Mexico, and its annexation to the United States. Then, as now, the rotten-end of this Republic was literally alive with sympathizers with the rebels, and, as usual, Liberty was the watchword and disguise of the freebooters, pirates, and plunderers. Great meetings were held then, as now, in almost all southern cities, and in many northern ones, with a view to cheer on *the oppressed* in the struggle for their rights. Slaveholders, slave-traders, and cold-blooded tyrants of every grade, poured forth their swelling words of sympathy with the oppressed and execration of the oppressors.[28]

But there was an important difference. In 1846 the anti-slavery, anti-expansionist forces had not been powerful enough to stop the federal government, as open agent of the slaveowners, from seizing Texas from Mexico. But in 1850–51, these forces had grown in strength and could prevent the federal government, anxious though it was to appease the slaveowners and to acquire Cuba, from effectively supporting the movement.

The failure of the Cuban people to aid López was no indication that they were satisfied with Spanish rule. But they had no confidence that López and his associates offered a worthy alternative. To most Cubans, the filibusters were robbers and plunderers, agents of rapacious forces of a foreign country who wished to dominate and exploit Cuba. Shortly after the Bahía Honda invasion, a long, anonymous poem appeared in Cuba. It reflected the spirit of anti-filibuster Cuban opinion:

> Oh pirates! report
>   to your compatriots
> How Cuba protects you,
>   how she invokes your support!
> And to those infamous bankers
>   who, for love of gold
> Order you to the slaughterhouse,
>   give affectionate thanks;
>   give thanks to the traitor

> Who even amidst so much anguish
> gives lying hopes of triumph
> and seductive promises.[29]

José Martí was correct in his conclusion that López invaded Cuba in the interests of the Southern slaveholders of the United States.

chapter 5

FILIBUSTERS AND CAPITALISTS

The death of López did not end the plans of Cuban and American filibusters for the incorporation of the island into the United States. A few weeks later, in September, 1851, several former associates of López in New Orleans formed a secret society called the "Order of the Lone Star." The Order spread rapidly in the principal cities of the South, even to New York City. Soon it had some 50 chapters in eight states, with a membership estimated at from fifteen to twenty thousand. As an intimate of the founders of the Order wrote, its chief purpose was "revolutionizing Cuba and annexing the 'Jewel of the Antilles' to the United States."[1]

With Quitman as head of the Supreme Council and González as military commander, the "Order of the Lone Star" initiated plans for a new invasion of Cuba. This was slated for June, 1852, in conjunction with the "Conspiracy of Vuelta Abajo," organized in Cuba by Francisco de Frías, López's wealthy brother-in-law, who had bought himself the title of Count of Pozos Dulces. By a revolt in Vuelta Abajo (the region which is now the province of Pinar del Río), assisted by the "Lone Star" expedition, the conspirators hoped to liberate Cuba from Spain and annex it to the United States.

In August, 1852, the conspiracy was unearthed by the Spanish authorities. The editor and printer of *La Voz del Pueblo Cubano* (The Voice of the Cuban People), organ of the conspirators, was condemned to death and garroted, and another editor escaped to the United States. López's brother-in-law and other conspirators were sentenced to prison.

The collapse of the conspiracy did not deter the filibusters. They opened an intensive propaganda campaign within the United States, conducting public meetings and publishing pamphlets. To those who made a point of the failure of the Cubans to support López in 1851, González answered that this must be attributed to poor timing, and he promised mass support in the island for a new expedition. He released to the press a "Manifesto to the American People" (reprinted in pamphlet form) describing the sufferings of the Cuban people and appealing for American aid for the filibusters.

In the South, persons of wealth and social position were lining up behind them, joining the "Order of the Lone Star," and giving other indications of their support for a new expedition. Prominent among the Southern annexationists, along with General Quitman, was Pierre Soulé, a French émigré who had settled in New Orleans. He was elected in 1848 to the U.S. Senate, where he became a leader of the extreme pro-slavery group, and, during the debate on the Compromise of 1850, an advocate of immediate Southern secession. He also agitated for Cuban annexation. In the South, he symbolized the spirit of "Young America," a movement whose chief aim was the annexation of Cuba. Soulé argued that, since it was impossible to buy Cuba from Spain, it was necessary to achieve its annexation by conquest—even if this involved a war with Spain.

While Soulé was engaged in his agitation, annexationist capitalists and politicians in the North were actually trying to foment a war with Spain. Outstanding among these was a New York capitalist, "Live Oaks" George Law, President of the United States Mail Steamship Company, which held a contract with the government to carry the mails bimonthly from New York to Chagres via Havana and New Orleans. He was also head of the "Steamship Crowd," a lobby in Washington which exerted continuous pressure on Congress for additional appropriations for steamship lines, and especially Law's mail line.

In 1850, Law made an agreement with Stephen A. Douglas, the "little giant" of Illinois, to use his lobby in Congress to push Douglas's project for a railroad (the Illinois Central) from Illinois to Mobile, in return for a support for supplementary appropriations for Law's mail line. The Law-Douglas alliance paid off, and Law saw that still more could be gained with Douglas in the White House. For Douglas favored the annexation of Cuba, and Law had much personally to gain from such a measure. A visit to the island in 1852 had convinced him that annexation would boom trade between Cuba and the United States. Not only would his steamship line profit, but through his connections, with Douglas in the White House and Southern Senators in Congress, all grateful for his activity in furthering annexation, he might secure a monopoly of the passenger traffic to and from the island.

When Douglas lost the Democratic nomination to Franklin Pierce, Law sought to achieve annexation by fomenting a war with Spain. All that was needed, he felt, was some act by the Spanish authorities in Cuba which would be played up as an insult to American honor and serve as a *casus belli*. The cession of Cuba to the United States could then be exacted as the price Spain must pay for the insult.

The *Crescent City* incident gave Law his pretext.

The *Crescent City* was an American mail steamer, owned by Law, which plied the waters between Cuba and the United States. The Havana authorities suspected William Smith, its purser, of obtaining political information detrimental to Spain and favorable to the annexationist cause, with the intent of publishing it in pamphlets in the United States, and then distributing them on the next stop in Havana. Captain General Valentín Cañedo, who had succeeded Concha in mid-1852, warned Captain Porter of the *Crescent City* that, in the future, any vessel with Purser Smith on board would not be permitted to land.

Law could, of course, have transferred Smith to a ship that did not stop at Havana. But then there would have been no incident to use as pretext for war with Spain. He sent the *Crescent City* to Havana with Smith still aboard. Arriving on the afternoon of October 3, 1852, it was barred by Cañedo from entering the harbor.

Law's agent in New York immediately sent a protest to the State Department, demanding either government protection or permission "to redress the grievance and repel the insult to our national flag, with such means, and in such manner as we shall deem equal and due to self-protection."[2] This call for war against Spain either by the government of the United States or by Law's private military forces was immediately echoed by the annexationists. The *Crescent City* had left Havana without discharging its mail or passengers, and sailed for New Orleans, where indignation meetings were held and resolutions passed urging the government to seek revenge, and, if necessary, to declare war. "War! War! give us war!" was the cry at one such meeting, at which Senator Judah P. Benjamin declared, to thunderous applause, that if Spain refused to give full satisfaction, then Americans had "the right to appeal to the God of battle and annex Cuba."[3]

Throughout the South similar meetings were held. The annexationist press cried that the time had come to seize Cuba, and if the government held back, Law "should convert his mail steamers into warships, put his muskets to use, and expel the Spaniards from Cuba with his own resources." The press assured the New York capitalist that he would "have no difficulty in finding men willing to join the 'crusade.'" The "Order of the Lone Star" let it be known that it had plenty of volunteers to offer. One of the organizers of the Order wrote to Quitman on October 14, 1852, "A Brigade is now being raised in anticipation of a war with Spain . . . already the 'grand password' has been given out, which is: 'Action! Action!! Action!!!'"[4]

The anti-annexationist press was not silent. It condemned Law for having provoked the international incident, and characterized the whole affair as "filibusterism in a new guise, but with the old spirit and the old hopes." It urged President Fillmore to order Law to desist from his provocation.[5] Fillmore did little until after the election of 1852, fearing that a stern policy would give the pro-annexationist Democrats another stick with which to beat the Whig policy toward Cuba. But once the election was over and the Democrats victorious, he took a firmer stand. He ordered the mails withheld from Law's steamer if Smith remained purser on one bound for Havana.

But Law was not to be intimidated by a lame-duck President. He would send his ship to Havana with Smith aboard, he told the press, and if Spanish officials seized her, the country would go to war. Otherwise, he was "mistaken in his estimate of the character and temper of the American people." He did what he said he would do, and sent the newer ship *Cherokee* to Havana instead of the leaky *Crescent City*. She carried no mails, no passengers, no naval commander, no insurance—only Purser Smith.

The maneuver infuriated Fillmore, who let Law know that he had no right to "threaten war on his own account for the purpose of real or imaginary injuries." If Law persisted in his conflict with the Spanish authorities in Cuba and lost one of his vessels, the government would do nothing to indemnify or protect him.[6]

Captain General Cañedo then took the wind out of Law's sails by accepting an affidavit from Purser Smith declaring his innocence of publishing anti-Spanish, pro-annexationist pamphlets and distributing them in Cuba. Cañedo then lifted the ban on the *Crescent City*, and allowed Smith to land in Havana. Law tried to create new warscares out of other incidents affecting his steamers, but the opposition of the anti-slavery-expansion forces was so strong that even the Pierce administration could do little to help him.

His efforts to provoke a war with Spain frustrated, Law remained determined to get Cuba into the Union. He joined forces with the filibusters to further this goal.

The great Democratic victory of 1852 had been celebrated with bonfires and torchlight parades in which banners were carried proclaiming such sentiment as "The Acquisition of Cuba Must Now Be Fulfilled," and "May the Queen of the Antilles Be Added to Our Glorious Confederacy under the Prosperous Administration of Pierce."[7] With "Young America" now in the saddle, the time was ripe for action. All that was needed was a military leader to replace the "martyred López," a man who, like the dead General, could be counted upon to do all in his power to bring Cuba into the Union.

The man the annexationists chose was General John A. Quitman.

On April 29, 1853, the *Junta Cubana* of New York called upon Quitman to lead an invasion of Cuba, and proposed to make him "exclusive chief of our revolution, not only in its military, but also in its civil sense." Quitman accepted on condition that "the details be placed on such footing as to insure success, and not to compromise my own character and reputation"; that adequate means be guaranteed, and that all Cuban patriots in the United States join in the movement. He also desired a pledge of co-operation from "respectable and influential" men in the island.[8]

For three months before taking this decision, Quitman checked on the reactions to an expedition. He conferred with the leaders of the "Order of the Lone Star"; he sounded out the attitude of the Pierce administration, and apparently was satisfied that he could count on its support. Quitman's biographer, Claiborne, writes that, on his way to a meeting with the *Junta Cubana* for the final agreement, the General stopped in Washington and communicated his designs to "distinguished persons" who assured him "not only that he had their sympathies, but that there could be no pretext for the intervention of the federal authorities. He left the capital buoyant with hope."[9]

In New York, where Quitman was to meet the Cuban *Junta*, a huge sendoff was given to the newly-appointed Minister to Spain, Pierre Soulé, en route to Madrid. The Cuban *Junta* led the demonstration, carrying the flag of the United States, the banner of the "Order of the Lone Star," and a number of other banners on which were inscribed:

> Oh pray, ye doomed tyrants,
> Your fates not afar,
> A dreaded Order now watches you—
> It is the Lone Star.

and:

> The Antilles Flower,
> The true key of the Gulf,
> Must be plucked from the Crown
> Of the Old Spanish Wolf.

A monumental representation carried in the parade by the Cuban *Junta* showed a tomb and a weeping willow. On the tomb were the words: "LÓPEZ AND CRITTENDEN. AGÜERO AND ARMENTEROS. They and their companions are not forgotten." Addressing a crowd of nearly 5,000 gathered outside Soulé's hotel, Miguel Teurbe Tolón, editor of *La Verdad*, speaking for the *Junta*, expressed the hope that when the Minister returned home, "a new star shining in the sky of Young America may shed its dawning rays upon your noble brow." Evidently aware that the Pierce administration had bestowed its blessings upon the proposed Quitman expedition, the *Junta* was confident that annexation of Cuba would soon be accomplished. They knew, as did Quitman, that in the instructions Soulé took with him to Spain from Secretary of State Marcy, the administration expressed the hope that Cuba would "release itself or *be released*" from Spain.[10]

On August 18, 1853, Quitman signed a formal agreement with the Cuban *Junta*, which appointed him the "civil and military chief of the revolution, with all the powers and attributes of dictatorship as recognized by civilized nations, to be used and exercised by him for the purpose of overthrowing the Spanish government in the island of Cuba and its dependencies, and substituting in the place thereof a free and independent government." He was invested with authority to contract loans, issue bonds, grant commissions, and raise military and naval forces. His civil powers were to cease as soon as a government could be organized in Cuba, but his military powers would continue until all Spanish forces were driven from the island. In the event of his success, he was to receive a reward of a million dollars.

Article II of the agreement specified that Quitman would protect slavery in Cuba, "establishing therein a free and liberal government which shall retain and preserve the domestic institutions of the country." The agreement said nothing about the annexation of Cuba to the United States, but there is little doubt that this was clearly understood by both parties. To be sure, when it was organized in New York in October, 1852, the Cuban *Junta* announced that it rejected annexationism. But this was for the record only; in all their public utterances, such as that by Tolón at the Soulé celebration, and in editorials in *La Verdad*, the leaders of the *Junta* made it clear that they expected and wanted annexation to follow liberation of Cuba from Spain. As for Quitman, it is ridiculous to suppose that the man who was dreaming of "Cuba as the nucleus of a slave empire" that would also "include Mexico, with himself as head of the empire,"[11] would have entertained the *Junta*'s proposal for a moment without positive assurance that annexation would be the ultimate goal. Indeed, Alexander M. Clayton, the new Consul at Havana, a confidant of Quitman and intimately acquainted with his plan, wrote to Quitman that he agreed that an "Independent Government after the fashion of Texas" would be "at first advisable." Then Cuba should be annexed to the Union in such manner as "circumstances may direct." If the North refused to allow Cuba to enter the Union, the South would secede and start a new government together with Cuba. "The acquisition of Cuba I regard as the only hope of the South," wrote another associate of Quitman. "Whether it comes into the Union or not, will matter little so far as the South is concerned. With the aid of Cuba, she can make her own terms either in or out of the Union."[12]

In effect, there was agreement among all three parties in the new expedition—the *Junta*, Quitman and his slaveowning associates, and the Pierce administration—that, after Cuba was "released" from Spain, this course should be followed: there should first be established an independent government which would then request annexation, and this would be carried through, as in the case of Texas, by a joint resolution which would require only simple majorities of the two houses of Congress.

Following his pact with the *Junta*, Quitman set up two executive committees subject to his orders—one at New Orleans and another at Savannah, Georgia. He gave these committees authority over all "local volunteer associations" in their respective regions. To evade the neutrality laws, Quitman planned to transport his filibusters to some point of foreign jurisdiction where he would organize them into a military unit. He would then stand ready to support an anticipated Cuban uprising.[13]

Quitman received hundreds of letters from men offering to join the expedition as volunteers or to raise commands of various sizes. Most of the volunteers, judging from the letters in the Quitman Papers, were from the South or the Southwest, many had served in the war with Mexico, and many frankly expressed their desire to go to Cuba to better their "fallen fortunes." Quitman accepted all volunteers and directed them to his subaltern, John S. Thrasher, in charge of enlistments in New Orleans.

Quitman himself concentrated on raising money. He expected the "Order of the Lone Star" to furnish at least $300,000, and also hoped for large sums from Cuba. With this money he expected to equip and transport some 3,000 men to Cuba.

Quitman originally planned to sail in February, 1854. But the enterprise encountered so many difficulties that a delay became necessary. For one thing, not all the expected funds were received. For another, Quitman received word that the Cubans were not yet ready to revolt. A number of wealthy planters in the island urged him to postpone his departure until after the Cuban sugar crop had been harvested in July.

On March 4, 1854, Felix Huston, former Commander-in-Chief of the Armies of the Texas Republic, and an organizer of the expedition, wrote to Quitman from New Orleans that he considered the enterprise "just at a dead halt," and thought "nothing can be done till next fall if then."[14] Quitman once again agreed to postponement.

While Quitman continued his preparations to invade Cuba, events in the island provided new and unprecedented momentum to the annexationist drive, as the "Africanization of Cuba" scare swept the South.

chapter 6

THE "AFRICANIZATION OF CUBA" SCARE

One reason for the decline of the annexationist movement in Cuba was the stiffening of Spanish resistance to British pressure to close the slave trade market, declare the trade piracy, and emancipate all slaves imported in violation of the treaties abolishing the slave trade. With Spain unwilling to take effective measures to prevent it, the slave trade flourished. Brazil, with British aid, was making progress in abolishing the slave trade; the Brazilian Parliament had passed laws defining the slave trade as piracy, and imposing severe penalties on apprehended slavers. Great Britain asked Spain to follow this example, and offered assistance. But Spain, pretending to act in ruffled national pride, rejected any British role in the solution of the problem. Meanwhile the trade continued, and for each "sack of coal" delivered to Cuba, the Captain General, other officials in the island, and the Queen Mother in Madrid, got their "take."

Meanwhile, too, the abolitionists in England and the sugar producers in the British West Indies who were finding Cuban competition impossible to cope with, were increasing their pressure on the British government to force Spain to stop conniving in violations of the slave trade treaties. In September, 1851, British Prime Minister Palmerston wrote to the Spanish Minister for Foreign Affairs: "It is high time this system of evasion should cease. His Majesty's Government demand from the Spanish Government a faithful and honorable fulfillment of the treaty engagements of the Spanish Crown and His Majesty's Government throw upon Spain the whole responsibility of any consequences which may arise from a longer continuance of a breach of faith in this respect."[1]

This was direct and forceful language, and indicated that British patience was wearing thin. Moreover, England was in a position to convert words into action. Not only could its navy protect Cuba from filibusters, but Englishmen held a large portion of Spanish bonds, the interest payments of which were overdue, and they could embarrass Spain by diplomatic pressure for payment.

In 1852 England had been ready to join with France and the United States to guarantee Spanish sovereignty over Cuba. Nothing came of the proposal because of the refusal of the United States. But Britain let Spain know that it would support continued Spanish rule over Cuba—provided Spain enforced the treaties abolishing the slave trade, and took steps toward the emancipation of the slaves. At the beginning of 1853, Palmerston plainly intimated that Spanish suppression of the Cuban slave traffic was the *sine qua non* of continued British support of Spanish ownership of Cuba. The British government went further. Its Ambassador at Madrid was informed —and he passed this information on to the Spanish officials—that although Britain would prefer to see Cuba in Spanish hands, it would not, as long as Spain did nothing about the slave traffic, interfere if the United States seized the island. For such an eventuality, "the government of Spain should be prepared!"[2]

When this forceful warning was given, Spain knew of the new expedition being prepared in the United States, and that the Pierce administration was abetting it. Under British pressure and the imminent danger of another and more powerful invasion, Spain decided on a new slave policy in Cuba. This, it expected, would guarantee British support against filibustering, and frighten the Cuban slaveowners away from annexationist agitators. Finally, it would raise a powerful ally of Spanish rule among the Negroes who could then be used to combat the filibusters and their associates in Cuba. Naturally, the Negroes would oppose annexation to the United States where slavery existed.

On September 23, 1853, Spain appointed the Marquis Juan de la Pezuela Captain General of Cuba and explicitly charged him with suppressing the slave trade. Pezuela was well known as an enemy of slavery. During a two-year term as governor of Puerto Rico (1849–1851), he had condemned the slave trade and aided the slaves in many ways, issuing decrees for the better treatment of the Negroes. An incorruptible official—a phenomenon among servants of the Crown—he had proved inaccessible to bribery.

Pezuela arrived in Cuba on December 3, 1853, preceded by rumors that he had instructions to end not only the slave traffic, but, as part of a secret agreement with the British, slavery itself. Almost immediately, he gave evidence that a new policy was in the offing. Previously, discussion of the slave question in the press had not been permitted. Now, on December 7, the *Diario de la Marina*, the organ of the government, began a series of articles discussing the forbidden subject. Believed to have been written by the new Captain General, the articles condemned previous government policy, called for the fulfillment of treaty obligations, and stressed the advantages of a free labor system as demonstrated by the Northern States of the American Republic.

Furthermore, Pezuela publicly praised the Bishop of Santiago de Cuba, Padre Antonio María Claret, long an object of vilification because he had agitated for improvements in the material and moral condition of the slaves. At the Bishop's request, he issued an order permitting the marriage of a white man with a Negro woman, which the slaveowners claimed was illegal. Finally, Pezuela established a militia in which free Negroes were to be enrolled as well as whites.

This would have been enough by itself to drive the slaveowners into hysterics. But Pezuela soon made it clear that he intended to do more. On December 23, 1853, he issued the first of several decrees: Negroes "known by the name of *emancipados* are all free"; anyone caught importing Africans would be heavily fined and banished from the island for a period of two years; and all governors and lieutenant governors who failed to advise him of clandestine landings in their respective provinces would be removed from office. Another edict provided for the introduction and regulation of Spanish, Indian, Yucatecan, and Chinese immigration.[3]

There was nothing actually revolutionary about these decrees, which simply sought to enforce existing treaty provisions. But Pezuela did not confine himself to words. He removed a number of officials, including the governors of Trinidad and Sancti Spíritus, for failing to prevent the landing of African slaves in their jurisdictions.

But Pezuela soon found himself up against more than opposition from the Cuban slaveowners and subordinates reluctant to carry out his orders. His major obstacle was the provision in the law of 1845 which prohibited intrusion in the plantations in pursuit of contrabands. As Pezuela pointed out, once the slave ship had landed its cargo in an obscure inlet, it was virtually impossible to pursue the trader further. Since a Negro bought in Africa for 40 *duros* was sold in Cuba for 700, since the long and broken coast line made it difficult to prevent landings, and since the authorities could not follow the slaves into the plantations, the slave traders readily risked the British blockade.

Pezuela's complaints, endorsed by the British, brought the necessary authorization from Madrid. In March, 1854, the inviolability of the plantations was nullified, and they could be searched to investigate their labor force.

On May 3, 1854, Pezuela issued his most celebrated decree. It authorized officials to enter all plantations suspected of contraband practices; provided for an annual registration of slaves after the August harvest; warned civil and military officers that they would be discharged if, on hearing of a disembarkation of slaves, they failed to notify the government within 24 hours; applied the same penalty to all lesser officials, "since it is not possible to effect an embarkation without the connivance of minor officials," and subjected all those convicted of slave smuggling to a two-year exile. "Now," said Pezuela, in concluding his decree, "the spectacle of an impotent authority and the impunity of a few capitalists must come to an end. Avaricious interests that place private gain above the national interest can no longer be tolerated."[4]

These measures filled the Cuban slaveowners with the wildest fears, and justifiably so. They recognized that the suppression of the slave trade, coupled with annual registration of the slave population, meant one thing—gradual abolition. Under Pezuela's decree, all slaveholders were to come before the local authorities and make a full declaration of their slave property. A slave whose master could not show a registered title to him, could be declared free on the spot. All slave arrivals in Cuba after 1820 were illegal entries and their owners possessed no clear title to them. The registration of slaves would bring these irregularities out into the open, and the illegally held slaves could be declared free at any moment the government chose. The death rate among the slaves on the island was extremely high and the birth rate correspondingly low. If their present supply were not replenished, and the slaves who had been smuggled in were declared free, the only slaves left would be those imported before

1820 and their offspring. It would not be long before scarcely a slave remained in the island.

To meet this threat, the Cuban slaveholders resorted to purposeful confusion. They could not attempt, before world opinion, to defend their right to import slaves in the face of treaties outlawing the slave trade; nor could they appeal for sympathy on the ground that the registration of slaves was unwarranted and that Negroes who had been brought into Cuba illegally should not be set free. So they raised the cry of "Africanization." They prophesied that the decrees already published were only the forerunners of more drastic ones. Spain would send hordes of Negroes to the island and free them after a short period of enforced contract labor. These "barbarous" Africans would, in time, submerge the whites. Spain would then decree complete emancipation and the Negroes would take over the island. "A general descent in the scale of morality would run throughout the entire population," and soon "civilization and Christianity" would perish in the island. It was all part of the "diabolical plot" of "Africanization." Spain had signed a treaty with Great Britain pledging herself to carry out this atrocious plan to reduce Cuba to a "howling wilderness."[5]

So furious was the assault on his edicts, so vicious the propaganda charging Spain with aiming at "Africanizing" Cuba at England's insistence, the Pezuela took pains to deny the charge: "This detestable invention is false in every way, offensive to our honor and glory, and wholly opposed to the sentiments of the Queen, and I now denounce it in the honorable name of the Queen." He assured the slaveowners that nothing would be done to interfere with their right to own slaves *"legitimately acquired."*[6]

But these words fell on deaf ears. The slave merchants and planters would be satisfied by nothing less than the immediate rescinding of all of Pezuela's decrees and his removal from office. When Pezuela and Spain refused to budge on these demands, they intensified the cry of "Africanization," and turned once more to the United States for help:

> In this state of things we turn our eyes to Washington, and with grief we see that there they do not know the danger that our lives and property are in, there they do not perceive the risk this country is in

of being Africanized. An immediate energetic remedy must be applied. Let the volunteers of the South or Filibusters as they have been called (if your Govt will permit them) come to our aid.[7]

But most Cuban slaveowners were convinced that a mere filibustering expedition could not succeed. They wanted the U.S. Army. In April, 1854, a number of influential slaveowners met with Consul William H. Robertson in Havana, urged that he persuade President Pierce to send American troops to Cuba, and outlined measures to be taken to prevent slave emancipation when the American Army landed. Robertson forwarded the suggestions of the Cuban slaveowners in his official dispatch under the heading: "Ideas that must be taken into consideration on composing the proclamation that will be addressed by the President to the Inhabitants of Cuba when the American Army shall come to the same."

The proclamation, hitherto unpublished, opened:

INHABITANTS OF CUBA.

The day of your political regeneration has come. . . . Cuba is free. . . . A brave and numerous army will hoist the star spangled banner in Cuba. It is the ensign of your liberty & the guaranty of your welfare. What will the desperate efforts of your oppressors be able to accomplish in order to uphold their tottering power?

Do not fear then, inhabitants of Cuba; the Am. Eagle will defend you from their rapacity & vengeance, because the Sons of Washington are your brothers. *The Eagle will protect your lives, your families, your property and the social condition of your country.* . . .

Let those of you who have heretofore lived upon the unlawful exactions, sacrificing to your avarice, a people worthy of a better fate, rise against the liberating army. But know that the hour of justice has arrived, know beforehand that the Federal Republic has in Cuba the sympathies of all honest & enlightened men *and the support of the planters & property holders for whom the Am. Union is a pledge of order & security.*

In forwarding the "proclamation" to President Pierce, Robertson urged him to use it word for word, "because in my opinion in this manner the general simpathies [sic] of the country will be attracted to the annexation cause, which is the true and important end that those simpathies [sic] must be directed to."[8] In other words, the "Africanization" scare could be used to justify the conquest and annexation of Cuba by the United States. With this purpose, the

American Consuls flooded the State Department with reports of the danger of "Africanization" of the island and with appeals for the government to send the U.S. Army.

In March, 1854, Secretary of State Marcy dispatched a secret agent, Charles W. Davis, to Cuba to investigate whether or not "the Africanization of Cuba is contemplated by Spain, and [whether] she is even engaged in making arrangements to carry the measure in effect." He was also to ferret out any British involvement in this "conspiracy." The government knew that Britain had been urging Spain "to adopt a policy adverse to the well-being of this country [the United States]," and that having abolished slavery in her own possessions, Britain "has been incessantly engaged in endeavouring to cause its abolition elsewhere." But it had, as yet, no evidence that "Spain has yielded to the wishes of Great Britain." If Spain did yield, then the President would ask Congress for immediate action: "Our forbearance is ceasing to be a virtue."[9]

Actually, the only "forbearance" that had ceased to be a "virtue" was the "forbearance" of the Negro people of Cuba, too long deprived of their natural right to freedom! The slaveowners were, indeed, fortunate that their right to enslave fellow human beings had been so long protected by Spain's armed forces.

After a three months' stay in Cuba, Marcy's emissary returned with a report that must have made the Secretary of State's hair stand on end. It charged Britain with seeking to emancipate all slaves in Cuba introduced after 1820, the "immediate result" of which would be "the destruction of the wealth of the Island, a disastrous bloody war of the races, a step backwards in the civilization of America— and in a commercial view, an immediate loss to the United States, it being one of the best markets for their produce, and in a political view, its loss would be incalculable as it would be a never ending source of embarrassments and danger to the whole Union." Pointing out that the slaves of Cuba had been "hardened by bad treatment and by compulsion to labor to which they are naturally indisposed" —the *hacendados* evidently were much more disposed to labor— Davis predicted that, upon emancipation, they would "destroy at one blow the productions of the Island," and armed with "the lifted torch and knife," proceed to "attack the whites they hate, and whose superior civilization they fear, and would not rest until they destroyed them or forced them to leave the Island." At the end of his report, Davis wrote:

> The conclusion is irresistible that the emancipation of the Island and consequent Africanization of the Island is the true object had in view, and to which the march is as rapid as circumstances will allow....
>
> The danger is the more to be dreaded from the neighborhood of a Black Empire [Haiti] whose example they [the emancipated slaves of Cuba] would feel proud to imitate and whose asylum they could fly to in case they were conquered. Should the United States remain passive spectators of the consummation of the plans of the British ministry, the time is not distant in which they will be obliged to rise and destroy such dangerous and pernicious neighbors.[10]

The conclusion to be drawn from Davis's hysterical report was obvious: send the U.S. Army to Cuba before Spain carried through the British-inspired scheme to "Africanize" the island! This, of course, was to be followed by annexation of Cuba.

Annexationist Cuban exiles in the United States sensed the value of the "Africanization" hysteria in their agitation. They were among the first to exploit it. The *Junta Cubana* issued a "Manifesto," signed by Betancourt, Goicuría, Hernández, and Valiente, warning that only a miracle could avert the bloody vengeance of the liberated Negroes, the utter desolation of Cuba, and the liquidation of its whites. It was up to the United States to perform that miracle by immediate armed intervention, not solely in the interest of Cuba, but in the interest also of preserving slavery in the Southern States. Ambrosio José González spelled out why the United States had to act at once:

> Shall she consent to have under the sway of England, obedient to her whisper, at sixty miles from her Southern border, on the path of her coasting trade, across the isthmian routes that command her Pacific and her eastern commerce, a colony—for what are they but colonists?—not of Germans, such as go to Ohio and Pennsylvania; not of Frenchmen, as inhabit Canada or occupied Louisiana, not of Spaniards, as peopled Cuba and Porto Rico, but of wild, untutored and ferocious Africans—the rallying tribes for a Jamaica and St. Domingo.[11]

Naturally, the Southern expansionist press swelled the outcry against "Africanization," and furiously beat the war-drums. An

"Africanized" Cuba was bad enough by itself, but with Jamaica and Haiti, it would fasten a belt of Negro republics around the coast of the United States. These Negro republics would kindle a conflagration throughout the South, endangering, through widespread slave insurrections, and through offering refuge to fugitive slaves, "the very existence of slavery." Better Cuba were "obliterated" than "Jamaicaized by negrophilism." "This ['Africanization of Cuba'] is monstrous," cried the pro-annexationist *Democratic Review*, "and we will not allow it. This continent is for white people, and not only the continent but the islands adjacent, and the negro must be kept in slavery in Cuba and Hayti under white republican masters."[12]

Early in 1854, Governor P. O. Herbert of Louisiana sent a message to the legislature on the "Africanization of Cuba" menace. He blamed it on British abolitionists, determined "to thwart and impede our progress." The United States could not afford to stand by idly and allow Britain to "Africanize" Cuba. Resolutions were introduced in the legislature supporting the governor's stand. In the State Senate, the Committee on Foreign Relations issued a report stressing that the "Africanization of Cuba" was fraught with danger to the South, since it would establish an African colony almost within sight of its shores. Furthermore, this would "materially affect the natural law of American progress by precluding forever the admission of Cuba into this Union." Finally, the Louisiana legislature adopted a resolution which called upon "the federal government [to] adopt the most decisive and energetic measures to thwart and defeat a policy contrived in hatred to this republic and calculated to retard her progress and prosperity."[13]

The resolutions were presented to Congress by the Louisiana Senators John Slidell and Judah P. Benjamin, with the remark that they expressed the views of the entire South. Slidell proposed further that the President be authorized to suspend the neutrality laws whenever he should deem it expedient to legitimatize filibustering expeditions to Cuba. He demanded immediate action, warning that no matter how great was the danger of the acquisition of Cuba by England and France, the possession of the island by either of these two strong naval powers "would be less dangerous to the South than the existence of a pretended independent black Empire or Republic."[14]

However, the Southern expansionists and their Northern allies were vigorously countered by the Northern opponents of slavery expansion. They saw in the "Africanization of Cuba" scare a trick to facilitate the annexation of Cuba, opening new territory for slavery and increasing the slaveowner power in the federal government. In a widely-reprinted editorial, the Frankfort (Kentucky) *Commonwealth* of May 10, 1854 declared bluntly:

> We believe the mainspring of the whole movement is the desire of annexing Cuba to the United States; and if there is any real apprehension that Cuba will be "Africanized," that event is dreaded, not because it would make Cuba a dangerous neighbor, but because it would put the island in such a condition that her annexation would not be desirable to the people of the Southern States, or indeed of any of the States. Africanizing Cuba would have about the same effect upon the filibuster projects as sinking her in the ocean; and there, we are inclined to think, lies the secret of all the extravagance about the terrible evils that are to come upon us from such an event.

Only "wild 'divine right of slavery' fanatics," declared the anti-annexationists, could think Spain so "utterly demented and blind to her own manifest interests" as to strike such a foolish blow at Cuban prosperity. But even if Spain liberated the slaves of Cuba, did she not have the right to do so? What business was that of ours? "*We cannot see that the United States have any right to interfere to prevent her from doing so if she chooses.* It is for her, not us, to decide what is expedient for one of her own colonies."[15]

Such attacks on the "Africanization" scare, voiced in editorials and in speeches and petitions to Congress, temporarily blocked the annexationist drive for immediate and drastic government action. Slidell's resolution remained "in profound oblivion" in the Senate Committee on Foreign Relations. The House of Representatives confined itself to asking the President for data.

The infuriated Southern expansionists warned that if the government continued to fail the South, they would take matters into their own hands. The problem was chiefly a Southern one, and that section was resolved "to defeat the 'Africanization' menace by some means, and at all hazards. It is from this portentous and deadly plot that we are to save ourselves."[16]

Before turning to examine the measures they took, some concluding words about the menace of "Africanization" are in order. There were, of course, Cuban and Southern slaveowners who believed the rumors of a British-Spanish conspiracy to convert Cuba into a Negro republic. But, for the most part, the "Africanization" scare was a pro-slavery annexationist device to achieve two goals: to repeal Pezuela's policies, and to gain support, especially among moderate anti-annexationists in the South and in the North, for the conquest and annexation of Cuba. The Spanish government, which bluntly denied any desire to "Africanize Cuba," charged that the reports were "spread about for the purpose of creating alarm amongst the owners of slaves, endeavoring, at the same time, to persuade them that the only means of avoiding the impending danger is to throw themselves into the arms of the United States." Dr. Portell Vilá correctly labels the attempt to equate Pezuela's policy with "Africanization" as "ridiculous," and calls it fabrication for "political ends."[17]

To put it more concretely, the objection to Pezuela's program was that it would immediately emancipate a considerable number of slaves in Cuba and end in complete abolition. This, as the New Orleans *Daily Picayune* frankly admitted on October 23, 1853, would render Cuba "worthless to the American Union, by fostering elements which would make it inadmissible into the confederacy." A free Cuba would be "worthless" to the slavery expansionists! It was freedom for the slaves of Cuba that the slaveowners could not tolerate. As C. Stanley Urban writes: "Conservative planters understood Africanization to mean the adoption of any system of labor which had for its ultimate aim the extinction of slavery, and they so interpreted the labor decree in the island in 1854." Everything else —"the Negro republic," "the burning of the sugar-producing properties by the torch," "the destruction and expulsion of the white race," "the disappearance of civilization and of Christianity"—was propaganda to confuse the real issue. As Robert Russell, a British visitor to the United States, reported: "The planters of the South cannot tolerate the idea of Cuba being made free, and they all declare that the United States would be justified in making war against Spain were she to free her slaves."[18]

chapter 7

THE QUITMAN EXPEDITION

In the spring and summer of 1854, the South rang with cries that the time was propitious for action to annex Cuba. England and France were involved in the Crimean War. Spain was convulsed by internal revolution.* Cuba was seething with discontent over Pezuela's labor decrees. Relations between the United States and Spain, as we shall see, were estranged over the *Black Warrior* affair.

These converging developments stirred hopes in the South that the Federal government would either send the army to Cuba, or, at the very least, so interpret the Neutrality Law as to allow filibusters to liberate Cuba before "Africanization" became a fact. Alexander Walker of the New Orleans *Delta* wrote to a member of the Pierce administration in June, 1854:

> First, you must understand that the cause of Cuba now overwhelms all others in this section. This whole corner of the Union has been Filibusterized. Cuba must be taken, and that shortly—but here the pro-Cuban feeling is manifested by a decided *penchant* for an expedition, as the only means of securing Cuba in such a state as to make her valuable to the South, and pass her through the process by which Texas entered the Union as a State—an equal among equals.[1]

The Pierce administration did not turn a deaf ear. However, the President, as we shall see, had his own plan to effect annexation, through forcing Spain to sell the island. While negotiations were proceeding, he decided to do nothing to antagonize Spain.

Meanwhile, Quitman, who had delayed his expedition, was busy

---

* Early in 1854, a liberal petition was submitted to the Spanish Queen demanding constitutional reform. When she replied by proclaiming a state of siege in Madrid and banishing the opposition leaders from the country, a revolution broke out in the city. The rebellion was soon joined by Valladolid, Zaragoza, and Barcelona, and the Queen capitulated.

with fresh preparations. He did not approve the plan to purchase the island, and reminded Pierce that a treaty of purchase, requiring a two-thirds vote of the Senate, would stand little chance of passing in the face of anti-annexationist opposition. He warned Pierce that if the administration vacillated "until the abolition plans of Spain can be matured, a fearful responsibility will devolve upon you and your advisers. You will be held accountable to posterity for the ruin of Cuba and perhaps that of thirteen states of this Union." These were, of course, the slaveholding states in the South. "To you," Quitman admonished Pierce, the issue of Cuba and its annexation to the United States "are mere questions of political considerations," but to the Southern slaveholders "they are questions of vital interests, affecting our happiness, our fortunes and our lives."[2] Quitman urged that Congress should repeal the Neutrality Law, let the filibusters leave for Cuba so that they could "procure its independence and subsequent annexation to the United States as a slave state."

Quitman believed, as did all Southern expansionists and their Northern allies, that to wait for the government to purchase Cuba, even if a treaty of purchase could pass the Senate, was to guarantee that it would be acquired only after Negro emancipation, when it had been made valueless to the South. Argued the New Orleans *Daily Picayune* on June 2, 1854:

> It is we believe, a well established principle of international law that a change of sovereignty does not affect in any way the rights of property nor the established codes and institutions of the country whose sovereignty is transferred. . . . These truths being admitted, as we suppose they will be by all, we would ask of those who have the management of the affairs of the Republic the following questions. Let us suppose that Cuba has been already sold to us. Does the Federal Government, in assuming the rights and duties of the sovereign, obligate itself to carry out the decrees of Captain General Pezuela? The answer obviously is yes.

Immediate action was thus essential. "Revolution and independence first, and annexation after, is the only possible way in which Cuba can be saved to the South," Mike Walsh, a New York annexationist, emphasized in a letter to Quitman. "Live Oaks" George Law, the New York war-mongering, pro-annexationist capitalist, lent Quitman a steamer, a large supply of rifles, and a considerable amount of cash. Southern expansionists, hailing the expedition as "the paramount enterprise of the age," contributed funds. Quitman, on his part, issued $100,000 worth of bonds, ranging in face value from $150 to $3,000, and selling at a discount of three dollars to one. Still short of the necessary funds to equip his expedition in the manner he deemed necessary, he issued, around May, 1854, a circular marked "confidential," but distributed with no great caution, in which he emphasized the perils of "Africanization" to the South and asked for contributions. He followed this up with a plan under which "each man admitted [as a volunteer] must pay fifty dollars to the cause . . . and bear his own expense to a seaport." This requirement cut down recruitments. On the whole, however, the $50-scheme elicited enough favorable response to permit Quitman to make definite plans. Late in May, Thrasher negotiated for steamers to carry the expedition to Cuba.[3]

All through these months of preparation, Quitman had been operating under the impression that he had the tacit approval of Washington. He openly communicated his project to important persons in the administration, and retained the impression that not only did he have the sympathy of the Federal government, but that it had no motive to interfere with the scheme. He had even assured the administration that he planned to avoid breaking the Neutrality Law (though he preferred Congressional repeal) to avoid embarrassing the government. He would equip and train his men outside government jurisdiction. Since the filibusters would leave as private citizens, the government would be absolved from interfering with their departure.

It came as a shock to the filibusters, therefore, when on May 31, 1854, the President issued a proclamation forbidding the formation "within the United States" of "all private enterprises of a hostile character" against a foreign nation. Pierce warned that the government would "prosecute with due energy all those who unmindful of their own and their country's fame, [dared] disregard the laws of the United States and our treaty obligations."[4]

While it is difficult to discover all the reasons responsible for the changed attitude of the administration toward the Quitman expedition, several are evident. Through espionage and the indiscretions of the promoters of the expedition, its "secrets" were well known to the Spaniards. The Spanish legation in Washington turned this information over to the Pierce administration, which could not continue to profess ignorance. To do nothing to halt the filibusters at a time when the administration was entering negotiations for the purchase of Cuba was to guarantee that Spain would give a cold reception to such overtures.

The day before he issued the proclamation, Pierce had signed the Kansas-Nebraska Bill. This infamous measure repealing the Missouri Compromise (which had restricted slavery in the territories), permitting Southern settlers to bring slaves into Kansas and Nebraska, and authorizing the inhabitants to vote whether they should enter the Union free or slave, had aroused intense opposition in the North. To open these Western lands to slavery was proof to millions in the North and West that the slavocracy and its tool, the Pierce administration, intended to extend slavery into the free territories over the opposition of the majority. If the administration, on top of this victory for the South, had permitted the Quitman expedition to depart unmolested, it would have further outraged the North.

Before Pierce issued his proclamation, he conferred with the Senate Foreign Relations Committee, informed the Senators of his intention and discussed it with them. John Slidell of Louisiana protested, but Pierce was adamant. He was resolved, he said, to acquire Cuba, but by methods other than filibusterism. When Slidell accused him of betraying the South, the President agreed to telegraph the District Attorney in New Orleans that decisive measures to annex Cuba were soon to be taken. He hoped that a knowledge of this would assuage the disappointment of the South. He had in mind the Southerners who were not even satisfied with the Kansas-Nebraska Act, since they knew that these areas were not suitable for slavery expansion, whereas Cuba was. Alexander H. Stephens of Georgia expressed the view of the Southern leaders when he wrote, in May, 1854, that while the Southern victory in the Kansas-Nebraska Act was significant, he doubted that it would produce an "actual extension of slavery. . . . We are on the eve of much *greater issues* in my opinion. The Cuba question will soon be upon us."[5] In an editorial entitled, "Nebraska and Cuba," the New Orleans *Daily Picayune* of June 9, 1854, stated frankly that Kansas and Nebraska by themselves were not important to the South. "The measure upon which the Nebraska principle will be tested is that of the acquisition of Cuba."

Federal action against the filibusters in New Orleans soon followed the proclamation. On June 19, 1854, Quitman and five others were cited in the U.S. Circuit Court at New Orleans for attempted violations of the Neutrality Law. All the accused, when brought into court, refused to answer questions on the Fifth Amendment grounds of self-incrimination. The Grand Jury chose to see no evidence of the actual organization of an invasion of Cuba, despite the recruitment meetings and the sale of Cuban bonds issued for that purpose. Judge John A. Campbell then required Quitman, J. S. Thrasher, and Dr. A. L. Saunders to post a $3,000-bond each as guarantee that they would not violate the Neutrality Act of 1818 for a period of nine months. Quitman and his associates posted the bond, but assailed the proceedings as an "unconstitutional, illegal and arbitrary exercise of power."[6]

Quitman and his confederates were hailed as heroes in New Orleans. At a public dinner in their honor during the Grand Jury proceedings, Federal Marshal J. M. Kennedy, who had the filibusters in custody, offered the toast:

> Cuba:
> We'll buy or fight, but to our shore we'll lash her;
> If Spain won't sell, we'll then turn in and *thrash* her.[7]

Though conceding that Pierce's proclamation and the Grand Jury had adversely affected the sale of Cuban bonds, Quitman did not end his preparations. In September, 1854, Samuel R. Walker went to Cuba to scout the ground, while George Law came forward with an offer of 5,000 muskets. *Apuntes Biográficos del Mayor General Juan Antonio Quitman*, a biography of Quitman, was published at New Orleans in Spanish to acquaint Cubans with their "liberator." In November, 1854, *De Bow's Review*, the leading expansionist monthly, published an article by Samuel R. Walker entitled, "Cuba and the South," which opened with the warning that the "Africanization" of Cuba was just around the corner. Everyone admitted "the necessity of action" to prevent "Africanization"; the only question was "what manner of action is best calculated to achieve the end in view."

War against Spain was "too dangerous," for on the firing of the first gun by an American ship of war, the Captain General would confiscate the Creole's property and emancipate all the slaves. "The United States, taking the island after the promulgation of such a decree, would hold but a worthless wreck . . . a crown robbed of its jewels" because the United States "could never again return the savage and brutal population to their servile state." Apart from the resistance of the emancipated slaves, "the fanaticism of the North would rear the banner of civil war to prevent such a consummation." On the other hand, if the island *were* purchased from Spain, it would be worthless to the Southern States since "it would introduce into our Union a State" burdened with Pezuela's decrees and others he might impose by the time the purchase was concluded. Then again, Spain would never sell. "No," Walker argued. "If we get Cuba, we must get it in another way; the road is open." Let the U.S. government hold off; Cuba would free herself in a short time, and the United States could acquire the island "as we acquired Texas." This, then, was "the best manner of action," to be pursued immediately, while the Crimean War distracted Europe. "With Cuba . . . what a splendid prospect of commercial eminence opens to the South! What wealth will float upon our waters! What a bright gem will she, 'the Queen of the Antilles,' be in the coronet of the South, and how proudly will she wear it." Walker's frank exposition of the ideology of the Southern slaveholding expansionists, "expressed the views of a wide section of the public in the Southwest."[8]

Slowly and laboriously the Quitman expedition took form, and in the early months of 1855, it appeared complete. About a million dollars had been raised; about 10,000 volunteers, chiefly from the Gulf States had been recruited. In February, 1855, Alexander H. Stephens urged Quitman to launch the expedition immediately: "Now is the time to act—now is the time to move—while England and France have their hands full in the East." Quitman, satisfied that he had enough money and men, and encouraged by reports that an uprising was being prepared in Cuba, gave orders for the filibusters to gather for embarkment. Detachments of volunteers started to slip out of New Orleans in the guise of "woodchoppers."[9]

But events had taken place that doomed this most formidable of filibustering expeditions. First, relations between Quitman and the *Junta Cubana* had turned sour. From the beginning, several Cubans had expressed irritation over the General's stipulation that a million dollars be put at his disposal before he would launch his expedition. This dissatisfaction spread as Quitman kept delaying his departure. Members of the Havana Club in Cuba kept clamoring for the expedition to sail, fearing that further delay would be fatal. Yet Quitman would not budge until at least $250,000 more was raised.

Quitman's explanations of his postponements especially incensed a group in the *Junta Cubana*, led by Domingo Goicuría and José Elías Hernández, who emphasized the need for haste, so that the undertaking would be completed while the Crimean War and the liberal revolution in Spain precluded European intervention. Getting nowhere with Quitman, they broke away from the General and the *Junta Cubana*, and began organizing an expedition of their own. In November, 1854, an advance guard of this expedition landed at Baracoa, at the extreme eastern end of the island, with a shipment of military supplies; it was immediately overpowered by the Spanish authorities.

This mishap seriously affected the Quitman expedition. Quitman had planned his invasion of Cuba to dovetail with an uprising to be led by Ramón Pintó, a liberal Havana businessman of Spanish extraction, who had been associated, from 1852, with the Creole annexationists as President of the Revolutionary Junta of Havana. But the landing at Baracoa put Captain General José G. de la Concha on his guard. (In September, 1854, Concha had replaced Pezuela as Captain General.) He learned from an informer that he and other leading officials in Cuba were to be shot on the night of February 12, 1855; that this would be the signal for a general uprising, which would be followed by Quitman's invasion and annexation to the United States as soon as military victory was attained.

Having discovered Ramón Pintó's plot, Concha did not wait. Ramón Pintó was seized and garroted, and 60 men, including several Spaniards, were sentenced to long prison terms. Crawford, the British Consul at Havana, wrote to Lord Clarendon on February 10, 1855: "The papers of those arrested were seized and I understand have been found to disclose a plan in combination with an expedition which was to have sailed about this time from certain parts of the United States in aid of the insurrectionists in the island."[10] *

Concha declared a state of siege, set up naval patrols along the Cuban coast, and demanded that the U.S. government take steps to prevent the planned filibustering expedition. On February 27, 1855, Concha wrote the epitaph on the filibusters' hopes. "I believe, in effect," he informed the Spanish Minister in Washington, "that I have dominated the internal situation completely; not only will parties in favor of filibusters not arise, but in case the filibusters come again they will be met with more hostility by the country than was the López expedition."[11]

This ruined Quitman's plan to dovetail his invasion with a revolt in Cuba. The uprising upon which Quitman depended was over before it began. The General saw that his chances of success had practically vanished.

Meanwhile, the Pierce administration had been getting clear evidence from the American people that the majority opposed any attempt to annex Cuba. The reverses suffered by "Young America" in the election of 1854 indicated a widespread reaction against the Kansas-Nebraska Act, but the administration's Cuban annexationist policy also figured in the defeat.† To permit the filibusters to leave for Cuba in the face of these returns was to court political suicide. The President, moreover, still hoped, as we shall see, to acquire Cuba by negotiation, which a filibustering expedition would prevent.

Pierce decided not to act publicly against the Quitman expedition. (To have done so would have required prosecution of the leaders.) He determined, instead, to deal with Quitman privately. At the end of February, 1855, Quitman made a trip to Washington. Whether he was summoned by Pierce or went to seek aid from the adminis-

---

* Another conspirator executed about the same time, though not in connection with the Pintó plot, was a Creole, Frances Estrampes. He had become a naturalized citizen of the United States and a member of the Cuban *Junta*. Without orders from that body, he had returned to Cuba with a cargo of arms to distribute in preparation for Quitman's expedition. Detected and arrested, he made a full confession, and was executed on March 31, 1855.

† "In 1852, Pierce had carried every state except Vermont and Massachusetts; in 1854, his party lost every northern state except New Hampshire and California." (Roy F. Nichols, *Franklin Pierce: Young Hickory of the Granite Hills*, Philadelphia, 1931, p. 365.)

tration is unimportant. What is important is that Quitman called at the White House. There he had interviews with Pierce, Marcy, and the Spanish Minister. Pierce and Marcy advised against the filibustering enterprise, and warned that the filibusters would not be allowed to leave U.S. territory. The Spanish Minister then showed Quitman exact information as to the formidable state of military preparations in Cuba, and emphasized that an attempt to invade the island must end disastrously.

Quitman resisted the pressure as best he could, and made a futile effort to get the neutrality laws repealed. Eventually he returned to New Orleans. Here his changed attitude led to a rapid crumbling of the filibustering front in the Southwest. The impression grew at Natchez and throughout the state of Mississippi that the expedition had been abandoned. Filibustering units were dismissed at Mobile and other Southern cities.

On April 30, 1855, Quitman informed the *Junta Cubana* of his irrevocable decision to abandon the enterprise. Claiborne, Quitman's biographer, attributes the General's withdrawal to want of money, and again to "precipitate measures originating in New York, without consent or knowledge of General Quitman [which] provoked the interference of our government and undoubtedly caused the failure of the great plan for the liberation of Cuba."[12] However, he passes over the major reason for the government's stand against filibustering: the anger of the North over the Kansas-Nebraska Act, which aroused increasing opposition to further extension of the slave power; and the overwhelming defeat suffered by "Young America," leaders of Cuban annexationism, in the election of 1854.

On Quitman's resignation from the command, the expedition collapsed. The *Junta Cubana* pledged itself to continue the struggle and made a vain attempt to obtain an accounting of over a million dollars collected by Quitman and his associates from the sale of Cuban bonds and from private donations. The *Junta Cubana* at New Orleans was dissolved *sine die*, and soon the New York division, disillusioned and disheartened, also disbanded. Goicuría, as we shall see, contracted with the adventurer William Walker for new filibustering expeditions. Quitman was consoled by a seat in Congress, and kept clamoring for the annexation of Cuba. In August, 1855, he delivered a speech before a huge audience in New Orleans in which he stressed that the salvation of the South lay in the annexation of Cuba, and predicted that "the South and the country would yet take the steps necessary to bring about this result."[13]

What became of the money Quitman collected is not known, but the fact that nothing was paid to the holders of Cuban bonds or other creditors gave the enterprise a bad reputation even among its former adherents. Goicuría, ex-Treasurer of the *Junta Cubana,* kept the arms and ammunition and the steamer *Massachusetts* in his possession.

On May 29, 1855, the New Orleans *Bee* reported the dispersal of the Quitman expedition. It concluded that Cuban annexation could not be achieved by filibustering action, but prophesied that some other method would soon succeed in annexing the island. It did not spell out what method it had in mind, but that there were other methods was soon to be demonstrated.

chapter 8

"MANIFESTO OF THE BRIGANDS"

When President Pierce issued his proclamation against the Quitman expeditionaries, he went out of his way to assure the Southerners that the administration had a scheme of its own to annex Cuba. The extremists among the annexationists had no faith in the administration's plans, but others were willing to wait and see, as long as they were "possessed of any information calculated to give any reasonable assurance that Cuba is to be taken."[1]

The administration's scheme began with the appointment of the prophet of Southern expansionism, Pierre Soulé, as Minister to Spain. His appointment was taken as evidence that the administration was resolved to obtain Cuba, by purchase if possible, but, failing this, by war. It will be recalled that Soulé had himself advised the Senate, in January, 1853, that it was necessary for the United States, in order to safeguard its social institutions (meaning slavery), to acquire Cuba, preferably by peaceful negotiations, but, if this failed, by conquest. He had reiterated this theme in addresses to the *Junta Cubana* before leaving America to take up his post in Spain.

These speeches and others, in Congress and in public, had not been overlooked in Madrid. Soulé's appointment was not only "an extremely injudicious one,"—it was hardly likely to forward the purpose of his mission. Indeed, it was only after advice from England and France that Spain agreed to receive a minister who so outspokenly advocated taking over its Cuban colony, by force if necessary. However, the instructions issued to Soulé indicated that the Pierce administration considered his reputation as an asset for its purposes. While Soulé carried no specific instructions from Washington to attempt to purchase Cuba, or to interfere in any other way with Spanish control in the island, Secretary of State Marcy made it clear that the administration expected Cuba, "in one way or another," soon to "release itself, or be released from its present colonial subjection." The Secretary hoped that Spain might "take a wise forecast of the future," and "give birth to an independent nation of her own race." Cuba would then "fall, necessarily, into the American continental system, and contribute to its stability instead of exposing it to danger"—the "danger" being, of course, emancipation of the slaves.

The language of Marcy's instructions to Soulé thus conformed to the standard annexationist timetable: first an independent Cuba, then its tumbling "into the American continental system." It is hardly surprising that Soulé interpreted Marcy's words "as a mandate for a transfer of sovereignty."[2]

Shortly after his arrival in Spain, following a series of bizarre incidents in Madrid, including a duel with the French ambassador, Soulé went to work. At first he sought to persuade the Queen Mother, María Cristina, to cede the island to the United States, pointing out to that greedy lady, much of whose private fortune was invested in Cuban real estate, that the cession would net her enormous profits. Then he suddenly dropped this approach and began a new one. In January, 1854, without authorization from Washington, he offered Spain a considerable loan, the collateral on which was to be Cuba. The loan would be used to pay off Spain's debt of about 400 million dollars, chiefly to British citizens and $600,000 to American citizens. Ever on the verge of bankruptcy, Spain had hardly been able to meet even the interest on this debt, and Soulé expected his offer to be accepted eagerly. But Spain was quite willing to continue defaulting and informed the American Minister that she did not need a loan.

On the last day of February, 1854, just when it appeared that Soulé's mission was getting nowhere, the American steamer, the *Black Warrior,* anchored in Havana Bay. On a technical violation of port rules, the ship and its cargo was seized by the Spanish authorities. The ship was returned to its owners within two weeks after its seizure on the payment of a $6,000 fine—later remitted.

The Pierce administration seized upon the incident as a pretext to foment war. In a message to the House of Representatives, accompanying the correspondence dealing with the incident, Pierce tied in the *Black Warrior* affair with the policy on slavery adopted by Pezuela in Cuba, which was "threatening the honor and security of the United States." He noted that in case "the measures taken for amicable adjustment of our difficulties with Spain should, unfortunately, fail, I shall not hesitate to use the authority and means which Congress may grant to insure the observance of our just rights, to obtain redress for injuries received, and to vindicate the honor of our flag."[3] When the House, controlled by Northern and Western anti-annexationists, refused him authority to pursue an aggressive policy, the President shifted to diplomatic strategy, relying on Soulé in Madrid to use the *Black Warrior* incident to browbeat Spain into ceding Cuba to the United States.

On April 3, 1854, Marcy sent a new set of instructions to Soulé. The Minister was now to broach the purchase of Cuba to the Spanish Secretary of State, and point out to him that, as a result of Pezuela's policies, Cubans had become more hostile to Spanish rule and readier to seek the protection of the United States. Spain, moreover, subjected Americans "to frequent acts of annoyance and injuries," interrupted American commerce, and interfered with American national rights. The United States could no longer tolerate this situation. Soulé was, therefore, authorized to offer a sum not in excess of $130,000,000, but if he were to meet with no favorable response:

> You will then direct your efforts to the next most desirable object, which is to detach that island from Spanish domination and from all dependence on any European power. If Cuba were relieved from all transatlantic connection and at liberty to dispose of herself as her present interest and prospective welfare would dictate, she would undoubtedly relieve this government from all anxiety in regard to her future condition.[4]*

The directive to purchase was definite enough, but the alternative option "to detach" Cuba from Spain certainly allowed latitude to a man eager to use every trick, including war provocation. The Presi-

---

* This paragraph was omitted in all published accounts of this correspondence until 1928, when it appeared for the first time in Henry B. Learned's "William Learned Marcy, Secretary of State, March 7, 1853 to March 6, 1857," (*The American Secretaries of State and Their Diplomacy,* edited by Samuel F. Bemis, vol. VI, p. 193.) Learned discovered it when he investigated the original sources in the National Archives.

dent and the Cabinet knew of these instructions and agreed to them.

Directly after receiving the new instructions, Soulé began conspiring with Spanish revolutionists at the same time that he assured the Queen of his support. At the same time, also, he renewed the subject of the purchase of Cuba with the Spanish government. To facilitate these negotiations, Pierce, it will be recalled, issued the Proclamation against the Quitman expedition. A little later, the Federal Grand Jury in New Orleans indicted Quitman and several of his associates.

In July, 1854, revolution erupted in Spain and a new government took over in Madrid. Soulé, who had had a hand in the revolution, thought the chances of obtaining Cuba brighter than ever. The naval powers of Europe were at war, leaving Spain without friends and unable to act, while political factions were jockeying for position. Dudley Mann, Assistant Secretary of State, who was vacationing in France, shared Soulé's confidence. "I look upon it [the purchase of Cuba] almost as good as accomplished," he wrote to Marcy in late August, 1854. The important thing now was "not to let the filibusters of Louisiana create any mischief."[5]

But, as usual with American attempts to purchase Cuba, just when the prospects were brightest they ended in failure. In late August, the liberal revolution in Spain was crushed. All the arrested conspirators implicated Soulé. Horatio J. Perry, the American chargé d'affaires at Madrid, grasped the full significance of the event when he informed Marcy that "the peaceable cession of the Island of Cuba by Spain at this time is impossible. . . . The policy which Mr. Soulé has represented at this Court and urged with all his talent and all his resources is a complete and utter failure."[6]

It is in this context that the historic conference of American ministers met at Ostend on October 9, 1854. The meeting grew out of a dispatch, dated August 16, in which Marcy directed the ministers to London, Paris, and Madrid to assemble at a place designated by Soulé, to consult on a Cuba policy. Soulé interpreted this suggestion as authorizing him to take new steps "to detach" Cuba from Spain. Assistant Secretary of State Mann, who met Soulé in France, described the Minister as more confident than ever that Cuba would soon belong to the United States. Mann shared this confidence. "When I join you," he wrote to Marcy on October 2, "I want to salute you with the exclamation, 'Cuba is ours, or as good as ours.' "[7]

The conference of ministers met at Ostend on October 9, and transferred its discussions to the quieter atmosphere of Aix-la-Chappelle on the 12th. Concluding their discussions six days later, the ministers communicated the results of their deliberations in a dispatch to the State Department, which came to be known as the "Ostend Manifesto."

In this notorious document, stigmatized by anti-annexationists as the "Manifesto of the Brigands," the three American ministers argued that the immediate annexation of Cuba was essential to the security and "repose" of the American Union. The changes recently organized in Cuba by Pezuela threatened an insurrection which might have "direful" consequences to the American people. The slaves of Cuba might emulate their brethren of Sto. Domingo. But, if Cuba belonged to the United States, she would not permit "the flames to extend to our neighboring shores, seriously to endanger or actually to consume the fair fabric of our Union." As long as Cuba belonged to Spain, she would be an "unceasing danger" and "a permanent cause of anxiety and alarm" to the United States. The dispatch urged, therefore, that an "immediate and earnest effort" be made to acquire Cuba at a price not to exceed $120,000,000. The purchase proceedings should be open and frank, so "as not to challenge the approbation of the world."

The whole world would benefit by the transfer. Spain could use the money to develop her "vast natural resources." She could extend her railroads and thereby secure a permanent and profitable market for her various productions. She could pay off her enormous bonded debt and thereby re-establish her credit. But suppose Spain, "deaf to the voice of her own interest, and actuated by stubborn pride and a false sense of honor," should refuse to sell. The answer was indisputable. Self-preservation was the first law of nature for states as well as individuals. It would remain only for the United States to inquire whether Cuba continued to threaten the "internal peace," and the existence of the "cherished Union," and

> Should the question be answered in the affirmative, then, by every law human and Divine, *we shall be justified in wresting it from Spain, if we possess the power,* and this, upon the very principle that

would justify any individual in tearing down the burning house of his neighbor, if there were no other means of preventing the flames from destroying his own house.

Under such circumstances, we ought neither to count the cost nor regard the odds which Spain might enlist against us.

In a private letter accompanying the Manifesto, Soulé urged Marcy to prepare for war. This was the moment, he wrote, "to be done with" the Cuban problem—now, "while the great powers of this continent are engaged in that stupendous struggle [in the Crimea], which cannot but engage all their strength and tax all their energies, as long as it lasts, and may, before it ends, convulse them all."[8]

There is some disagreement among historians as to which of the three ministers—Soulé, Buchanan or Mason—had the greatest share in the writing of the iniquitous "Ostend Manifesto." But there is general agreement that it is a shameful page in American history. According to one historian, when the "Ostend Manifesto" was received by the Pierce cabinet, on November 4, it "filled the President and all the members ... with amazement." Why it should have had this effect is exceedingly strange. Nearly all the ideas, and, indeed, many of the exact phrases used in the Manifesto, were taken from Marcy's instructions to Soulé.[9]

Fortunately, the pro-slavery, annexationist forces, which the Pierce administration served, no longer dominated the American political scene. On November 4, the day the "Ostend Manifesto" arrived in Washington, New York voted every Democrat in Congress from that state out of office. This was only one of a series of electoral disasters for the administration. By the time all the returns were in, the Democrats had lost control of Congress. This was the answer of an electorate angered over the Kansas-Nebraska Act, and it was a repudiation of the administration's belligerent Cuban annexationist policy, as well.

Although the "Ostend Manifesto" was not made public immediately, but was dispatched in secrecy to the State Department, the New York *Herald* printed a digest of the document so that the general tenor was understood. The public reaction was so hostile that Pierce and Marcy did not dare to give their full support to the designs on Cuba. The administration, already repudiated at the polls, debated its reply to the three ministers. On November 13, Marcy sent the answer. It has usually been interpreted as a severe rebuke, refuting every phase of the Manifesto. But if one reads the text in the National Archives, it becomes clear that he did not entirely repudiate the Ostend document. True, Marcy notified Soulé that if Spain were not willing to sell Cuba to the United States, the negotiations should be temporarily discontinued. This is interpreted by most historians as a sudden reversal in the administration's Cuban policy due to the crushing defeat the expansionists had suffered in the election of 1854. But it is important to note that Marcy also instructed Soulé to reopen negotiations for the purchase of Cuba whenever a favorable opportunity arose. He then went on to explain that Spain's refusal to sell would not in itself be a cause for seizure of the island. Only a "material change in the condition of the island" which might involve "immediate peril to the existence" of the United States, would require such action. But in that event, "there is no doubt that the case will be promptly met by the deliberate judgment and decisive action of the American people." Frequent annoyances to American commerce with Cuba were nevertheless almost certain to continue; and it was "scarcely reasonable to expect that a peace thus rendered precarious will remain long unbroken." The President was, therefore, determined to have all difficulties with Spain speedily adjusted. He would "exceedingly regret" having to resort to "coercive measures" in order to "vindicate our natural rights and redress the wrongs of our citizens." Soulé should press for a settlement of the *Black Warrior* affair, and bring it to a close only when Spain disavowed the acts of her officials, censured their behavior, and offered a full indemnity for the losses sustained. This course would show Spain how difficult it would be for her to maintain the "present" state of things in Cuba, and should induce her to see "the reasonableness" of the demand to sell the island to the United States.[10]

Thus Marcy's dispatch upheld much of the "Ostend Manifesto." There was the reference to the Pezuela policy in Cuba which, if carried to the point of emancipating the slaves, would justify the seizure of the island; and it would be the United States alone who would determine that the Spanish policy constituted a "clear and present danger" to her (the Southern slaveholders') security. There was the emphasis on strong diplomatic pressure accompanied by a threat of war to force Spain to dispose of Cuba. The major difference was that the *Black Warrior* affair should be used as a club to compel Spain to sell. "He [Marcy] merely added an intermediate step to the procedure recommended in the Ostend Manifesto," notes Robert B. Leard.[11]

Soulé was not content "to linger" in Madrid "in languid impotence," waiting for a favorable opportunity to reopen the purchase question, and he sent in his resignation. The following day he attended a session of the Cortes and heard a speech branding the sale of Cuba an insult to Spanish honor, receive wild applause.

Shortly after Soulé left for Washington, Spain cut the ground from under the war-mongering annexationists by meeting American demands in the *Black Warrior* case. She conceded that the port authorities should have allowed the captain of the vessel 12 hours in which to present a correct manifest, offered reparations for the unjustifiable confiscation and fine, and proposed to bring the offending Cuban officials to trial. Pierce and Marcy reluctantly accepted Spain's terms.

On December 1, 1854, Congress reconvened. Immediately Representative August R. Sollers of Maryland demanded from the President all pertinent correspondence relating to the "Ostend Manifesto." Not until the last day of the short session of Congress, March 3, 1855, did a resolution embodying this demand pass. Pierce then sent in a carefully edited selection from the Marcy-Soulé correspondence. The vital "detach" paragraph of the instructions of April 3, 1854, was omitted.

Newspapers throughout the country printed the expurgated dispatches in full. The reaction was swift. Except for the Southern expansionists, the American people condemned the "Ostend Manifesto." "Atrocious," "Disgraceful," "Indefensible," "Robbery," "Immoral"—these were some of the terms applied to it. "How could you order the conference at Ostend?" the noted historian George Bancroft asked Marcy during the height of the newspaper publicity, and Marcy sought to disassociate himself from it. "The robber doctrine I abhor," he wrote. "If carried out it will degrade us in the eyes of the civilized world. Should the administration commit the fatal folly of acting upon it, it could not hope to be sustained by the country and would leave a tarnished name to all after times."[12] Coming from the author of the "detach" dispatch to Soulé, this was, indeed, a startling statement. But then Marcy had taken care to have the "detach" paragraph of the instructions omitted in the public release.

Nonetheless, Marcy's letter indicated that the time had passed for putting the "robber doctrine" into effect. Even that staunch annexationist, Lewis Cass, advised Marcy to halt the war agitation in the administration organ, the *Washington Union*. "I am tired of them," he wrote from Detroit in April, 1855, "and so is the [Democratic] party and the country. We cannot get Cuba honestly at present. We have nothing now to do but to sit still."[13]

The administration had no choice but to follow this advice. Soulé's vacated Spanish post went to ex-Senator August Caesar Dodge of Iowa. His instructions included the sentence: "The President regards the incorporation of Cuba into the American Union, essential to the welfare both of the United States and Cuba, as one of those inevitable events the occurrence of which is merely a question of time."[14]

Thus the curtain was rung down on the Cuban annexation campaign of the Pierce administration. Every device to annex Cuba had been tried—purchase, filibustering, and provoking a war—and each had failed. The majority of the American people rejected the "robber doctrine." It was this rejection and not, as some historians have insisted, the "relative moderation" of the Pierce administration,[15] which thwarted one after another of the conspiracies to annex Cuba for the benefit of the slave power. The Kansas-Nebraska Act did not sate the appetite of the Southern slaveowners, but the bitterness it provoked in the North demonstrated to all but the rabid expansionists that the annexation of Cuba would break up the Union. Before this danger even the annexationist-obsessed Pierce administration had to retreat.

The policy pursued by the Pierce administration, in the interests of the Southern slaveowners, did not succeed in obtaining possession of Cuba. But it did succeed in halting the steps being taken in Cuba toward the gradual abolition of slavery. As a result of menacing protests over Pezuela's conduct as Captain General in Cuba, coupled with demands for his removal by the slave merchants and planters in the island, Spain was forced to replace him. The man who succeeded Pezuela was José de la Concha who, for the second time, took command in Cuba. Immediately after his arrival, Concha announced that, while he intended to suppress the slave traffic, Pezuela's decrees permitting tracing and registering of slaves on the plantations would be abrogated. Thus in one and the same proclamation, he asserted that the slave traffic would be suppressed and guaranteed that it would continue by abolishing the only effective method of suppressing it.

While the United States government welcomed Concha's revocation of Pezuela's decrees, it was determined to make certain that this was now Spain's fixed policy. In August, 1855, A. C. Dodge, American Minister to Spain, informed the Spanish Secretary of State that his government wished to impress upon Her Majesty how important it was that there be no return to the Pezuela policies, instigated by "the Abolitionists of Great Britain and elsewhere [who] were seeking through the medium of Cuba and its authorities to interfere with and undermine or abolish slavery in the southern states." Dodge joyfully reported back to Washington that the Spanish Secretary of State had informed him that the United States need have no fear. No agreement existed with Britain to destroy slavery in Cuba. "He said that Spain regarded slavery as an indispensable element for the prosperous development of the resources of Cuba."[16]

Thus, due largely to pressure from the United States, accompanied by threats of war and of seizure of Cuba, Spain's first sincere effort to extinguish the slave trade in the island, liberate the *emancipados* and prepare the way for gradual abolition of slavery, was nullified. Ironically, Spain's retreat only gave new life to the Cuban annexationist campaign in the United States. The New Orleans *Daily Delta* had stated bluntly on June 25, 1854, when it seemed that Pezuela's policies would be carried out: "Without the stable institution of slavery, Cuba would be worthless to the United States." With slavery, Cuba remained, until the Civil War, a prize coveted by the Southern expansionists. While Spain continued to maintain slavery, the annexationists hatched new plots to acquire Cuba.

chapter 9

LAST OF THE FILIBUSTERS

The retreat of the Pierce administration from the pronouncements of the "Ostend Manifesto" and the disbanding of the Quitman expedition signified the end of almost a decade of steadily mounting efforts to attach Cuba to the United States as a slave state. It also marked the end of the sporadic uprisings in Cuba designed to coincide with invasions from the United States. Agitation to annex the island continued after 1855, but it never recovered the strength it had in the previous decade.

Three factors combined to reduce enthusiasm for the annexation of Cuba to the United States. These were the comparative tranquility within Cuba itself; the disillusionment of the exiled Cubans in the United States; and, finally, the ever increasing opposition of the Northern states.

Relative quiet prevailed in Cuba for several years after Captain General Concha suppressed the annexationist conspiracy of Ramón Pintó. For one thing, Concha relaxed his iron-fisted policy as peace returned to the island. For another, although Concha issued decrees against participation in the slave trade, he won the slaveowners over by putting a stop to Pezuela's policy of gradual abolition. Since his decrees against the slave trade proved ineffectual, the slave merchants, as well as the planters, were content. Though the planters were suffering from the repercussions of the economic crisis of 1857 in the United States, they were generally satisfied with Concha's rule. It was only when Concha proposed that the Cuban government be empowered to exile, by decree, anyone suspected of being involved in a slave expedition, that voices of discontent once more were heard among the wealthy classes. The home Government, having congratulated itself that the "ever faithful isle" appeared to be more faithful than ever, was immediately alarmed, and disallowed

Concha's proposal as too arbitrary. Concha, balked in his determination to stop the slave traffic, resigned in disgust and left Cuba in December, 1859.

General Francisco Serrano, who succeeded Concha as Captain General, was himself a progressive who believed in reforms for Cuba. He carried instructions from the Liberal government in Spain, headed by Leopoldo O'Donnell, to encourage reform hopes "in so much as they do not become dangerous." Emboldened by these instructions, Serrano, who was married to the daughter of a rich Creole family in Cuba, took steps to win the good will of the Cubans. Along with vigorous, though not very successful, measures to terminate the illegal entry of African slaves, he sought to meet the planters' chronic need for labor by admitting 100,000 Asians as contract laborers.

Serrano's conciliatory attitude was also reflected in his extending to Creoles the privilege enjoyed by the *Peninsulares*, since 1834, of meeting informally and advising the government on matters of policy. Many men prominent in Cuban economic and intellectual life accepted the Captain General's invitation, and the residence of Miguel Aldama, Cuban reformer and slaveowner, became the center for these informal meetings.

One thing these discussions among prominent Cuban *hacendados*, business, and professional men made clear: annexation to the United States had lost prestige as a solution for Cuba's problems. As Ramiro Guerra y Sánchez puts it, annexationism lay revealed "as an inferiority complex and a conservative solution to preserve slavery within the island." Even pro-slavery elements in Cuba abandoned their efforts to achieve union with the United States, because they foresaw the impending conflict between the states and the consequent abolition of slavery. The majority of Cuban slaveowners turned instead to reform, their hopes buoyed by the era of tolerance under Serrano. But the idea of independence also began to make itself felt, especially among the Cuban masses, and this was to increase when, as usual, the era of tolerance came to an end.[1]

Nor did the sentiment for annexation survive among the majority of the Cuban exiles. Frustrated and disillusioned by the failure of the Pierce administration to follow through on its annexation policy, and by the rupture with Quitman, most of the exiles became indifferent if not hostile to the United States. After the Cuban *Junta* of New York disbanded in 1855, its outstanding leaders, Valiente, Betancourt Cisneros, and el Conde de Pozos Dulces, took up residence in Paris.

Among the remaining émigrés, two parties now formed. One renounced annexation and favored independence. Speaking for the lower and middle-class Cuban Creoles who began to favor emancipation, they sought to attract the anti-slavery forces in the North with the vision of a Cuban Republic in which slavery would be abolished.

The second exile group was made up of the bitter-end annexationists. Although they complained of Quitman and the Pierce administration, and their confidence in the slaveholding expansionists had declined, they still believed that an expedition, properly organized and prepared, would succeed. Their leader was Domingo Goicuría. In 1855, Goicuría was living in New York. Fifty-six years old, he wore a long flowing grey beard which he was reputed to have vowed "never to shave until his native country was freed from the Spanish yoke."[2]

He certainly had curiously contradictory ideas as to how this was to be achieved. On June 10, 1855, in a public manifesto to all Cubans, Goicuría asserted that the United States had failed the Cubans and that rather than beg for American aid, the price of which was annexation and Negro slavery, Cubans must adopt as their ideal both independence and emancipation. Yet, a few months later, Goicuría joined forces with William Walker, the "grey-eyed man of destiny," and darling of the Southern slaveholding expansionists of the mid-1850's, in a filibustering venture which was to begin with the seizure of Nicaragua for the American slaveholding interests and end in the annexation of Cuba.

In 1853, after an unsuccessful career as doctor, lawyer, editor of the pro-annexationist New Orleans *Crescent*, and politician, Walker led a filibustering expedition to the Mexican State of Lower California. Brought to trial in San Francisco for violating the neutrality laws, after being ejected by the Mexicans, Walker was promptly acquitted and the fine imposed on his associates was never paid. In the South, he was acclaimed as a hero, and, after the collapse of the Quitman expedition, Walker was looked to as the man to save the slave system by seizing new territory in Latin America for slavery expansion.

In 1855, Walker fitted out an expedition of "emigrants" to invade Nicaragua, ostensibly on invitation by a native revolutionary faction. Goicuría perceived in Walker's Nicaraguan venture a stepping-stone for an invasion of Cuba, to be followed by its annexation to the United States. If Cuban volunteers could be transported to Nicaragua as "emigrants," they could evade the neutrality laws of the United States. Accordingly, Goicuría dispatched an agent to Walker and offered him men and supplies for the Nicaraguan expedition in return for a pledge by Walker to turn to Cuba as soon as his position in Nicaragua was consolidated. Walker's response was eager, especially since Goicuría was said to be in possession of some $200,000 of unspent Cuban funds.

In January, 1856, a written agreement was drawn up between Walker and Goicuría's agent, Francisco A. Lainé, a survivor of López's *Pampero* expedition. It stipulated that the Cubans were first to aid Walker with men and resources in "consolidating the peace and government of the Republic of Nicaragua." After this, Walker was to "assist and cooperate with his person and with various resources such as men and others, in the cause of Cuba and in favor of her liberty."[3] Nothing was said in the agreement about the future status of Cuba thus "liberated" from Spain, but Goicuría was left with the impression that annexation to the United States would follow.

After the contract was signed, Goicuría left for New Orleans where, as a representative of Walker, he tried to sell Nicaraguan bonds. Returning to New York, he became associated with the capitalist, Cornelius Vanderbilt, one of America's "Robber Barons," whose Accessory Transit Company held a monopoly on steamboat navigation in Nicaraguan waters. Vanderbilt saw immediate profits in the Nicaraguan venture, and helped finance Goicuría and his Cuban followers. George Law, an old capitalist conspirator for Cuban annexation, lent his muskets to Walker.

In late February, 1856, Goicuría's command of 250 men left New York. Arriving in Nicaragua, they joined Walker's forces and played an important part in capturing Granada, then the capital. Goicuría was commissioned as brigadier-general, and other Cubans were given important posts on Walker's staff. The Cubans, in turn, hailed Walker as their future liberator and, at a banquet in his honor, toasted him as "the hope of Cuba."

Walker installed a Nicaraguan puppet as President, with himself as effective head of the state, and the Southern expansionist press in the United States let loose with loud cheers. Now that Walker controlled Nicaragua, they expected him to complete his task by ousting Spain from Cuba and annexing it to the United States as a slave state. "The fate of Cuba depends on the fate of Nicaragua, and the fate of the South depends upon that of Cuba," editorialized the New Orleans *Daily Delta* on April 18, 1856.

Ever mindful of the interests of the Southern slaveholders, the Pierce administration lost no time in recognizing Walker's regime. In a message to Congress on May 15, 1856, Pierce actually boasted that the new government of Nicaragua had been established with "the assistance and cooperation of a small body of citizens of the United States."[4] This naturally infuriated Central Americans. A document entitled "Protest of the Executive Power of New Granada, against the recognition by the United States of the intrusive Government of Nicaragua," pointed out that the United States declared filibusters outlaws when not in power, and respectable authorities when in. New Granada viewed the President's message to Congress with "painful and profound surprise." Peru saw in the clasping of Walker's guilty hand a signal to similar marauders from the slave states. Still stronger were the protests from Guatemala and San Salvador. Minister Irisarri, speaking for these countries, in a letter to Marcy on May 19, 1856, attacked the Monroe Doctrine as a device behind which the United States could freely commit aggression against all of Latin America:

> The origin of this doctrine was the invention of Mr. Monroe, President of the United States, who sought to establish as a principle that the United States had the exclusive right of interference in the political affairs of this continent, prohibiting all intervention on the part of European nations. The pretended right, however, was not admitted by any of the fifteen Spanish American republics, nor by the Empire of Brazil, and if European nations had not thought fit to take a serious view of that declaration until now, this is of little consequence, & can have no effect in making the other nations of America consider themselves as subjected to this species of protectorate which

they have not asked for, and which must not be imposed upon them by force. Such guardianship is highly injurious to the rights of those nations whose inherent sovereignty and independence are conceded.

Irisarri charged that the movement to conquer Nicaragua was part of a broader plot "to master, as of now, other Central American Republics, Mexico, Cuba, and the Isthmus of Panama, leaving for later the extension of their domination to the Tierra del Fuego [the tip of South America]." Scornfully, he reminded the United States that its haste to recognize the Nicaraguan government set up by Walker was unprecedented in its relations with the Latin American nations.

This nation [the United States] has never proceeded with a similar haste to recognize the governments of Spanish America when they presented less difficulties and in which they could not find a similar reason for recognizing these governments for similar selfish reasons. Before they resolved to recognize Chile and Buenos Aires, the government of the United States sent to those countries commissioners to gather information about the nature of these governments, as well as their forces and resources to preserve their independence. And they spent several years in gathering such information.[5] *

These protests made no impression on the Pierce administration, nor did they impress the Cuban members of the Walker movement, bent on following up the Nicaraguan invasion with one in Cuba, which would end in its annexation to the United States. Now that Walker had been recognized by the United States, they fondly believed the fulfillment of their dreams was at hand.

Armed with recognition, Walker sent Goicuría to London as representative of Nicaragua at the Court of St. James. Goicuría, expecting that an expedition would soon be on its way to Cuba, left Nicaragua in August, 1856, and proceeded to New York. He never reached England. A quarrel broke out between Walker and Goicuría and, by November, the Cuban filibuster had withdrawn from the Nicaraguan project.

Goicuría had joined forces with Walker because he saw in Walker's venture a promise of liberation of Cuba and of annexing it to the United States. But after he left Nicaragua, Goicuría received

---

* For a discussion of the attitude of the U.S. government toward recognizing the South American Republics after they were founded, see Volume I, pp. 131-136.

letters from Walker indicating that he did not contemplate annexing either Nicaragua or Cuba to the United States, but rather organizing a military federation of the five Central American states, which were to be conquered in turn. To such "a powerful and compact federation based on military principles," Cuba would be added. He planned to establish close connections with the South and, after creating a tropical slave-labor federation, to invite American slaveowners to emigrate there with their slaves. First an "entente cordiale" would bind the South and Walker's slave-labor federation together; then, after the South seceded from the Union, which Walker regarded as inevitable, a formal merger would create a vast slave empire composed of the seceded states and Walker's Central American domain, with Cuba occupying a key place in the empire.

As a first step in realizing this dream, Walker, on September 22, 1856, after consulting with Pierre Soulé in Nicaragua, revoked the decree abolishing slavery. (The interdiction against slavery in Nicaragua had been passed in 1824 by the Federal Constituent Assembly of all the Central American States.) Walker also reopened the slave trade, and instituted vagrancy and contract-labor laws which imposed forced labor on the Nicaraguans and reduced them to virtual peonage.

There was immediate jubilation in the South. To the extreme slaveholding expansionists, Walker's action marked the beginning of a Southern empire which would oust Spain from Cuba, and restore slavery in all of Central America and the West Indies. Cuba, all of Central America and Mexico should be conquered, and with the seceded South, form a tropical empire.

With the re-establishment of slavery in Nicaragua, Goicuría knew his mission to England (to neutralize her when the invasion of Cuba would occur) was futile. He knew that, under the pressure of her anti-slavery forces, England, much as she might welcome the weakening of American trade in the Caribbean and Central American areas, would not permit the re-establishment of slavery in these regions. With the largest navy afloat, she could easily destroy any invasion of Cuba. Finally, Goicuría also knew that Cuba, liberated by an expedition from Walker's Nicaragua, would never be acceptable as a state to the North. While this did not trouble Walker, who was obsessed with his imperial dreams, Goicuría wanted annexation of Cuba to the United States, and that aim would now be doomed by any association of Cuban annexation with slavery expansion.

"I cannot now in any way continue with my connection with you," Goicuría informed Walker. Furious over the collapse of his plans, he sent his correspondence with Walker to the New York newspapers, thereby exposing Walker's pro-slavery designs in Central America and other parts of Latin America.[6]

Although Goicuría had broken with Walker, other Cuban exiles in Nicaragua continued to work with the adventurer, waiting for the day when the invasion of Cuba would begin. But it never did take place. Costa Rica declared war on Nicaragua, convinced that its own independence was threatened by the "pirates who sailed from the coasts of the United States." Other republics of Central America, alarmed by Walker's expressed ambitions, formed an alliance for the maintenance of their sovereignty. Added strength, in the form of men, wealth and technical assistance, was given to this coalition by Cornelius Vanderbilt, who sought revenge on Walker for revoking his monopoly in Nicaragua and giving it to a rival concern.

To the disappointment and chagrin of the South, Walker was defeated by the Costa Ricans. However, he surrendered on May 1, 1857, to the U.S. naval forces which had intervened in the war, and abandoned Nicaragua—but not before his men had leveled the historic city of Granada and left behind a lance, thrust into the scorched ground, bearing a pennant with the boast: "Here was Granada."

In late May, Walker and his men, including his Cuban contingent, returned to New Orleans where they were welcomed as heroes. In a speech, Walker pictured himself as the savior of slavery, and pointed to Cuba, with its slave institutions, as the model for Central America. He called on the South to help him liberate Cuba, upon whose base he would create a slave empire in Central America. This was a goal he was "determined never to abandon."[7]

With the aid of the South and the assistance of his Cuban followers, among whom Charles Bienvenue and Donatien Augustin, old Cuban filibusters, were most active, Walker planned a new attempt on Nicaragua, after which, he assured his Cuban recruits, he would invade Cuba. In April, 1859, while Walker and his associates were engaged in this work, news came that a filibustering expedition, headed by José Elías Hernández, had sailed from New York for Cuba. Bad weather prevented their landing, and they were forced into Port-au-Prince, Haiti, where they were interned.

In August, 1860, Walker led his last filibustering expedition to Central America. He landed in Honduras, evading American and British naval forces stationed off the coast of Nicaragua to intercept him. He planned to proceed into Nicaragua by land, but the English intervened, captured him and surrendered him to the custody of Honduras, where, on September 12, 1860, he met his death before a firing squad. Several of his Cuban followers died with him.

The Southern press wept for its "hero." But the Northern press shed no tears. "He has created a deep distrust of all North Americans throughout the entire Isthmus," declared the Washington *Daily National Intelligencer* of September 26, 1860, on learning of Walker's execution. "Our Government is regarded as ambitious, deceitful, and treacherous by those who, before General Walker visited them, looked upon our Republic for imitation. He has prepared the way for the predominance of European, particularly English, influence from the gulf of Panama to the southern boundary of Mexico. It is well that expeditions with such results should end." The reference to the growth of European influence in Latin America was to the fact that in 1858, the Presidents of Costa Rica and Nicaragua, frightened by Walker's activities which, they knew, were winked at by the United States government, issued a manifesto declaring that Central America was menaced by annexation to the United States unless help was secured from Europe, and they were therefore placing their countries under the protection of England, France, and Sardinia!

This astounding development brought the following comment from the Springfield (Mass.) *Republican* in its issue of June 24, 1858:

> This is the fruit of our Ostend Manifestoes and our filibuster expeditions. Our government stands properly at the head of the American powers, and should have had a commanding influence, but a filibustering administration has driven them to seek foreign alliance and support, and for this growth of foreign influence upon the continent we have only ourselves to blame. . . . Of what avail is our reiteration

of the Monroe Doctrine, so long as we repel our neighbors from all friendly associations and compel them to seek the aid of the European governments.

The liberal New England paper went on to suggest that the United States immediately take measures to re-establish friendlier relations with its neighbors to the South. As a first step in this direction, it proposed that the government abandon, once and for all, its rash attempts to annex Cuba.

Such sage words of advice made, as usual, no impression on the die-hard annexationists. A year later, in 1859, a new attempt, this time by the Buchanan administration, was made to annex Cuba.

chapter 10

END OF THE ANNEXATIONIST ERA

Since he was an open advocate of Cuban annexation, James Buchanan's nomination as the Democratic candidate for president in 1856 pleased the slavery expansionists in the South. Although his connection with the "Ostend Manifesto" led to his being denounced by the Republican party as the spokesman for "the highwayman's plea that 'might makes right,'" it endeared him to the Southern expansionists. When Buchanan won by a squeak, the New Orleans *Delta* pointed out that he owed his election to the South, and should therefore live up to the "letter and spirit of [the] Ostend Manifesto."[1] But for almost two years, Buchanan did nothing publicly to fulfill these expectations. Behind the scenes, however, he was hatching a new scheme to annex Cuba.

In August, 1855, Dodge, the American Minister to Spain, had informed the U.S. Government that he was convinced that "all the treasure of the earth could not purchase Cuba," and that any ministry favoring it would be "instantly expelled from power and be exposed to popular fury."[2] Buchanan, however, thought he had found a way around this difficulty. The solution was offered by Christopher Fallon, Philadelphia banker and financial agent of the Spanish Queen Mother. Fallon proposed to Buchanan that he be empowered to use his connections with the European bankers who held Spanish bonds—the Barings in London, the Rothschilds and Léon Lillo et Cie. of Paris—to force Spain to sell Cuba to the United States. Spain, it will be remembered, owed about $400,000,000, more than half to Britain, and $600,000 to Americans. Repeatedly during the 1850's, Spain had failed to meet even the annual interest, to say nothing of reducing the debt. Now Fallon suggested that the United States use the major creditors to exert pressure at Madrid to force Spain to sell Cuba to the United States. With the purchase money, Spain would be able to pay her accumulated interest and perhaps also a portion of her principal.

Having received the go-ahead signal from Buchanan, Fallon left for Europe with a letter from the President making his wishes known in general terms. (Buchanan wrote that if Fallon's report proved encouraging, he would "receive more formal instructions.") Fallon conferred in Paris, Rome, and Madrid, and even held an interview with the Queen Mother. He reported to Buchanan that the bankers would be delighted to see Spain sell Cuba and the purchase money used to pay the bondholders. But their pressure, he saw, would not be enough to carry it through. Spanish politicians of both parties had to be bought off. "Then the party in power would negotiate the sale and be driven out of office by indignant public opinion. The 'opposition' coming in, would find Spain committed to the sale, and 'reluctantly' fulfill the contract, and each side subsequently would collect its commissions." Fallon suggested that a new minister be sent at once to Madrid with no written instructions to negotiate for Cuba but with a large fund of secret-service money at his disposal.[3]

Buchanan seized happily upon this suggestion, and appointed August Belmont as official briber. A New York banker and American agent of the House of Rothschild, Belmont was the ideal choice for this assignment. For one thing, he had for years been working for the acquisition of Cuba. For another, he had proposed bribery as early as 1853, and had even held discussions in Paris, "with several gentlemen of influence in Spain." With "a secret fund of $40,000 or $50,000 . . . placed at my disposal," he had told Secretary Marcy, he could practically guarantee the transfer of the island to the United States.[4] But Marcy had ignored the suggestion.

Chosen by Buchanan as Minister to Madrid, Belmont was eager to carry out the special secret mission of annexing Cuba through bribery. But the Senate refused to approve the appointment, and, instead of the shrewd, unscrupulous New York banker, the President had to settle for William Preston, a former Congressman from Kentucky.

Preston was approved by the Senate, but this still left unsolved the problem of where the bribe money was to come from. The secret-service fund, proposed by Fallon, could never furnish the needed amount. A Congressional appropriation was obviously the only answer. Buchanan decided to ask openly for the money.

On December 6, 1858, he broached the subject in his annual message. The annexation of Cuba, he began, would be a victory for the forces of "light and civilization" inasmuch as through it, "the last relic of the African slave trade would instantly disappear." Having made this gesture to anti-slavery Northern opinion, the President emphasized that Cuba commanded the mouth of the Mississippi and hence "the immense and annually increasing trade, foreign and coastwise, from the valley of that noble river." As long as the island remained under the control of "a distant foreign power," this trade was exposed to dangers in time of war and subjected to "perpetual annoyance in time of peace." The United States should therefore purchase the island. Since the success of negotiations might depend upon the "making of an advance [payment] to the Spanish Government immediately after the signing of the treaty, without awaiting the ratification of it by the Senate," Buchanan suggested that Congress grant him a "large appropriation" for that purpose.[5]

On January 10, 1859, John Slidell of Louisiana, a veteran Cuban annexationist, introduced a bill in the Senate to make the President such a grant. The bill was referred to the Committee on Foreign Relations. Two weeks later, the Committee made its recommendation. It cited documents to show that the acquisition of Cuba had long been contemplated by the U.S. government. Jefferson, John Quincy Adams and, indeed, almost every President since the 1830's had favored it.

> The ultimate acquisition of Cuba [the Committee declared] may be considered a fixed purpose resulting from the political and geographical necessities which have been recognized by all parties and all administrations, and in regard to which the popular voice has been expressed with a unanimity unsurpassed on any question of national policy that has heretofore engaged the public mind. The purchase and annexation of Louisiana led, as a necessary corollary to that of Florida, and both point with unerring certainty to the acquisition of Cuba.

Spain could not long keep Cuba. The question was "shall it fall to European powers, become independent, or be annexed to the United States?" The first two alternatives were unacceptable to the

United States! The only possible solution was annexation, and the only practicable way to acquire the island now was by purchase, negotiations for which could only be successfully carried on by the means suggested in the President's message. Congress should therefore appropriate $30,000,000 for his special use.[6]

Robert B. Letcher, former Governor of Kentucky and Minister to Mexico, wrote angrily that this fund was intended "to bribe Spanish traitors to assist in the purchase of Cuba. . . . If we mean to rob Spain of Cuba we ought to have as much sagacity as a common thief has and that is to do the job *gracefully* and *safely*."[7]

The Senate debate precipitated by the brazen recommendation of the Committee on Foreign Relations lasted over a month. The opposition to the "Thirty Million Dollar Bill" was led by the Republicans, but since they had only 20 Senators out of a total of 62, the only way they could prevent its passage was to keep it from coming to a vote until the end of the short session of the 35th Congress. Hence every time the Democrats moved for a vote, a Republican Senator would take the floor. John Breckenridge, a leading annexationist, declared furiously that "we talk too much and do little" about acquiring Cuba, and Judah P. Benjamin of Louisiana, another prominent annexationist, fairly wept as he declared that the annexation of Cuba was "now within our power," but the nation was being talked out of its choicest prize.

The Republican Senators were backed in their opposition to the bill by anti-annexationist and anti-Administration papers throughout the country. Spain, went the argument, did not wish to sell, the Cubans did not wish to be bought, and the people of the North and West were not "willing to be . . . taxed to prolong the life of tropical slavery for another generation." In addition to all this, the very idea of placing $30,000,000 in the hands of Buchanan to do with as he pleased was to commit "a crime against the national welfare."[8]

Some Southerners also opposed Buchanan's purchase plan, especially after he had stressed that one result of the annexation of Cuba would be the closing of the illegal African slave trade. These Southerners predicted that this would force Cubans to adopt free labor, and, sooner or later, to emancipate their slaves, thereby making Cuba worthless to the South. To overcome this obstacle, Miles

Taylor, Congressman from Louisiana, proposed a bill guaranteeing the permanence of slavery in Cuba after it was purchased, thus making certain that it would enter the Union as a state dominated by the slaveowners. With this assurance, the majority of the slavery expansionist newspapers supported the "Thirty Million Dollar Bill." "Cuba, if she come to us at all, it will be as a slave community," the Charleston *Mercury* gloated on February 28, 1860.

But the Republican obstructionist tactics, backed by Northern opinion, kept the bill from coming to a vote. Although they numbered less than one-third of the Senate, the Republicans, by their unity and adroit manuevering, blocked the Democrats. To be sure, the latter were able to defeat a motion to table the bill, but when Congress adjourned *sine die* without voting on the measure, it was clear to all but the die-hards that the "Thirty Million Dollar Bill" was doomed.

Buchanan, however, was too much of an expansionist at heart to give up. Though he had no funds on hand, he sent William Preston to Madrid with full power to negotiate the purchase of Cuba. Preston reported back that although Spain refused to discuss the subject, he was certain that, with thirty millions at his disposal as bribes together with pressure by bondholders, a deal could be concluded. This assurance was all Buchanan needed to make another try for the necessary funds. In his third annual message to Congress, December 19, 1859, the President pressed for the "Thirty Million Dollar Bill," the need for which remained "unchanged. I therefore again invite the serious attention of Congress on this important subject. Without a recognition of this policy on their part it will be almost impossible to institute negotiations with any reasonable prospect of success."

But efforts to push an appropriation through the Senate failed. On May 30, 1860, its most active advocate, Slidell, acknowledged defeat, but warned that "I shall bring it before the Senate at the next session."[9] Slidell, as we shall see, kept his word, but by that time the secession of the Southern states was in full swing, and the chances of getting his bill adopted were infinitesimal.

Both branches of the split Democratic Party, in the crucial Presidential campaign of 1860, advocated acquiring Cuba. The Republicans did not mention Cuba at their convention in Chicago, but their opposition to its annexation during the debate on the "Thirty Million Dollar Bill" made any statement unnecessary. Abraham Lincoln, the Republican candidate, had already declared that as long as one slave continued to toil on Cuba's sugar plantations, no consideration should be given to annexing the island. Senator Stephen A. Douglas, heading one of the two Democratic tickets, had advocated, in his famous debate with Lincoln, that: "When we get Cuba we must take it as we find it, leaving the people to decide the question of slavery for themselves, without interference on the part of the Federal Government, or of any State of this Union." But Lincoln had rejected this "specious kind of moral neutrality on slavery," and in November, 1860, a majority of the people of the North also rejected it when they elected Lincoln to the White House.[10] The Cuban question itself had been forced out of the campaign by the more immediate issue of secession; but those who cast their votes for Lincoln were also voting NO on annexation.

The Cuban question re-emerged, however, during the critical winter of 1860–61, when the Southern states withdrew from the Union and established the Southern Confederacy, with Jefferson Davis and Alexander H. Stephens, both aggressive Cuban annexationists, as President and Vice President. With the framework of the Union crashing about his ears, James Buchanan made his last effort to annex Cuba. In his fourth annual message, December 3, 1860, Buchanan reiterated "the recommendation contained in my annual message of December, 1858, and repeated in that of December, 1859, in favor of the acquisition of Cuba from Spain by fair purchase." He was certain that annexation would "contribute essentially to the well-being and prosperity of both countries in all future time."[11] Though these were now empty words, John Slidell reintroduced his "Thirty Million Dollar Bill."

This produced an uproar in the North. The people, the President was told by the Northern press, would never consent to the passage of such a "monstrous," "lawless and piratical" bill requiring the spending of millions of dollars for a territory that "the next day may assert her right of secession."[12] Nor was the South interested, now that it was engaged in destroying the Union. Once the South formed a separate Confederacy, Jefferson Davis had declared in July, 1860, at the Mississippi Democratic Convention, Cuba would be acquired. And the Confederacy would not haggle with Spain; it would simply move in and conquer Cuba.

The possibility of annexing Cuba as part of a deal to keep the seceded states within the Union was ended by Lincoln's rejection of the Crittenden Compromise. This proposal to appease the slaveowners would have permitted slavery in all territory "now held or hereafter acquired" south of the old 36°30′ line. This would allow the South to expand into Cuba, Mexico, and Central America. On January 11, 1861, Lincoln wrote to Senator Hale of New Hampshire: "If we surrender, it is the end of us and of the government. They will repeat the experiment upon us *ad libitum*. . . . A year will not pass till we shall have to take Cuba as a condition upon which they will stay in the Union. . . . There is in my judgment but one compromise which would really settle the slavery question, and that would be a prohibition against acquiring any more territory."[13]

On the eve of the Civil War, William H. Seward, Lincoln's Secretary of State, proposed a war on Spain as a means of solidifying the Union. This hoary device of averting a domestic crisis by the distraction of a foreign war, had the added lure that the annexation of Cuba might bring the South back into the Union. But Lincoln rejected Seward's mad project.

The plan of the Southern leaders to build a slavery empire with Cuba as its base was abandoned after the Civil War started as it became evident that the war was not going to be a walkover. The slaveowners had to win friends for their cause in Europe, and it was necessary to disavow all designs on Cuba. The Confederate leaders lost little time in renouncing all intentions of annexing Cuba, in order to acquire diplomatic recognition from Spain. In July, 1861, they sent Charles Helm to Havana to direct shipping through the Federal blockade. Helm explained to the Captain General that earlier Southern ambitions to annex Cuba had grown out of the necessity of a political balance against the North in the U.S. Senate. An independent Confederacy had no such need, he said, and he urged the Cuban authorities to so inform Spain. And in August, the Confederate Commission to Europe was urged to hurry to Madrid to ask for recognition. The three representatives were told to stress mutual interests in slavery as the binding tie between the Confederacy and Spain, and to disclaim all Southern designs on Cuba, pleading the balance of power in the old Union as the former Southern motive for the acquisition of the island.

The annexationist press in the South approved of these steps. The time had come to pull down the flag of Cuban annexation. The New Orleans *Delta* (March 7, 1861) declared:

> If there was a time when political interests, perhaps political necessities caused the South to desire the acquisition of Cuba, as a slave State, in order to equalize the balance of sectional power, that time has passed away together with the necessities and the desires which characterized it. There is no longer any sectional balance to be equalized, there is no longer any danger to the South from a preponderance of Free State Representatives in our National Councils. For those evils we have found a remedy [secession] much more desirable and much more decisive than the acquisition of Cuba.

With this funeral oration over the lost cause of Cuban annexation, the leading annexationist paper in the United States closed the era of piratical invasions, threats of war, bribery schemes, and purchase plans!

There was no single reason for the failure of annexationism, but we should note that the decisive role was played by the majority of the Cuban people and of the American people. The Cuban annexationists had the support only of the slaveowners, and this support vacillated with the rise and decline of threats to slavery. The mass of the Cuban people, as the filibusters discovered, gave no support to the annexationist conspiracies. As Abraham Lincoln put it, "their [the filibusters'] fault was that the real people of Cuba had not asked for their assistance."[14] And without the support of the masses, "the real people of Cuba," the filibusters fell easy prey to Spanish military power.

In the United States, many groups, including conservative merchants, bankers, and even some Southerners, fought annexation vigorously. But one group was responsible more than any other for the failure of annexationism: the abolitionists and free-soilers of the North. They were determined to limit slavery to the South, and to end the domination of the federal government by the slave power. The acquisition of Cuba, with its slave economy, would prolong and extend slavery and give the slaveowners an even louder voice in the halls of Congress. In state after state throughout the North, they denounced the annexation of Cuba as a plot of the slave power, and again and again their protests forced the slavery expansionists and their allies in the North to retreat. In August, 1855, in a speech at New Orleans, John A. Quitman said flatly: "The anti-slavery sentiment in Congress . . . alone prevents the annexation of Cuba."[15] Two years later, on July 21, 1857, the New Orleans *Courier,* summing up the reasons for the defeat of every effort thus far to annex Cuba, admitted that one factor, and one factor alone, was primarily responsible: the opposition to Cuban annexation by the abolitionist and anti-slavery-extension forces in the North. "Their political opposition to slavery is so bigoted that they will never assent to the addition of another foot of territory over which they think slavery will be extended."

Annexationism continued to exert some influence both in the United States and Cuba down to the end of the nineteenth century. But it never again was the force it was in the pre-Civil War era. In the United States, it was eventually replaced by a new "Manifest Destiny," the "Manifest Destiny" of American imperialism, which replaced direct annexation with economic colonization and political domination of the island. In Cuba, it was clear by the end of the 1850's that annexationism no longer offered a way out for the island. After trying reformism as an alternative, many Cubans chose another way—the fight for independence.

chapter 11

CUBA DURING THE AMERICAN CIVIL WAR

The period in Cuban history that began with the administration of General Francisco Serrano, in November, 1859, was marked by the *política de atracción* (policy of attraction). This policy took account of the growing desire for independence following the decline and virtual disappearance of annexationism. Serrano realized that Spanish dominion could not be preserved under an antiquated colonial system. To arrest independence tendencies, he took the lead, it will be remembered, in inviting the participation of the Creoles in government affairs. Serrano's "policy of attraction" was continued by Domingo Dulce, who succeeded him as Captain General in August, 1862. Thus he encouraged the establishment of schools for the children of the poorer classes, who had only the limited primary instruction of the few existing charity schools,* and he followed Serrano's lead in inviting the participation of Creoles in government affairs.

Taking advantage of this extended period of tolerance, the leaders of Cuban economic and political affairs first organized the *Círculo Reformista* (Reformist Club), and then converted this organization into something entirely new in Cuban history: the *Partido Reformista* (Reformist Party). Though political parties were illegal in Cuba, the Reformist Party was tolerated by Serrano and Dulce. Thus a new situation emerged in the development of

---

* In 1864, the municipal government of Havana partially rectified this situation by establishing three elementary schools. Rafael María de Mendive, a distinguished poet and journalist, who had dedicated himself to "furthering the advancement and improvement of the society in which he lives," was appointed director of the Elementary School for Boys, which opened on March 19, 1865. One of his students was José Martí Pérez, then twelve years old. Martí's contact with Mendive, and his studies under the great teacher, left an indelible imprint on the future Cuban liberator.

the Cuban reform movement. Reformism now had its own party; its leaders were José Morales Lemus, José Manuel Mestre, the Count of Pozos Dulces, José Antonio Echeverría, and Miguel Aldama. Most of them were wealthy sugar planters. Aldama was one of the richest men in the island, a multimillionaire owning five of the most valuable estates, large railway holdings, and the most splendid private residence in Havana. Several, especially Pozos Dulces and Aldama, had actively supported the annexationist movement as a means of protecting slavery in Cuba. But the desire to liberate Cuba from Spanish tyranny, as well as the force of economic development, had brought about a change in their position on slavery.

To combat the growing influence of the reformers in the Cuban government, a counter-organization known as the *Partido Incondicional Español* (Unconditional Spanish Party) was formed during Serrano's administration. Composed mainly of Spanish merchants and the leading slavocrats, this party fought every move to extend the liberties of the Cuban people, which they feared would cost them their long-standing privileges. Its organ, *El Diario de la Marina*, repeatedly warned the Captain General that any concession to the reformers threatened Spanish dominion over Cuba. But Serrano and Dulce were convinced that the Spanish Party's policy would lead to precisely what they were warning against, and they favored the *siglistas*, as the reform group was called, from their organ, *El Siglo* (The Century), founded in May, 1863. After the editorship had been rejected by José Antonio Saco, it was placed in the hands of the Count of Pozos Dulces. Under his direction, *El Siglo* rapidly gained popularity, and, in its head-on debates with *El Diario de la Marina*, it was recognized as the voice of the Creole reform movement.

In *El Siglo*, the Reformist Party publicized a program which included: a charter for Cuba; curtailment of the absolute powers of the Captain General; the right of petition; freedom from arbitrary arrest and illegal confiscation of property; Cuban representation in the Cortes; the extension of the civil, commercial and criminal codes of Spain to Cuba, and a gradual solution of the slave problem, through suppressing the African slave trade and removing all obstacles to white immigration. The Reformist Party proposed that a study be undertaken of existing slave institutions, and that an effort be made to solve the slavery problem without harm to the interests of the proprietors.

As we have seen in the preceding volume, the political and administrative reforms proposed by the Reformist Party were not new.* They had been advanced during the first and second reform movements. It was in their new attitude toward the slave trade and slavery that the reformers of the 1860's took an inportant step forward. In the first movement, led by Arango y Parreño, the reformers had staunchly defended slavery and the slave trade. In the second movement, led by Saco, the reformers had called for the prohibition of the slave trade, but advocated the continuance of slavery. Now, the reformers attacked not only the slave trade but the indefinite prolongation of slavery. They advocated the abolition of slavery, provided it took place gradually and did not seriously jeopardize the interests of the slaveowners.

This program represented a remarkable evolution of thought among the wealthy Creole leaders of the reform movement, however limited it may appear compared with the needs of the times. To be sure, the reformers did not speak for those interested in maintaining the institution untouched. But they themselves had belonged, for many years, to the die-hard slavocrats, and their changed attitude represented a growing, though by no means decisive, trend.

What was responsible for this new trend? No single explanation can account for it, but several influential factors are evident.

One was the growing understanding among the Cubans who sought independence that slavery prevented the unity necessary for its achievement. The Cuban exiles were the first to reach this conclusion, for they had learned that they could not depend on help from the United States to oust Spain from Cuba. If they were united, the Cuban people could muster enough strength to oust Spain by their own efforts, but such unity was impossible while slavery remained. Many wealthy Creoles who detested Spanish tyranny were loath to risk their material stake in slavery. Over their heads hung the threat that Spain would meet revolution with a decree emancipating the slaves. The Cuban exiles, and a small group of planters in the island, were ready to counter this threat by proposing emancipation themselves. The Republican Society of Cuba

* *See* Volume I, pp. 75–77, 83–85, 87–88, 95–97, 170–82, 197–98.

and Puerto Rico, an organization formed in the 1860's by exiles dedicated to the struggle for independence, declared that "the firm plan of the Society is the independence of the Antilles and the absolute liberty of its inhabitants without distinction of race or color."* Some Cubans, particularly among the exiles, went farther and proclaimed the need for unity of Negro and white as a precondition for a successful revolt. "Both are needed against the common enemy," declared a group of Cuban revolutionaries. "Let them get together that they may be able to shake off the double yoke."[1]

This was, of course, the most advanced position, which in the early 'sixties was shared by few of the Creole planters. The farthest the majority was willing to go was gradual abolition. And they were willing to go that far primarily because slavery was no longer proving profitable.

According to the Census of June, 1862, there were 368,550 slaves in the island. This number constituted approximately one-fourth of the population, which totaled 1,359,238—728,957 whites; 34,050 Asiatics; 743 Yucatecans; 4,521 *Emancipados*; 221,417 free Negroes, and 368,550 slaves. (The percentage of Negroes, free and slave, to whites in the population had declined from 58.5 in 1841 to 43.2 in 1861.) The slaves were employed in the following economic activities:

In the cities (largely as a servant class)	75,977
On the sugar plantations	172,671
On the coffee plantations	26,942
Other agricultural occupations	92,960

It is obvious from these statistics that the Cuban coffee industry of the first half of the nineteenth century based almost entirely on slave labor, was no longer an important employer of slaves. Coffee production had swiftly declined after 1848, when the United States reduced its importation of Cuban coffee in retaliation against the

---

* The Republican Society of Cuba and Puerto Rico, founded in New York on April 7, 1866, was the successor to the *Sociedad Democrática de los Amigos de América*, established in New York in 1864, and devoted, as the preamble to its Constitution declared, "to promote the intimate union of the peoples . . . and the league of governments and to carry forward the great plan of assuring liberty and independence to those countries of the New World. . . ." (*Constitución de la Sociedad Democrática de los Amigos de América*, New York, 1864.)

high Spanish tariff on North American flour. By 1862, when the Cuban reformers began to advocate gradual abolition, the few Cuban coffee planters had no pressing reason to oppose this program.

But it was the sugar industry that dominated the economy of Cuba, and it was the decline of the slave system in that industry that swayed the Cuban reformers. This decline was influenced by several factors.

Already, by the 1850's, the Cuban sugar industry was being forced to meet competition from European beet sugar by using more efficient methods of production. This involved heavy investment in machinery. By 1860, the steam engine was in general use in the mills. In their drive to "produce more, better and cheaper," the Creole planters put themselves heavily into debt to the Spanish bankers and entrepreneurs at usurious interest rates. Except for a few, in and near Havana, the planters lacked the capital for mechanization. The majority, therefore, had to depend on Spanish capitalists, who exacted one percent per month interest from planters near Havana, and two and a half to three percent per month for others, varying with the distance from the capital. In addition to this, Spain raised the taxes on Cuban sugar production, while other European countries subsidized the competing beet-sugar producers. But although mechanization in the mills and refineries lowered the cost of production, the cost of slave labor mounted. Until 1845, the price of a *bozal* (a recent arrival in the island) was approximately 300 pesos; by the period 1855–60, it had risen to 1,250 to 1,550 pesos. The price of slaves kept rising because of the gradual suppression of the slave trade—the slave population increased by only 43,470 from 1849 to 1860 whereas in the period 1828–1841 it had increased 135,828—but the conditions of slave labor kept productivity low.

One sign of the decline of the slave system was the introduction into sugar mills of specially trained white workers, paid in wages, who worked beside the slaves during the grinding season. On October 19, 1852, the Boston *Journal* reported: "BOSTON MECHANICS FOR CUBA. The bark, *Sarah Olney* . . . sailed this noon for Matanzas. She carries a large amount of machinery, mostly sugar mills. Quite a number of machinists from South Boston also go out on her, making between 39 and 40 who have gone from that part of our city this year. They nearly all find employment in running the mills upon the various plantations during the sugar season, and return to their families and friends to spend the summer." The Census of 1862 revealed that the sugar industry, slaveholding pre-eminently, already employed 41,661 white workers. Not only was slave labor becoming more costly, but the uneducated slave was unable to operate efficiently the refinery machines. More and more planters began to ask themselves: why support a slave who was not an efficient worker throughout the year when the same man, once free, could be educated to learn the operation and be employed during part of the year at low wages?

Another sign of the decline of the slave system was that it had become more profitable for small planters to rent their slaves to understaffed larger planters. Slaves rented for from 25 to 30 pesos per month, and for 30 to 40 pesos at harvest time. This practice of renting slaves had begun as early as the 1840's, but by 1860, it had become an important feature of sugar production. Here was concrete evidence of the decline of the slave system and the rise of the wage-earning system. A mixed system of production was emerging which included slave labor, contract labor, and free labor. The undermining of the slave economy was already in progress.

While economic circumstances were working against the continuance of slavery in Cuba, a great Civil War was being fought over this very issue in the United States. To be sure, Lincoln, despite his hatred of slavery, had not yet raised the issue of emancipation, insisting that his sole war aim was to preserve the Union. Despite growing pressure from the Negro people, led by Frederick Douglass, and white abolitionists who insisted that the Union could not be preserved unless the federal government made emancipation a key objective in the struggle, the Lincoln administration did not, for more than a year, budge from its position. But by the fall of 1862, Lincoln finally came to realize that national salvation required the abolition of slavery and the recruiting of Negro soldiers in the Union Army. On January 1, 1863, Lincoln issued the Emancipation Proclamation, which declared all persons held as slaves in the States and parts of the States, the inhabitants of which were in armed rebellion against the United States, "then and thenceforth free." Shortly thereafter, Lincoln granted permission to Governor Andrews of Massachusetts to recruit two Negro regiments for the Union Army. By 1864, there were about 200,000 Negroes fighting for the Union cause, and when Lincoln was asked to stop enlisting Negroes, and to dismiss all already in the service, he replied:

> There are now in the service of the United States nearly two hundred thousand able-bodied colored men, most of them under arms, defending and acquiring Union territory. . . .
> Abandon all the forts now garrisoned by black men, take two hundred thousand men from our side, and put them in the battlefield or corn field against us, and *we would be compelled to abandon the war in three weeks.*[2]

Inevitably these events had a profound impact upon developments in Cuba.

The Spanish merchants and slave traders favored a Confederate victory for the sake of preserving slavery in Cuba. The majority of the Creole population, however, especially the Reformist Party leaders, though they still depended on slave labor, identified themselves with the North, as the side of civilization and progress. Even after the Emancipation Proclamation, despite its threat to the Cuban slave economy, the Creoles, as a class, generally remained sympathetic to the North. At the close of 1863, when the Lincoln administration was taking further steps to implement the Emancipation Proclamation, Pozos Dulces wrote editorially in *El Siglo* that "the name of Lincoln is destined to occupy a glorious page in the book of great men, and the place which he occupies in history is already fixed by the passions and miseries of the present moment. The American Union, founded by Washington and preserved by Lincoln, will transmit both of these names to the most remote posterity."

Some Cuban historians, including Ramiro Guerra y Sánchez, have interpreted this and similar Reformist writings as evidence of the abolitionism of the Reformist Party.[3] Such idealism, however, did not play a large part in the decisions of the Cuban reformers, who were timid abolitionists at best.

By 1860, Louisiana sugar production had become a serious competitor to Cuban sugar in the American market. Protected by tariffs, its sugar culture had made noticeable advances. Between 1825 and 1861, Louisiana sugar production had grown from 30,000 to 459,-

410 hogsheads, with good prospects for further advances. Most sugarhouses in Louisiana in 1861 were modern plants operated by steam.

To the relief of the Cuban planters, the Civil War changed all this.

> From a record production of 459,410 hogsheads in 1861 [writes a student of the Southern cane sugar industry] valued at more than $25,000,000, the crop declined in 1862 to 87,000 hogsheads which, despite the high prices prevailing in 1863, was worth only $8,000,000. . . . But the bottom was not reached until 1864 when the cumulative effect of inadequate capital, inefficient and inadequate labor force, and widespread destruction of capital equipment resulted in a crop of only 10,000 hogsheads, valued at less than $2,000,000. Although more than 1,200 plantations . . . had produced the record crop of 1861, in 1864 only 175 plantations . . . still were making sugar.[4]

The Cuban planters anticipated that a victorious North would remove all duties on Cuban sugar so as to sell more manufactured goods to the island. This, of course, would complete the ruin of sugar production in the South. After all, wrote Pozos Dulces, Louisiana sugar could compete only because of artificial stimulants, "thanks to protective rights and differentials imposed upon ours. . . . In the event of a Northern victory, Cuba's sugar will replace those which are artificially protected, and, in exchange, the Northern manufacturers will be able to sell at better prices the products needed in Cuba to give a better impulse to its own production." On the other hand, a victorious South would impose higher tariffs on Cuban sugar, perhaps even prohibit it entirely. As Raúl Cepero Bonilla points out: "The ruin of the sugar industry of the South which the triumph of the North foreshadowed in the judgment of Pozos Dulces, gained for the abolitionists of Lincoln the sympathy of the Cuban slaveowners."[5]

Hence they uneasily swallowed the Emancipation Proclamation, recognizing it as essential to Northern victory. But Pozos Dulces could not refrain from expressing regret that it had been found necessary. "We regret," he wrote in *El Siglo*, "that the necessities of war had to precipitate a catastrophe that we believe must be everywhere a work of time and economic and social progress." Lest its slaveowner readers interpret the paper's sympathy for the North as a sign of abolitionism, he avowed the Reformist Party's belief that "property should be duly protected and guaranteed no matter in what form it should happen to present itself."⁶

Just as the *Peninsulares* desired a Southern victory, since "a divided United States would assure Spanish domination for a long time," many Creoles believed that a Northern victory would weaken Spain's grip. Some even linked the cause of abolition, symbolized by the North, to the cause of independence. The Negroes, they knew, would support no revolution not linking their freedom with independence, and the white Cubans could not successfully drive out the Spaniards without the help of the Negroes, who still made up nearly half of the population. The contribution of the Negroes to Northern victories in the Civil War strengthened this argument.

Others, realizing that slavery was a doomed institution, believed that steps should be taken to prepare at once for gradual abolition before the impact of the Civil War brought a more immediate and drastic solution. By this they meant that the Negro, slave and free, aided by Negro and white allies inside and outside of Cuba, influenced by the Emancipation Proclamation, might rise up to put an immediate end to slavery. "It is reported from Havana," the London *Times* announced on May 9, 1865, "that a wide-spread dissatisfaction exists among the slaves in Cuba, and that an insurrection is apprehended."

"The Emancipation Proclamation and other abolitionist decrees of Lincoln," writes Emeterio S. Santovenia, "made the privileged ones in Cuba uneasy, but they made the ones who worked for their living enthusiastic." The slaves, learning of the Emancipation Proclamation through their own grapevine, began chanting a song of their own coming liberty:

> *Avanza Lincoln! Avanza!*
> *Tú eres nuestra esperanza.*
>
> Go forward, Lincoln! Forward!
> You, Lincoln, are our hope.⁷

The tragic news of Lincoln's assassination produced "an unparalleled demonstration of grief" in Cuba, especially among the Negroes "who could no longer hasten to the wharves of the Island's capital and wait for news of the redeemer of his race." In Havana the mourning for Lincoln (*luto de Lincoln*) was so widespread that it became "a public demonstration of grief." Men and women wore black ribbons displaying a picture of Lincoln and a device representing the American eagle. José Martí, then 12 years old, joined in the mourning. "For two men I trembled and wept on learning of their death, without knowing an iota about their lives," he wrote later, "for Don José de la Luz [y Caballero] and for Lincoln."

So frightened were the slaveowners by the public expression of grief, that they took pains that none of the many eulogies to Lincoln, published in Cuba after his assassination, contained references to his part in the abolition of slavery in the United States. Referring to the elegy in Lincoln's memory, *La Voz del Cielo* (The Voice of the Sky), published in Havana in 1864, Emeterio S. Santovenia writes: "As in the rest of the verses published in Cuba on the death of Lincoln, abolition of slavery is not mentioned."[8]

A number of Cubans, several of them slaveowners, began to advance plans for gradual abolition in the midst of the Civil War. Most of these plans involved payment of indemnities for liberated slaves, although some made exceptions of slaves fraudulently introduced in violation of the treaties. When the Civil War ended in victory for the North, public opposition to the slave trade intensified, and there was a flood of abolitionist plans. The first was reflected in the organization of the *Asociación contra la trata* (Association against the Slave Trade), organized to carry out the plan of a young Havana lawyer, Dr. Antonio González de Mendoza, who had freed his own slaves. Members listed in a public register were to pledge themselves not to buy Negroes smuggled into the island after November 19, 1865. Leading reformers—José Manuel Mestre, José Morales Lemus, José Silverio Jorrín, Juan Poey, el Conde de Pozos Dulces, José Antonio Echeverría and other Cuban intellectuals— joined the Association, and even some *Peninsulares* backed it. Failing to win approval from the Spanish government, the Association's plans remained on paper. But its very formation was a sign of the growing opposition to the slave trade.

All the abolitionist plans of the period immediately following the American Civil War had two things in common. All called upon Spain to outlaw the slave traffic as piracy, and to punish it as such.

All agreed that abolition should be gradual without "disturbing the habits of subordination and respect instilled in the slaves," and without disturbing the peace and security of the island. "What is singular," José A. Echeverría wrote to Saco in June, 1865, describing the various proposals for abolition, "is that there isn't anyone who recommends the more or less rapid abolition of slavery." "Look at the example of the United States," cried Fermín Figuera, a Cuban who, in 1866, proposed a 25-year plan of gradual abolition. "A disastrous Civil War is not necessary. A plan of gradual emancipation with compensation is possible and much more intelligent."[9]

However timid the Cuban brand of abolitionism, it is clear that as a result of economic forces and the impact of the American Civil war, abolitionist sentiment was growing in the island. It is also clear that it was impossible to maintain slavery any longer on the old basis. That Creole abolitionism was inspired more by the economic disadvantages of slavery and by hatred of Spanish domination than by humanitarian feelings or abstract love of human liberty does not negate its ultimate significance. After all, the decision to emancipate the slaves in the United States during the Civil War was motivated more by the necessity to preserve the Union than to put an end to "a stupendous crime against human nature."[10] But that did not cancel its great significance. As Carlos Rafael Rodríguez notes: "In the decree of liberty for its Negroes, the United States defined also the future of the Creole slaveowners."[11]

chapter 12

BIRTH OF CUBAN WORKING-CLASS CONSCIOUSNESS

"In the United States of America," wrote Karl Marx, "every independent movement of the workers was paralyzed so long as slavery disfigured a part of the Republic. Labor cannot emancipate itself in the white skin where in the black it is branded."[1] This statement applied with equal force to Cuba. As we have pointed out in a previous volume, the Cuban economy was based primarily on slavery, and slave labor bred a contempt for work, and created a society in which there was no respect for labor. As long as Negro slavery dominated Cuban economic life, it was impossible for the white workers to establish effective trade unions to improve working conditions.*

All this does not mean that there were no organized efforts of Cuban workers during the slave regime. The beginnings of the labor movement in Cuba, as in the United States, took place during the slave era, although the militancy and effectiveness of the movement were limited by the existence of slavery.

The first group of Cuban workers to organize for the improvement of their conditions were the cigar makers. The late 1850's witnessed an important change in the status of these tobacco workers. Prior to this period, they had enjoyed enormous bargaining strength because of the scarcity of skilled craftsmen in the industry. So great was this scarcity that many cigar makers abandoned work in the shops whenever they wanted to, sure to find jobs when they were ready for them. Employers were eager to hire them and even promised them wages in advance to induce them to leave the shops in

---

* *See* Volume I, pp. 187–88.

which they were employed. Not a few cigar makers left one job after another owing employers for wages paid in advance.

This was the era in which the status of the cigar maker was that of a highly paid, skilled aristocrat of labor who had no trouble in securing work, and felt little need for combining with other workers in the trade to strengthen his bargaining power. As a popular tune of the period put it:

> I like the cigar makers
>   because they are always singing.
> Happy, they are working,
>   earning much money.
> They wear good hats.
> They wear expensive shoes.
> They wear good pants,
>   a good watch, a good watch-chain.
> And they stop on their corner,
>   and plant their flag.[2]

Gradually, this situation changed. For one thing, in July, 1851, the government in Cuba, responding to an appeal from manufacturers of cigars, complaining of the losses they suffered from advances in wages to workers who abandoned their employment, instituted a system known as *libretas* (passbooks). All journeymen tobacco workers of both sexes were required to present themselves within 30 days at the Secretariat of the Industrial Section of the Royal Economic Society, where they would receive their passbooks. In the future, when a journeyman left the shop in which he was employed, the employer would note in the passbook the state of his account, and especially if he owed any labor for wages advanced. No shopowner could employ a journeyman who owed an employer for advanced wages unless he (the shopowner) first paid the sum to the previous employer. Moreover, any employer who induced journeymen to abandon the shops in which they worked by promising them wages in advance, would be subject to a fine of not less than 100 and not more than 500 pesos.

Although the passbook system was primarily designed to end practices which were disorganizing production in "one of the principal industries of the country," it could be and was used to reduce the bargaining strength of the individual cigar maker. The blank pages in the passbook could be used by an employer to note the fact that the cigar worker was a "trouble maker and agitator" in the shop, and such workers found it increasingly difficult to secure employment in other shops.[3]

But the major change in the status of the cigar workers occurred because of a reduction in production resulting, for the first time, in widespread unemployment among the artisans. Fernando Ortíz points out that "already in 1856 there were in Havana numerous cigar makers out of work due to the fact that in 1855 there were exported, besides a great deal of leaf, no less than 357,582,500 rolled cigars. These had been exported to the United States to saturate the market before the tariff was raised on March 3, 1857."[4] (Although the Act of 1857 revised many rates downward and even placed several raw materials on the free list, it raised the duty on tobacco.) The market for tobacco products in the United States was further reduced by the Panic of 1857, resulting in an economic depression which lasted until 1858.

These economic calamities, coming after the great cholera epidemic of 1855 in Cuba, convinced many workers, especially the cigar workers, of the need for united activity to improve their conditions. This feeling first found expression in the formation of Mutual Aid Societies.

In 1857, Adolfo Ramos, an artisan in Havana, asked for and was granted permission to establish a "Mutual Aid Society of Honest Workers and Day Laborers." The Society's constitution revealed that it would admit as members "all *white* people of good education who lived in the parish of Our Lady of El Pilar." Other Mutual Aid Societies founded during this period contained a similar constitutional provision, as well as one which provided that a candidate for membership as well as his family had to "enjoy good health." This last provision is understandable in view of the fact that the main purpose of these societies was to aid the members and their families in the event of illness or death. "The only goal of this Society," read a typical introduction to the constitution of these associations, "is to supervise the necessary means of enabling the honest artisans and day workers who belong to it to recover their health, for they earn their subsistence and that of their families only by their personal labor."

The exclusive *white only* character of the membership of the associations led the free Negro workers to organize their own Mutual Aid Societies. Several were founded in the late 1850's. In 1858 the free Negro, Antonio Mora, asked for and was granted permission to organize a Mutual Aid Society in the parish of San Nicolás de Bari, under the patronage of the "great power of God." In the introduction to the constitution which accompanied the request, Mora wrote: "Considering how useful and beneficial it would be to the proletarian class to create a means capable of making its misfortunes less calamitous, of making its cruel sufferings more tolerable, various dark-skinned individuals have planned to form a Society with the name which is at the head." All who wished to become members had to meet the following qualifications: (1) to be a Catholic; (2) to be a free person; (3) not to have a bad reputation; (4) to be of decent behavior and of quiet character; (5) to have a known skill, and (6) that he, his wife, his children and his parents should enjoy perfect health at the time he requested permission to join the organization.[5]

Mutual Aid Societies, primarily composed of white artisans, spread into the interior of the island. All of them, like those in Havana, combined the character of mutual aid and semi-religious organizations. They were confined to one parish and operated under the protection of a celestial patron whose fiesta was solemnly celebrated by the members of the Society. On such occasions, as at other public functions to which they were invited, the members came carrying their insignias and banners and dressed in similar clothing.

It is in these Mutual Aid Societies that we find the embryo of the Cuban labor movement and the precursors of the future trade unions. Whatever their limitations, they represented the beginnings of an understanding in working class circles that in contemporary capitalist society, with its inevitable cycles of depression and unemployment, in which the power of the employer to discharge a worker whenever he no longer needed his services was unlimited, and in which the individual worker could not earn enough, even when employed, to provide for himself and his family in time of illness and death, co-operation among the workers for their mutual help was essential. In these societies the workers learned to lend each other assistance, and out of this experience emerged a real sense of class solidarity. The rise of this consciousness was marked by an important event in the history of the Cuban working class: the publication of *La Aurora*, the first newspaper in Cuba dedicated to serve the interests of the workers.

La Aurora was basically the idea of Saturnino Martínez. Born in Asturias, he came to Cuba as a boy and learned the trade of cigar making. Self-taught, he rapidly achieved recognition as a poet. Nominated as a member of the public library of the *Sociedad Económica de Amigos del País* (Economic Society of the Friends of the Country), Martínez studied there at night after a daytime spent rolling cigars in the factories of Partagás. He soon conceived the idea of publishing a newspaper dedicated to the artisans, and through his contact with the outstanding Cuban intellectuals of the time in the Society, he obtained moral encouragement. With the means for publication provided by workers in the tobacco factories, *La Aurora* came off the press with its first issue on Sunday, October 22, 1865. At the top of the first page of the eight-page, two-column edition was the masthead:

LA AURORA
A WEEKLY NEWSPAPER DEDICATED TO THE ARTISANS

Then followed the announcement: "Its purpose will be to illuminate in every way possible that class of society to which it is dedicated. We will do everything possible to make ourselves generally accepted. If we are not successful, the blame will be in our insufficiency, not in our lack of will." The first page also contained a lengthy editorial on the development of the sciences and arts and the spread of human intelligence. "Fortunately," it observed, "we belong to a century which cannot remain wrapped in oblivion. . . . We belong to a time in which ideas are being extended to all the classes, and in which the workers are proceeding to gain the rank which too long unjustly has been denied to them." Within "the limits of what a publication of the character of ours would be permitted," *La Aurora* would play its role in appeasing the hunger of the workers for knowledge of science and literature, and attempt to diffuse "light among the masses of society."

Verses and articles of a literary character, and translations of three songs of Béranger, among them *"La Santa Alianza de los Pueblos"* (The Holy Alliance of the Peoples) filled the remaining pages of the first issue.

Assured of continuing support from the tobacco workers of Havana (of whom there were in 1863, 15,128 working in 516 tobacco factories) and from workers in other occupations and sympathetic intellectuals, *La Aurora* continued to publish week after week.

La Aurora regularly published the writings of leading Cuban intellectuals—Antonio and Francisco Sellén, Luis Victoriano Betancourt, Joaquín Lorenzo Luaces, José Fornaris, Fernando Urzais, Alfredo Torroella, Felipe Poey and others—who contributed articles, poetry and fiction, and, especially in the case of Torroella* and Luaces, did so with full consciousness that they were putting their talent at the service of a class unjustly exploited. In addition to the works of Cuban writers, *La Aurora* carried translations of foreign authors, among them Schiller and Chateaubriand. It also featured reviews of new books and plays, as well as news of current trends in the intellectual world.

The attention *La Aurora* paid to works of literature does not mean that it neglected the immediate day-to-day problems facing the workers. It exposed the tyranny of the factory owners, denounced the lack of sanitary conditions in many workshops, the abuses of the foremen, and the brutal treatment of apprentices. On June 27, 1866, *La Aurora* wrote bitterly: "Do you know that in certain tobacco factories, they still use that thing which has a knot on the end and sounds, when used, like the cracking of a whip? And do you know that at the edge of La Zanja, according to what people say, there is a factory owner who puts shackles on the children he uses as apprentices? They say that the other day at lunch time, because one of them took a little wine at the table, he split his head open. And the world marches on!"

La Aurora also called attention to the problems of older workers who, having given the best years of their lives to enriching their employers and no longer being able to produce as much as when

---

* In a tribute to Alfredo Torroella, delivered on February 28, 1879, José Martí referred to him as "the bard of the poor, of the slaves, of the martyrs." (*Obras Completas*, La Habana, 1946, pp. 731–34.) The reference to the slaves is undoubtedly to Torroella's drama, *El Mulato*.

they were young, were callously forced to take on the most menial tasks in order to eke out an existence. In the January 29, 1867 issue, it dealt with this problem as it related to the cigar workers and offered a plan to alleviate the misery of the older workers:

> All crafts and trades have their aspirations, which generously nourish the hope of the individual who practices them. But cigar making has the misfortune to offer the worker only a terrible descent at the end of his career, that is to say, he has to go from the heights to the depths, from the table to the barrel of stripping tobacco.
>
> We know individuals who, having dedicated themselves from their childhood to the rolling of this rich leaf which by itself alone constitutes the principal of wealth of this country,* have almost reached the height of perfection in this craft. But what good will it have done them once their vision has decreased or they have completely lost their dexterity? What happens when they get older? What do the employers care about the skills these workers acquired in the course of twenty or thirty years? Others will be seated at the front of their shops, and the old workers will go to the barrel.
>
> In order to avoid an old age of misery and poverty for this class of artisans, and to stimulate them, at the same time, to work steadily, the people who run the workshops should assign them a premium which they can only obtain as a result of a fixed number of years during which they work constantly in the same shop. Moreover, when they reach an age when they can no longer carry out their function as operatives, they should be assigned some other employment in the same establishment which would be adaptable to their circumstances, either as foreman, agent, associate, or other job, which would give them a subsistence without the necessity of reducing their intelligence to the miserable labor of opening leaves.

Actually, *La Aurora* had little faith that its proposal for a form of pension system would be adopted by the employers. Although the latter, it pointed out, had themselves once been workers, they were now concerned only with increasing their profits. They forgot entirely "those who have contributed to enriching them."

La Aurora persistently campaigned for the formation of Mutual Aid Societies by the Cuban workers. "In their bosom," it declared in recommending the Societies to the Carpenters and Masons, "they can find warmth and support in the dark winter of necessity." More-

---

* Actually, sugar constituted the principal wealth of Cuba. But as a tobacco worker himself, Saturnino Martínez, who wrote this editorial, was inclined to exaggerate.

over, José de Jesús Márquez, one of the regular contributors, used the columns of La Aurora to advocate the formation in Cuba of Consumers' Co-operatives based on the principles of the Rochdale Pioneers of England. (The Society operated on the basis of a plan whereby profits were divided among purchasing members according to amounts of purchases.) As a result, a co-operative was set up in Havana in June, 1866, by an Association of Cigar Makers, and within a month, this venture was so successful that it was followed by two other stores, all organized on the Rochdale Plan. On July 15, 1866, La Aurora reported that the co-operative movement was spreading among workers throughout the island.

Of all the campaigns initiated and carried through by La Aurora, the one that left its most lasting impression on Cuban society was the "Lector System," the system of readings in the work shops. In the same year in which he founded La Aurora, Saturnino Martínez interested Don Nicolás de Azcárate, director of the Liceo (High School) of Guanabacoa, in the possibility of instituting educational readings in the cigar factories. Azcárate met with the workers of the factory El Fígaro, who were eager to undertake the experiment, and he prevailed upon the owners to permit the readings. One of the workers was chosen as the reader, and the others contributed to his earnings from their own production while he was so engaged. On January 7, 1866, La Aurora announced joyfully: "Reading in the shops has been started for the first time among us, the initiative for which belongs to the honored workers of El Fígaro. This constitutes a giant step in the march of progress and general advance of the artisans because in this way . . . they will go on little by little becoming familiar with books, in such a way that they will be their best friends and the greatest entertainment."

The factory of Don Jaime Partagás was next. Here "two magnificent reading stands," paid for by the workers, were set up for the readers. The stands were inaugurated at a ceremony on February 3, 1866, during which Saturnino Martínez, one of the workers, made a speech in which he referred to the charge that artisans were interested only in material things. He continued: "If in Cuba we had a Cobden or a Bright who had made us familiar with the great questions with which we are dealing, perhaps we would have succeeded in getting rid of the iron cloak which oppresses us. But thanks to the great step we have just taken, we will not remain long sunk in darkness."*

The shops of *El Fígaro* and Partagás became a national attraction. Foreign visitors made it a practice to stop in to see the readings, among them U.S. Secretary of State William H. Seward. After observing the workers listening to the readings while wrapping cigars, visitors were apt to remark admiringly: "This is not what we had been led to believe of this class of artisans."⁶

One after another, shops in Havana, petitioned by their workers, instituted the reading system. *La Aurora* carried weekly reports of the progress of the movement, as well as a list of the newspapers and books that were being read aloud: the reformist newspaper *El Siglo*, the books, *Battles of the Century*, *Political Economy* by Florez y Estrada, *The King of the World*, a moral and philosophical novel by Fernández y González, a two-volume *History of the United States*, a two-volume *History of the French Revolution*, and a six-volume *History of Spain* by Galeano. When the management of the *Caruncho* shop refused to grant the workers' request for readings, *La Aurora* challenged it to give a good reason for the action, and then proceeded to demolish the arguments advanced. Angered by *La Aurora's* campaign, the owner threatened to have the weekly suspended. *La Aurora* refused to be intimidated, and shot back on March 25, 1866:

> One of the principal businessmen of this capital has threatened to suspend our innocent *Aurora* if we have the temerity to continue to concern ourselves with Readings in the Shops, especially as it relates to his factory. We did not know that there are businessmen capable of suspending a publication which did not injure anybody and was authorized to exercise its functions in public. But thanks to the activities of this gentleman, now we know that any stripper of tobacco leaves has *facultades omnímodas* for such things. What does *El Diario de la Marina* say to this?

The reference to *El Diario de la Marina* was not accidental, for this reactionary organ of absolutism had already launched a ferocious campaign against the readings in the shops on the ground that they were implanting "subversive ideas" in the minds of the workers. *La Aurora's* reply in its issue of March 18, 1866, is a historic

* Richard Cobden and John Bright were leading English reformers.

statement: "*El Diario de la Marina* has openly declared itself against readings in the shops. We who have been the instigators of the idea are happy about this, since its opposition proves that the practice is a good one."

The battle to maintain and extend the readings, waged by the artisans without any help other than *La Aurora* and *El Siglo*, was a bitter one. In the end, however, the forces of reaction triumphed. On May 14, 1866, the Political Governor, Don Cipriano del Mazo, prohibited readings in the "different kind of workshops"—thereby proving that the practice had spread from the tobacco industry to other industries. The decree noted with alarm that once the readings were tolerated, "the meetings of the artisans were converted into political clubs," and that the reading of newspapers "passed on to that of books which contain sophisms or maxims prejudicial to the weak intelligence of persons who do not possess the critical faculties and the learning necessary to judge with accuracy the output of writers who ... often expose the peace of nations to grave dangers." All this distracted the workers from their main duty, that of applying themselves "assiduously to their work." To tolerate this situation "would constitute a grave defect in the law which prohibits political associations as well as anything else which can introduce confusion, anarchy and disturbance in society." Therefore:

> 1. It is prohibited to distract the workers of the tobacco shops, workshops and shops of all kinds with the readings of books and newspapers, or with discussions foreign to the work in which they are engaged.
> 2. The police shall exercise constant vigilance to enforce this decree, and put at the disposition of my authority those shop owners, representatives or managers who disobey this mandate so that they may be judged by the law according to the gravity of the case.[7]

What a commentary on the absolutist mentality of the oligarchy that controlled Cuba! The slightest effort on the part of the Cuban working class to acquaint itself with issues other than those relating directly to their work could not be tolerated. (The decree falsely attributed the readings to elements outside of the working class who were trying to impose them on the artisans, ignoring the fact that they were instituted in each shop as a result of a petition from the workers.) What was it that so frightened the ruling class? It was not the reading from *El Siglo*, for there was nothing especially radical in the reformist newspaper, and it did not go beyond respectfully urging administrative reform from Spain. But the recounting, in several books read in the shops, of the history of the American and French Revolutions could not but help to expose Spain's arbitrary rule in Cuba, and show how the people of the United States and France overthrew tyranny by revolutionary upheavals. Then too, Don Alvaro Florez Estrada's *Political Economy* contained passages which alarmed the Cuban ruling groups. Among them was the observation:

> The monopoly of teaching throughout time has been the aim of those interested in perpetuating abuses, in the same way that industrial monopoly has always been the goal of those manufacturers whose products, because of their inferiority and high price, could not sustain the competition of foreign goods.

Again:

> We do not have any illusions. Society will not become organized as it should be as long as the obligation to work is not extended to all members of society, and as long as the right of the worker to dispose of the fruit of his labor is not a right religiously observed. There is no other alternative: either continue the struggle of the two parties in which human kind has been divided or give to labor the recompense it should properly have. My view directs itself to the latter.[8]

What the authorities feared was that the workers, hearing such words, would understand clearly who and what were responsible for their miserable status in Cuban society. And this could not be permitted!

The order of May 14, 1866, prohibiting readings, was published in the leading newspapers. Nevertheless, readings in some form continued, for a year later Captain General Francisco Lersundi issued another decree in which he noted that while the earlier order had resulted in a reduction in the amount of "reading of books and newspapers of exaggerated ideas in various shops," the practice not only continued in "clandestine meetings, [but] as the worst things are transmitted with great speed . . . this pernicious practice has been extended all the way into the island by political groups not only in the workshops but in other fields as well."* Hence he strictly or-

---

* Lersundi was referring to the fact that readings were occurring on the plantations, especially among the tobacco pickers.

dered the police and military forces to use "all the means at your disposal, to see to it that associations for readings be dissolved wherever they exist, and that the readings be not allowed to continue in any shape or form."[9]

Under Lersundi's iron despotism—next to Tacón he was the most hated Captain General in Cuban history up to this time—the decree against readings in the workshops was strictly enforced, and the practice was suspended until it was revived again in the 1880's, when the Cuban labor movement made its appearance in its modern form. Before this, in the 1870's, the practice was carried over to the United States by Cuban cigar makers who emigrated to New York, Tampa, and Key West.

La Aurora continued to educate the workers after readings in the factories were prohibited. But the paper was under constant surveillance. Every issue came under the scrutiny of official censorship. It is understandable, then, why *La Aurora* failed to report a historic event in the development of the Cuban working class—the first strike in Cuba, a strike of the cigar workers in the factory of H. de Cabañas y Carvajal in 1866. Even though Saturnino Martínez, editor of *La Aurora*, directed the strike, and along with 16 other workers was scheduled to be deported from Cuba, the paper carried no notice of these events. Nor did it report the fact that the deportation order was annulled as a result of a successful defense of the strikers by José Ignacio Rodríguez, a distinguished lawyer who was also Secretary of the *Sociedad Económica de Amigos del País*. Any issue of *La Aurora* which reported such events would promptly have been banned by the censors. It is probable that the same reason accounts for the failure of the paper to comment on the all-important issue of Negro slavery in Cuba.

Even in its censored form, *La Aurora* came under continual attack by the reactionaries. In the November 4, 1866, issue, reporting the fact that the previous month had marked "the completion of a year of the life of our publication," Martínez noted that throughout the entire year, "we have been denounced as anarchists, revolutionists, seditionists, socialists, enemies of foreign capital." He expressed surprise that "so much perversity can be attributed to an innocent little newspaper which has no more aspiration than to be useful to the working class, in whose bosom we have been formed, and where we still keep the tools with which we have always earned and still earn the bread of our family."

In May, 1868, *La Aurora* was compelled to suspend publication temporarily, and was only permitted to reappear in a new format as a "Weekly of Science, Literature and Criticisms." But it was only a reprieve. In October, 1868, with the outbreak of the Ten Years' War, *La Aurora* was forced out of existence permanently by the authorities.*

The period of *La Aurora*'s existence, 1865–68, marked the beginnings of working-class consciousness in Cuba. It was a period in which the workers began to understand the causes responsible for their exploitation, and to take the first steps through mutual aid societies, co-operatives, strikes, and trade unions to protect themselves from the evils inherent in the wage system. In this development, the readings in the factories and the articles in *La Aurora* made notable contributions. To be sure, the solutions offered in *La Aurora* to the problems facing the workers were often utopian and reformist, and this continued to exert an influence on the Cuban labor movement for years to come. But it does not alter the significant fact that the main message preached by the men associated with *La Aurora* was one that was indispensable for the future of the Cuban working class. This was the doctrine that there was a battle between the workers and their employers; that in order to emerge victorious in this struggle, the workers had to achieve an understanding of the society in which they lived, through education, and then, with this understanding, act as a united body with common interests to achieve their goals.

* Martínez, however, continued his crusade to bring education to the workers in *La Unión*, which he founded in 1873, and *La Razón*, which appeared as a weekly from 1876 to 1884.

chapter 13

HIGH HOPES FOR REFORM

In January, 1865, Francisco Serrano, returning to Spain from Cuba, addressed the Cortes on the necessity of immediate reforms in the island's economic, political and social structure. Among other things, in this famous speech, he advocated the right of Cuba to representation in the Cortes.

News of the speech aroused a wave of excitement in Cuba. On May 12, 1865, a memorandum, signed by 24,000 persons claiming to speak for a cross-section of all groups in the island—except the Negroes, of course—was addressed to Serrano. The memorandum congratulated him on his speech and asked him to present to the Cortes demands of the signers, which may be summed up under three heads: (1) reform of the tariff system; (2) Cuban representation in the Cortes and political and civil rights equal to those of the metropolis; (3) abolition of the slave traffic. "The commerce in Africans continues," the memorandum noted, "a repugnant and dangerous cancer of immorality. . . . Private interests here have proven themselves more powerful than the honor and conscience of the nation."[1]

The absence of any mention of the abolition of slavery was not accidental. On this subject the reformers were deliberately silent. A meeting had been held at the home of José Ricardo O'Farrill to discuss a plan for gradual abolition that might be incorporated in the memorandum. Most of the discussion had revolved about the plan proposed by the Spaniard, Francisco Montaos, director of *La Prensa*, a Havana newspaper. It had divided the slaves into five groups, setting a value on each according to age. The slave would either buy his freedom at the sum prescribed for his age group (*coartación*) or the payment would be made from a fund set up to carry out gradual emancipation.

Most of the reformers present at the meeting had opposed the plan, and made it clear that the majority of the Creole proprietors would oppose that or any other abolition plan. After the meeting, O'Farrill and other Creole reformers had joined with the anti-reform group in a joint memorandum to Captain General Dulce asking him to bar further discussion or publication of Montaos' plan.

One argument advanced against including any mention of abolition in the memorandum was that it would destroy all chances of winning over the "Unconditional Spanish Party" to join in the petition. This hope proved vain. After the scuttling of Montaos' plan, the two groups sought common ground on a reform program that excluded abolition, but they were too divided on other issues to reach agreement.

A month after it received the reform memorandum, the Spanish government was handed a petition from the Spanish party in Cuba. Its signers declared that they were not opposed to administrative or tariff reforms, but desired to avoid the growth of "factions" among "ignorant people." They therefore opposed all political reforms as well as Cuban representation in the Cortes. Such political assimilation with Spain would be dangerous because of the diversity of the races in the island. Finally, Madrid was urged to remember that political reforms given to "an ignorant and factious people" had been mainly responsible for the separation of the continental American colonies from Spain. She was respectfully warned not to repeat that mistake.[2]

Fortunately for reform hopes, the government of Spain had now come into the hands of the Liberal Union Party, headed by Leopoldo O'Donnell, with Antonio Cánovas del Castillo as colonial minister. Though barely more than nominal liberals, they recognized the wisdom of meeting the rising reform pressure at least part way. Moreover, the government was under increasing pressure from foreign powers, and from the growing abolitionist movement in Spain itself. Furthermore, England was now not alone in demanding that Spain act. The United States, no longer dominated by the slave power, had, for the first time, joined Britain in notes to Spain on the slave trade. To be sure, the American note did not go as far as England's, which called upon Spain to declare the slave trade piracy and liable to the severe penalty for that offense. The American note asked only that Spain take stronger measures against the trade. But, though more polite, the effect of the American note was strengthened by the agitation in the United States for a boycott on Cuban imports if Spain failed to respond.* Consequently, in reply to the British and American notes in October, 1865, the O'Donnell government, though refusing to commit itself on declaring the slave trade piracy, did undertake to enact a more stringent law against the slave trade at the next session of the Cortes.

Having committed itself on that demand in the Reform memorandum, the O'Donnell government decided to take other measures to pacify the Creole Reform Party. Thus it was that two steps were taken almost simultaneously: the introduction early in November, 1865, in the Cortes, of the "Law for the Suppression of the Slave Trade"; the other, on November 25, 1865, a Royal Decree establishing a *Junta de Información de Ultramar* (Board of Overseas Information or Colonial Reform Commission) for the study of reform proposals. The Commission was to be limited to the following objectives:

(1) On the bases which must be founded the Special Laws which according to Article 80 of the Constitution of the Monarchy (adopted in 1836) must be presented to the Cortes for the government of the provinces of Cuba and Puerto Rico.

(2) On the manner for regulating the work of the Colored and Asiatic population, and on the methods for facilitating immigration. . . .

(3) On the treaties of navigation and commerce that should be celebrated with other nations . . . and the administration of customs.³

"They [the Royal Commission] will not come to answer; but to discuss," Colonial Minister Cánovas wrote to Captain General Dulce on December 12, 1865. But the government's proposal even to discuss the question of colonial reforms aroused stormy opposition in Spanish conservative circles. In spite of mounting opposition from conservatives, Madrid authorized the election of 20 Cuban and

---

* On March 25, 1865, even before the Civil War had ended, the *National Anti-Slavery Standard*, the leading abolitionist journal in the United States, raised the question of a boycott of Cuban products. In an editorial entitled, "The Example of Our Emancipation," it predicted that the abolition of slavery in the United States was bound to influence the end of slavery in Cuba. But to speed the process, it was proposed that freedom-loving Americans boycott Cuban products. Since Spain depended mainly on Cuba for her income to run her kingdom, the boycott would force her to abolish slavery in the island.

four Puerto Rican commissioners who were to come to Spain to present their views on needed colonial reforms. Partly to appease the conservatives and partly to avoid the risk of election of men who favored radical reforms, the government instructed the municipalities in the two colonies to set high property qualifications for voting. And to make doubly sure of a conservative victory in Cuba, Dulce was instructed to divide the electorate of the municipalities into four groups: property, industry, commerce, and the professions. The division of industrial and commercial interests was arranged in a way that would magnify the electoral power of the anti-reform party.

To everybody's amazement, the reformers won a smashing victory in the elections. Of the 16 Cuban commissioners elected, 12 were Creole reformers. (Three of the four commissioners elected in Puerto Rico were reformers.) Among them were the leading men in Cuban society, José Morales Lemus, Miguel de Aldama, el Conde de Pozos Dulces, José M. Mestre, José A. Echeverría, Manuel de Armas, and the most respected of all Cubans of the era, the exile José Antonio Saco, who was triumphantly elected by the municipality of Santiago de Cuba even though he had not yet agreed to accept the post, and, in spite of a spirited campaign of the Spaniards of the area to get a pro-Spanish representative elected.

The election returns of March 25, 1866, thus marked the overwhelming triumph of the reform cause; together with the victory in Puerto Rico, they proved decisively that the Creole population of the Antilles was virtually unanimous for colonial reform. The Negroes, of course, had no voice in the elections. "The reformist agitation which moved Cuba," writes José L. Franco, "only reached the white population. The Negroes and mulattoes, free or slave, were forbidden to express their opinions."[4]

On July 9, 1866, after four months of investigation and discussion, the Cortes passed the "Law for the Suppression and Punishment of the Slave Trade." The new law more precisely defined complicity in the slave trade. Now any person connected with the trade was liable for heavy fine and imprisonment. (The death penalty was reserved only for those who resisted arrest, and for those whose cruelty resulted in death or grave injury to the slave.) The other advance in the new law was the provision for the registration and census of all slaves in Cuba and Puerto Rico "so that at no time can negroes be taken for slaves when they have been introduced in contravention to this law." Men of color who were not inscribed in this registration were to be considered free men. Fines and imprisonment were to be levied on anyone found guilty of violating the provision for registration.

Many critics, especially the newly-organized Spanish *Sociedad Abolicionista* (Abolitionist Society), felt that the only effective way to end the slave trade would be to abolish slavery itself. ("We will never tire of saying it," declared the Society in a memorandum to the Cortes, "that while slavery exists, all efforts to suppress the slave traffic will be futile. Long and painful experience has proven it."[5]) Nevertheless, the first part of the O'Donnell government's twofold program—suppression of the slave traffic and colonial reforms —had been largely achieved. (After 1866 the slave trade declined, mainly because the new law was better enforced than any previous measures.) The fact that the Cortes had withstood the opposition of the wealthy slave interests in Cuba and Spain who raised the old cry that any legislation touching the slave problem would lead inevitably to the emancipation of the slaves, the "Africanization" of Cuba, the destruction of its economy and the end of Spanish domination in the island, augured well for the future of the Reform Commission.

Unfortunately, in July, 1866, even before the Reform Commission met, the Liberal Union Ministry of Leopoldo O'Donnell fell from power. Under the new Narváez government, the Cortes was suspended for six months. This so-called *Moderado* (Moderate, in the sense of conservative) regime was hostile to colonial reforms, especially anything that touched slavery. (One of its first acts was the suppression of the Spanish Abolitionist Society.) Cánovas, the chief champion of Cuban reform, was forced to flee Madrid for having presented a memorandum of the deputies asking for the re-opening of the Cortes.

By the time the Antillean Commissioners gathered in Madrid, it was doubtful that the government would even convoke the Reform Commission. But, deciding that it was wisest to make the best of a distasteful situation it had not created, the new ministry called for a convocation on August 11, 1866. However, it made sure of control by naming 21 persons to represent the Peninsula as against the

20 elected in the Antilles. The worst the reformers had expected was that the government would name an equal number, which would, in itself, have been a setback, since Spanish interests were already represented by four commissioners from Cuba and one from Puerto Rico, elected by the *Peninsulares*. With the reactionary forces in a clear majority, the outlook was not bright.

It was thus with considerable trepidation that the Cuban Reform Commissioners met in the Salon of the Colonial Ministry on October 30, 1866, for the first meeting. Their gloom deepened when they heard Colonial Minister Alejandro de Castro announce that the sessions would be secret, and that it was forbidden to release news to the press. Obviously the government feared that public opinion favored the reform cause, and was taking precaution against pressure to alter the status quo.

The first obstacle to be overcome by the reformers related to the agenda for the conference. The Royal Decree of November 25, 1865, it will be recalled, had limited the Commission to three general objectives. But flushed with their overwhelming victory in the election of delegates, the Cuban Commission had arrived in Madrid with a long list of reform demands. They wanted an end to the "exceptional state" in which Cuba had been governed since 1825; they wanted the separation of political and civil power from the military to be further implemented by nomination of a governor-general by the Crown to represent the executive power, and of a captain general to command the army; constitutional rights for all Spanish subjects; an insular assembly for administrating affairs "peculiar to the island"; a new territorial and civil organization of the island with provincial councils and deputations; municipal governments popularly elected (by taxpayers); representation in the Cortes; tariff, customs, tax and administrative reforms; and, finally, efficacious measures for ending the slave trade, with the recommendation that it be declared piracy as was done in Brazil in 1850.

The question was whether the government would even grant these requests a hearing or would restrict the discussion within the limits defined in the Royal decree. This question was speedily answered. Alejandro Oliván, President of the Conferences, announced that all the demands of the Commissioners would be discussed freely.

A detailed examination of the many sessions, exhaustive debates,

High Hopes for Reform • 155

committee reports, recommendations and projects that made up the work of the Reform Commission of 1866–67 would require a book in itself. Space permits only a summary of the economic, political, and social questions debated by the Commissioners.

The proposals of the reformers in the economic sphere called for the elimination of customs duties on all merchandise imported into the island. Since this would mean a loss in revenue for the Metropolis, the reformers suggested recouping that revenue by an income tax of six percent levied on farmers, businessmen and professionals. This, in their eyes, would more equitably distribute the tax burden.

In case complete free trade were not feasible, the reformers asked that custom duties be lowered, and articles of prime necessity, such as flour and foodstuffs (which came largely from the United States) be admitted duty-free.

In the political arena, the reformers were equally aggressive in their demands. In the report prepared by a commission headed by Morales Lemus, the chief demand was for representation in the Cortes on the basis of one deputy for each 45,000 inhabitants. In the islands themselves, an Insular Council and Insular Assembly, popularly elected, would assist the governor, and would be consulted on insular finance and administrative policy. The islands were to be divided into administrative subdivisions, each provided with a responsible Provincial Council and Assembly. In addition, the number of municipal governments was to be increased and made more representative and responsible.

On civil rights, the reformers asked that all the rights of the Spanish Constitution be applied to the Antilles. Other demands (throwing considerable light on the oppressive nature of Spanish colonial government) included the free exercise of a profession, equality of access to civil employment according to merit and capacity, the right to acquire property and the protection thereof, freedom from arbitrary arrest and search, and the same civil and criminal codes as in the Peninsula. Also, the Captain General's power to suspend civil liberties in emergencies—and in Cuba the emergency had been in existence since 1825*—was to be subject to control by the Insular Council and Assembly. Arbitrary tribunals were to be abol-

* See Volume I, pp. 104, 119, 170, 172, 176.

ished, and it would be forbidden to reduce a free citizen to servitude for failure to fulfill any law or contract.

The rights demanded by the reformers were termed by them as "inherited by man and the essential condition of his existence." If she denied them, Spain would be committing a crime against God and nature.[6]

The Reform Commissioners from Cuba and Puerto Rico had had little difficulty in formulating their recommendations in the economic and political fields. There was practically no disagreement among them on these issues. But when it came to the "social question," the Reform Commissioners were anything but united. On November 27, 1866, at the third session of the Commission, the Puerto Rican Reform Commissioners—José Julián Acosta, Segundo Ruiz Bélivis, and Francisco M. Quijano—exploded a bombshell by declaring that the moment had arrived for the abolition of slavery in Puerto Rico. In a dramatic resolution, they denounced slavery as a "miserable institution," and declared: "The delegates of Puerto Rico demand today, as always, the abolition of slavery with or without indemnification, if it cannot be done in any other way; abolition without regulation of free labor or with it, if it is considered absolutely necessary."[7]

Two Commissioners associated with Cuba, Luis Pastor and Domingo Sterling, both nominated by the government, came to the support of the Puerto Ricans. But the other Cuban Commissioners were horrified, and announced that they would "not accept immediate abolition" even as a matter for discussion. But the Cuban Commissioners were powerless to prevent the discussion, even though, in discussing emancipation in any form, they were exceeding their instructions. No discussion of reforms in the Antilles could possibly be conducted without consideration of how they would affect the slave system. Then again, international opinion forced the question into the Commission's proceedings. "The abolition of slavery is an urgent question," argued one Commissioner, "because the whole world is concerned with it." "When morality, religion and public convenience demand it," declared another, "when the United States has just sacrificed the life and well-being of millions of its inhabitants in order to achieve the abolition of slavery at the doorstep of our Antilles, it is impossible to continue with the illusion that we can delay the solution of the problem."[8]

Although the Cuban reformers were unable to cut off discussion on the abolition resolution, they made their opposition to emancipation clear in their famous *informe*, drawn up by José Antonio Echeverría and signed by all of the Cuban Commissioners. They congratulated the Puerto Ricans on the fortunate circumstances of their island which made it possible to consider immediate abolition. But, the Cuban Commissioners lamented, their island was not so lucky. In Puerto Rico slavery was weakened and destined shortly to disappear, whether or not Spain moved to abolish it. In Cuba, on the other hand, slavery still constituted the dominant form of production.

The Cuban reformers could not, of course, defend slavery. It was too late in the day for that. On the contrary, they reiterated, in the *informe*, their moral opposition to slave labor: "We recognize and we support the right of the slave to return to the enjoyment of his liberty." But this lofty sentiment was always followed by a qualifying statement such as: "But the undersigned reserve the right to present those ideas which they consider convenient for the future prosperity and conservation of the island, because such ideas must be in harmony with the political laws that will be asked for at the opportune moment."[9] By this they meant subordinating the solution to the slave question to the political reforms demanded by the Cuban *hacendados*. In other words, they insisted that political power in Cuba be securely under the control of their class before they would be willing to consider the slave.

In contrast, the Puerto Rican reformers felt that the slave question was primary, partly because Puerto Rican slavery, being less rooted and less important economically, permitted them to think so, but also because they had learned more from the struggle against Spanish oppression than had their Cuban counterparts. They understood that the existence of slavery had been used by Spain as a means of maintaining the political status quo. They had reached the conclusion that abolition would have to precede the general program of reforms desired by both islands. The Cuban reformers, however, wanted power securely in their hands, after which they expected to build a white Cuba, closing the slave traffic to cut down the number of Negroes in the island, liberating the slaves but expelling them from Cuba. Cuban reformism thus admitted that "humanity and progress require the breaking of the chains of the slave," but hoped to accomplish this simultaneously with the elimination of the Negro from Cuban society. "We want the predominance of the white race," they cried in the conferences of the Reform Commission.

To proposals for abolition the Cuban reformers put up a stubborn resistance. Their island simply could not endure the consequences of such changes "in the means of production; nor can it prepare for them, nor attend to the removal of the obstacles which are in the way of such a useful and noble purpose."[10] Nevertheless, in the end, the Cuban Commissioners were forced to retreat and agree to the consideration of plans for abolition *prior* to the enactment of economic and political reforms. After weeks of debate, they yielded to the proposal that a committee of commissioners be appointed to study the means of extinguishing slavery, but insisted that gradual and not immediate abolition would be the only procedure considered. This condition was accepted, and the Puerto Rican and Cuban Commissioners prepared separate plans for abolition.

The final days of the Reform Commission were given over to discussion of the emancipation question. On April 10, 1867, the Puerto Ricans (Acosta, Bélvis, and Quijano) submitted their plan. Indemnification of the slaveowners was to be financed through a foreign loan, and they fixed the indemnity value of slaves according to age. (Children under seven years and adults over 60 years were to be valued at 100 pesos each; those between eight and 15 years, and 40 and 61 years, at 200 pesos each, and those between 16 and 40 at 400 pesos each.) The total for the 41,000 slaves in Puerto Rico was calculated at 11,993,800 pesos. But the Puerto Rican Commissioners made it clear that "in any case, with or without indemnification, slavery must not endure one day more."

On the last day of the Conference, the Cuban reformers presented their project. The document was drawn up by José Antonio Echeverría and signed by all the Reform Commissioners with the conspicuous exception of Saco. The Cuban plan for gradual abolition included a prologue in which the reasons for emancipation were summarized, and the bold statement made that "The immorality of slavery would suffice by itself to make its abolition indispensable." But this was, as usual, qualified by a long list of dangers to be avoided, and the warning that every necessary step should be taken, during the course of emancipation, to guarantee that the white race would dominate the island with the implication that forced emigration of Negroes should be encouraged.[11]

With these considerations, qualifications, and warnings, the Cuban Commissioners proposed that gradual abolition take place in several stages. The most important general provisions of the Cuban plan were:

1. That the African slave trade be totally suppressed. (No mention, however, was made of declaring the slave trade piracy.)

2. That those born of slaves henceforth be declared free.

3. That slaves whose names do not appear in the census or register be declared free.

4. That no emancipation be decreed without providing for previous indemnification to the owners.

5. That no plan be adopted without previously consulting the corporations of the island.

The plan would establish an annual lottery to supply funds "in order to improve the condition of the slaves and rescue them from their present state." The slaves would be divided into age groups. Drawings would be held for each group, and a certain number of slaves would have their freedom purchased through lottery funds. Meanwhile *coartación* would continue permitting some slaves to work out their own liberty. Slaves 60 years and older would be set free, likewise those under seven, but the latter would remain under patronage, even if their numbers were drawn in the lottery, until the age of 18. A certain proportion of slaves, beginning with the older ones, would be set free until, after seven years, all slaves were freed.

Indemnification was figured at 450 pesos for each slave, the Cuban plan thus making certain that the slaveowners would be handsomely compensated after they had already extracted huge profits from the system. The total cost of emancipation was calculated at 117,599,000 pesos, which meant that the Cuban slaveowners would come into a goodly sum for having kept 300,000 human beings in bondage.

Both the Puerto Rican and Cuban plans received the approval of the majority of the Commissioners. But approval was not unanimous, even among the reformers. Saco, it will be remembered, refused to sign the Cuban document.*

On the last day of the Conference, April 16, 1867, the Colonial Minister, Alejandro de Castro, entered the conference hall to read the Royal Decree terminating the Reform Commission. He congratulated the delegates on their work, and on their complete or near unanimity on so many of the reports, recommendations, and projects. He reviewed the conclusions of the Commission in the economic and political fields as well as on the "social question." Castro ended his speech with these hopeful words: "The work done by this Commission is of such importance that not a moment can be lost in its application."[12]

On this optimistic note, the curtain rang down on the celebrated *Junta de Información de Ultramar*. Some delegates, like Morales Lemus and Saco, were certain that nothing would come of the five and one-half months of tedious labor. But most of the Commissioners were more optimistic. After all, the Commission had started its work in an atmosphere of gloom following the overthrow of the liberal government, and there had even been the prospect that the demands of the reformers would not be placed on the agenda. Yet every demand had been thoroughly discussed, and though the Cuban Commissioners had been forced to permit abolition to be added to the agenda, they had staved off immediate emancipation and had accomplished their main purpose. That the economic and political demands had been adopted by the Conference, even though more than half of the Commissioners had represented the interests of the government, was a helpful sign. So too was the fact, implicit in the words of the Colonial Minister Castro, that the government approved of the spirit of these recommendations.

But the reformers did not depend only on the benevolence of the

* A year later, in an article in *La Política*, a Madrid newspaper, Saco gave his reasons for not signing the document. Once again he emphasized the racist argument: "if there is black humanity in Cuba there is also white humanity . . . remember Haiti." Saco argued further that Spain would be unable to find 140,000,000 pesos for indemnification. He warned that the proprietors were prepared to go to extremes to protect their slave property, and predicted separation from Spain if abolition were carried into effect in Cuba. (José A. Saco, *La Esclavitud en Cuba y la revolución en España*, Madrid, 1868, pp. 2–15.)

government. They had emphasized during the sessions that reform in the direction of self-government and economic freedom was the only way Spain could preserve the loyalty of her overseas possessions:

> The islands of Puerto Rico and Cuba have anxiously watched the march of events in the mother country. They witnessed and studied with profit the convulsions of the Hispanic-American republics and the struggle in the neighboring Federation of the United States, and neither the upheavals nor the causes of progress and backwardness in one or the other are unknown to them.[13]

The "march of events" in Cuba would soon prove that this veiled threat of the reformers was not an idle one!

chapter 14

FAILURE OF REFORM AND OUTBREAK OF THE WAR FOR INDEPENDENCE

The Cuban reformers returned elated, only to find the island seething with disappointment and discontent. While they, in Madrid, had been discussing liberalization, Cuba was being ruled by a Captain General, Francisco Lersundi, who typified Spanish tyranny. Lersundi swept away the concessions granted the Creoles under Serrano and Dulce, and harshly repressed all liberal tendencies.

The Reform Commissioners' accounts of the encouragement that they had received from spokesmen for the government on the final days of the Conference raised hopes throughout the island. But these hopes were swiftly shattered. It soon became apparent that Colonial Secretary Alejandro de Castro had been speaking for himself. The Narváez government did nothing at all on the Commission's recommendations. In disgust, Castro left the Colonial Ministry.

Having blasted the hopes of Cubans and Puerto Ricans, the Narváez government added insult to injury. On February 12, 1867, the Spanish government imposed a new tax on the colonies, a levy of six percent on the net income of real and industrial properties, and the Colonial Government was authorized to assess new taxes up to 12 percent if necessary in order to cover administrative expenses. Ironically, the colonial delegates themselves had suggested this tax, but they had done so on the understanding that customs duties would be abolished, along with other antiquated taxes that restricted commerce. The government abolished certain of these taxes, it is true, but not the heavy customs duties. Furthermore, the decision had been taken without consulting the island's representatives in any way.

To make matters worse, the new taxes were imposed during an unprecedented depression in Cuba that threatened economic ruin. In December, 1866, the Industrial Bank and the Bank of Commerce in Havana had stopped payment, and there was fear that the Spanish bank would follow. With the prospects that the sugar crop would suffer a drastic decline in volume and prices, the new imposts aroused anger and despair throughout the island.

Thus, after the high hopes for reform, slavery remained untouched in Cuba, and Spain continued the oppressive regime of the *facultades omnimodas*. She not only retained the burdensome customs duties, but imposed a tax of from six to ten percent on incomes of all types of business in the island. The Reform Commission of 1866–67 had proved to be one of the grimmest farces in Spanish history.

Protest swept through Cuba and Puerto Rico, but availed nothing. Those reformers who advocated implementation of the Commission's recommendations in the press, were either driven from the islands or silenced by the colonial governments. The efforts of Morales Lemus, Pastor, and other reformers who were still in Madrid, to influence the government also proved unsuccessful. Though defeated at the elections for the Commissioners, in the end the Spanish Party emerged triumphant. For this victory, the *Peninsulares* in Cuba were willing to pay the price of another arbitrary tax.

"These facts demoralized the *Partido Reformista*," Morales Lemus conceded. The Cuban reform movement collapsed in disillusionment and bitterness. *El Siglo*, its organ, suspended publication. When Pozos Dulces resigned the editorship on April 14, 1868, Don José de Armas y Céspedes took his place and sought to prolong its life; but, as he said, it was "like the woman of Malabar, throwing herself into the blaze after the disappearance of her husband."[1]

Many Creoles were now ready for armed rebellion, especially in the eastern provinces (Oriente) where there no longer lingered the slightest hope of reform in Spanish policy. The wealthy Creoles of Oriente turned the Masonic lodges of the towns of Bayamo, Manzanillo, Holguín, Las Tunas, and Santiago de Cuba into conspiratorial centers, and to these efforts the lodges of Havana and Camagüey lent their support and co-operation. The "Freedom Anthem," later to become the National Hymn of the Republic of Cuba, was composed by Pedro (*Perucho*) Figueredo and orchestrated by Manuel Muñoz, both from Bayamo, and was played under the very eyes of the Spanish military government:

> Haste to the combat, Men of Bayamo,
> Whom the country proudly watches.
> Do not fear a glorious death.
> For to die for the fatherland
>   is to live.
> To live in chains is to live overwhelmed
>   by affront and infamy.
> Hark to the clarion's call!
> To arms, valiant ones!

Before they had gone far with preparations for armed revolt, these white Cubans came face-to-face with the question of the Negroes. Without their support, the white Cubans could never succeed. But the Negroes would support no revolution that did not link their freedom and rights with the independence of Cuba. Unless this problem was successfully solved, the revolution would be still-born.

The solution was offered by the Republican Society of Cuba and Puerto Rico, founded in New York in April, 1866, as the successor to the *Sociedad Democrática de los Amigos de América*. Encouraged by the triumph of the North in the Civil War and by the victory of the Mexican revolutionary masses, led by the great Benito Juárez, against Maximilian's attempt to impose an empire on Mexico with French bayonets, and, most of all, by Spain's humiliating retreat from Santo Domingo,* the Republican Society of Cuba and Puerto Rico raised the call for revolution. Penetrating the vigilance of the colonial authorities, the Society gained wide circulation in Cuba for its *Voice of America*. Cuba and Puerto Rico, the organ thundered, must be free and republican, and the Republican Society proclaimed "liberty for all the inhabitants of Cuba and Puerto Rico without distinction of race and color."[2]

This call sent a shudder through many wealthy white Cubans and

---

* In 1861, Santo Domingo, fearful of being absorbed by Haiti, gave up its independence and submitted once again to the Spanish Crown. Four years later, after rediscovering what Spanish colonial administration meant, it rose up in revolt a second time. After losing 10,000 soldiers, Spain was forced to pull out. Spain's failure in Santo Domingo refuted the argument of men like Saco that Cuba was not big or strong enough to win its independence.

all of the *Peninsulares*. They saw in it not merely the abolition of slavery, but the elevation of the masses in the island, Negro and white, to a place of importance, if not dominance.

But not all wealthy and influential property owners were frightened by this appeal. Some had already begun to favor gradual, compensated abolition. This was true especially in the eastern provinces where, as we have seen, the effects of foreign competition and technological change was reducing the profit margin in sugar production. The coffee and cattle enterprises of that part of the island had also been adversely affected, especially by Spanish fiscal policies. Under these new economic pressures on the plantation system, many owners were deciding that slavery was becoming unnecessary and even burdensome. These and other influences made it possible for prominent Cubans to consider uniting with the Negroes for mutual benefits—the struggle against Spanish rule. But to consider did not yet mean to act. Deep racist prejudices and apprehensions stood in the way.

Although carefully watched by the white authorities for any sign of revolt, many Cuban Negroes, especially the free Negroes, were aware of and greatly excited by the rising discontent in the island. They knew of the report in favor of gradual abolition submitted by the Cuban Commissioners, and of the opinions of progressive white intellectuals on slavery, and even of the appeal of the Republican Society of Cuba and Puerto Rico. They waited to see if the revolutionary movement would extend its hand in unity, offering liberty to those who joined its ranks.

But in Santiago de Cuba there was a Negro family that was doing more than wait. This was the free Negro family of Marcos Maceo and Mariana Grajales. Marcos Maceo, a small dealer in agricultural products, was born in Venezuela, but registered himself, at the time of the baptism of his son, Antonio Maceo y Grajales, as a native of Santiago de Cuba. He did this to avoid the decree—enacted after the slave revolts of 1844, in which free Negroes were active—expelling all free men of color who had come from another country.

His son, Antonio Maceo, whose name was soon to ring throughout Cuba, had three teachers for short periods, but received most of his education at home and in the streets. He went to work at the age of 16, transporting agricultural products by muleback. At an early age he showed interest in the political issues of the day, learned to hate slavery which he saw during his trips into the countryside, and the Spanish despotism that sustained it. Antonio Maceo caught the attention of the lawyer, Don Ascencio de Ascencio, who introduced him to a group of "merchants, industrialists, and friends of Ascencio's household, [and] formed a circle of intelligent friends for the young mulatto." The fact that these influential white Cubans welcomed the young Negro to their discussions indicates how far in advance of the rest of the island was the anti-Spanish movement in Santiago de Cuba.

In 1864, Maceo became a member of the Masonic Lodge of Santiago de Cuba, and entered the inner revolutionary circle. Thus, as a young man, Maceo was already associated with the most anti-Spanish elements in the island, and, when the struggle for independence began, he unhesitatingly joined the actives. In this he not only had the support of his father, who also joined the revolutionary movement, but his mother's warm encouragement as well. Indeed, as a passionate patriot and foe of the Spaniards, this Negro woman, Mariana Grajales, one of the outstanding women in Cuba's revolutionary history, swayed her entire family to the cause of independence.[3]

In August, 1867, the leaders of the *Junta Revolucionaria* of Bayamo sent Pedro Figueredo to Havana to seek the co-operation of the Reform movement. At a meeting with Morales Lemus, Figueredo was at first informed that the Reform Party would place a credit of three to six million pesos in the United States to advance the revolutionary cause. But as Figueredo was about to leave Havana with this encouraging news, he was told by Morales Lemus that his group had decided to cancel the offer. He gave as their reason the desire of the reform leaders to await the outcome of the presidential election of 1868 in the United States. If the expected election of Ulysses S. Grant occurred, they believed that one of his first acts would be "to liquidate Spanish domination in the island of Cuba, leading eventually to its annexation to the United States." In fact, Morales Lemus informed Figueredo, the Cuban reformers had been advised by a leading American military figure, a close associate of General Grant, that for this plan to be carried through "it was necessary that Cuba should remain quiet because a revolution would bring widespread bloodshed and ruin of properties."*

Figueredo had to inform the Revolutionary Junta of Bayamo that the leaders of the western district refused to co-operate in a revolutionary struggle against Spain. Whatever the pretext they used to justify their stand, the fact remains that the reform leaders were not prepared to join in the struggle for independence.⁴

Though they naturally would have preferred a united national movement, the revolutionary leaders in Oriente did not give up their conspiratorial activities. On the contrary, they began organizing an armed revolt. The Revolutionary Junta of Bayamo had been organized by the Masonic lodge in that town, and lodges in other towns now followed this example. In Manzanillo, Carlos Manuel de Céspedes, Borges, Isaías and Bartolomé Masó initiated a revolutionary junta, and in Camagüey, the Masons, led by Salvador Cisneros Betancourt, did likewise. Secret societies and Masonic lodges all over Oriente, in which Cubans and Dominican émigrés joined together, were consolidating a real revolutionary organization.

To co-ordinate the rising revolutionary activity, Francisco Vicente Aguilera called a meeting on August 4, 1868, on a farm named *San Miguel de Rompe* in the district of Las Tunas. The gathering was presided over by Carlos M. de Céspedes, the oldest delegate in attendance. Born at Bayamo on April 18, 1819, Céspedes had completed his education at the University of Barcelona, Spain. He settled in Madrid and became involved in revolutionary activity. Banished to France, he resumed revolutionary activities on his return to Spain, and was then imprisoned. When he returned to Cuba, he began organizing the struggle for independence along with Aguilera, Figueredo, and others in the Oriente district. A man of letters

---

* The military figure referred to was General William T. Sherman, who had visited Cuba in November, 1866, while on a diplomatic mission to Mexico. In his autobiography, Sherman merely writes: "At Havana we were very handsomely entertained, especially by Señor Aldama, who took us by rail to his sugar-estates at Santa Rosa, and back by Matanzas." (*Memoirs of General William T. Sherman*, New York & London, 1913, vol. II, pp. 416–17.) He says nothing about any political discussions with Cubans regarding the future status of the island. Nor is there any reference to such discussions in the William T. Sherman Papers in the Library of Congress. There are two letters to Sherman, in Spanish, dated Havana, November 25 and 26, 1866, but both deal with Mexican rather than Cuban affairs.

as well as a soldier and a slaveholder, Céspedes delivered a moving plea at the meeting for immediate revolutionary action, ending with these words: "Gentlemen, the hour is solemn and decisive. The power of Spain is decrepit and worm-eaten; if it still appears great and strong to us, it is because for more than three centuries we have contemplated it from our knees."[5]

But the assembled group, though moved by this impassioned speech, were not yet ready. Some favored a last attempt at reform; others, annexation to the United States. Even those who favored independence felt that insufficient preparations had been made for war. Again, most of the plantation owners urged that armed insurrection be postponed until after the grinding of the sugar-crop, arguing that this would enable them to contribute more effectively to an armed struggle. And throughout the discussion, the question of slavery kept arising. All agreed that Negro manpower was needed for the cause, and that Negroes could not be expected to join unless the revolutionary movement decided to abolish slavery. But few were yet prepared for such a step. On the contrary, those who still urged a last attempt at reform argued that the chaos of revolutionary war would endanger control over the slaves.

Unable to agree, the gathering set a date for a new session at which all pending questions would be resolved.

While the revolutionaries kept postponing the time for action, events in Spain gave a new stimulus to the advocates of reform. On September 18, 1868, the reactionary and inefficient Spanish Bourbon monarchy fell before the attacks of liberals, led by military and naval personalities, and the Queen fled to France. *La Revolución Gloriosa* (the "Glorious Revolution"), as it was immediately named, instituted a Provisional Government which decreed universal male suffrage, freedom of the press, association, education, and religion in peninsular Spain. It also promised the colonies a share in these reforms, assuring the people in the Antilles that the Revolution "was not carried through for the sole benefit of the inhabitants of the Peninsula, but also for our loyal brothers overseas."[6]

Although concerned over the fact that several members of the new government were abolitionists, the Cuban reformers hailed the "Glorious Revolution" and the promise of colonial reforms, hoping that this would forestall the struggle for independence. But the hard-core revolutionists had resolved, after the mockery of the Colonial Reform Commission, that "This is the last deception." They had lost all faith in Spanish promises, and the fact that men like Francisco Serrano and Domingo Dulce, who had long been calling for colonial reforms, were leaders of the liberal revolution did not impress them. The conservatives still exercised considerable influence in the Provisional Government and there was every likelihood, judging from Spanish history, that in the end it would be they, and not the liberals, who would dictate colonial policy. Furthermore, in Cuba itself, the reactionary Captain General Francisco Lersundi adhered to the exiled Queen Isabel, and continued to enforce the oppressive Bourbon colonial policies.

Actually, Céspedes felt that the confusion reigning in Cuba since the first news of the "Glorious Revolution" was propitious for the independence movement, and he urged the revolutionaries to strike immediately. But the sugar planters still called for delay until they could finish their grinding operations. Though Céspedes was impatient to act immediately, the rebellion was tentatively set for December 24, 1868.

While the Cubans delayed, the Puerto Rican revolutionaries rose in revolt. Since 1863, the Puerto Rican revolutionary, Dr. Ramón Emeterio Betances, had been organizing revolutionary activity in the island. This activity blossomed forth briefly in the *Grito* (Cry) *de Lares* of 1868. On February 24, 1868, a revolutionary Junta, founded in the town of Lares in Puerto Rico, began to plan the immediate liberation of the island. One of its members was Mariana Braceti, known as *Brazo de Oro* (Golden Arm), an indication of the important role assigned to women in the Puerto Rican revolutionary movement. "Because of the persecution and terror against persons organizing the independence movements," notes Jesús Colón, "secret societies had to be organized. . . . As the underground work had to be intermingled with the everyday activities . . . women were a 'natural' for this kind of work." Commenting on the fact that Mariana Braceti was made a member of the Lares Revolutionary Junta, he observes that this occurred at a time "when women were not allowed from the home without a chaperon and when they were not considered for anything outside of home and church."

On September 23, 1868, the historic rebellion of Lares broke out, and the Revolutionary Junta proclaimed a Puerto Rican Republic. Unfortunately, Dr. Betances was unable to furnish the uprising the needed arms and munitions, and despite heroic resistance, the small revolutionary forces were overwhelmed. One incident of the battle was long to be remembered in Puerto Rico. Ana Martínez Pumajero, wife of a leader of the Lares rebellion and mother of a son who was also involved in the struggle, saw her house ransacked and destroyed by the Spanish soldiers. She promptly set up housekeeping under a mango tree. When the Spanish authorities asked "in the name of the law" for her son's whereabouts, she answered, "In the name of the laws of honor and patriotic love, and on a pledge of death not to talk, I do not know where in the mountains my son is."[7]

Then an event occurred which forced into immediate and unexpected action those in Cuba who were pledged to fight.* Demands by the Spanish tax collectors for the sums called for by the new law forced the property owners either to pay or rebel. They chose the latter course. Luis Figueredo, on his farm, *El Mijial*, eight leagues from Holguín, hanged the Spanish tax collector, putting himself by this act into outright rebellion.

A hurried meeting took place on the plantation *Muñoz*, near Las Arenas, and on October 3, another assembly was held on the farm of Manuel de Jesús Calvar in the *Ranchón de los Caletones*. At these meetings, areas of command were assigned to various groups, and arrangements were made to advance the revolution from its scheduled opening on Christmas Eve.

Almost immediately after the October 3 meeting, another event occurred which forced the revolutionists to disregard previous plans and take immediate action. A telegram from Captain General Lersundi to Colonel Udaeta, governor of Bayamo, was intercepted by a telegrapher friendly to the revolutionaries. It read: "Cuba belongs to Spain and for Spain she must be kept no matter who is governing. Send to prison D. Carlos Manuel de Céspedes, Francisco Vicente Aguilera, Pedro Figueredo, Francisco Maceo Osorio, Bartolomé

---

* According to the Spanish authorities, there was close communication between the revolutionists in Puerto Rico and Cuba. General Pavía, governor of Puerto Rico, wrote to the Spanish Minister of War: "It is not to be doubted that connivance existed between the chiefs of this island and those of Cuba." (José Pérez Moris, *Historia de la insurrección de Lares*, Barcelona, 1872, p. 333.)

Outbreak of War for Independence • 171

Masó, Francisco Javier de Céspedes. . . ." The conspiracy had been discovered. The wife of one of the rebels, Trinidad Ramírez, had revealed the plan in confession to her priest, who had convinced her that it was her religious duty to inform the authorities.[8]

Without waiting any longer, Carlos Manuel de Céspedes, accompanied by only 37 men, all planters from the province of Oriente, proclaimed the independence of Cuba—the historic "Grito de Yara" —from his plantation, *La Demajagua*, near Yara, in the vicinity of Manzanillo, on the morning of October 10, 1868. On the same day, Céspedes liberated his slaves and incorporated them into his small and ill-armed force. He likewise issued a previously drawn manifesto stating the causes of the revolt and listing its officers, with himself as General-in-Chief. Bartolomé Masó was named Lieutenant General and second in command, and Manuel de Jesús Calvar, Brigadier General. Francisco Vicente Aguilera, one of the original organizers, was not assigned any post, revealing, at the very beginning, the dissensions that were to plague and weaken the struggle against Spain.

The manifesto, issued in the name of the *Junta Revolucionaria de la isla de Cuba*, declared that the revolt was due to arbitrary government, abusive taxation, corrupt administration, exclusion of Cubans from government employment, exclusion of Cubans from the Cortes, deprivation of political, civil, and religious liberties, and particularly rights of assembly and petition. Explicit references were made to the failure of the Colonial Commission of 1866–67.

> . . . as great nations have sprung from revolt against a similar disgrace, after having exhausted pleadings for relief, as we despair of justice from Spain through reasoning and cannot longer live deprived of the rights which other people enjoy, we are constrained to appeal to arms and to assert our rights in the battle-field, cherishing the hope that our grievances will be sufficient excuse for this last resort to redress them and to secure our future welfare.

The announced objectives were the culmination of the demands of Cuban agitators developed over half a century:

> To the God of our conscience, and to all civilized nations, we submit the sincerity of our purpose. . . . We only want to be free and to see all men with us equally free, as the Creator intended all mankind to be. Our earnest belief is that all men are brethren. We respect the

lives and property of all peaceful citizens even though they be Spaniards resident in this territory; we admire universal suffrage which assures the sovereignty of the people; and we desire the gradual indemnified emancipation of slaves, the free interchange with nations which use the principle of reciprocity, national representation to decree laws and taxes, and, in general, we demand the religious observance of the inalienable rights of man. We constitute an independent nation because we believe that beneath the Spanish roof we shall never enjoy the complete exercise of our rights.[9]

Following the Declaration of Independence, the provisional goverment of the Republic of Cuba was organized at Bayamo!

The manifesto proclaiming Cuban independence basically represented the interests and reflected the views of the Cuban landowners in the eastern provinces who sought an important position for themselves in the island, and who wished to end commercial restrictions on their economic development—both of which, they were convinced, could not be achieved under Spanish dominion. Its policy on slavery differed in no way from that advanced by the reformers before the Reform Commission of 1866-67—gradual emancipation with indemnification. Both the reformers and the organizers of the revolution movement of 1868 proposed a conservative solution to the "social question," a solution which was to follow the achievement of political and economic freedom. The abolitionist section in the manifesto was to be put into operation *after* the revolution emerged victorious. "When we have made the Republican flag triumph," said Carlos M. de Céspedes, "and we have forced the representatives of the Spanish government to leave Cuba precipitously, the revolution will take care of this vital question."[10]

Clearly, then, the immediate emancipation of the slaves played no part in the action taken at Yara. Nevertheless, the momentous decision in the *Grito de Yara* to raise the banner of revolt against Spanish rule was the most important event in Cuban history up to this time. What is especially significant is that this small band of men was determined to pursue the revolt against incredible odds. For, given this determination, it was inevitable that most of the leaders of the revolution would be forced to understand that victory could not be achieved without involving the Negro masses in the struggle. Just as military necessity eventually forced the Lincoln administration to proclaim immediate emancipation, so, too, in the War for Independence in Cuba, military necessity compelled the leaders of the revolution to adopt a similar policy. And when military necessity made this decision inevitable, the Cuban masses succeeded in transforming the character of the revolution, imbuing it with a democratic and abolitionist purpose. It was this that caused José Martí to call "the first constitution of independence on October 10, 1868 . . . the only day of redemption the Negro has known in Cuba."[11]

But all this belongs to the following chapters. Let us close the discussion as the cry *"Independencia y Cuba libre!"* is being picked up and relayed throughout the island. A new Cuban spirit was arising, one beautifully imaged by the poet Miguel Jerónimo Gutiérrez, who was himself to die for the independence of his country:

> The Cuban is no longer the stupid Sybarite
> Who languished, intoxicated, delighted,
> Drinking the poison cup of pleasure.
> He is no longer the slave who bows down
> Before the despots in humble adoration.
> He is the brave fighter, the warrior
> Burned brown by the fire of the sun.
> He is the soldier whom the infamous "fifth"*
> Did not recruit to serve the King.
> He is the noble patriot who is determined
> To be independent or die a hero.[12]

---

* The reference to the "infamous 'fifth' " is to the practice used by the Spaniards in recruiting troops for service in Cuba. The soldiers were chosen by lot; every fifth man chosen was sent to Cuba.

chapter 15

THE TEN YEARS' WAR:
THE EARLY PHASE, 1868-1869

On October 10, 1868, Cuba entered a new phase in its history—the phase of active and continuous revolution. What turned out to be a Ten Years' War (1868–1878) had begun.

In Havana, an official Spanish newspaper dismissed the news from Oriente as inconsequential, announcing derisively that "a handful of deluded, badly armed fellows had uttered a cry of rebellion in Yara."[1] There was good reason for this early contempt for the *mambises*, as the Cuban rebels were called. The first patriot forces consisted of just 147 volunteers who did not have a weapon apiece: 45 fowling pieces, four rifles, and a few pistols and machetes comprised their entire military equipment. Since they were forced into action before their organizational system had been completed, the leaders of the rebellion operated in their respective areas with little more than the slaves of their plantations and without close contact between them. No wonder the Spanish authorities took the rebellion lightly.

As the rebel leaders, with the motley crew of badly-armed patriots at their disposal, engaged the Spaniards in a series of minor skirmishes, the revolt developed rapidly. The patriot army grew by leaps and bounds as the Cuban masses, white and Negro (free and slave), joined the movement, especially in the rural areas. On October 12, Céspedes already had 4,000 men; towards the end of the month, his army numbered 9,700, and on November 8, 12,000.* Many were Negroes who were to form a considerable part of the Cuban army

---

* It is difficult to arrive at an exact estimate of the size of the Cuban army at any given time during the Ten Years' War since widely different reports appeared in various sources, and while the Spanish authorities always tended to minimize the size, the Cubans generally exaggerated it.

throughout the revolution; nearly all were operating without uniforms and with an amazing variety of weapons. Oftentimes the Cuban troops overpowered enemy contingents entirely through the element of surprise and with few arms other than the machetes with which all the rebel soldiers were already equipped when they joined the ranks.

Half-armed, ragged, ill-fed, but burning with revolutionary zeal, the patriot forces defeated the Spaniards at Yara, Baire, and Jiguaní, the last accomplished by troops under the command of General Donato Mármol. On October 15, they laid siege to Bayamo, a city of ten thousand people, and on the 19th, captured the city. Céspedes established the government of the Republic of Cuba in the captured city.

With each new victory, more and more recruits were added to the rebel forces. At the same time, the revolutionaries received aid from another source, which proved to be very opportune in view of their lack of military experience. A group of Dominican exiles, led by Máximo Gómez, destined to become one of the great figures of Cuban independence, Luis Marcano, and Modesto Díaz, utilizing the experience gained in the Dominican wars against Spain, became the instructors of the Cubans in military strategy and tactics. The military experience of these men was to prove invaluable for the revolutionary cause.

With these reinforcements, the rebels defeated Spanish detachments, cut railway lines, and soon gained dominance over vast sections of the eastern portion of Cuba. On October 28, Holguín rose in arms; on November 8, the patriots had advanced within a mile of Santiago de Cuba, the capital of the Eastern Department. On November 4, a group of Cubans in the province of Camagüey, led by Ignacio Agramonte y Loynaz, raised the standard of revolt. Agramonte was aided by the arrival of an expedition from foreign areas with a large supply of war materials under the command of General Manuel de Quesada, who had won his rank in the Mexican Army. The expedition also brought Manuel and Julio Sanguily and a group of Havana youths. On February 9, 1869, the whole of the district of Las Villas rose in arms under the direction of General Federico Cavada, a Colonel in the U.S. Volunteer Service during the Civil War.

As the number of skirmishes multiplied, as Cuban victories mounted, and damage to Spanish forces increased, the Spaniards awoke to the seriousness of the situation. Captain General Francisco Lersundi dispatched a powerful military column under the command of the Count of Valmaseda to drive the Cuban troops and government from Bayamo. At the same time, he ordered the activation of the members of the infamous institution called *Voluntarios* (Volunteer Corps). In addition, he created a state of martial law by decreeing that all cases of rebellion and sedition should be handled by specially created Military Commissions. All insurrectionists were to be treated by the military tribunals as traitors.

The Volunteers had been organized originally to meet the threat of the López expeditions by Captain General Concha, who later gave formal recognition to the Corps. In the principal cities, especially Havana and Santiago de Cuba, Volunteers were organized into infantry battalions and squadrons of cavalry. The highest rank among them was that of Colonel.

The purpose of the Volunteers was to reinforce the regular army in emergencies. They maintained the "home front" in cities and towns, relieving the Spanish soldiers of garrison duty so that they could move out to battle. The Volunteers were led by members of the island oligarchy—the great landholding, slaveowning and commercial families who had grown rich on sugar plantations and the slave trade. The Corps itself was composed mostly of Spaniards, chiefly bachelors, who had left Spain as adventurers, eager only to make money. Despising the Cubans and itching for a chance to cow the Creole population, they eagerly responded to Lersundi's call to duty, and as we shall see, soon chalked up a bloody record of lynchings and mass murders in cities and towns "without parallel in history."[2]

So important were the Volunteers in the maintenance of Spanish dominion in Cuba, that without this organization it is extremely doubtful that Spain could have continued the war. When the revolt at Yara began, Spain had only 7,000 regulars in the island. The Volunteers enabled Lersundi to contain the rebellion until reinforcements arrived. From 40,000 to 73,000 Volunteers were enlisted on the Spanish side during the command of Lersundi, and, in order to arm them, 90,000 Remington rifles were purchased in the United States.

Now armed and organized, the Volunteers became a powerful force for a reactionary policy toward the rebellion. Spurred on by *La Voz de Cuba*, a paper founded by Gonzalo Castañón, a Colonel in the Volunteer organization, the Volunteers made it clear that they would tolerate nothing short of complete extermination of the rebels and their sympathizers. Since they knew that Spain depended upon them for the conservation of the island, the Volunteers did not hesitate to attempt to force their reactionary policy upon the Metropolis and its officials in Cuba. Soon the Volunteers, backed by the powerful economic interests who controlled them, began to play a decisive role in colonial policy.

Under Lersundi, of course, the Volunteers had no need to exercise their power to insure a hostile policy toward the insurgents. He was their hero and had outlined the policy they were to insist upon early in the rebellion. On October 24, 1868, 80 distinguished citizens of Cuba, several prominent Spaniards and a group of Cuban liberals including José Manuel Mestre, José Morales Lemus and Miguel Aldama, held an interview with Lersundi. A liberal government was in power in Spain following the "Glorious Revolution" of 1868, and the Cuban reformers were still convinced that the Provisional Government, headed by Marshal Prim, would grant the long hoped-for reforms to Cuba and extend to the island the same rights that it offered Spain. But Lersundi was conducting himself as if the Queen, who no longer occupied the throne, were still reigning. Replying to Mestre, who conducted the interview and who appealed for colonial reforms and "national unity" as a means of ending the rebellion quickly, Lersundi called the insurrectionists "incendiaries, assassins and robbers," and rejected the peace proposals.[3]

It was clear that nothing could be expected from Lersundi. But the Provisional Government in Spain was beginning to be concerned about Lersundi's intransigent attitude. His blind refusal to deal with the members of the Reform Party not only made any hope of reconciliation impossible, but brought additional aid to the rebels. He forced many wavering reformers to make the choice between joining the rebellion or submitting to autocratic colonial rule. The reformers also became fearful of their lives as the Volunteers began to unleash a wave of vengeance against all advocates of change. As a result, several prominent Creoles, including Morales Lemus and Miguel Aldama, joined the rebel cause. They and other reformers, in choosing the rebel side, fled the island and set up Juntas in the United States and in Latin American countries to collect and send material aid to the revolution.

With the rebellion spreading in the face of Lersundi's reactionary policy, the Madrid Government was forced to reconsider the manner of putting an end to the insurrection. Finally, the decision was reached to remove Lersundi and send a liberal governor to the island, who would hear the claim of the Cuban reformers and seek a peaceful solution. General Don Domingo Dulce, a former Captain General who already had a liberal reputation in Cuban affairs and was a friend of the Creole reformers, was selected as the man to inaugurate the new policy. He arrived in Cuba on January 4, 1869, authorized "to modify taxation and to govern by liberal standards." He carried with him an emergency three-point reform program: freedom of the press, freedom of assembly, and representation for Cuba in the Cortes.[4]

The majority of the Cuban reformers had not yet chosen rebellion, and they hailed Dulce's arrival with joy. Here, it seemed, was the opportunity of bringing peace through a policy of conciliation. But the reactionary forces, opposed to all concessions to the Cubans, were strengthened by the outcome of the battle for Bayamo. The Spanish column advancing on the city, reinforced by troops added in Las Tunas, had been stopped by a brilliant attack led by Captain Antonio Maceo. But in the next advance of the Spaniards, the experienced Valmaseda outmaneuvered his inexperienced adversary, General Donato Mármol, heading the Cuban division of 4,000 untried Negroes armed only with machetes, and 500 colored and white troops, armed with an assortment of rifles and various types of firearms. Valmaseda surprised the main body of the Cuban forces in El Saladillo, defeating them completely. More than 2,000 Cubans, most of them recently freed slaves, died in this battle.

On January 15, Valmaseda entered Bayamo, only to find it a smouldering ruin. The Cuban defenders of the city had burned it to the ground, with the unanimous consent of its inhabitants, when they realized that they could not resist a siege led by forces equipped with artillery.

The defeat of the rebels at El Saladillo and the capture of Bayamo enhanced the prestige of the advocates of the policy of exterminating the rebellion by military power and terror. But Dulce was proceeding with his mission under the illusion that he represented the real power in Cuba. Shortly after arriving, he suppressed the Military Commission and declared a stay of proceedings of the political cases which the body was judging. Then he declared a general amnesty for all who had suffered imprisonment or punishment for political reasons, and for all rebels who would surrender their arms within 40 days. Dulce also sent two peace commissioners to talk with Céspedes, the revolutionary chieftain. Finally, he issued a series of decrees giving a more liberal character to the government.

Most important of the decrees was the one granting freedom of the press and of assembly. The termination of the censorship of the press was greeted with joy by the *Habaneros*, eager to express themselves on the burning question of the day. No less than 77 periodicals were issued between January 10 and 28. One was the students' news sheet, *La Patria Libre* (The Free Fatherland) which contained a dramatic poem by José Martí. Another was *El Siglo,* an underground student paper, which published Martí's sonnet, "The Tenth of October." The sonnet closed: "God be praised that at last Cuba breaks the hangman's noose that oppressed her, and raises her head proud and free."[5]

The spate of publications revealing support of the rebels and contempt for the Spanish authorities infuriated the antagonistic Spanish Party, especially the Volunteers. At their meetings, the leaders of the Volunteers cursed Dulce with unspeakable fury, accusing him of being in the power of the Cuban reformers.

But the Volunteers did not confine their hatred of Dulce's policy to words. To prevent any *Habanero* from joining the rebels, all exits from Havana were guarded, and the Volunteers summarily imprisoned any Cuban caught without a pass. Anyone suspected of sympathizing with the separatist cause was similarly treated. The Military Commission had been abolished, but the Volunteers operated through their own Commission.

The Villanueva Theatre was presenting a comedy, and rumors

reached the Volunteers that one of the actors sang a rebel refrain during the performance; that the audience wildly applauded the song, and that women who attended the theatre wore tunics of blue and white, the colors of the Cuban revolutionary flag. It was also rumored that a performance supposedly given for the benefit of the poor was actually to raise funds for the revolution. The enraged Volunteers laid plans to teach the actors and the audience a lesson. On the night of January 21, the Volunteers opened fire on the defenseless audience, shooting men, women, and children in the theatre and in the open streets to which the panic-stricken audience fled. When the civil authorities arrived, it was with difficulty that they restrained the Volunteers from burning the theatre to the ground.

The Volunteers prowled the streets throughout the night, attacking homes which they believed were occupied by rebel sympathizers. For three consecutive days after the frightful massacre, terror reigned while the city was at the mercy of the Volunteers. Buildings were fired upon; Miguel Aldama's palace was sacked, and after seizing jewels and valuables, the Volunteers destroyed everything they could not carry off.

The pro-Spanish press reported these incidents proudly, and placed the blame not upon the Volunteers but upon the Cubans and Captain General Dulce. *La Voz de Cuba*, champion of the Volunteers, carried a bitter indictment of Dulce, accusing him of working secretly for the revolutionary cause.

As the Volunteers continued to promote every kind of disturbance in the capital, Dulce kept issuing proclamations to the *Habaneros* urging them to remain peaceful, to "have faith in your authorities," and assuring them that "justice will soon be done."[6] But these were empty words, and no one realized this better than Dulce himself. His prestige and authority had already ebbed away. He knew that the real power in the city of Havana was held by the Volunteers, and that he must either resign or appease the intransigents. He decided on the latter course. The date for the surrender of arms by the rebels was February 20, 1869. But already by the 12th of the month, Dulce had suspended all political guarantees. Further to please the reactionaries, Dulce pressed military activities against the rebels, and began wholesale deportations of persons suspected of being in sympathy with the rebellion. When a boy of 18 yelled *"Viva Cuba libre!"* at a departing boatload of exiles, Dulce, yielding to the demand of the Volunteers, had the boy judged by a military tribunal and shot. Furthermore, he endorsed the bloody proclamation issued on April 4, 1869, by Count Valmaseda, commanding in the eastern district, which decreed that in rebellious areas all males over 15 caught absent from their plantations without adequate excuse would be shot; all houses not occupied by Spanish forces or not displaying a white flag were to be burned; and all women and children not living in their own houses or with relatives were to be concentrated in certain fortified towns.

But nothing Dulce did could convince the Volunteers that he was reliable. They sent a committee to the Captain General advising him to resign. Before Dulce could decide the matter definitely for himself, the Volunteers took matters in their own hands. Troops burst into the palace of the Captain General, demanding that he leave immediately for Spain. On June 5, General Dulce embarked for Spain.

While awaiting the arrival of the new Captain General, Antonio Caballero de Rodas, the Volunteers began to consolidate their position still further. They founded the first *Casino Español* (Spanish Club), supposedly for social purposes, but actually to provide a center where the wealthy leaders of the Volunteers, together with the rich Cuban sugar planters who shared their views, could meet to determine policies aimed at forcing the authorities to uphold the position of the Spanish Party. When Caballero de Rodas arrived on June 28, 1869, he authorized the Casino plan, and soon Santiago and other cities boasted a *Casino Español* headquarters, as in Havana, for the wealthy contractors, slaveholders, and bureaucrats. Through the *Casino Español*, the Volunteers began to exercise political control over whole localities with little regard for the Spanish Government.

Actually, the fact that the Madrid Government meekly accepted the expulsion of Captain General Dulce indicated that the reactionary cause had triumphed. The policy of the Volunteers was now the policy of Spain, and the short-lived attempt at political reforms was abandoned. The Spanish Government made it clear that the rebels must submit to the last man or face annihilation. They must surrender completely before reforms could even be considered.

The fact that peace negotiations failed miserably should have come as no surprise to anyone familiar with the true state of affairs in Cuba and Spain. In both countries, the groups that wanted war and insisted that the revolt must be wiped out at all costs were all-powerful, and those who favored a more liberal policy either had insufficient influence or capitulated quickly to the reactionaries. The intransigents in the island of Cuba comprised the clergy (with some notable exceptions), the contractors, the bureaucracy, the well-to-do merchants, the bankers, the sugar factors, the dealers in slaves, and the majority of the great slaveowning sugar planters who held the best lands in Cuba. For years they had grown rich on Cuban poverty, and they were determined to continue to suck the lifeblood from the island. They were joined in their opposition to a peaceful settlement by strong allies in Madrid. Manuel Calvo, a rich Spanish merchant with investments in Cuba, headed a powerful lobby against liberal measures for the island, a lobby made up of men whose interests were closely connected with Cuba and its slave system. Their henchmen in the Colonial Ministry exerted every ounce of strength to protect these interests. The Church, epitome of reaction, and the military were also indefatigable defenders of these interests. Many officers, in an army heavily overstaffed with high ranking officers, looked forward eagerly to a long war in Cuba for wealth, advancement, and prestige.

There were Spaniards who favored granting Cuba home rule similar to that enjoyed by Canada, or incorporation into Spain as a federal province, and even a few like Pi y Margall, one of Spain's outstanding intellectuals and leader of the Republican movement, who dared to propose independence for Cuba. And there were many Spaniards who were shocked by the gangster-like activities of the Volunteers. But they were in a distinct minority, and their influence counted for little when arrayed against the merchants, the Church, the military and the others whose interests would be disastrously affected if Cuba were lost. Moreover, the liberals were very good at issuing lofty statements about the need to grant reforms and stay the bloodshed, but when it came to the showdown, they invariably showed their true colors by kow-towing before the reactionaries, and eventually ended up in the reactionary camp.

Whatever they might quarrel about, and quarrel they did incessantly, all political parties in Spain agreed on one issue: the necessity of keeping the Castillian banner flying over the "Pearl of the Antilles."* And no government that wanted to hold on to the island could afford to alienate the Spanish Party in Cuba, enforced by the powerful Volunteers. Concha, who created the Volunteer Corps, admitted that the Volunteers exploited patriotism in order to defend the vested interests of the island's privileged class. But Concha quickly added, "It is not possible to govern the island without the confidence of the Spanish Party."[7]

In short, the reactionary forces in Cuba and Spain, whose commercial and other interests were dependent upon an enslaved Cuba, set the policy as early as the spring and summer of 1869. Those who differed with this policy were silent or helpless. Thus the advocates of a war of extermination triumphed.

Against this background, the Ten Years' War unfolded.

* The Spanish Socialists, whose influence increased rapidly in Spain following the revolution of 1868, paid no attention to the struggle in Spain's oppressed colony. In none of the resolutions adopted by the Socialists at their conventions from 1868 to 1878 is there even a reference to the war in Cuba. To a large extent, this resulted from "the anarchist influence in the Socialist movement, with its indifference to political issues." (Max Nettlau, "*Bakunin und die Internationale in Spanien, 1868–1873,*" *Archiv für de Geschichte des Sozialismus und der Arbeiterbewegung*, vol. IV, 1914, pp. 277–92.)

chapter 16

THE TEN YEARS' WAR:
THE WAR UNFOLDS, 1869-1870

Having decided on a war of extermination, the Spanish Provisional Government of General Prim began a full-scale military build-up. Thousands of youths and men were mustered in Spanish villages and hamlets and loaded in ships at Cádiz and Vigo to fight and die in Cuba. From November 1868 to December 1869, Spain sent to the Cuban War her best group of generals and officers to command 35,000 veteran soldiers and thousands of others not too well-trained. In addition, she sent 14 warships and a train of artillery equipped with Krupp cannons of the latest model.

On the sea, of course, Spain held complete sway; the revolutionists had no navy at all, and by the end of 1869 Spain had a powerful fleet based upon Cuba—about 50 vessels of 400 guns, including the iron-clads *Victoria* and *Zaragoza*. This was no small advantage, for it often enabled Spain to keep outside aid, in the form of arms and men, from reaching the Cubans. Still, in spite of Spain's vigilance, considerable material did reach the Cubans early in the war. In June, 1869, the Cuban *Junta* in the United States claimed that seven or eight expeditions had reached Cuba from American waters. Altogether, the *Junta* had, by then, succeeded in delivering more than 20,000 small arms, 22 small cannon, and a large number of men, of whom most were Cubans and others veterans of the Union and Confederate Armies. General Thomas Jordan, a well-known Confederate officer, landed in Cuba in May, 1869, and was soon made Cuban chief of staff.

With these supplies of arms and ammunition, the Liberating Army was, for several months, able to offer strong resistance to powerful Spanish forces and to win important victories. On June

23-24, 1869, under the direction of General Thomas Jordan, the revolutionary army repulsed superior Spanish forces near Holguín, 20 Americans being among those slain. Under Jordan and Agramonte, the *insurrectos* kept the Spanish forces at bay in the province of Las Villas.

By the late summer of 1869, the Cubans were confronted by a severe shortage of arms and ammunition. The Federal Government, as we shall see, stopped the flow that had been coming from the United States, and although supplies did come through from Latin America and Jamaica, it was a mere trickle compared with the needs of the insurgents.

Faced with a great inferiority in numbers and material of war, the insurgents were forced to adopt the only logical military strategy—guerrilla warfare. The rebels could not sustain the heavy losses of frequent large-scale battles of traditional warfare. Their limited numbers and lack of sufficient war material in contrast to Spain's greater resources in men and arms, and their insecure supply lines, precluded orthodox strategy. Consequently the basic aim of the rebels was attrition—to wear down Spanish resistance. The main policy of the *insurrectos* was to discourage and tire the Spanish armies and the Spanish government; the great hope in this strategy lay in making the war economically disastrous for Spain, thus forcing the Spaniards to sue for peace. This meant that the rebel fighting units sought to create the greatest economic dislocation possible by cutting railway and telegraph lines, destroying sugar mills and other valuable property, preventing all profitable production, and generally paralyzing the commercial and economic activity of the island.

The type of strategy employed by the rebels meant innumerable small skirmishes and few large battles. Occasionally the rebels were unwittingly drawn into large-scale combat, and at rare intervals, they entered into it for prestige and morale purposes. But the *insurrectos* usually avoided a large battle unless they believed they held a decided edge and unless it was on the terrain in which they preferred to operate.

Armed with machetes, a variety of firearms, and scanty supplies of ammunition, the guerrillas roved the woods and poured out of ambuscades. They cut railway lines and aqueducts, destroyed communications, and burned the plantations and estates of those not in sympathy with their cause. Often after the Spaniards had removed roadblocks and rebuilt burnt bridges, the road was cut again in their rear by rebel groups. Spaniards held possession of every seaport and most of the towns on the island; the small and poorly armed guerrilla bands of insurgents often controlled the mountain ridges and forests less than a mile away. Their aim was to confine the Spanish Army to the cities, and then, by cutting the roads, isolate the units and force them to surrender. When troops were sent out to quell them, the guerrillas hid in the fastness of the interior where the enemy dared not follow them. The Spaniards shelled, strafed and fired at the unseen enemy, and returned to boast of having "cleaned up" the rebels in the area. But no sooner was the report made than resistance burst forth again. Thus the pattern continued throughout the long war.

What the Cuban army lacked in numbers, in experience and training in warfare, in arms and equipment, was often compensated for by a thorough knowledge of the country, the effective use of guerrilla strategy, greater immunity to cholera and other diseases that flourished in the island, and above all, patriotic devotion. The most important asset for guerrilla warfare is an ideal; the rebels were fighting for the liberation of their country from Spain's tyrannical yoke, and this gave them the popular support without which a guerrilla movement cannot be effective. Such help was often the key to Cuban successes in the Ten Years' War, in spite of the inferior number of their armed soldiery in comparison with that of the enemy. The *guajiro* and the *campesino*, the slave and the free Negro, not only moved steadily into the ranks of the Liberating Army, but aided and shielded the patriotic fighters against the Spaniards, even though in doing so they risked their own lives.

The guerrilla warfare carried on over a period of years by the rebels was commanded by the indomitable Gómez, García, and Agramonte.* All three were masters of guerrilla strategy, but General Gómez developed this type of fighting to a high point of perfection. According to the plan he outlined, the *insurrectos* were divided into highly mobile small units, operating continually on the move and never allowing more than momentary peace in any one area.

---

* Agramonte was the only one of the three who did not survive the war. He was killed in 1873 in a skirmish at Jimaguayú.

The fighting was of the revolving and hit-and-run variety, with no fixed battle lines. It was conducted by many self-sufficient units; but the revolutionary army did have an effective over-all command and organization, which permitted concentration at any given time.

The outstanding leader of the guerrilla units was the Negro revolutionary, Antonio Maceo, who was to prove himself one of the great guerrilla fighters of all time. In skirmish after skirmish at the very outset of the war, particularly in those of El Cristo and El Cobre, the young Negro showed such exceptional courage, initiative, and leadership that he was quickly promoted, first to the rank of sergeant and then to the rank of captain. Maceo won further recognition for his meritorious conduct during the campaign of Bayamo. His unit was one of the few which maintained discipline after the defeat of El Saladillo, and, under Maceo's command, constantly harassed and inflicted damage on the rear guard of the Spanish column. On January 16, 1869, Maceo was promoted to the rank of commander, and was allowed to operate with independent forces, although he was still under the organizational jurisdiction of General Mármol.

With greater freedom to formulate his own tactics, young Maceo began to operate brilliantly in guerrilla actions around Mayarí and Guantánamo, and, as early as January 26, 1869, received a promotion to lieutenant colonel of the Liberating Army. Too often among Cuban military leaders, intrigues and personal aspirations got in the way of the necessary effective military operations. But in Maceo's encampment there was no other objective but winning military victories and securing the pronounced aims of the revolution. Maceo instilled in his men the concepts of discipline, duty and the aims of the revolution, and the soldiers, in turn, showed him not only respect but love. He set them a high example, for he never seemed to rest. The majority of his troops relaxed after a combat, but Maceo, with his escort, was immediately roving the area, preparing the next ambush of the Spanish troops, taking advantage of the terrain with the sureness and care of an experienced officer grown old in the career of arms. Gómez, under whose instructions Maceo was to develop fully the art of guerrilla warfare, noted that the Negro commander displayed from the first month of the war an uncanny ability to prepare all the details before entering into combat; that he took all the essential precautions which would keep his troops covered in case of a surprise, and that his retreats were well planned and occurred in successive stages.

On many occasions, Spanish officers were disastrously fooled by Maceo's whirlwind attacks against greatly superior numerical forces. When the initial attack was repulsed, and the seemingly desperate retreat was followed up by the Spaniards, they found themselves suddenly trapped in a well-prepared ambush on unfavorable terrain. Maceo delighted in outsmarting the Spanish generals; again and again he decoyed them into situations that were disastrous to his opponents.

When not fighting, Maceo took advantage of the old *palenques,* the abandoned shelters constructed at one time or another by fugitive slaves in the most hidden of forests or in the most inaccessible mountain fastnesses. In these natural sanctuaries, he established crude hospitals, workshops, living quarters for the families of the troops, and food stores which were operated by his mother and wife, Mariana Grajales and María Cabrales. Whenever conditions permitted, he used the sloops of the network of illicit traffic operating in the Caribbean to import medicines, salt, ammunition, and other indispensable necessities in small lots from Jamaica, Santo Domingo or Haiti. The other main source of war materials, and thus a constant preoccupation and objective in all military engagements, was the taking of booty from the enemy. Through these three sources, Maceo managed so that neither food nor munitions were lacking. The 200 men who composed his forces were relatively well fed, well dressed, and well shod.

Maceo's military successes continued unchecked. In the period from February to May, 1869, he defeated the Spaniards in several bitter clashes, in one of which, May 14, 1869, his father was killed at his side; and in another, shortly after, Maceo himself was wounded in an attack. This was the first of the innumerable wounds which were to cover Maceo's body from head to foot before his death during the Second War for Independence. He was carried back to one of his hidden rest camps, where his wife and mother nursed him back to health. A few weeks after he was wounded, Maceo and his wife suffered the death of their two small children, victims of the hazards of war.

During the periods when he was not fighting, and those of forced rests as a result of his frequent wounds, Maceo sought to improve his education beyond the meagre "schooling" of his boyhood. Dr. Félix Figueredo, a man of broad culture, spent hours lecturing to Maceo on history, politics, and political science, and supplied him with books to read.

In the attack on the fort of the sugar plantation of Arroyito in Santa Cruz de Villalón, Maceo captured the fort, the prisoners guarding it, and all the arms. And in each of his incursions into the zones rich in sugar cane, Maceo fulfilled one of his basic reasons for fighting: he freed the slaves of the sugar mills, and explained to the liberated Negroes that one of the major purposes of the war was to wipe out slavery in Cuba. And the Negro slaves, now free men, "swelled the ranks of the Liberating Army."[1]

While the various rebel guerrilla units were concentrating on winning military victories, the revolution was passing through a series of crises.

The men who raised the banner of revolt at Yara, though great Cuban patriots, were nonetheless themselves men of wealth and spokesmen for the interests of the Cuban landowners in the eastern provinces. These men wanted a revolution that would eliminate Spanish domination over the island, but they also wanted to make sure that it was their class, the *hacendado* class, that controlled the course of the revolution and would dominate the scene once Cuba was liberated.

But from the first day of the war, the essentially conservative character of the insurrectional movement, headed by Céspedes, came into conflict with the aspirations of the popular classes, who flocked into the ranks of the Liberating Army. The Cuban lower classes, Negro and white, who made up the bulk of the revolutionary army, were fighting not only for the liberation of their country from Spanish tyranny, but also for reforms of many aspects of life in Cuba—especially for greater political power in the hands of the common people, and the abolition of slavery. Inevitably a conflict emerged between these two types of objectives.

This cleavage came to the surface before the war was a month old. At Yara, the Republic of Cuba had been organized and Céspedes was, without a dissenting vote, chosen to be its acting head. Thus

Céspedes was literally invested with dictatorial powers, combining in himself the offices of commander-in-chief of the army and head of the government. This monopoly of power by one individual may have been necessary in order to bring order to the revolutionary movement as soon as possible. But what may have been justified as a temporary expedient aroused discontent among the revolutionists when Céspedes showed no inclination to relinquish any of his powers. Most outspoken in their criticism were the Camagüeyans, led by Ignacio Agramonte. The Camagüeyans were frankly dissatisfied with the way Céspedes hugged complete authority, and they demanded that the centralized power of the commander-in-chief be reduced and that a principle of federalism be introduced, thus permitting greater authority in the hands of the respective districts. To pursue this objective, Agramonte was selected to arrange an interview with Céspedes. The two men were not able to reconcile their views, and developed a personal antagonism toward each other that was to grow in intensity as the war unfolded.

An even more fundamental cleavage within the revolutionary ranks grew out of the issue of slavery. Céspedes, in his first manifesto as chief of the revolutionary Junta, October 10, 1868, said that "we desire the gradual indemnified emancipation of slaves." But even this narrow objective was to be put into operation *after* the revolution emerged victorious. To act on the question before victory was achieved, as Céspedes saw it, would lose the support of the *hacendado* class, particularly the rich Western planters (perhaps 1500 in number), essential for the triumph over Spain. In his concern that the *hacendados* be protected in all their property, including slave property, Céspedes, on November 12, 1868, announced that summary execution by a firing squad would be the fate of "the soldiers and chiefs of the Republican forces who, faithless to their sacred mission, shall burn, rob or defraud the peaceful citizens, *and those who introduce themselves into the farms whether to stir up or remove their work crews.*" Thus the slaveowners were assured by the top leadership of the revolutionary movement of the peaceful enjoyment of their work crews.

But there were many in the revolutionary ranks who felt that the entire policy of appeasing the propertied classes in the hope of winning them to the revolutionary cause was not only futile but disastrous to the success of the revolution. The hopes of receiving support from the *hacendado* class were proved illusory soon after the outbreak of the war. The *hacendados* of the West or richest part of Cuba, with few exceptions, not only refused all help to the revolutionary cause, but placed themselves on the side of the Spanish government. To a great extent, the same was true even in Oriente; the *hacendados* of the sugar zone of Santiago de Cuba quickly pledged their support to Spain, and even turned over 10,000 pesos to the Spanish authorities for the purpose of "exterminating the revolution." [2]

Obviously to cling to the policy of appeasing the *hacendados* would gain nothing since the slaveowners, convinced that their investment in slavery was best protected by the Spanish authorities, had, in the main, already cast their lot with Spain. At the same time, the policy seriously weakened the appeal of the revolution to the Cuban masses, and caused the many Negroes already in the rebel army to question the anti-slavery aims of a struggle for which they were prepared to give their lives. Finally, it held back the thousands of Negroes ready to join the revolutionary ranks, for although slaves incorporated into the revolution had been declared free, a formal decree abolishing slavery throughout the island had not been issued, and without such a decree, the status of the Negro in the Liberating Army was uncertain.

It did not take long for the conflict over a correct policy relating to slavery to come to a head. Céspedes, it will be recalled, had established the capital of the rebel government in Bayamo, the first town of any size taken by the Liberating Army. On October 28, 1868, ten days after the city was captured, the Revolutionary Municipal Council of Bayamo, two of whose members were Negroes, petitioned Céspedes to proclaim the immediate abolition of slavery. The petitions pointed out that it was naive to expect the slaveowners to support the revolution, while the failure to proclaim immediate abolition weakened the fighting capacity of the Liberating Army, and interfered with the ability of the revolutionary movement to attract sympathy from abroad.

Céspedes, exercising his dictatorial powers, rejected the petition. But recognizing the growing opposition to his timid policy on slavery, in his proclamation of Bayamo, December 27, 1868, he decreed a cautious measure of abolition calculated to please the outside world, without really antagonizing the propertied classes of Cuba. Céspedes publicly recognized "that a free Cuba was incompatible with a slavist Cuba." But he promptly added that abolition was contingent upon the final success of the revolution. Meanwhile, the Republic would respect slave property; fugitive slaves belonging to rebel proprietors would not be admitted into the revolutionary ranks without the consent of their owners. However, the slaves of those who had been convicted of being enemies of the country and openly hostile to the revolution would be confiscated and declared free without indemnification for their owners.

Céspedes' proclamation was hardly an advance in the direction of emancipation. Cuban slavists who sided with the revolution could, if they wished, continue to enjoy the fruits of slave labor. Nor did Céspedes recognize the liberty of the slaves who joined the revolution. The Negro slave could not enroll himself into the ranks of the Liberating Army *unless his master authorized it*, and the proprietors who handed over their slaves to the revolutionary service without liberating them, kept their property.[3]

The Revolutionary Assembly of the Central Department, an outgrowth of the Revolutionary Committee of Camagüey, criticized the inadequacies of Céspedes' decree; it called for a more decisive policy to abolish slavery immediately, and on February 26, 1869, issued a declaration which began: "The institution of slavery, introduced into Cuba by Spanish Dominion, must be extinguished along with it." It then announced that slavery was abolished throughout the Central District; that the slaveowners would be indemnified in due time; that all who were liberated by the decree would, if suited for it, be welcomed in the Liberating Army, "enjoying the same compensation and the same consideration as other soldiers of the Liberating Army."[4]

Although the decree had no effect in the areas of greatest slave concentration—according to the Census of 1869, the Occidental District had 300,989 and the Central and Oriental Districts, 62,297 slaves—and though the rebel forces did not yet control enough territory to give it the necessary backing, it was an important statement of aims, and revealed the rising opposition to Céspedes' conservative policies. Céspedes himself, recognizing this opposition, conceded that the time had come to end his dictatorial regime and to begin operating on democratic principles. A call was issued for a constitutional convention to meet at Guáimaro, a town 35 miles from Puerto Príncipe, to draw up a fundamental document for Free Cuba and establish a functioning democratic Republic.

The Constitutional Convention met at Guáimaro on April 10, 1869, with delegates present from Villaclara, Sancti Spíritus, Jiguaní, Holguín, and Camagüey. A Constitution was adopted which provided for a republican form of government to consist of executive, legislative, and judicial departments. The legislative power was vested in a House of Representatives in which there was to be equal representation from each of the four states into which the island of Cuba was divided—Oriente, Camagüey, Las Villas, and Occidente. Céspedes was elected president and Manuel Quesada commander-in-chief.

The 24th article of the first Constitution of Free Cuba, drawn up by the Camagüeyan delegates, declared that "all the inhabitants of the Republic are absolutely free." This was certainly a victory for the popular forces. So, too, was the replacement of absolute rule by a representative form of government, and the provision in the Constitution that the House of Representatives "shall not abridge the Freedom of Religion, nor of the Press, nor of Public Meetings, nor of Education, nor of Petition, nor any inalienable right of the People."[5]

But the conservative elements were not so easily defeated. They scored important victories at Guáimaro. For one thing, the Convention declared that the rebels were fighting for annexation to the United States as well as independence; and the Congress of the Cuban Republic, established by the new Constitution, followed this up by asking the government of the United States to admit Cuba into the Union. It was freely admitted during the discussions that annexation was the safest way to guarantee that the more radical elements in the revolutionary movement would not emerge triumphant following independence.

The victory of the conservatives was especially evident in the failure to carry into effect the constitutional provision abolishing slavery. The Constitution of Guáimaro had proclaimed all the inhabitants of the Republic entirely free, but on July 6, 1869, the

House of Representatives rejected the Constitution, and instituted instead the *Reglamento de Libertos* (Rule of the Freed) which continued slavery in the Republic, though in a more discreet form. The slave, who was now called *liberto,* was compelled to continue to work for his master, but the latter was not obligated to feed, clothe or even to pay him wages. This system, which remained in force until December 25, 1870, was "forced labor," pure and simple. In short, the top leaders of the revolutionary movement, still anxious not to antagonize the *hacendados,* especially of the Occidental District, refused to make "entirely free" all the inhabitants of the Republic.

While it is true that in the Occidental District, where the Liberating Army had not penetrated, the provision in the Guáimaro Constitution abolishing slavery had little practical effect, it nevertheless did serve, at first, to stimulate the exodus of fugitive slaves who sought, by various means, to escape to the regions where the rebels exercised control. But when the news reached the slaves in Occidente that they were exchanging slavery of the lash for "forced labor" the exodus was seriously hampered. This, of course, permitted the sugar planters to continue production without interference, and contributed to Spain's ability to conduct the war. Finally, the nullification of the abolition clause of the Guáimaro Constitution had a dampening effect on the morale of the revolutionary soldiers, many of whom, especially the Negroes, felt that the real objectives of the war of liberation were being sabotaged by the conservatives.

Fortunately, the revolutionary spirit of the Liberating Army survived the shock of seeing the abolition provision of the Constitution betrayed. In fact, many of the guerrilla units, like the one led by Maceo, continued to liberate the slaves when they captured sugar plantations and mills, and either recruited the freedmen into the rebel army or set them to work on land confiscated from loyalist planters. The more revolutionary commanders sent emissaries to urge Negro slaves in the Western District to escape to Las Villas and Camagüey, where they would be under the protection of the Liberating Army, and where "their masters may lose all hope of recovering them."[6]

Under the pressure of the popular forces, Céspedes made a sharp turn in a more revolutionary direction. In October, 1869, he decreed the "destruction of all the cane fields of the island." "Better for the cause of human liberty, better for the cause of human rights, better for the children of our children, that Cuba should be free, even if we have to burn every vestige of civilization from the tip of Maisí to the tip of San Antonio, so that Spanish authority shall be eliminated."[7] (Maisí was the eastern tip and San Antonio the western tip of the island.) A month later, Céspedes formally approved the revolutionary practice of urging the slaves on the plantations to rise up.

Thus, by the end of 1869, even though "forced labor" was in operation, the revolution, under the pressure of the popular forces, was becoming more and more completely abolitionist in character. By this time, too, the Liberating Army had attained better organization and greater combat efficiency, although the lack of adequate arms and other supplies retarded its effective use. In the fall of 1869, Adjutant General Thomas Jordan, writing from the scene of action, reported that "hundreds of brave men are standing in my sight almost naked, some quite so, and few with shoes of any sort." Early in 1870, General Quesada reported that the 61,694 Cuban soldiers were equipped with 13 pieces of artillery, 16,000 rifles and guns, 3,558 pistols and revolvers, and 60,075 machetes.[8]

The overwhelming superiority of the Spanish military machine forced the rebels to abandon the province of Las Villas—the most western province of the rebellion—and to fall back to Camagüey. Nevertheless, the Liberating Army, under the direction of General Thomas Jordan and the celebrated Agramonte, continued to offer strong resistance to the powerful Spanish forces in that province. And rebel guerrilla bands were so effective that Spanish troops could hardly stir in Oriente beyond fortified lines without meeting surprise attacks. The guerrillas kept the Spaniards in Santa Clara, Camagüey and Oriente in a state of constant turmoil.

Unable to defeat the guerrillas, the Spanish troops and the Volunteers vented their fury in terror. Hapless men, women, and children were driven into concentration camps—many forced to walk for days to get there. Vast areas, suspected of aiding the rebels, were destroyed, the male inhabitants shot. Only blackened walls of huts remained. In Santiago and its environs, peaceful citizens were killed just so that their houses might be sacked and their crops sold by military officers. Throughout Cuba, arrests mounted.* The Spanish troops showed no quarter to rebel soldiers; prisoners were given "the usual four shots in the back."[9]

Yet it was apparent that despite this "utmost barbarism"—the phrase of a shocked newspaper in Madrid—Volunteers and Spanish army alike were failing to master the revolt. It was also clear that this savage but unsuccessful colonial war was causing severe strain on the government in Spain itself. There was open talk in Madrid of having to fight for "five or more years." There was whispered talk of a refusal of the Spanish soldiers to face up to the brilliant guerrilla tactics of the rebels, of a refusal to go through with military plans against the rebels which would involve serious casualties, of gross inefficiency at the top. "Spain is losing the war in Cuba," a number of newspapers in Madrid stated openly. The guerrillas, cholera, smallpox, yellow fever, and malaria were exacting a deadly toll. Again and again the government had advertised that the revolt was crushed, but it soon became evident that the army had not mounted anything that could be called an offensive against the rebels, except in the communiqués of the High Command. De Rodas and Valmaseda boasted of constant "victories," but even the Spaniards conceded that they were imaginary triumphs which had no foundation in fact. Indeed, early in January, 1870, Spaniards confessed to A. E. Phillips, the American Consul in Santiago, "that it is impossible to suppress the insurrection, and the only inducement for continuing the war is that the commanding officers are filling their pockets."[10]

Almost four months later, on March 24, 1870, *La Discusión* of Madrid made the same confession in a bitter editorial:

> For 18 months we have sustained a very difficult and bloody struggle in Cuba. Forty thousand Spaniards have put their feet upon that burning soil, where many of them have found sepulture. Forty million dollars have gone out from our poor and miserable coffers. What have we accomplished? Nothing—absolutely nothing. It is painful thus to

---

* Because he wrote a letter accusing a student of being an apostate for having marched in a parade with the Spaniards, José Martí, though still a boy, was arrested by the Volunteers and condemned to six years at hard labor in the government quarries. He spent six months of backbreaking stone-cutting, which left him a physical wreck, half blind and with a hernia caused by a blow from a chain. Some friends secured a pardon for him, but to keep him from further seditious activities, the authorities deported him to Spain.

speak, but we can do nothing less. The insurrection is not conquered. It will continue to have more or less force, and it will hold out long enough to consume all our resources, which are very few, and to cause the death of many, very many Spaniards. And suppose, after all, we should obtain some results. In the end it would be hard, it would be painful, if we should meet with the same fate in Cuba as happened to us in Santo Domingo. To fight to water the soil with our blood, and after so much heroism, after so much self-abnegation, yes, then to leave the sepulchers of our soldiers to the hand of the enemy.

We agree that the insurgents are badly whipped; yes, we admit that our reported victories may be true ones, but who can conquer a people fighting for liberty? The insurrection, so far as it concerns the question of being subdued, may at any moment assume greater proportions. It is certain that the contest will be ceaselessly renewed.[11]

"Who can conquer a people fighting for liberty?" *La Discusión* asked frankly. Certainly not Spain by herself. Spain was faced with a challenge in Cuba that she was failing to meet with the resources at her disposal. She was losing the colonial war. The regime was weakened in Spain itself. But Prim and his associates had important support elsewhere, especially in the United States. Spain had used and was using armaments manufactured in the United States. Without such supplies, the Spanish could never have maintained the destructive and cruel war against the Cuban people.

Now came the crucial test. Would Spain continue to enjoy the friendship of the government of the United States and all that went with it?

chapter 17

THE UNITED STATES AND THE INDEPENDENCE OF CUBA, 1868-1869

In daring to raise the banner of independence against a vastly superior foe, the Cuban revolutionists were encouraged by the belief that their heroic struggle would win the support of all people who were enjoying their own freedom. As the Cuban poet, Antonio Hurtado del Valle, wrote on the eve of his departure for Mexico to mobilize aid for the Cuban cause:

> I do not come here as daring Cortés,
>   seeking dried-out
>   in some granite mountain
>   an abundant deposit of gold;
> I do not come like some adventurer,
>   to convert into degraded slaves
>   a noble, candid, innocent people....
> The thirst for riches does not bring me here.
> Nor do I come to destroy with a rude hand
>   the well-being of an independent people.
> I come alone, a Christian troubadour,
> To beg, in my sorrowful poem,
>   perhaps of the resounding air,
>   that an American people will raise an obelisk,
> To establish the liberty of Cuba.[1]

In the former Spanish colonies in America, Cuba's appeal for help did not fall on the "resounding air" and die. The Mexican Congress authorized President Juárez to recognize the Cubans as belligerents, and gave orders that the Cuban flag should be admitted in the ports of that nation. Cuban belligerency was acknowledged by Peru (which also recognized her independence), Mexico, Bolivia, Colombia, Chile, Venezuela, and other Latin American Republics. In taking this stand, these governments acknowledged that the fight

Cuba was waging was identical with the one they had conducted a half century before against Spanish domination. As the House of Representatives of Colombia put it: "The cause for which the Cuban patriots fight is the same for which Colombia fought incessantly from 1810 to 1824."[2]

Latin American support for Cuban independence went further than expressions of sympathy. It also expressed itself in important contributions of arms, military experience, money, refuge for émigrés, diplomatic protection, and so forth. Not a few Latin Americans, from Mexico to Chile, gave their lives as combatants in the Cuban Liberating Army.

Important as was this assistance, the Cuban cause was nevertheless especially dependent upon the policy of the government of the United States. Recognition of the right of belligerency of the Cubans by the United States would have spelled disaster for the Spaniards, for it would bring with it the free shipment of arms, and imply the promise of eventual diplomatic recognition. Without it the Cuban rebels would be seriously, if not fatally, handicapped. Without vital supplies, even the valiant soldiers of the Liberating Army could hardly be expected to mount effective offensive actions and bring the war to an early end.

Naturally, Spain bent every effort to prevent the accordance of belligerent status to the Cuban patriots. Comparatively poor herself in the natural resources, especially iron and steel, necessary to wage a modern war, she was able to obtain arms and ammunition from Europe and the United States. Thus she was able to cope with a revolutionary army in Cuba that had to fight largely with machetes, in a situation where five men were waiting to use every rifle that reached the front.

The Cuban revolutionists expected that the character of their struggle entitled them to the support they needed from the United States. As President Céspedes wrote to President Grant:

> The ideas which the Cubans defend and the form of government which they have established, written in the Constitution promulgated by them, at least make it obligatory for the United States, more than others, to be inclined in its favor. If for exigencies, requirements of humanity and civilization, all the nations are obliged to be interested in Cuba, asking for the recognition of the war it is carrying on against

Spain, the United States has the duty imposed upon it by the political principles it proclaims and diffuses to take the leadership in this direction.... Our fight, like all those in its class, will be long, but your Excellency can do much to shorten it, on proclaiming the justice of the government of the United States recognizing our belligerency and our independence.[3]

From the outbreak of the Cuban Revolution, a large section of the American public proclaimed its sympathy with the insurgents and began to demand the recognition of Cuban belligerency. "The first gleam of the sword of freedom and independence in Cuba secured my sympathy with the revolutionary cause," wrote Frederick Douglass, the greatest Negro leader of the nineteenth century in the United States, "and it did seem to me that our government ought to have made haste to accord the insurgents belligerent rights."[4] Douglass was voicing the sentiments of the majority of the American people. "The American press, people, and Congress sympathize with the Cuban rebels and want them to succeed," the London *Times* stated on March 29, 1869. On March 25, 1869, the House of Representatives began consideration of a resolution reported from the Committee on Foreign Relations, declaring that the United States sympathized with the people of Cuba "in their patriotic efforts to secure their independence and establish a republican form of government," and pledging the support of Congress to the President whenever he should "deem it expedient to recognize the independence and sovereignty of such government." On April 9, with a large majority of both parties voting for it, the House adopted this resolution by a vote of 98 to 25.[5]

The news of the action of the American Congress was greeted with cheers by the Cuban patriots in their armed camps. The American Consul at Havana reported that the rebels were now "sanguine of success," expecting that momentarily the United States would recognize the belligerency of the Cuban Republic.[6]

But while the American people had spoken through Congress, petitions, and mass meetings calling for recognition of Cuban belligerency, it was up to the administration in Washington, headed by President Ulysses S. Grant, to decide whether the popular desire would be carried into effect. On March 19, 1869, Grant's Cabinet was forced to make its first decision in the formulation of a

Cuban policy. The question concerned the reception to be accorded a representative of the insurgent government who, it was rumored, had arrived in New York. Official recognition of the Cuban representative would have meant recognition of the insurgent government. Nearly all members of the Cabinet, led by Secretary of State Hamilton Fish, were vehemently opposed to any action that would lead to recognition of Cuban belligerency. Only one member of the Cabinet spoke up for speedy recognition. He was John A. Rawlins, Secretary of War. But in the face of the opposition from other members, he did not press the issue. President Grant, moreover, decided to drop the matter for the time being.

A few days later, on March 24, José Morales Lemus, the representative of the revolutionary government, arrived in Washington and attempted to secure official recognition. But Fish refused to receive Morales Lemus formally, and was careful to remind him that he "must not address me officially" since that might be construed as recognition of the Cuban revolutionists. He told Lemus "that we intend to observe perfect good faith to Spain, and whatever might be our sympathies with a people, wherever, in any part of the world, struggling for more liberal government, we should not depart from our duty to other friendly governments, nor be in haste to prematurely recognize a revolutionary movement until it had manifested capacity of self-sustenance and of some degree of stability."[7]

Already in the first weeks of his secretaryship, Fish had revealed that he would bend every effort to prevent recognition of Cuban belligerency. The aristocratic New Yorker frequently expressed support for "people . . . struggling for more liberal government," but he did not include the Cubans in this category. "He placed a low estimate upon the intelligence and moral qualities of much of the [Cuban] population," Allan Nevins, Fish's biographer writes. "He doubted the aptitude of the conglomerate of Indian, Negro, and Spanish blood for self-government and thought . . . that evolution under Spanish tutelage might be better than revolution. Moreover, he felt a certain friendliness for Spain."[8] What Fish's biographer does not mention is that the Secretary of State also believed that Cuba would eventually be taken over by the United States, and that, meanwhile, it was the best American policy for the island to remain under Spanish control. It is true that Fish did not respond affirmatively when José Morales Lemus informed him that the Cuban Congress at Guáimaro had agreed "to propose the immediate annexation [of Cuba to the United States]." But this path to acquisition of the island would have meant war with Spain. The Spanish commentator, Gabriel Rodríguez, argued that Fish really wanted to acquire Cuba, but did not think it was necessary to go to war for it. Once the island had been devastated by war, Spain would be willing to sell it to the United States. Until that time, however, it would suit the interests of the United States to have the island remain under Spain's control.[9]

As early as April 6, 1869, Fish pointed out at a Cabinet meeting that the wisest policy for the United States to follow was to allow the "madness and fatuity of the Spanish Dominion in Cuba" to continue until such time as all the civilized nations would come "to regard the Spanish rule as an international nuisance, which must be abated, when they would all be glad that we should interpose and regulate the control of the Island." Only the United States, Fish emphasized, could have the privilege of stepping in and taking control of Cuba. In October, 1869, Fish told the German Minister in Washington that while "it is not our interest to acquire Cuba at the present," the United States would never consent that "the Island pass into the possession or under the control of any other European Government."[10] This was the old policy of favoring possession of Cuba by a weak power like Spain until such time as conditions were ripe for the United States to step in and annex the island. Such a policy naturally ruled out an independent Cuba.

These, however, were not the arguments Fish advanced officially against recognition of Cuban belligerency. He told Morales Lemus that the United States had to wait until the Cuban revolution "had manifested capacity of self-sustenance and of some degree of stability." The Cuban revolution manifested the capacity to sustain a war for ten years with a good deal of stability, but throughout that long period, Fish stood adamant against recognition of belligerency. The Republic of Cuba, he said again and again, was no government at all; it had no capital; held no ports; could receive no envoys, and had no territory definitely under its control. All this rendered it impossible for any responsible power to recognize Cuban belligerency, to say nothing of Cuban independence.

Fish ignored, of course, what the Latin American Republics understood when they recognized Cuban belligerency—that to apply traditional principles of international law to a war of liberation such as was being waged in Cuba was to favor the colonial oppressor. To expect a full-blown government to be rapidly established in a long, narrow island, with its poor communications and scantily populated areas, was to set up impossible conditions for recognition. To meet the conditions set by the United States for recognition of their belligerency, the Cubans would have had to abandon their entire strategy; for guerrilla strategy, the key to the revolutionary struggle, forbade the Cubans to try to hold towns or fortified places. Yet this was being used by Fish to justify non-recognition of belligerency.

Even the pro-Spanish *Voz de Cuba*, published in Havana, conceded in October, 1869, that the Cuban rebels had a functioning government: "Is it possible that in Guáimaro, four days' journey from Havana—two by sea, and two by land—there should have existed for the last eight months a Government of traitors; that they should have been holding sessions, issuing decrees, publishing papers, and exercising all the rights of sovereignty?"[11] This government, established at Guáimaro on April 10, 1869, was functioning sufficiently well to alarm the pro-Spanish Party in Cuba, but not well enough for the friends of Spain in the American government. Governments-in-exile, without a capital, a properly organized administration, and an effective army, had often been recognized by responsible powers. Why not then a government which operated inside Cuba and whose army was engaged in constant battle? That this army, because of the nature of guerrilla warfare, lacked the stability of the traditional military machine only proved the need to recognize a new aspect of military operations.

An important argument raised by Fish in opposition to recognition of Cuban belligerency grew out of the *Alabama* claims against Great Britain. At this very time, Fish was building the justice of American claims on the ground that Britain had, without sufficient justification, conceded belligerent status to the Southern Confederacy during the Civil War, thereby causing the damages inflicted by the Southern ship *Alabama* (built in England) on the Northern merchant marine. To recognize Cuban belligerency, Fish argued, would undermine the basis of the American claim.

The representatives of the Cuban Republic in Washington were not unsympathetic to the problem created by the *Alabama* claims for the United States. But they pointed out that the administration should draw a distinction between a war fought by the Southern Confederacy to overthrow a democratic form of government in the United States and a war fought in Cuba to establish a democratic form of government. At least the administration should acknowledge publicly that selfish considerations rather than principles of international law motivated its refusal to recognize Cuban belligerency. *The Nation* went even further. It found the argument that Cuban belligerency ought not to be recognized because it would damage the American position toward England "one which is as unworthy of the friends of Cuba as of its enemies. . . . If the United States has reached such a pass that the only rules of law it acknowledges are such as suit its temporary convenience, it has to all intents and purposes dropped out of the family of civilized nations. The effect on our policy in the *Alabama* case, and our duty in the Cuban case, are two separate things."[12]

"Spain has scarcely a friend in the United States," declared the London *Times* on May 6, 1869. It was mistaken. Spain had many friends in the United States: businessmen engaged in commercial relations with Cuba; Americans who owned property and slaves in Cuba and were afraid of the effect of the revolution on their interests; and all who looked forward to the day when Cuba would be annexed by the United States and believed Spain should control the island until then. And Spain had a warm friend in Grant's Cabinet, Hamilton Fish. Although Fish was often critical of Spain's conduct in Cuba, he invariably managed, as we shall see, to pursue a policy which saved Cuba for Spain until "we [the United States] should interpose and regulate the control of the Island."

With two exceptions, the other members of the Cabinet were also inclined to favor Spain. The exceptions were Postmaster General John A. Creswell and Secretary of War John A. Rawlins. Rawlins, especially, championed the Cuban cause. He had been Grant's right-hand man during the Civil War, and as the General's chief-of-staff had kept him from bad associates and errors of personal conduct. His influence on the new President was considerable, and it was largely due to this that Grant was, at first, inclined to favor the recognition of the belligerency of the Cuban insurgents.

It was later revealed that Rawlins had received $28,000 in Cuban bonds from the New York *Junta** which, though worthless at the time, would have a value if the Cuban cause triumphed. This information was turned over to Fish by the Spanish Minister in Washington as proof that Rawlins had a pecuniary interest in the success of the insurrection. Exceedingly poor, Rawlins probably figured that the bonds would take care of his family after his death—if Cuba was victorious. After Rawlins' death, the Cuban *Junta* contributed $20,000 in Cuban bonds to a fund for his family. Some of Rawlins' friends contended that the $28,000 in bonds referred to by the Spanish Minister had also been given to his family after the Secretary of War's death, but the evidence does not sustain this view.

Those who knew Rawlins intimately testified that his motives for supporting Cuba's struggle were in keeping with his liberal principles. He had hailed the overthrow of Maximilian's empire in Mexico; he sympathized with Ireland in her efforts to oust the British oppressors, and he believed that the United States should take the lead in freeing the Western Hemisphere from "the influence and dangers of monarchism." He also used expressions that were associated with the doctrines of "Manifest Destiny"—he hoped to see "the aegis of our power spread over this continent"—but he was a sincere friend of the oppressed, and Cuba's struggle for freedom and independence moved him deeply.[13]

Unfortunately, death was stalking Rawlins—he suffered from tuberculosis—and conscious of his approaching end, he worked feverishly to impress upon Grant the necessity of "more speedy action" in granting belligerent rights to the Cubans. Fish was aware that Grant was leaning more and more to Rawlins' position, and that this position was widely supported in Congress and throughout the country. On June 14, 1869, Fish received this letter from Iowa:

---

* *Juntas* were organized in New York, Washington, Tampa, Philadelphia and Boston. The most important group was the "Central Republican *Junta* of Cuba and Puerto Rico of New York," with José Morales Lemus as president. It published its own newspaper, *La Revolución*, held concerts to raise money, sponsored mass meetings, fitted out a number of expeditions to the island, and issued bonds in the name of the "Republic of Cuba." Copies of *La Revolución* are in the New York Public Library.

No time should be lost in according belligerent rights to the Cuban Patriots. Give a bold Example & encourage the popular spirit to be free.... Cuba is to be free but inactivity at Washington will get no credit in the result....

You fellows that sit in Easy Chairs need to mingle with the people & journey West for ten days. You would then give belligerent rights to the Cubans. It is their due and it is due to the people of the U.S. that they have their due.[14]

To stave off recognition of belligerency, Fish hit upon an alternative device which would have the effect meantime of maintaining the status quo. This was to reach some sort of settlement with Spain to end the Cuban insurrection. The first steps in this direction were unofficial in character. In June, 1869, Paul S. Forbes, an international businessman and representative of the bankers who held Spanish bonds, was named as special and confidential agent with advisory powers. He was on intimate terms with General Prim, and had reported to Fish that the leader of the Spanish Provisional Government had hinted at Spain's willingness to sell Cuba to the Cubans in order to retrieve the nation from bankruptcy, though he suggested that Spanish sensitiveness on parting with any of its empire might be an obstacle. The international bankers, who stood to gain a fortune through the rise in the value of the Spanish bonds if the deal went through, were enthusiastically in favor of the plan. Forbes recommended to Fish that the United States act as mediator between Spain and Cuba, and guarantee for the Cubans a sum to be agreed upon for which Cuba would be given her freedom.

There was a good deal of conflict in the Cuban *Junta* over going along with Fish's plan. Some members felt that the whole idea was a device to prevent recognition of Cuban belligerency. (Rawlins, incidentally, shared this view.) Finally, Fish obtained the consent of Morales Lemus and the *Junta* to proceed with the plan to buy Cuba for $100,000,000. He then offered Spain the good offices of the United States in order to terminate the war upon the following basis: (1) the independence of Cuba to be recognized by Spain; (2) the abolition of slavery in Cuba; (3) Cuba to pay Spain an indemnity not exceeding $100,000,000 for the renunciation of her sovereignty in the island; (4) the guarantee by the United States (if Congress agreed) of this payment; and (5) a complete armistice during negotiations.

These five conditions were to be transmitted to Madrid by General Daniel E. Sickles, the new Minister to Spain. In an accompanying note, Fish added the threat that if Spain did not accept the good offices of the United States, and if the state of things did not change in Cuba, it would not be fair to detain for a longer time the recognition of the right of belligerency of the Cubans. "An early recognition of belligerent rights is the logical deduction from the present proposal and will probably be deemed a necessity on the part of the United States, unless the condition of the parties to the contest shall have changed very materially."[15]

While Sickles was en route to Madrid, Fish, in order to prove to Spain that the United States was still a friend, urged Federal officers to increase vigilance against filibusters and to destroy all expeditions organized to land men and arms in Cuba. He gave instructions that if such expeditions escaped, they were to be pursued even beyond the territorial waters of the United States, and, if required, the military and naval forces of the government were to be called upon. An expedition organized by the New York *Junta*, consisting of 800 to 1,400 men and equipped with Spencer carbines, revolvers, sabres, two batteries of 12-pounder, and several 60-pounder guns, was intercepted late in June, 1869, by the federal authorities and nearly all of the men taken prisoner.

Fish found the first reports from Madrid most encouraging. Before Sickles arrived at Madrid, Forbes had had several meetings with Prim and Manuel Silvela, the Foreign Minister. He informed Fish that Prim was ready to bring about Spain's withdrawal from Cuba (and even Puerto Rico), but insisted on $150,000,000 as the price. Spain, said Prim, would give up Cuba only to relieve its finances. Unless this object was accomplished, "we never will do it." He was therefore firm in his stand for $150,000,000. While these conversations were taking place, the session of the Cortes was terminated "in order to negotiate quietly."

Arriving at Madrid on July 21, Sickles began negotiations with the Spanish officials. The American Minister was soon able to report to Fish that "if a way could be found to settle the question in such a manner as to do justice to Cuba without infringing upon the honor of Spain, the government would be greatly gratified. There is no intention or desire among the liberals of Spain again to work the Island of Cuba on the old selfish system." But, as we have seen, the "liberals of Spain" were at the beck and call of the powerful commercial and exporting interests, the military, the clergy, and the office-holding class who were determined to hold on to the wealth they derived from Cuba. The influence of these groups on the course of the negotiations was soon felt. Upon consulting the Cabinet, Prim found inflexible opposition. Nevertheless, Prim, ever the opportunist, saw that the U.S. offer might still be artfully exploited to hold back American recognition of Cuban belligerency, for as long as negotiations continued, it was unlikely that the Grant administration would act in this matter.

Prim, therefore, formulated new conditions. The Cubans were to be induced to lay down their arms at once. During a complete amnesty, which Spain would grant, an election of Cuban deputies to the Cortes was to be held. Through the Cortes, a plebiscite would then be called, in which the Cubans could vote upon the question of independence. If the majority declared for independence, Spain would grant it, the Cortes consenting. Cuba was then to give a satisfactory sum guaranteed by the United States. If the Cubans were to accept this program, Prim declared, they could "have their liberty without firing another shot."[16]

Prim conceded that there were difficulties in the execution of his plan. Actually, he knew that he had advanced impossible conditions. The Cubans would not lay down their arms prior to similar action by the Spaniards. The group within the Cuban *Junta* which had opposed the negotiations from the beginning, led by J. M. Macías, was voicing bitter opposition to continuing the "farce," insisting that Cuba belonged to the Cubans and that it was outrageous to ask the poverty-stricken people to pay another penny to the nation which had so long oppressed them. Even Lemus, who disagreed violently with the Macías group, refused to accept Prim's conditions. In answer to a question as to whether this proposal was acceptable to the Cubans, he replied: "No. We cannot trust the Spaniards. We will not lay down our arms; nor will we accept an amnesty. We have been fighting for nearly a year and have gained too many advantages to accept such a proposition as that. Prim is only playing for time. We must have an armistice or nothing."[17]

Whatever faint hope remained for adoption of the original American plan was exploded when, early in September, 1869, Becerra, Acting Secretary of State, an enemy of any plan to relinquish Cuba, purposely let the contents of the American plan leak out. The resulting enraged outcry from all the groups interested in retaining Cuba as Spain's rich colonial preserve forced Prim to reject the American offer of good offices. Thus ended the efforts of the United States to act as mediator in the war between Spain and Cuba. There had never really been a chance that Spain would concede the independence of Cuba. Indeed, the only ones to benefit from the months of negotiations were the groups in the United States and Spain who had sought all along to use the mediation scheme to hold back American recognition of Cuban belligerency.

On several occasions during the negotiations, Grant, pressured by public opinion and influenced by Rawlins, had made up his mind to recognize Cuban belligerency, and had even directed the preparation of a proclamation to that effect. The date of the proclamation was left blank. It stated that in order to prevent cordial relations between the United States and Spain from being affected by the "grave events" in Cuba, and, in order "to avoid the damage which might come to the citizens of the United States and to their navigation and commerce from the want of clear provisions by which to adjust their conduct," and in order that the laws of the United States might be enforced, the citizens of the country were warned to observe neutrality. Neutrality by the United States in the Cuban war meant recognition of Cuban belligerency.

But each time Grant raised the question of issuing the proclamation, Fish convinced the President that the chances of Spain's accepting the American conditions for ending the war were bright, and on each occasion Grant delayed. But Fish went even further. In August, 1869, Grant instructed Fish to issue the signed proclamation, but the Secretary of State deliberately refused to do so. On July 10, 1870, Fish boasted that he had in August, 1869, prevented "the issuing . . . of the proclamation of Cuban belligerency which he [Grant] had signed, and which he wrote me a note instructing me to sign (which I did) and to issue (which I did not)."[18]

On August 31, 1869, at a Cabinet meeting, Rawlins, who had risen from his deathbed to plead the cause of Cuba, accused Fish of a cynical policy toward the Cubans, and of utilizing the negotiations with Prim to prevent Grant from issuing his proclamation. Rawlins demanded that America act at once, and advanced a long, able, and impassioned argument for recognition of Cuban belligerency. But Fish was again able to convince Grant that negotiations should continue, and that an impulsive recognition of belligerency would destroy all that Forbes and Sickles had accomplished in discussions with Prim.

Again Fish triumphed. Grant agreed not to issue a proclamation of neutrality at once, as Rawlins had demanded, but to let negotiations continue until October 1, by which date, if nothing had been accomplished, a proclamation would be *considered*. On September 4, Fish wrote jubilantly to George Bancroft in Berlin: "There is a very strong pressure throughout the country for the recognition of belligerency in favor of the Cubans. Thus far the administration has resisted it."[19]

It will be recalled that in his instructions to Sickles, accompanying the American offer to mediate the war in Cuba, Fish had held out the threat that if Spain did not accept the terms and the state of things did not change in Cuba, it would not be fair to hold off any longer the recognition of the right of belligerency of the Cubans. Yet no declaration of belligerency followed the refusal of the American offer, and conditions remained the same in Cuba. Fish was still sympathetic with the new regime in Spain, partly because Sickles believed that his friends in the Spanish Cabinet were "apparently in earnest for a complete accord with the United States." But Fish was also influenced by the fact that the chief pressure in the administration for recognition had been eliminated by the death of Rawlins on September 5, 1869. In his dying moments, Rawlins had appealed to Postmaster-General Creswell: "There is Cuba, poor, struggling Cuba. I want you to stand by the Cubans. Cuba must be free. Her tyrannical enemy must be crushed. Cuba must not only be free, but all her sister-islands. The Republic is responsible for its liberty. I will disappear; but you must concern yourself with this question. We have worked together. Now it is up to you alone to watch over Cuba."[20]

Mixed with the sorrow felt by many Americans was a feeling of relief in certain quarters. As the foes of Cuban independence saw it, Rawlins had died opportunely. But for "Cuba, poor, struggling Cuba," his death was a tragedy.* Grant wept over the loss of his counsellor, but he quickly forgot the cause to which Rawlins had dedicated his last months. Grant and the expansionists were now interested in a new and different cause—the annexation of the Dominican Republic.

An effort to annex the Negro republic of Santo Domingo had been made during the previous Johnson administration, but despite the pressure of businessmen who were deeply interested in exploiting the resources of the island, it had ended in failure. Grant, an advocate of national expansion, sent General Orville E. Babcock, military secretary to the Chief Executive, to Santo Domingo on a warship with definite instructions from Secretary Fish to resume negotiations for annexation. Babcock was connected with American businessmen who held speculative concessions in Santo Domingo, the value of which would be greatly enhanced by annexation. He met with President Buenaventura Báez according to instructions, and, on September 4, 1869, signed an agreement providing for a treaty of annexation between the United States and the Dominican Republic.

Now Grant could go ahead with his scheme to annex Santo Domingo while letting Spain dominate Cuba until the United States was ready to take over that island too. As for the Cuban people fighting against great odds for freedom and independence, the comment of the Charleston *Courier* was appropriate: "Cuba can now expect but little more aid from the United States. The advocates of independence within her limits must, therefore, depend upon their own energies."[21]

---

* The Cuban *Junta* sent a special representative to Rawlins' burial in the Congressional Cemetery. On February 13, 1931, the centenary of Rawlins' birth was celebrated in Cuba (it was practically ignored in the United States), and he was referred to as one of the staunchest friends Cuba had ever had. In 1947, the National Congress of Cuban Historians called Rawlins "the best friend of Cuba among the North American governing officials of all times." (Declaration of National Congress of Cuban Historians on Relations Between Cuba and the United States, 1947," reprinted in Antonio Núñez Jiménez, *La Liberación de las Islas*, La Habana, 1959, pp. 466–467.)

chapter 18

THE UNITED STATES AND THE INDEPENDENCE OF CUBA, 1869-1870

With Rawlins dead, and with Grant's attention riveted on pushing the annexation of the Dominican Republic through the Senate, the prospects for the continued success of Fish's Cuban policy appeared bright. But the pressure for a declaration of belligerency continued to mount, for American public opinion was more than ever in favor of the Cubans. The reports of further Spanish atrocities in Cuba, and the fact that Spain was constructing 30 gunboats in the United States while the federal authorities continued to seize expeditions to land men and arms for the Cuban patriots, accentuated the pressure for a declaration of belligerency. At the request of Peru, the government of the United States had refused to let the ships leave the yards in which they were being built. Peru was then nominally at war with Spain and, as we have seen, sympathized with the Cubans. Through her Minister in Washington, she protested against the release of the gunboats, pointing out that even if these warships were not used against Peru, they would release other Spanish vessels for use. Fish had eagerly acceded to the request, seeing in it another argument for delaying recognition of belligerency. He pointed out to Grant that Spanish anger would lead Madrid to act in a way that would give a stronger basis for recognition in the future.

But this did not last long. In December, 1869, orders were given for the release of the gunboats, and they left New York Bay to supplement the Spanish fleet blockading Cuba. The surest sign of the change in Grant's attitude toward the Cubans can be seen in his reaction to the release of the gunboats. Although he put up a mild protest, Fish noted in his *Diary* that the President did not believe a state of war existed any longer in Cuba, and while he did not think that Spain would gain control of the island, he had lost all confidence in the rebels—"the Cubans are inefficient and have done little for themselves—come here in large numbers and make trouble for us."[1] This in December, 1869, when Cubans were fighting and dying, waging one of the bitterest guerrilla wars in history!

The section dealing with foreign affairs in the President's first annual message to Congress, December, 1869, written by Fish, reflected the same cold-blooded views. There was an expression of sympathy "with all people struggling for liberty and self-government," but that was as far as Grant was prepared to go. The contest in Cuba had at "no time assumed the conditions which amount to a war in the sense of international law, or which would show the existence of a *de facto* political organization of the insurgents sufficient to justify a recognition of belligerency."[2]

The President's message aroused widespread resentment. The government of the United States had lavished special tokens of sympathy and friendship on Spain. But when it came to Cuba, it spoke only in generalities. How much longer, asked the friends of Cuba, would the American people allow their good name to be dragged through the prisons of Spain and the blood and misery of Cuba?

In spite of Grant's message, the agitation for recognition of belligerency continued. In the first week of January, 1870, López Roberts, the Spanish Minister in Washington, was so disturbed about this mounting demand for recognition of belligerency that he urged Madrid to employ the strategy of declaring the rebellion virtually at an end. On January 6, 1870, Caballero de Rodas, in Havana, following Roberts' instructions, announced in the *Gaceta Oficial* that the rebellion was extinguished, and that civil tribunals were again functioning. Roberts replied that the ruse was "completely satisfactory, the insertion of the announcement [in American papers] having produced a very good impression on public opinion here."[3]

Roberts claimed too much for the Spanish strategy. Actually, few Americans took seriously Spanish announcements that the rebellion had been crushed, for they were soon made ridiculous by rebel victories. What lent more credence to such a report in January,

1870, was the fact that the government of the United States participated in the propaganda campaign.

To still the clamor for recognition of Cuban belligerency, Fish resorted to an especially cynical tactic. He arranged with T. B. Connery, Washington correspondent of the New York *Herald*, to publish an article claiming that the Cuban revolution was practically dead, and that therefore the movement for recognition of Cuban belligerency was a waste of time and energy. On January 7, 1870, the *Herald* carried the article under the headlines:

DISCOURAGING REPORTS FROM CUBA
MISMANAGEMENT OF THE CUBAN JUNTA IN NEW YORK
CAUSE OF THE FAILURE OF THE REVOLUTION

Connery wrote that official reports and private letters shown him by a "high official"—Fish—proved that "the revolution of the patriots is on its last legs. Their forces are reduced to a mere handful of armed and unarmed men." The Cuban generals were proposing surrender. "This last fact I am assured is beyond question." The Cuban *Junta*, riddled with dissension, was falling apart. The failure of the Cuban revolution, according to the State Department, was due primarily to the inefficiency and blundering of the *Junta*. Connery reported that Fish had told Lemus at the outbreak of the war that Cuba could buy arms from the government of the United States, but could not organize expeditions from U.S. territory. Instead of taking this advice, the *Junta* had squandered its resources in organizing armed expeditions. This forced Fish, against his will, to halt the expeditions, and had turned the administration from friendship for Cuba to hostility. Both the President and Fish had been ready, indeed "anxious," to issue a proclamation in favor of the Cubans, but the "high official" explained that "the reckless management of the *Junta* deprived them of the opportunity of doing so." Indeed, a proclamation was actually drawn up and ready to be issued, "but disaster after disaster [for the Cubans] followed, and the President was reluctantly compelled to withhold his signature to the proclamation." Now it was too late to consider recognition of belligerency. The Cuban revolution was over. True, Spain had lost a large part of her army in Cuba, but this could be explained by the fact that "cholera, yellow fever and general sickness did more to kill off the Spaniards than the Cuban bullets and sabres."

Commenting editorially on Connery's article, the *Herald* announced that it was time to drop the demand for recognition of Cuban belligerency. "There is no longer any rebellion in Cuba, and the revolution has turned out to be a lamentable failure. . . . To grant belligerent rights at this stage would make the American people the laughing stock of the nations." The only thing left to do was to annex Cuba. "In the bosom of the great Republic, they [the Cubans] will be free, prosperous and happy."

Since a number of newspapers reprinted Connery's dispatch and supported the *Herald's* editorial conclusion, it is clear that Fish had hit upon an effective strategy to hold back recognition of belligerency. Nevertheless, the article did not go unanswered. The Cuban *Junta* vigorously denied that there was any dissension in its ranks. As for the revolution being on its last legs, all reports from Cuba and in the Madrid press proved that the contrary was the case, and that rebel military operations were growing more effective. The argument that the *Junta* could have purchased arms from the government of the United States, and, instead, wasted its resources on fruitless expeditions, simply failed to take into account that at no time were the *Junta's* efforts to obtain arms favorably received in Washington. On the contrary, *Junta* representatives were coldly rebuffed whenever they raised the question of making such purchases. The Cuban representatives were therefore compelled to act without the approval of the federal government, or else watch their fellow countrymen fighting in Cuba continually handicapped by lack of arms. That many expeditions failed to leave the United States was more a proof of the administration's appeasement of Spain than of an incorrect policy pursued by the *Junta*. Finally, the contention that a proclamation recognizing the belligerency of Cuba was about to be issued, but had been withdrawn because of disasters that befell the Cuban cause, was a feeble excuse that had no basis in fact. "Our memory does not record a single disaster as having happened in the whole of that month [September, 1869], neither great nor small."[4]

The *Junta* could have added that it was the height of cynicism for Fish to plant a story picturing himself as a champion of the recognition of Cuban belligerency who was prevented from fulfilling his desire to announce such recognition by unfortunate developments in Cuba. For, as we have seen, Fish deliberately refused to issue the proclamation when ordered to do so by President Grant, and used every device at his command to prevent its issuance. The story of the Cuban collapse was only the latest of Fish's devices to gain his objective at the expense of the Cuban patriots. What made his action in this instance particularly vicious was that Fish was then in possession of a dispatch from Consul Phillips in Santiago, dated January 3, 1870, which stated:

> The insurrection continues in full force, and frequent encounters take place, as is seen by the frequent arrivals of wounded Spanish soldiers. The Cubans being better armed and disciplined than formerly, in many cases take the offensive, and, having their ranks increased by desertion from the Spanish army are becoming bold and fight well. . . . I am inclined to believe . . . the insurrection will continue for a long time, as it is impossible for any force that Spain can send to exterminate the rebel force, owing to the climate and topography of the country.[5]

Small wonder that the New York *Tribune*, denouncing Connery's article, concluded on January 8, 1870, "the Cuban patriots have to fight 'hard lying' here [in the United States] as well as the Spaniards."

Fish's "shrewd stroke"—the phrase is that of Allan Nevins, his biographer[6]—had its effect. But it did not stem the drive for recognition of Cuban belligerency. On February 11, 1870, John Sherman introduced a resolution in the U.S. Senate for recognition of belligerency. On the 18th, Representative Banks introduced a resolution of a similar nature in the House. At the same time, meetings were held throughout the country to rally support for passage of the resolutions, and petitions urging such action flooded Congress. Editorials kept hammering away at the theme that it was up to Congress, representing the will of the American people, to act. "Speak at last!" Horace Greeley's New York *Tribune* pleaded on February 23, 1870. "Speak out, we entreat the representatives of the people, and speak at once! . . . Something must be done for Cuba—the more we can honestly do the better. Speak at last!"

The judicial murder of the Cuban patriot, Domingo Goicuría, on

May 6, 1870, still further increased American hostility to Spain. Goicuría had returned to Cuba from the United States and was in hiding in Havana, when he was betrayed to the Spanish officials. He was immediately condemned to death, and after being carried through the streets of Havana in a hideous parade, was garroted near the Príncipe Castle. The whole proceedings took only a few hours.

By the end of May, the agitation for adoption of the joint resolution recognizing Cuban belligerency had become so intense that Fish felt only one type of action could prevent its passage—a special message by the President to Congress emphatically opposing recognition, around which the supporters of the administration might be rallied. When Fish first read the draft of the message he had drawn up, Grant approved every word of it, with the exception of a small paragraph. The next day, however, he objected to having it sent as a message, preferring that it be submitted as a report from the State Department. The reason he gave for desiring this procedure was a trivial one—that the style was so different from his that it would be recognized at once that he had not written the message. But a few days later, Grant revealed the real reason: he feared that the message proposed by Fish would have an unfavorable effect upon some Senators who were supporting the treaty to annex Santo Domingo, but who, being pro-Cuban, might oppose him on Santo Domingo if he came out strongly against recognition of Cuban belligerency. But Fish removed this obstacle by pointing out that the "noisy agitators" who favored recognition of Cuban belligerency opposed the Dominican annexation. He was correct. The friends of the Cuban rebels in Congress for the most part opposed Dominican annexation because they realized it diverted attention from Cuba and jeopardized the future of the Cuban Republic, since it would strengthen the hands of the annexationists. Grant then consented to having copies made of Fish's proposed message, and arranged for it to be sent to Congress.[7]

On June 14, the President's special message was received by Congress. As far as he could see, Grant pointed out, nothing had changed since his annual message of the preceding December to justify recognition of Cuban belligerency. The rebels, avoiding major battles, continued to limit their operations to attacking the rear-guard of the Spanish troops. Certain Americans who were holders of bonds of the Cuban Republic wanted to compromise their country. The war was still being carried on "with a lamentable disregard of human life and of the rules and practices which modern civilization has prescribed. . . . Each [side] commit [*sic*] the same atrocities and outrage alike the established rules of war." There was no *de facto* government in Cuba sufficiently in power to justify a declaration of belligerency, a question which "is one of fact, not to be decided by sympathies for or prejudices against either party." Furthermore, such a declaration might disrupt American trade. In the beginning of the war, the Spanish government had initiated a system of exile, councils of war, executions of suspected persons, summary expropriation of their possessions and other arbitrary measures by executive decrees. There thus arose the question of the rights of American citizens in Cuba. These problems had forced the American government to remonstrate with the Spanish government. But the situation had improved. Spain had agreed to the establishment of a Joint Commission to settle American claims.[8]

The message infuriated the pro-Cuban forces in Congress. Representative Cox called it "the most impudent message ever sent to Congress," while Representative Swann labelled it "an insult to its members and to the country." Banks charged that a person in the pay of Spain had prepared the message.

The New York *Sun* announced furiously on June 15, that the "Government at Washington had been sold to Spain. . . . When General Grant came fresh from the Western prairies . . . his heart was full of patriotism and his sympathies were warm for the struggling Cubans. But in the corrupt and enervating influences of Washington and under the demoralizing teachings of Hamilton Fish he has become another man—almost no man at all." The *Sun* suggested that Fish was qualified to serve as the King of Spain for whom General Prim was looking.

On June 16, 1870, Spain won its most decisive victory in the war against Cuba up to this date. On that day, in the House of Representatives, as a result of Grant's message, the resolution for granting belligerent rights to the Cubans was defeated by a vote of 100 to 70. The House then passed a resolution authorizing the President "to remonstrate against the barbarous manner in which the war in Cuba had been conducted"—presumably by both the

Spaniards and the insurgents. The Senate soon stifled even this mild resolution. "The event has justified the message," declared the London *Times* on July 1, 1870, "for now Congress is estopped from further movements to help Cuba." Had the resolution carried, Fish would have resigned, and this would have been disastrous for Spain.

Grant liked the vote "very much." A few weeks later, in attempting to reassure Fish of his confidence in him, Grant thanked his Secretary of State for having "almost forced me" into "signing the late Cuban message, and I now see how right it was."[9]

Spain and the Spanish Party in Cuba shared Grant's enthusiasm for the vote. Not only did it mean that the Cuban rebels would have to continue fighting with hardly enough arms to go around, but it removed the pressure for action to put an end to the system of slavery in Cuba.

We have spoken above of the various maneuvers resorted to by the opponents of recognition of Cuban belligerency to prevent a proclamation of recognition by the government of the United States. There was the argument that no action should be taken along these lines lest it disrupt the negotiations to persuade Spain to grant the Cubans independence as part of the sale of the island. This, of course, proved to be an illusion. Then there was the argument that the Cuban revolution was on its "last legs," and nothing would be accomplished by a declaration of belligerency. This was quickly proved false. Still there was another argument which was resorted to from the outbreak of the war by the foes of recognition of Cuban belligerency. This was the contention that Spain was going to institute colonial reforms in Cuba, the most important of which would be the abolition of slavery.

It is difficult to say whether the men who advanced this argument really believed that Spain would ever abide by reform promises made to Cuba. But what is definite is that they knew that one of the strongest reasons for American sympathy for the Cuban rebels was that they had declared for the abolition of slavery and were presumably fighting for that objective among others, and that as the war continued, the revolutionary government was forced, by pressure from popular forces, to live up to its abolitionist principles. Consequently, men like Fish kept warning the Spaniards that unless they promised to abolish slavery and did something to fulfill the promise, it would become more difficult, if not impossible, to prevent the recognition of Cuban belligerency.

Those in the Spanish government who appreciated the truth of this warning made promises to abolish slavery. For a time such promises were enough to help forestall any action in favor of Cuban belligerency by the Grant administration. But soon promises were not enough, especially since the Cuban Republic was moving more decidedly in an abolitionist direction. On December 23, 1869, Fish warned López Roberts that it was "important to have action and results, and not mere promises."[10] Otherwise it would not be possible to hold the line against the recognition of Cuban belligerency.

Faced with the fact that she was having increasing difficulty in suppressing the rebellion in Cuba, and with an ever-rising sentiment in the United States for recognition of Cuban belligerency, Spain was forced to pursue a course that would conciliate the American government for the time being. This meant doing something about abolition. On May 7, 1870, the new Colonial Minister, Segismundo Moret y Prendergast, vice-president of the Spanish Abolitionist Society, wrote to the Captain General of Cuba: "Not another day must pass without doing something about this. France and England will not help us while we are slaveholders, and this one word [slavery] gives North America the right to hold a suspended threat over our heads." Three weeks later, on May 28, 1870, Moret presented to the Cortes his "Preparatory Law for the Abolition of Slavery in the Spanish Antilles." His statement to the Cortes on why the law was needed was a remarkable tribute to the Cuban independence fighters:

> The Government has chosen this moment to present the law because it was the last opportunity. Think, *Señores*, that our enemies [the Cuban rebels], familiar with North American customs and language, in contact with their statesmen, have been able from the first moment to give to the insurrection a special character, presenting it as the flag of liberty against the flag of tyranny, as the principle of colonial autonomy against the principle of oppression by the Metropolis, as the principle of independence against the pretensions of Europe.

The time had passed, Moret warned, for the "promises and descriptions of other epochs." It was necessary to say to the world and particularly to the United States: "We give you definite proof; here is the project . . . slavery is dead, and is finished forever in Spanish dominions."[11]

After all this rhetoric, one might conclude that the Moret Law, approved by the Cortes and published in Madrid on July 4, 1870, ended slavery in Cuba. It did nothing of the sort. The law provided that all children of slave mothers born after its passage should be free, but the new-born were to be subjected to a state of patronage (*patronato*) until the age of 18. The master, now called a *patrón*, was obligated to care for the young Negroes (*patrocinados*), but he also had the privilege of utilizing their labor without pay until they had reached the age of 18. From then on the Negro youth was entitled to "half the wages of a free man." The law also provided that all slaves born between September 18, 1868, and the publication of the law might free themselves upon payment of $50. But to gain this sum, they would have to spend some of the best years of their lives in servitude.

The only slaves declared free immediately under the Moret Law were those aged 60 years or more. But as the Spanish Abolitionist Society pointed out in its protests against the law, this was hardly a sacrifice on the part of the owners, since few slaves in Cuba reached the age of 60 years, and those who did were scarcely useful any longer. Actually, the aged slaves who had produced wealth for their masters for over half a century and might be supposed to have earned the right to support in their few remaining years, were to be turned adrift. If these old freedmen (*libertos*) chose to remain in the houses of their masters, they were obliged to work "according to their capabilities" on the plantation or in the house.

The new law in no way altered the essential nature of slavery, that is, of forced labor with threat of physical punishment for those who were recalcitrant. Although the use of the whip was temporarily withheld, pending the publication of the regulations for putting the law into effect, the principle of corporal punishment was still preserved. Stocks, irons, and imprisonment remained in full force.

Fish was correct when he declared that the Moret Law was not an honest emancipation measure: "It may rather be called a project for relieving the slaveowners from the necessity of supporting infants and aged slaves, who can only be a burden, and of prolonging the institution as to able-bodied slaves."[12] This correct evaluation did not, however, move Fish to change his attitude toward Spain.

The debate in the Cortes on the Moret Law made clear that the limited character of the measure was largely due to the fact that the conservative group did not take seriously the danger of recognition of Cuban belligerency by the United States. There was justification for this feeling. It is true that Fish instructed Sickles on June 20, 1870, while the bill was still in debate, to state in a "friendly but decided manner," the American government's disappointment with the bill. But Fish said nothing about the effect of the proposed law on the administration's policy in relation to recognition of Cuban belligerency, and his failure to do so, as well as Grant's special message opposing recognition, were pointed to in the Cortes as proof that that body's unwillingness to pass an emancipation act that went beyond the Moret Law would in no way affect relations with the United States on the one issue that was crucial.[13]

After the Moret Law was passed, there was a widespread demand that Washington inform Spain in no uncertain terms that if the deficiencies of the law were not immediately remedied and slavery abolished in Cuba, the belligerency of the rebels would be recognized. Spanish agents in the United States were alarmed by this development, especially since Charles Sumner, Chairman of the Senate Committee on Foreign Relations, who until now had opposed recognition of Cuban belligerency, had criticized Grant for accepting the Moret Law, and was demanding such recognition if Spain failed to pass a truly effective abolition measure. But in Spain there was not the same sense of alarm. The Spanish government relied upon Fish and Grant to stand firm against the demand for recognition of belligerency. As Moret wrote to Captain General Caballero in Cuba on August 13, 1870: "I hope that public opinion in the United States which today is not very favorable to the [Moret] law will be rectified shortly in the same manner as that of their Government." He went on to praise Fish and Grant for holding the line against recognition in the face of the public clamor for such action. About the same time, Antonio Gallenga, visiting Cuba to write a book on the insurrection, noted that "the Cuban slaveowners feel confident" that "the policy of the Cabinet at Washington" would not change regardless of the failure to carry through any meaningful action in the direction of abolition.[14]

As long as the Spanish government felt confident that it had the sympathy of Fish and Grant, it would do nothing to alienate the sympathies of the Volunteers and the wealthy loyalist class in Cuba. And as long as the Cuban slaveowners felt confident that they had nothing really to fear from Washington, they would, through their agents, the Volunteers, force Spain to toe the line. Both in Spain and Cuba the sympathy of the American people for the rebels was discounted. It was the administration and not the people who decided whether or not to declare a state of belligerency in favor of the rebels. The Grant administration had made it clear early in the war that it would not recognize belligerency, and Spain and the loyalist elements in Cuba felt confident that that position would remain in force.

Many of the Cuban revolutionists still had confidence that the American people, sympathizing with the struggle for Cuban independence, would force their government to render it assistance. But, with or without American recognition and assistance, they were determined to fight on.

chapter 19

THE TEN YEARS' WAR:
THE MIDDLE PHASE, 1871-1875

On December 27, 1870, General Prim was mortally wounded in Madrid by an assassin. He died three days later. If Prim had lived, it has been argued, the Cuban problem would have been solved without further bloodshed. Had he not sent an agent to the New York *Junta* with an offer of autonomy, and other agents with the offer of independence for Cuba, provided that the Cubans indemnified Spain by a payment of $200,000,000, guaranteed by the United States? A month before his violent end, he sent Juan Clemente Zenea, Cuban poet and rebel, as intermediary to Cuba to negotiate with insurgent leaders. Zenea carried a safe-conduct from López Roberts, Spanish Minister in Washington. Perhaps, it is argued, the government of Amadeo—the young Prince of Savoy, Italy, whom Prim had selected as the constitutional monarch of Spain—with Prim directing it, would have been able to maneuver the sale of Cuba through the Cortes.

But this speculation ignores the all-important and ever-present fact that the prosperous slave interests in the Western province of Cuba, the privileged mercantile groups, the colonial bureaucracy, and the military officials were all fattening on the war, and they were not prepared to yield an inch to bring it to an end. During the many political changes in Spain that followed Prim's death, these groups continued to dominate the policy toward Cuba.

The ruling oligarchy in Cuba celebrated Prim's death by showing their contempt for his endeavor to negotiate a settlement with the rebels. The day he died, Valmaseda threw Zenea into prison, and several months later, to the delight of the Volunteers, he had the poet shot.

Throughout the better part of 1871, the Spanish government, with Don Amadeo seated shakily on the throne, tried to give the impression that it exercised full authority in Cuba. But it kept silent as the Spanish regulars and the Volunteers continued to commit atrocities and violate the lives and property of unfortunate Cubans. Then on November 27, 1871, news came from Cuba which showed that the Volunteers still controlled policy in the island. On that day, a party of medical students at the University of Havana entered a cemetery. Soon reports reached the Volunteers that the students had "profaned" the grave of Colonel Gonzalo Castañón, editor and Volunteer hero who had been assassinated, presumably by rebels. Without bothering to establish proof of the allegation, the Volunteers demanded that vengeance be taken on the students.

A mob, led by the Volunteers, dragged the students to the palace of Captain General Crespo, who was ruling temporarily in Valmaseda's absence. Crespo came forth upon the balcony to face the mob which was screaming for blood. Thoroughly frightened, the Captain General did not dare disperse the mob. A Council of War was called. After an all-night session, eight students were condemned to death, including one boy who had been in Matanzas during the episode at the cemetery. They were shot at four o'clock the same morning. Some thirty others were sentenced to the chain gangs from four to six years.

On the first anniversary of the execution of the students, the principal street corners of Madrid were plastered with printed posters reminding the passers-by of the "terrible day on which eight sons were stolen from the earth and a people wept at the grave of eight martyrs." The broadside, entitled *El 27 de Noviembre de 1871*, was signed by two of the surviving students who were then in Madrid, but it was from the pen of José Martí, already a leader among the Cuban exiles in Spain. Typically, Martí emphasized that "there is a limit to weeping over the graves," and he called upon all Cubans to swear "an oath of infinite love of country . . . over their bodies."[1]

After he arrived in Spain in 1871, Martí had looked forward to the day when Spain would become a Republic. Then, perhaps, Cuba might live harmoniously and peacefully with Spain. But the news of the killing of the medical students wrought a complete change in Martí's outlook. The bloody incident destroyed forever all desire on his part for anything less than the complete independence of Cuba, and he made a vow to devote his life to this cause.

Still, Martí believed that a Spanish Republic might result in the withdrawal of the army from Cuba and the granting of independence to the island. In February, 1873, occurred the event Martí and all other Cuban exiles had been waiting for. Early in the year an artillery corps of Vitoria mutinied. When the Cortes dissolved the corps, Amadeo abdicated. The Cortes met on February 11 in joint session, ushered the king out of Spain, and proclaimed the Republic immediately thereafter.

Martí was in the press box at the Cortes on that historic February 11. But his joy was diminished when he heard a Republican deputy, in hailing the new-born Republic, salute the unity of Spain and Spanish Cuba. Four days later, Martí sent an extensive essay, entitled "*Cuba y la Primera República Española*" (Cuba and the First Spanish Republic), to Don Estanislao Figueras, the head of the new movement. How, he asked, "can Spain deny Cuba the right to be free, which is the same right she used to achieve her own freedom? How can she deny this right to Cuba without denying it for herself? How can Spain settle the fate of a people by imposing on them a way of life in which their complete, free and obvious wish does not enter at all? . . . A Republic that did these things would be a Republic of ignominy."[2]

Martí's essay was published in pamphlet form. But the Republic paid no attention to it whatsoever. Before they assumed power, the Republicans had advanced the position that autonomy under a future Spanish federal republic was the solution for Cuba. The Cortes declared the form of the republic to be federal. But that was as far as the Republicans went in fulfilling their pledge. By March, 1873, it was clear that the new Republican regime in Madrid was as intent as the old monarchical one upon exterminating the Cuban patriots. Preoccupied with internal order and security, the Republic gave the reactionaries in Cuba a freer hand than they had ever enjoyed. Six years of military failure in Cuba had taught the Spanish Republicans nothing. The position remained the same: there would be no change in a Cuban policy "while there is one single rebel in there with a gun in his hand."[3] This emphatic repetition of the status quo formula for Cuba was a feature of the brief life of the first Spanish Republic.

The one important action of the Republic in the area of colonial reform was the adoption of a law by the Cortes in March, 1873, abolishing slavery in Puerto Rico. While this was a great victory for the Puerto Rican slaves and abolitionists, it is important to bear in mind that unlike Cuba, slavery had never been deeply rooted in Puerto Rico.

After the Republic had succumbed in January, 1874, and a year later, when Cánovas, the conservative statesman, re-established the monarchy under Alfonso XII, it was clear as never before that the Cuban question would only be settled by force of arms. Even the most optimistic of the Cubans living in Madrid understood now what Martí had been saying for months: that nothing could be expected from Spain, and that Cuba's future would be decided only by the Liberating Army.

While Spain passed from a monarchy to a republic and back again to a monarchy, the fighting in Cuba had never ceased. The rebel guerrillas offered permanent resistance, and even as the pro-Spanish press loyally boasted of how the Spanish forces were riding roughshod over the rebellion, it revealed that the insurrection was still alive. In a letter to Bancroft Davis, March 7, 1871, Sickles wrote of the new Captain General: "Valmaseda out-telegraphs de Rodas. The latter put down the insurrection every month *morally*, the former demolishes it every night *materially*. Yet it still lives and will not die."[4]

Nevertheless, the rebels had been pushed back steadily from the Western districts, and by the fall of 1871, the rebels were offering victorious action only in the province of Oriente. In his *Diary*, Gómez frankly portrayed the bleak picture that confronted the rebels:

> The state of the Revolution [in October, 1871] was hardly encouraging, since the only portion which sustained itself with apparent advantage over the enemy was the one I commanded . . . [especially] the occupation of the rich territory of Guantánamo. . . . Everything else held out only the prospects of ruin and decadence for the Republic. Bayamo was lost and disorganized; the Venezuelan General

Manuel Garrido who commanded it had been disgraced; Camagüey was sustained only by a spearhead of valiant men led by the audacious and noble Agramonte and with the rest [of the province] in the power of the Spaniards; Las Villas was totally abandoned with the remnants of the army drifting from Camagüey to Oriente. That was the state of things in those memorable and bitter days.[5]

Only one policy, Gómez insisted at a meeting with President Céspedes at this time, could remedy this dangerous situation. This was to invade the Western provinces. Fortunately for Spain, up to this point in the war, Matanzas, Havana and Pinar del Río provinces, the richest part of Cuba, had never been invaded. Indeed, commerce there had actually increased during the revolt, and their sugar production had maintained a fairly constant level.

The principle strategy of the rebellion, as we have seen, was to make the revolution a tremendous and unbearable economic burden for Spain. But as long as fighting and destruction were confined to Oriente, this strategy could not be truly effective. The strategy had to be applied to the whole of the island or else the rebellion would remain restricted in its effects and gradually lose its impetus. It was essential, Gómez argued, to invade the Western provinces, paralyze production and create a chaotic situation in the areas. The advancing Liberating Army, carrying the banner of emancipation, could strike the economic life of the Occident at its most vital point. Once the slaves fled in large numbers to join the revolutionary movement, production would be completely disrupted. Spain would be deprived of the means and resources to wage war; the wealthy oligarchy that ruled Cuba and dictated policies to Spain would be compelled to call for abandonment of the war effort. On the other hand, to continue to leave slavery and economic production in the Western provinces untouched was to fight the Spanish with one hand tied behind one's back.

> While liberty is not given to the thousands of the slaves who are groaning today in the jurisdiction of Occidente, the most populated and richest of the island; while exportation by the enemy of the production of the great sugar plantations established there is not impeded . . . the revolution is destined to last even much longer, Cuban resources will be drained, and lakes of blood will run unfruitfully in the fields of the island.[6]

Gómez's famous plan for an invasion of the West was much like that used by the Union Army in the American Civil War, once the Lincoln administration realized that the emancipation of the slaves (and the consequent disruption of the Confederate economy) was the key to Union victory. As long as the slaves continued to work for the Confederacy, the Union forces were seriously handicapped. Not until the Emancipation Proclamation was carried into the South by the Union Army, the slaves induced to run away from the plantations, and the productive forces of the Confederacy disrupted, did the Union cause begin to make rapid headway.

General Emilio Cavada of the Liberating Army, who had fought with the Union forces in the Civil War, urged the revolutionary government to apply the lessons of that conflict. He cited the example of General Benjamin F. Butler of the Union army who had invaded the South: in order to destroy the resources of the Confederacy, he had encouraged the slaves to flee from Confederate owners to the Union lines. Cavada called repeatedly for an invasion of the West and the liberation of the slaves in that area by the revolutionary army.

Cavada's proposal met with fierce opposition from the conservative representatives of the *hacendado* class in the revolutionary government, and was rejected. Gómez's plan for the invasion of the Occidental district fared no better. Céspedes agreed that there was an urgent need to destroy the industrial capacity of the great sugar-producing district. But he refused to countenance Gómez's plan, arguing that it was a hopeless venture and that the rebel army must wait for more supplies. The Liberating Army, he pointed out, had hardly 7,000 men in the two provinces of Oriente and Camagüey. Moreover, the rebel army had no artillery and suffered a constant lack of ammunition. To this Gómez replied that the army in Oriente had proved the ability of the rebels to win victories against overwhelmingly superior forces, and that it could duplicate this feat in the West. But Céspedes remained adamant.

A month after the discussion with Gómez, Céspedes did approve of sending a military expedition to the rich province of Las Villas which, if successful, would open the door to a broader invasion of the West. But there was such great opposition to the proposal by the opponents of a western invasion that the plan was dropped, a decision which brought relief to the conservative forces in the revolutionary government, to the *hacendados* for whom they spoke, and to the wealthy émigrés who were opposed to military action against the plantations they had left behind in Cuba.

Gómez returned to the zone of Guantánamo where fighting raged throughout the rest of 1871 and into 1872. Maceo, who led the Cuban forces under the orders of Gómez, won tribute after tribute for his courage and success. Gómez praised his "valor, skill and activity." Martínez Campos, the Spanish general, after failing to defeat Maceo with 1,000 men, declared: "It is impossible to end the war by means of arms." On April 16, 1872, a month after Maceo had been promoted to the rank of full colonel, President Céspedes wrote to the Negro commander:

> A few days ago I received the news that the operations of the enemy in Guantánamo had been completely paralyzed. This fact which can be due to various causes, is primarily due to the brilliant operations and heroic efforts of the Cubans who fight against the Spaniards in that district. Those have been operations and efforts which have obtained the sort of glory that is justly associated with your name and which is confessed and recognized by all.[7]

Although the Cuban victories in Guantánamo were important, Gómez knew that it was necessary to strike out to the West if the revolution was to make real headway. Realizing that he could not gain approval of his larger plan to invade the entire Occident, Gómez proposed that the government endorse a plan whereby the main forces of the Liberating Army would concentrate at Holguín, and then continue operations until a junction was effected with the forces of Agramonte in Camagüey province which had been virtually isolated for months.

At a meeting which lasted from May 26 to June 7, 1872, Gómez succeeded in persuading the government to accept his plan. But before it could be put into operation, Gómez was ordered to divert men from the expedition to protect the members of the government. When Gómez refused to obey the command, Céspedes removed him as commander of the province of Oriente for disobedience. Once again Gómez's plan was abandoned.

On June 20, General Calixto García, who had been second in

command in Oriente, took over Gómez's position as commander of the province. Maceo, named Brigadier General on June 8, in recognition of his valuable service to the Republic, took charge of the Second Division of the First Corps of the Liberating Army. On July 1, the whole army of Oriente united under Calixto García to wage offensive warfare. During the next four months, the rebels won victory after victory in the district of Guantánamo, in many of which Maceo with his unit played a leading role. This period of unbroken success for the Cubans was initiated in the battle of Rejondón de Báguanos where the rebels were led by General Manuel de J. Calvar. Maceo received the principal credit for obtaining a brilliant victory over more than 400 Spanish soldiers conducting a convoy from Holguín to Baraguá. "First when it seemed that the Spanish battalion might break through the Cuban ambush," wrote Fernando Figueredo, a witness of the battle, "there was heard at the vanguard a discharge which made the earth tremble. It was Maceo who . . . had flown to our aid, and majestically arranging an ambush received the Spaniards. . . . The enemy was completely demoralized. There was no longer any hope of resistance."[8]

The Cubans seized 146 rifles, 14,000 cartridges, many bags of clothes, and the archives of the battalion. This victory over a numerically superior enemy had a stimulating effect on the rebel soldiers. "The Army of Oriente," Fernando Figueredo noted, "was inspired by the victory and marched from that moment from one triumph to another."[9]

The campaign in Oriente was climaxed by the capture of Holguín by the rebels on a plan originally conceived by Gómez. Maceo, assisting General García, won new fame in the victory. The Spaniards repeatedly condemned the Negro commander to death as a bandit, but they could do nothing to carry their decrees into effect.

The resignation of Captain General Valmaseda late in 1872 was a direct result of the success of the Cuban campaign. Unfortunately, at this very promising point in the war, internal dissensions in the leadership of the government, which had been brewing all along, reached a climax. The successful march of military operations had to be suspended temporarily while the conflict within the government was resolved.

The adoption of the Constitution at Guáimaro had stemmed the rising opposition to Céspedes' absolutist rule. But it soon made itself felt again. Harassed continually by the Spanish columns, the members of the House of Representatives of the Cuban Republic could rarely meet, and by 1873 many of them had been killed or had died. In this situation, Céspedes had assumed all civil powers, assigning a secondary role to members of his Cabinet. In a manifesto of October 24, 1873, he asked for even more authority.

At the beginning of the war, Céspedes had the support of the conservatives, who regarded him as an effective spokesman of the wealthy propertied classes and as a defender of their interests. The President's early stand against immediate abolition of slavery and the policy of stirring up slave revolts also won him the support of the conservative elements. But as Céspedes began to see the necessity of a forthright abolitionist position and "the policy of the incendiary torch," he lost the support of the conservatives. However, his action in assuming complete authority and interfering in military matters, especially his removal of Gómez from command, kept the revolutionists who approved of his policy on slavery from rallying to his support. In short, Céspedes was isolated in the revolutionary movement. He lost the support of the conservatives by his more radical policy towards slavery and the incendiary torch without, at the same time, winning a solid following among the popular forces. When to this is added personal jealousies—there was a wide feeling that Céspedes showed too much partiality to members of his family —and political opportunism, it is not difficult to understand why a political crisis arose.

Matters came to a head on October 27, 1873, when several members of the practically defunct House of Representatives called a meeting of the body at Bijagual without inviting President Céspedes. All the principal military chieftains of Guantánamo, Santiago de Cuba, Holguín, Jiguaní, Bayamo, and Las Tunas also attended the meeting. More than 2,000 soldiers accompanied their officers.

The main business of the assembly was the removal of Céspedes, and the isolation of the President became clear when none of the groups at Bijagual, conservative or revolutionary, came to his defense. Since Vice-President Francisco Vicente Aguilera was on a mission abroad, the President of the House of Representatives, Salvador Cisneros Betancourt, was proclaimed President of the Republic. A message was sent informing Céspedes of his removal.

With the main decision taken, those present swore allegiance to the Constitution. Cisneros then named his Cabinet: Francisco Maceo Osorio, Secretary of State; Antonio Hurtado del Valle, sub-Secretary; General Vicente García, Secretary of War and Treasury; Fernando Figueredo Socarrás, sub-Secretary of Dispatch, and Federico Betancourt, Secretary of the Council. The officers and their soldiers returned to their respective camps.

Now that there was a new government, General Gómez revived his campaign for an invasion of the West. He proposed that the invasion move into Las Villas and then carry the revolution to Havana itself. He pointed out once again that as long as the Occidental district kept on grinding its sugar, exploiting the slaves, and nourishing the Spanish treasury with the necessary funds for exterminating the revolution, the Cuban Republic, regardless of whether Céspedes or Cisneros was President, could not survive. The only hope for a definite victory lay in applying the torch to the mills and other centers of production in the Western provinces and liberating the work crews, depriving the *hacendados* of the resources with which to help Spain fight the rebellion. "Five hundred men . . . under the command of the then Brigadier General Antonio Maceo was the only force which I asked of the government," Gómez wrote in his *Diary*.[10]

The new administration received Gómez's appeal coldly, thereby demonstrating that the conservative spokesmen for the *hacendados* still exercised a great influence in determining revolutionary policy. The reason given was that the situation in Oriente was too dangerous to spare troops for an invasion of the West. In addition, President Cisneros had his attention fixed on the arrival of new filibustering expeditions of arms and men from the United States. One of them, that of the *Virginius*, was to meet a tragic end.

In January, 1874, García and Maceo obtained an important victory at Junurún-Melones against three Spanish battalions and a unit of guerrillas under the command of the famous Colonel Federico Esponda. The Spaniards were completely routed, leaving behind 150 dead, including five officers, and taking with them more than 200 wounded. With this victory, the situation in Oriente improved to a point where the government was unable any longer to postpone Gómez's long-delayed plan for a western invasion.

At the beginning of February, 1874, a meeting was held of all the highest ranking generals of the Liberating Army, the President, his Cabinet, and the House of Representatives. The gathering took place at San Diego de Buenaventura, situated in the southeastern corner of the province of Camagüey. Here Gómez delivered a lengthy presentation of his plan, demonstrating that the western invasion was not only necessary but feasible. Supported by all of the rebel generals, except Secretary of War Vicente García, Gómez succeeded in convincing the government to grant him permission to put his plan into effect. There was some opposition to Gómez's proposal to make Maceo second in command, on the ground that the Negro general was needed in Oriente. But Gómez insisted that Maceo was essential for the success of the invasion, and he had his way.

On February 4, 1874, Gómez formed a force of 500 soldiers from Oriente and Las Villas (300 infantry and 200 cavalry), and with the approval of the government, named Antonio Maceo general of the division, second in command only to himself. The long-awaited invasion of the West, the main source of wealth for Spain, was about to begin.

"The news," wrote a contemporary, "caused a kind of invigorating dizziness. Nothing else was thought about in Oriente. Everything appeared small, insignificant, when compared with the prospect of invading the fields of Occidente.... Nothing else was talked about except the invasion, and everyone wanted the march to begin right away."[11] Pieces of paper were passed from one Cuban patriot to another. On them were written the words of the hastily-prepared "The Hymn of Las Villas." Quickly put to music, it became one of the most popular songs of the entire war. Although it is impossible to convey the beauty of the Spanish verse in a literal translation, the following gives the spirit of the song:

> There are green valleys, brothers,
>   Where the golden sugar cane grows.
> There the greedy despots
>   Are enjoying our wealth.

> Do you not see the lucky tyrants
> > Who are sustained with the sweat
> Of the African's miseries?
> > A gross insult to their sorrows.
>
> Corrupt air of bacchanales
> > Is breathed alone by youth.
> Lubricious pleasures and immoral,
> > Rob them there of virtue.
>
> We must save the Cubans
> > From such a system of corruption.
> And it is a noble enterprise, brothers,
> > To bring redemption to these people.
>
> The generous peoples of Oriente
> > Call up the flower of their warriors,
> And with you march the valiant
> > Battling Camagüeyans.
>
> Raise up a hymn that rises to the sky
> > And which, plowing rapidly across the sea,
> Teaches the world that Cuba knows how
> > To overthrow its tyrants.
>
> And that in the breast of the Cubans
> > Heaven has placed all the vigor
> Of American torrents
> > And the volcanoes of Ecuador.
>
> Hurrah! to Las Villas! Because the voice
> > Of the people which weeps there calls to us
> On the shores of the Agabama
> > And on the banks of the Damují.[12]

On February 10, 1874, the Cuban invading army of 500 rebel soldiers defeated 2,000 artillery-equipped veteran Spanish troops, under General Manuel Portillo. The victory was largely due to the skilful maneuvers organized by General Gómez, but the tremendous efforts of the rebels were inspired by Maceo. Colonel Manuel Sanguily, a participant in the battle, thus described the action of the Negro General in a crucial moment:

The Spaniards had been driven to the right, and around four hundred had sheltered behind a parapet. . . . The Orientales reached it under a tremendous fire from their opponents. We do not know if the troops from Oriente hesitated or not, but it is certain that General Maceo, like a colossus, was seen seizing the soldiers nearest him by the collars and belts and propelling them against the Spanish positions like projectiles.[13]

Maceo did not stop fighting after the Spanish retreat. He attacked the rear guard furiously.

Another Cuban victory followed, on February 16, in the battle of Las Guásimas against overwhelmingly superior Spanish forces. Once again the victory was the result of the combination of Gómez's brilliant strategy and Maceo's skilful and courageous leadership in action. Maceo, given the responsibility of superior command by Gómez, marched with 200 cavalry and 50 infantry against the Spanish column of 2,000 men sent from the city of Camagüey with cavalry, infantry, and artillery. In all, the Spaniards poured 6,000 men and six pieces of artillery into the battle. But, battered constantly by Maceo and his soldiers, the Spaniards had to retreat. The Spanish suffered 1,037 dead and wounded and the Cubans 174. Maceo, once again wounded at the end of the victorious battle, was one of the Cuban casualties.

The Cuban victory, inspiring as it was to the rebel cause, had its drawbacks. So much ammunition and other war materials had been consumed in the five-day battle, to say nothing of the dead and wounded, that the invasion of the West had to be called off for the time being. Actually, the decision to fight such a large-scale battle was not in keeping with Gómez's basic strategy—namely, to rely on guerrilla attacks and invasions of the production units in the areas and to avoid major battles against superior Spanish forces. Although the Cubans might win such battles and would suffer much fewer losses than the Spaniards, they could hardly afford such victories with the small number of fighting men and limited resources on hand.

Gómez announced the postponement of the western invasion; yet he fully expected to obtain aid from the government in carrying through his plan later. But when in May and June, 1874, Gómez proposed to the government a revival of the project of invading the

West, he came up against a series of obstacles, some old and some new.

The invasion of the West had always been opposed by the conservative representatives of the *hacendado* class in the revolutionary government. They had repeatedly emphasized that the revolution, if it wanted to get the support of the *hacendados* of the Occident, had to protect their property—mills and slaves—from "the horrors of the insurrection." They further argued that "the policy of the incendiary torch" was bound to antagonize the émigrés who looked forward to the day when they could return to their plantations in Cuba. And, without their support, how could expeditions be organized from outside the island to bring much needed supplies to the rebel fighters?

The conservative pressure on the government intensified while Gómez and Maceo were leading their small army westward. But now another argument was added: the danger of Negro domination of Cuba. The conservatives had watched Maceo's emergence to a position of importance and leadership in the Liberating Army with growing concern. If, led by Maceo, the Liberating Army should move through the West, freeing the slaves as it went, would not the liberated Negro population seek to dominate Cuba and make Maceo, their champion, the foremost figure in the island? "Do we liberate ourselves only to share the fate of Haiti and Santo Domingo?"[14]

During the invasion of the West in February, 1874, the conservatives launched an all-out campaign of slander against Maceo, particularly among the troops of Las Villas, charging him with seeking to use the invasion to build a foundation for a Negro-dominated Republic. This campaign produced results. When Gómez proposed a revival of the invasion of the West, the troops of Las Villas refused to accept Maceo as their commander. While it was not unusual in the Ten Years' War for units of one area to refuse to accept a commander from another region,* the opposition to Maceo, in this instance, stemmed primarily from capitulation to racial prejudice and swallowing the bogey of "Negro domination," a fear created by the conservative opposition to the invasion.

---

* It was also not unusual for troops of one region to refuse to fight outside their area, a tendency which weakened the Liberating Army.

Since the troops of Las Villas were to occupy a prominent place in the campaign through that province, Gómez was forced to capitulate and Maceo was recalled to Oriente. But realizing that the reason advanced by the forces of Las Villas that they could not accept Maceo as their chief because "he was not from Las Villas" was only an excuse to cover their objection to him because he was a Negro, Gómez designated Lt. Colonel Cecilio González, "a man as black as ebony," as the leader of the campaign. "Of this one they cannot say he is not from Las Villas, because he was born in Cienfuegos," Gómez stated in announcing González's appointment. "And the white racists of Las Villas had to accept the Negro González as their chief," notes the Cuban historian, Emilio Roig de Leuchsenring.[15]

The final irony was that even with Maceo out of the way, the government refused to approve Gómez's request for a revival of the invasion plan. José Morales Lemus, spokesman for the wealthy émigrés and a long-time opponent of a western invasion, warned the government that an invasion of the Occident district, and the application in this area of "the policy of the incendiary torch," would jeopardize all possibilities of securing aid from the government of the United States, which, he predicted, would shortly recognize Cuban belligerency. The Spaniards, he emphasized, were spreading propaganda in the United States that an invasion of the West, if successful, would bring on "Negro domination of the island," and that "she [Cuba] would be converted into a second Hayti." This was hurting the Cuban cause.[16]

Thus the revolution was restricted to the least important economic section of the island, and the most important districts continued to provide Spain with the resources to carry on the war. How important this factor was regarded by the Spaniards is revealed in a report of April 25, 1874, from Henry C. Hall, American Consul in Havana. Hall informed the State Department of the proceedings of a Board composed of ex-Captains General of Cuba. He continued:

> The Board entertains no hope of a speedy suppression of the insurrection; in fact it is indirectly admitted that it may be a work of years. But the hope is expressed that it may be kept within its present limits and that the sugar production of the Western Departments of the island may be kept up; as long as this production continues means will

not be wanting for sustaining the Government and combatting the insurrection; to this end it is recommended that all the resources of the Government should be directed.[17]

As for the expected aid and recognition of the revolution from the United States, that proved once again to be an illusion.

chapter 20

THE UNITED STATES AND THE INDEPENDENCE OF CUBA, 1871-1875

On December 23, 1871, General Daniel Sickles returned home from Spain to confer with the President. Asked by a reporter what the chances were for achieving the promised reforms in Cuba, he replied: "It is, perhaps, doubtful whether, as things are in Cuba, any radical measure of colonial reform could be carried out through the Spanish authorities in the Island without provoking a more serious rebellion [among the Volunteers] in Havana than was begun at Yara in October, 1868."[1] Sickles' frank revelation of who was determining Spanish policy in Cuba provoked an outburst in the press. All along, the Grant administration had been assuring the American people that the liberals in Spain would soon institute far-reaching reforms in Cuba, and that recognition of Cuban belligerency would damage the chances of securing such changes. Now Sickles made it clear that it was futile to hope for such reforms; that the entire policy of the Grant administration—that of trying to push Spain in the direction of reform—rested on quicksand.

In April, 1872, Hamilton Fish conceded that the United States had been able to obtain from Spain only "promises." Several months later, he made an even more startling confession, demolishing the administration's chief argument against recognition of Cuban belligerency. On October 24, 1872, Fish told the Spanish Minister to Washington, Don José Polo de Bernabé, that the continuation of the war in Cuba without apparent probability of success on either side was producing "a state of things which will justify, if not require, a recognition of belligerency. That four years of contest without any advantage of arms by Spain over the insurgents exhibit a condition under which no complaint can be made if other powers recognize it as war."[2] In other words, it was possible, if the administration wished to do so, to *justify* recognition of the Cuban rebels on the basis of the situation in the island.

Instead of following this position logically, Fish pursued his usual tactic of delay while trying to push Spain in the direction of reforms in Cuba.

On October 29, Fish sent a long official communication to Sickles (known as "No. 270") in which he pointed out the failure of the Spanish authorities to execute the feeble Moret Law of July, 1870, and bluntly blamed this upon the efforts of the Cuban slave interests. Unless the reforms were immediately carried into effect, "Spain must not be surprised to find, as the inevitable result, a marked change in the feeling and in the temper of the people and of the government of the United States."[3]

Spain, of course, was not impressed. She had heard harsh words before from the Grant administration, and even threats of action to recognize the belligerency of the Cuban rebels. But the action had never been forthcoming, and there was no reason to suppose that the situation would be any different this time. However, when the Grant administration threatened to boycott Cuban sugar through a discriminatory tariff, the Spanish government decided that it would have to take some step to conciliate the Americans. After all, the United States bought 75 percent of the Cuban sugar production; and American boycott would drive the sugar planters into bankruptcy, and deprive Spain of the resources with which to carry on the war. On December 2, the Zorrilla government in Spain stated that it would send to the Cortes a bill of immediate abolition for Puerto Rico. Polo even told Fish that Spain might concede similar concessions to Cuba if only the United States would drop the threat to boycott Cuban sugar production.

Fish was satisfied. Grant's message to Congress in December, 1872, said nothing of the boycott; indeed, it had nothing of importance to say about Cuba except to praise Spain for instituting new regulations to enforce the Moret law, and to hope that she would "voluntarily grant additional measures of reform."[4]

A few days after Grant's message to Congress, a call was circulated in New York City by Negro citizens for a meeting to be held at Cooper Institute in behalf of the "Cuban Patriots," and to take proper action "to advance the cause of freedom." The key speeches were delivered by Samuel R. Scottron and the Reverend Henry Highland Garnet, chairman and secretary respectively of the Cuban Anti-Slavery Committee. They noted that the Negroes in the United States had been reluctant up to now to criticize the Grant administration's Cuban policy. They had believed it to be necessary to support the Republican Party, the Party that had adopted the constitutional amendments abolishing slavery and granting citizenship and suffrage to the Negroes. But the time had come when they could no longer keep silent. "Let the colored people of America avail themselves of the sacred right of petition to assist the struggling patriots of Cuba, and disenthrall from the most tyrannical slavery five hundred thousand of our brethren now held as chattel slaves by the government of Spain." The Grant administration should immediately concede the Cuban Republic belligerent rights. The Cuban patriots had done much to justify such recognition even under international law. But one thing, in the eyes of Negro Americans, was enough justification. They had abolished slavery, and "an actual state of freedom" existed in the Cuban Republic. Moreover, "the colored inhabitants battle side by side with the white, holding the rank of officers, and in numerous instances, colored officers [are] commanding white troops."*

The Negro citizens at the mass meeting unanimously declared themselves on the side of "the Cuban Patriots, who have already decreed and put in practice the doctrine of the equality and freedom of all men." They viewed "with abhorrence the policy of the Spanish government for the last four years" in the island of Cuba, and declared that "it is our opinion that the success of the Spanish arms will tend to rivet more firmly the chains of slavery on our brethren, re-establishing slavery where it does not now exist and restoring the horrors of the African slave trade and the Coolie traffic," and that, on the other hand, "the success of the Cuban Patriots will give to the whole inhabitants of the island, freedom and equality before the law."

* In a letter to the meeting, General Thomas Jordan, formerly of the Cuban Liberating Army, emphasized that the "former slaves are fighting bravely in the ranks of the Cuban army not in separate organizations, as in the United States, but in the same companies side by side with the white people, and I have seen white men commanded by blacks."

Resolved, That we, therefore, after four years' patient waiting, deem it our duty, and do hereby petition our government at Washington, the President and Congress of the United States, to accord to the Cuban Patriots that favorable recognition that four years' gallant struggle for freedom justly entitles them to.[5]

The New York *Herald* of December 15, 1872, urged the Grant administration to bear in mind the fact "that the voice of this Cooper Institute meeting is the voice of all our citizens of African descent, including especially those four millions lately released from the shackles of slavery." But the voice of Negro Americans made as little impression on the administration as had countless other appeals for recognition of Cuban belligerency. Spain had promised to act against slavery, and that was enough to satisfy Fish. And when on February 13, 1873, definite news came that a Republic had been established in Spain, Fish had another excuse for not acting. Now Spain was certain to take definite steps to abolish slavery in Cuba, and to institute other reforms. Now was no time for the United States to do anything but to congratulate the people of Spain and Cuba.

Spain did keep its word to abolish slavery—but only in Puerto Rico. "But," writes Allan Nevins, "the lash and the slave-pen still existed for half a million Cuban Negroes."[6]

In informing Polo in December, 1872, that the U.S. threat to boycott Cuban sugar production was being suspended, Fish had added: "It will be held for further consideration awaiting the action of the Spanish Government." But when there was no "action" so far as slavery in Cuba was concerned, the demand arose for a revival of the plan to deliver a blow against the great Cuban sugar interests. It was rejected by the administration. Nothing must be done to pressure the Republic in Spain, Fish insisted, for Cuba's best hope for the future rested with the new government. General M. Quesada, representative of the Cuban Republic, publicly charged that the administration had capitulated to pressure from Americans who did business with Cuba and those who owned plantations and slaves in the island.* These men, he said, "exert a great influence" in Washington, and they had persuaded the administration to drop a measure which would have driven them into bankruptcy along with the

---

* In his annual message, 1871, Grant had proposed action against Americans who owned slaves in Cuba, but nothing was done.

Cuban slaveowners. It was this group, too, which had influenced the decision against recognition of Cuban belligerency. "Between the interests of certain American merchants and the duty of recognizing Cuban belligerency, the balance was inclined in favor of the former."[7]

In October, 1873, Grant, acknowledging that the people demanded it, raised the question of recognition of Cuban belligerency in the Cabinet, and the idea was supported by some of the members. Fish still opposed recognition, but he informed Sickles of the growing trend in the administration in favor of it. Only sympathy toward the Spanish Republic had, for some time past, restrained the government, Fish wrote on October 27, "from a very decided position toward Spain," but unless more than promises were given, action would be taken.[8]

Four days later, an incident occurred which led the vast majority of the American people to believe that recognition of Cuba belligerency—indeed, even war between the United States and Spain—was about to occur. On October 31, the steamer *Virginius*, carrying the American flag, a crew of Americans and Englishmen, and 103 Cubans as passengers, was seized some miles off the coast of Jamaica by the Spanish war-vessel, *Tornado*, after a chase which had started near Cuba. The ship had also carried arms and ammunition for the Cuban rebels, but these had been thrown into the sea during the chase.

The *Virginius* was brought at once to Santiago de Cuba. The Military Governor of the port and province, General Juan Burriel, convoked a court martial and, on November 4, four of the prisoners —General Washington Ryan, an English citizen, and three prominent Cuban insurgents—were shot.* Burriel then ordered that the rest of the crew and passengers be tried immediately by a Spanish military court as pirates, notwithstanding the fact that the ship had been seized in English waters, that it bore the flag of the United States, and that no arms and ammunition had been found aboard. On November 7, after a secret trial, without counsel or opportunity to be heard in their own behalf, Captain Joseph Fry, an American,

---

* All four men had been tried by the Spaniards and sentenced to death two years earlier, and were shot as soon as they were identified. Two of the Cubans were General Bernabé Varona, called "Bembeta," famous for his long opposition to the Spaniards, and Pedro de Céspedes, brother of President Céspedes.

and 36 others were executed. On November 8, 12 more were shot, making 53 in all. The men were executed with savage cruelty. The remaining persons captured on the *Virginius* would all have been shot in the same manner. But on November 7, the British frigate, *Niobe*, with Captain Sir Lambton Lorraine commanding, arrived at Santiago. Lorraine protested against the executions and the right of Spain to pursue and capture a vessel outside of territorial limits. He threatened to bombard the city if the slaughter was not stopped. This threat stayed the murder of the 102 remaining persons captured on the *Virginius*.

Throughout the United States a loud clamor arose. Some voices called for war with Spain; many demanded immediate recognition of Cuban belligerency, and still others urged American intervention in the Cuban struggle to put a stop to the barbarities. Indignation meetings were held in Pittsburgh, Boston, Baltimore, New Orleans, New York, and other cities, and resolutions were adopted urging immediate recognition of Cuban belligerency.

"The Administration does not need the stimulus of public meetings," Fish wrote. "It is 'fired up.' "[9] But not so "fired up" that it was ready at last to recognize the Cuban Republic. Fish still insisted that recognition "would have been the assertion of what does not exist; there is not at this day [November 17, 1873] the evidence of any organized government of what is called the republic of Cuba ... simply a brave, persistent defiance of Spanish rule, and a long-continued guerrilla fighting." (At least Fish now admitted that the rebellion was not on its "last legs.") Furthermore, recognition of belligerency would not "benefit" the Cubans. Fish conceded that he had not been able to persuade "these Cuban gentlemen"—leaders of the *Junta*—to go along with him on this point, but "at least Mr. Lemus admitted to me that he agreed with me in this view." Since José Morales Lemus had more than once advocated policies which were inimical to the success of the Cuban Revolution, it was not difficult for Fish to win him over to the State Department's point of view. It was men like Morales Lemus whom Martí had in mind when he wrote that "there are Cubans who serve the interests of the United States while dressed up as patriots."[10]

On November 29, after voluminous correspondence between Fish and Sickles, and lengthy negotiations first in Madrid and then in

Washington, a protocol was signed by Fish and Polo which provided that General Burriel, the Spanish commander under whose direction the executions had taken place, was to be punished; Spain was to restore the *Virginius* and the survivors, and, on December 25, was to salute the American flag. If, however, before that date, Spain should prove to the satisfaction of the United States that the *Virginius* was not entitled to carry the flag and was, at the time of the capture, carrying it improperly, the salute was to be dispensed with. An investigation was begun late in November of the persons connected with the *Virginius*, the result of which was to prove that the vessel had been secured fraudulently. So the salute to the flag was dispensed with.

Although the protocol of the agreement had been signed, by December the final settlement of the dispute had not been reached. Grant, irritated by the delay in the final arrangements, spoke of recognition of Cuban independence. Fish, as usual, persuaded him to wait. It was decided not to limit the time for a final settlement of the *Virginius* dispute.

The delay served Fish's purposes well. The panic of 1873 which had started in September, when the banking house of Jay Cooke & Co. closed its doors, was in full swing by the end of the year as thousands of workers joined the ranks of the unemployed. The economic depression engrossed public attention to the exclusion of almost every other issue. Cuba was again forgotten. Indeed, when the Senate convened in early December, it was so little concerned about relations with Spain, that Grant said to Fish humorously that he believed "if Spain were to send a fleet into the harbor of New York, and bombard the city, the Senate might pass a resolution of regret that they had cause for so doing, and offer to pay them for the expense of coming over and doing it."[11]

On December 16, 1873, the *Virginius* was turned over to American authorities. While being conveyed to Charleston, the vessel, in poor physical condition, sank off Cape Fear.

It took more than a year before a final settlement of the *Virginius* dispute was reached. Spain, having admitted the illegality of the capture and the wrongfulness of the executions, agreed on March 2, 1875, to pay an indemnity of $80,000 to cover all the claims of the United States. Spain paid the indemnity some time in advance of the date required, a fact which Fish acknowledged as "evidence of friendly dispositions, and strengthens hope of speedy adjustment of all outstanding questions."[12] But neither Cuban independence nor the continuation of slavery in Cuba was included among the "outstanding questions" to be adjusted!

The *Virginius* affair thus passed into history without altering the friendliness of the Grant administration for the Spanish government or its hostility toward the Cuban Republic. General M. Quesada bitterly accused the U.S. government of pursuing the "Machiavellian policy" of prolonging the status quo in Cuba, "which will leave the Cubans unable to obtain their independence through want of the requisite arms and materials—the Spaniards at the same time unable to suppress their efforts—until both parties become so weakened that the island will fall an easy prey to the government [of the United States]."[13]

One result of the *Virginius* affair was the resignation of General Sickles as Minister to Spain. The transfer of negotiations from Madrid to Washington, thus taking the affair out of his hands, was taken by Sickles to mean a lack of faith in his conduct of the case. (It was Sickles' opinion that the policy pursued by the U.S. government was not vigorous enough.) He therefore resigned on December 6, 1873.

His successor was Caleb Cushing, who before the Civil War had advocated the annexation of Texas and Cuba, and had organized, with his own money, a regiment to serve in the war against Mexico. In his instructions to Cushing, Fish wrote that the government of the United States had only one desire for Cuba—"its elevation into an independent republic of freemen, in harmony with ourselves and with other republics of America."[14]

When this pious statement was published in *Foreign Relations* late in 1874, it must have caused the representatives of the "other republics of America" in Washington to ask themselves: "Is there no limit to the cynicism of the American Secretary of State?" To link the policy of the U.S. government toward Cuba with that upheld by the Latin American republics was unjustified at any time since the outbreak of the Cuban rebellion, but in 1874 it was vicious. To understand why, it is necessary to relate the little-known story of a noble effort by the Latin American republics, led by

Colombia, in 1872–74, to achieve Cuban emancipation and independence, an effort which was frustrated by Hamilton Fish.

The story begins on September 26, 1872. On that day, the Minister of Foreign Relations of Colombia, Don Gil Colunje, addressed a circular to all the republics of Latin America and to the United States, proposing joint action, under the leadership of the United States, to achieve the independence of Cuba and the abolition of slavery in the island. This historic document, a copy of which, in English, is in the National Archives, in Washington, D.C., opened: "The people of Cuba, after having proclaimed to the world their determination to be free and independent, are now, and have been for four years past, engaged in a daily struggle with their mother country, seeking to accomplish the work of liberation which they began." It was impossible to say when this bloody conflict would end since "neither of the two combatants show any signs of willingness to yield." Yet to allow the war to continue would guarantee that "the beautiful soil of the island" would soon become "but a field of ruin and desolation." On the other hand, the achievement of Cuban independence would not only bring about "the enrollment of another people among the nations of the world," but it would also signify "the final and absolute disappearance from this continent of that stigma, so disgraceful to humanity which is called *slavery*."

The United States, Colunje pointed out, had made an attempt to end the war through mediation early in the conflict, but the effort had failed. However, in his message to Congress of December, 1869, President Grant, referring to the failure of the U.S. effort, had added: "It is hoped that the good offices of the United States may yet prove advantageous for the settlement of this unhappy strife." These words were clearly applicable to the situation in the fall of 1872; hence the government of Colombia considered itself "fully justified in proposing, as it hereby does, to that of your Excellency, that all the governments of Spanish America, in accord with that of Washington, enter into common action for the obtainment from that of Spain, of the recognition of the independence of Cuba." Should Spain demand payment for such recognition, "such an obstacle could be easily removed by the said governments paying, *pro rata*, the amount necessary to reimburse her. This step would signify nothing further than a desire to attain the much-wished-for result, since, the perfect right of Cuba to become a nation being admitted, as it is, the payment of a price for her ransom would be without either reason or justice." Actually, Cuba, whose resources were still ample, "would be able, at no very remote period, to cancel the debt thus contracted with the mediating governments," should she be required to do so. Colunje concluded:

> Such, sir, are the views in accordance with which my government desires to act in relation to the Cuban question, and it flatters itself with the belief that they will receive the hearty support of the governments which it addresses, since it is not in harmony with the character of sister Christian nations to remain passive spectators of a work of subjugation like the one in question, which is attended with so much suffering and productive of such disastrous results.[15]

Here, indeed, was a proposal that should have produced an affirmative response from all the governments to which it was addressed. And with the 19 republics of America, North and South, speaking as one for the independence of Cuba and the emancipation of its slaves, Spain would have been forced to yield. Since the plan offered to reimburse Spain for the loss of her colony, it took care of her pride, battered as it was anyway by four years of war in Cuba, and since it ruled out the annexation of Cuba by the United States, the proposal was certain to win the support of the European powers whose liberal-minded citizens were bound to rally to its support.

The Colombian Circular did evoke an immediate response from all of the Latin American governments to which it was addressed. But they waited to see what the United States would do before adopting a public stand.

Fish knew that the success of the Colombian plan depended on the attitude of the government of the United States. He had instructed all U.S. Ministers in Latin America to report to him on the reaction of each government to the Circular, and had learned that all approved of the project and were prepared, if necessary, to contribute to the payment of an indemnity to Spain in return for the liberation of Cuba. Each government had raised only one condition —that the United States must join the Latin American republics and act as mediator.

Fish then proceeded to torpedo the grand move to secure the independence of Cuba. The United States would have nothing to do with the Colombian plan, he informed Francis Thomas, American Minister to Peru, a country enthusiastically in favor of the project. For one thing, the government of the United States resented the reference in the Colombian Circular to the failure of its mediation efforts in 1869 to bring the war in Cuba to an end. "This is contrary to the fact. No such measure has been undertaken." In the second place, there was no guarantee that the Colombian project "would be successful." Finally, Colombia had no right to propose the United States as an arbiter without first consulting her:

> It is certain . . . that our zeal in behalf of the step proposed by Colombia would not be increased by her having taken it for granted that our intervention would in any event be employed. The measure would have been much more acceptable to us whatever might be the probability of its success, if, before the Circular had been issued, we had been consulted as to our disposition to accept the function of an arbiter.[16]

Thus with the life of the Cuban Republic and the freedom of hundreds of thousands of Cuban slaves at stake, the U.S. Secretary of State rested on the niceties of diplomatic procedure to doom a project which had the greatest possibility thus far in the Ten Years' War to achieve an end to the bloody conflict, the independence of Cuba, and the emancipation of its slaves. Fish's objection to Colombia's reference to the failure of the 1869 mediation effort was absurd. As we have seen, such an attempt had been made and had failed. It is significant that Fish made no reference to the quotation from Grant's message to Congress which acknowledged the mediation effort and related its failure.

Fish raised still another objection to the Colombian project which was equally without foundation. When the Colombian Minister called upon him in person to urge reconsideration of the decision not to support the plan, Fish read him a lecture.

> I replied [he wrote in his diary] that some of the most earnest and intelligent republicans of the present age had inaugurated the revolution in Spain, and were now endeavoring to establish permanently a republican government; that . . . the future of a republican government in Spain and its dependencies was hanging upon this issue, involving not only the question of a republic for 1,500,000 in Cuba, but

for 14,000,000 in Spain. It behooves those who were considering this question to think of the effect of pressing Spain in her present emergency with questions such as he contemplated.[17]

"Fish," a Cuban historian has correctly noted, "adopted the attitude that the Republic of Spain should triumph, and for this it was necessary to condemn the Republic of Cuba to death." This position he adhered to in spite of the fact that Fish knew that with regard to Cuba, the Republicans of Spain were no different from the monarchists, the liberals no different from the reactionaries. As President Céspedes put it in a letter to the U.S. government, March 22, 1873, urging support for the Colombian plan, "in the name of humanity, of respect for republican principles of civilization": "The Republic of Spain is as determined as the old monarchy to deny independence to Cuba, exterminate its patriotic men and women, and rivet the fetters upon the slaves of the Antilles."[18]

An attempt was made by Colombia to revive the plan in 1874 after the fall of the Spanish Republic, but again it failed because of the refusal of the United States to co-operate. Even though, with the disappearance of the Spanish Republic, one of his chief arguments against the project had been removed, Fish still refused to join a grand Pan-American combination to bring pressure upon Spain to secure the independence of Cuba and the emancipation of the slaves.

Small wonder, then, that when Fish's instructions to Cushing were published late in 1874, Latin American officials who had been associated with the Colombian project laughed scornfully at the Secretary of State's assertion that the United States desired for Cuba "its elevation into an independent republic of freemen, in harmony with ourselves and with other republics of America." If anything, this shameful episode in American diplomatic history proved that the government of the United States still clung to the traditional policy of opposing the independence of Cuba, and was still waiting for the laws of "political gravitation" to bring the island within the American Union.

On July 1, 1875, a patriotic Cuban woman, a great-granddaughter of Diego Velázquez, the first Spanish conqueror of the island, sent an anguished letter to Hamilton Fish from Key West. She pleaded for American aid for Cuba's "army of Patriots now struggling to be freed from Spanish Tyranny."

> I earnestly appeal to your government through your honorable Self in behalf of Noble Cuba—to recognize her. Extend to her a helping hand that she may extricate herself. Let peace resound througout [sic] the island. Oh America, A Christian nation. Stop the immense bloodshed and destruction of her property. Save our women and children from destruction.... We want freedom and Independence. We as a people wish to become a Republic. ... Just think of 26,000 able bodied men ready to fight—had they proper arms. Many are fighting with common knives and stones. ... Go back in history and you will find they were better armed and equipped than the brave army of General Gómez is at present. ... Oh God, help Cuba and her people. My dear Christian Friend, Let me hear from you at your earliest consideration.[19]

The letter was never answered. But Fish had long since given the answer of the government of the United States: No recognition, no aid for the Cuban insurgents.

chapter 21

THE TEN YEARS' WAR:
THE FINAL PHASE, 1875-1878

The first few months of the year 1875 found the Cuban rebels in their most promising position thus far in the war. They had a strong grip on the provinces of Oriente and Camagüey, where they moved at will in the country, and where the Spaniards controlled only the towns and strongly garrisoned areas. "We could call ourselves almost masters in Oriente and Camagüey," General Enrique Collazo recalled. "The government of the Republic exercised its functions in these provinces with entire and complete liberty."[1]

In addition, General Máximo Gómez, disregarding official objections to the plan, had finally succeeded in the first phase of his cherished dream of invading the province of Las Villas. On January 6, 1875, Gómez crossed the *trocha*, a long fortified line which the Spaniards had erected in an effort to prevent penetration of the West.* Immediately, Gómez, *el hombre de la tea* (the man of the torch), unleashed a devastating campaign in the province of Las Villas. "The objective," he told his officers and soldiers, "is the destruction of the plantations which sustain the enemy, principally the mills from which the *hacendados* derive their wealth and with which they support Spain's war effort." The flames that destroyed the plantations and the mills, he wrote, "will snatch the slave from the domination of his master." In little over a month, Gómez burned 83 mills.

In carrying out this campaign, Gómez was fulfilling his main pur-

* A *trocha* is a ditch, with an embankment on one side, and with entanglements of wire projecting over the edge to prevent the passage of an army. A large area in front of the ditch is cleared away, and fortresses and watch towers constructed at intervals of about a mile.

pose in joining the Cuban revolutionary struggle. In August, 1896, in the midst of the second War for Independence, Gómez told Fermín Valdés Domínguez that the exploitation of the Negro slaves had moved him to join the Cuban Liberating Army, hoping thereby to end these "shameful and intolerable injustices" in that island. In his *Diary*, Valdés Domínguez recorded the following statement by Gómez which he says is reported verbatim:

> . . . my business of wood and other things brought me to different mills, and in one of them I saw a poor Negro being lashed with a whip . . . in front of all the other workers. I couldn't sleep all night. It seemed to me that that Negro was one of the many I learned to love and respect when I lived with my parents in Santo Domingo.
>
> Through my relations with Cubans, I then entered into the conspiracy; but I went to war, bearing these memories in my soul, in order to fight for the liberty of the Negro slave; and it was then that, realizing there also existed what could be called white slavery, I united the two ideas in my determination. To them I consecrated my efforts. But in spite of the years that have passed since then, I cannot forget that I accepted the principles of the revolution in order to fight for the liberty of the Negro slave.[2]

Gómez's success in penetrating the province created panic among the Spanish bureaucrats and slaveowners of Las Villas, and this alarm was felt even in Havana where, for over six years, those who sympathized with Spain had lived tranquilly, confident that the rebels would never succeed in penetrating the *trocha*. A series of rapid changes in the post of Captain General of the island followed, which ended with the selection of Valmaseda for the third time in the war.

The *mambises*, encouraged by Gómez's success in Las Villas, redoubled their efforts in other provinces. There was common talk that the year 1875 would see the end of the war and of Spanish despotism in Cuba. There was even a decline of divisionist tendencies in the revolutionary government. "There was greater unity than at any other time," Enrique Collazo recalled, "and a general will to give priority to military measures for winning the war." President Cisneros bestowed official blessings on Gómez's plan, and issued an order to the various generals to select specified numbers of soldiers to send to the vigorous commander and to aid him "to carry the war to Matanzas and Havana."

"Fortune was smiling on us," wrote General Collazo, "and the future looked happy and agreeable."[3] But the great hope of victory by the end of the year through united effort was to be demolished. Dissension reared its head once again in the revolutionary movement.

A year before, it will be recalled, Vicente García had been the only general to oppose openly Gómez's plan for an invasion of the West. Although he was an excellent general and occupied the post of Secretary of War in the revolutionary government, García constantly fought the Cisneros administration, claiming, on the one hand, that it was not sufficiently revolutionary, and, on the other, that it should not countenance Gómez's "policy of the incendiary torch." García thus attracted both radical elements who wanted reforms in the government and conservatives who opposed Gómez's revolutionary methods. He was also supported by the relatives and associates of the former president, Carlos Manuel de Céspedes, despite the fact that García was one of the first to demand Céspedes' removal from office.

While Gómez was awaiting reinforcements in Las Villas, García, using as an excuse some disagreement he had with General Calvar, renounced his allegiance to the government of the revolution. He immediately called a Council at Lagunas de Varona on April 27, 1875, of all elements dissatisfied with the state of the revolution. The announced purpose of the meeting was to demand substantial reforms in the revolutionary government. All the troops of the zone of Las Tunas, where García had a large following, went to the meeting, and many in Oriente province left the battlefield to the enemy. Maceo, however, furious at García's sabotage of the war effort, worked actively both to hold the front against the Spaniards in Oriente and to reinforce Gómez's army.

Essentially, however, García's move resulted in disrupting the whole revolutionary movement. But when Cisneros pointed this out to the protest meeting, García and his followers were unmoved. Finally, Cisneros offered to resign. The offer was not accepted, but the government was paralyzed. Gómez withdrew his forces from Las Villas, and military activity on almost every front came to a halt. Later, the House of Representatives accepted Cisneros' resignation and named Juan B. Spotorno, president of the House, interim President of the Republic. Spotorno remained Provisional President until March 29, 1876, when the House elected Tomás Estrada Palma President of the Republic.

Estrada Palma did make some efforts to invigorate military operations so long dormant. He met with Gómez and discussed a revival of the invasion of the West. Gómez, eager as ever to put his plan into full operation, moved once again into Las Villas. Thus after a year of relative inactivity there were new hopes of united efforts against Spain. But once again these hopes were to be frustrated.

In his interview with Gómez, Estrada Palma, who had close links with the Cuban exiles, assured the Dominican general that military supplies were on the way from the United States and that the chances of recognition of Cuban belligerency were never brighter. On both points the new President proved to be extremely overoptimistic.

Military supplies to further the revolution were not coming through; the wealthy Cubans in the United States upon whom Estrada Palma depended for funds to purchase these supplies were refusing to contribute. Whatever money was raised came from the tobacco workers in Key West, Tampa, and other cities. These Cuban workers had emigrated to the United States with a considerable part of the tobacco industry at the outbreak of the Ten Years' War. (The number of tobacco workers in Key West grew from 3,000 in 1868 to 18,000 in 1870. Most of them were Cubans.) Throughout the long years of conflict, they had contributed monthly quotas from their meagre wages to the revolutionary cause, and when they learned that Gómez's invasion of the West required additional contributions for military supplies, they immediately increased their quotas. (Some even sold their clothing and contributed the money to the fund drive.) But the rich Cuban exiles who had millions deposited in New York banks, safe from taxation and confiscation by Spain, refused to part with any of their wealth to help Gómez's invading army. Gómez himself acknowledged that the failure of the wealthy exiles to come through with funds for military supplies immobilized the invasion of the West. "The poor Cubans responded well, and if Miguel Aldama and men like him had responded immediately to what was asked of them, who knows how far we could have gone."[4]

Ten Years' War: The Final Phase • 257

Estrada Palma's assurance to Gómez that U.S. recognition of Cuban belligerency was just around the corner was no more accurate than his statement that military supplies were on the way. It is true that President Grant occasionally referred to the necessity of recognizing the Cuban Republic, and public demand for such a step was always present. But Fish dismissed this demand for recognition of Cuban belligerency as due primarily to "the wonderfully persuasive influence of Cuban bonds scattered broadcast among [a] noble array of newspapers." He could not, however, entirely ignore it. In November, 1875, he pointed out, in a private letter to Minister Cushing in Spain, that it was apparent the first week of the coming session of Congress would witness a "shower of resolutions" for the recognition either of belligerency or independence. To prevent Congress from acting, Fish came up with a new maneuver; he dispatched a lengthy instruction to Cushing, known by its number as "266," which concluded that in the absence of any prospect of a termination of the war in Cuba, "the time is at hand when it may be the duty of other Governments to intervene, solely with a view of bringing to an end a disastrous and destructive conflict, and of restoring peace in the island of Cuba." But neither Cuban independence nor abolition of slavery in Cuba were made conditions for peace. All the United States asked was an end to the fighting in the island, and the cooperation of the European powers, especially England, to achieve this goal. Its real purpose was revealed by Fish when he wrote that while negotiations were being conducted with Spain, Congress would have no reason to "run off on demagogism and sentimental sympathy" for the Cubans.[5]

Nothing came of No. 266. England refused to join in putting pressure on Spain to end the war in Cuba; indeed, only Italy was prepared to support the plan. Fish was criticized in the U.S. press for having consulted the powers of Europe on what should be considered purely an American question, and thereby violating the Monroe Doctrine. *The Nation* of February 3, 1876 found it "a singular spectacle" to see the United States ten years after requiring the withdrawal of the French from Mexico in obedience to the Monroe Doctrine, inviting all the European governments to repeat the Mexican experiment in Cuba. What was more to the point, but was not referred to in the American press, was that while Fish had rejected a proposal to unite with the Latin American republics to bring pressure on Spain to end the war in Cuba on the basis of independence for the Cubans and abolition of slavery, he did not hesitate to propose unity with the European powers to bring pressure to end the war without the granting of independence and abolition of slavery.

Fish, however, was satisfied. A major purpose in sending dispatch No. 266 was to forestall action by Congress recognizing Cuban belligerency or independence and to keep the control of such matters in the hands of the administration. This objective was achieved. Congress held off action when Grant, in his annual message of December, 1875, intimated that negotiations to end the war were in progress. The effect of the message, Fish wrote jubilantly to Cushing, "was all that could be desired, and left the Administration master of the question without apprehension of resolutions of recognition, etc."[6]

Meanwhile, dissension was increasing within the revolutionary movement. A clear sign of this was the vicious campaign against Antonio Maceo. As before, he was accused of seeking a Cuban Republic dominated by Negroes. Ugly rumors circulated that Maceo was waiting for an opportunity to lead the Negro soldiers against the whites and seize power. He was accused of not obeying the decisions of the government and of favoring Negro over white officers. These slanders represented the feeling of important elements in the revolutionary camp. Colonel Ricardo Céspedes told the Spaniards after he became a prisoner of war that he and other officers of the Liberating Army "saw ruin coming in the support given to the colored element." Naturally, the Spaniards spread this statement widely throughout Cuba.[7]

Maceo had ignored the slanders for months, but he conducted himself so as to prove that they were lies spread by foes of the Revolution to sow confusion, alarm and dissension in the revolutionary ranks. He told his officers and men that there were no black and white soldiers. All were Cuban warriors, and all were entitled to enjoy equality. There should be no domination of one race over the other in the future Republic.

By May, 1876, Maceo realized that his silence only encouraged the racists to intensify their slanderous campaigns. On May 16,

1876, he wrote to the President of the Republic from his camp in Baraguá. It is worth quoting this famous letter of protest and refutation in full:

> Antonio Maceo y Grajales, native of the city of [Santiago de] Cuba, Brigadier General of the Liberating Army, and at present Chief of the Second Division of the First Corp, respectfully states:
> That for some time I have tolerated acts and conversations which actually I discredited because I believed they only came from the enemy, who, as everybody knows, has used all weapons to disunite us to see if by this means he can defeat us. But later, seeing that the issue was growing, I tried to see where it came from, and at last I am convinced that it does not come only from enemy sources, but, painful for me to say, it comes from our own brothers who, forgetting the republican and democratic principles which should guide them, have followed personal political ends.
> Therefore, in view of this development, I believe that it is my duty to appeal to the Government which you represent, so that when you understand the reasons which I shall present at a later point, you will proceed with justice and resolution, taking the necessary measures to clear all doubt as to my conduct and to remove the slightest smear from my name. The desire all my life has been, is, and will be to serve my country, defending its proclaimed principles. This I have done many times. The cause must triumph and sacrosanct principles of liberty and independence must remain safe.
> I have known for some time, Mr. President, through a person of good reputation and prestige, that a small circle exists which has manifested to the Government that it "did not wish to serve under my orders because I belong to the colored race." And later, through different channels, I have learned that they are now accusing me of "showing favoritism to the colored over the white officers in my command." In doing so they are serving their own particular political interests; by this method they hope to destroy me as they have not been able to do so by other means. They are trying to do this to a man who entered the revolution for no other reason than to shed his blood to see the slaves and his country free. After learning what was occurring, I spoke to one of the men who belongs to this circle and I became more convinced than ever of their evil goals. In planting these seeds of distrust and dissension, they do not seem to realize that it is the country that will suffer the consequences.
> And since I belong to the colored race, without considering myself worth more or less than other men, I cannot and must not consent to the continued growth of this ugly rumor. Since I form a not inappreciable part of this democratic republic, which has for its base the

fundamental principles of liberty, equality, and fraternity, I must protest energetically with all my strength that neither now nor at any other time am I to be regarded as an advocate of a Negro Republic or anything of that sort. This concept is a deadly thing to this democratic Republic which is founded on the basis of liberty and fraternity. I do not recognize any hierarchy.

Those who are to mold the future nation must prove themselves now. The men who act in the manner which I have described can never form a part of that nation if it is to be the sort of country for which we are fighting. They are as much the enemies of the revolution as those who are fighting openly and directly against me, and they must be treated as such.

If for some unbelievable reason I should be denied my just demands, I shall be forced to leave the cause in which I had so much hope; if politics is to have the upper hand, then I must ask for my passport to some civilized land. This does not mean that I am looking for an excuse to quit the war; the country needs its good sons as never before, and I am not the kind who tires so easily, in spite of the eleven wounds which I proudly carry in my body. I shall never tire of fighting so long as I believe the goal to be worthy of the effort.

I am addressing this letter to you because I want to see the truth prevail and because I expect the guilty to be discovered and punished.[8]

Unfortunately, the government did nothing to meet Maceo's demand; the slanders against the great Negro leader continued, and the Spaniards continued to raise the bogey of a Negro Republic. Nevertheless, Maceo did not carry out his threat to resign his post and leave the country. On the contrary, he continued to oppose all who used the racial issue to destroy the revolution, just as he opposed men like Vicente García who tried to use the need for reforms to destroy the revolutionary government.

"Unity to fight the common enemy." This was the keynote of Maceo's messages to the revolutionary commanders. He worked actively to get García and all other rebel chiefs to forget personal differences and unite for the success of the revolution. But he failed. Dissension in the revolutionary ranks increased with each month. In September, 1876, General Carlos Roloff informed Gómez that the officers of Las Villas would not accept the Dominican's continuance as commander of the forces of the province. "I did not answer a word," Gómez wrote in his *Diary*, "and immediately turned over the control of the forces with which I expected to fight the last battle against the Spanish army. On that same day I retired to the plantation, *La Reforma,* with my heart broken by so many deceptions."[9] Gómez shortly left the plantation to become Secretary of War and Commanding General in Oriente under President Estrada Palma. But his removal from command in Las Villas had doomed the whole plan for offensive action in the West.

As long as most of the activity of the Spanish army in Cuba was defensive, this internal dissension was not fatal to the Cuban cause. But in the spring of 1877, the situation changed. In the previous fall, General Arsenio Martínez Campos had arrived in Cuba at the head of 25,000 additional reinforcements for the Spanish army. His plan was to abandon defensive warfare, invade the rebel territory near Las Villas, and from there move east to the province of Oriente.

With special authority as the Commander of the entire Spanish field army, Martínez Campos opened a vigorous offensive in the months of March and April, 1877. He decreed that any rebel caught with arms in hand would be executed. At the same time, he developed a shrewd policy to take advantage of the divisions within the revolutionary camp. General Martínez Campos made a concentrated effort to get in touch with all the dissenting elements; he sent prisoners of war back into the revolutionary ranks to create greater dissensions; he offered money to those who seemed likely to lay down their arms; and he circulated the complaints, accusations, rumors and heated remarks of one rebel group against another, playing up, for example, the bogey of a Negro Republic if the rebels won. Along with these tactics, General Martínez Campos made peace overtures and requested interviews with the legal government of the revolutionists. On May 5, 1877, he issued a proclamation which rescinded all orders of banishment "for political motives," and lifted the penalties imposed on insurgents (except for the leaders of the insurrection) who presented themselves for pardon before the end of the war.[10]

Heavy losses by the insurgents resulted from Martínez Campos's military offensive; the revolutionary cause was further imperilled by the desertions of the rebel officers and soldiers in Las Villas, who were under the influence of Vicente García, and the rebellion of the soldiers of Holguín, led by the Negro chieftain, Limbano Sánchez, known as "the Lion of Holguín." Efforts by Maceo and Gómez to convince García and Sánchez and their followers to lay aside all differences in the face of the need for unity once again failed. Rebel morale was rapidly sinking, and some revolutionary leaders talked of peace without independence, in spite of their oath not to do so. On August 7, 1877, Hamilton Fish, who had left the office of Secretary of State, wrote with the utmost delight: "The end [of the Cuban trouble] is approaching,"[11]

The policy of the U.S. government toward Cuba was not changed by Fish's resignation as Secretary of State. This policy was summed up as follows by the Cuban League of the United States in a statement issued in August, 1877: "Until now, it appears that the conduct of the Administration at Washington has had for its object a continuation of Spanish dominion in Cuba; partly because certain high commercial interests deem it to their advantage, and partly because the Treasury department did not deem it wise to diminish, either in whole or in part, the millions of dollars which the national treasury derives from the importation of fruit from the Spanish Antilles."[12]

The situation in Oriente, where Maceo and Gómez kept up the fighting spirit of the rebels by attacking Spanish columns, was still fairly stable. Unfortunately, at this critical stage of internal and external threat to the revolution, Maceo was wounded in battle. "This development," Gómez wrote sadly in his *Diary*, "leaves me in a very grave situation since there is no chieftain who can command the same influence as Maceo. Meanwhile, the Spaniards are increasing their operations."[13]

For a time it was believed that Maceo would not live, but the Negro General not only lived; he accomplished another of his seemingly impossible deeds. He was protected by a small bodyguard of eight men, commanded by his brother, José Maceo. An informer advised General Martínez Campos of the gravity of Maceo's wounds, of the small size of his escort, and of the exact place where he could be found. Martínez Campos immediately dispatched a column of 3,000 men, who completely surrounded the area containing Maceo's bodyguard. On September 27, 1877, less than two months after he had received his seemingly fatal wounds, and as the Spanish troops were approaching, Maceo got off his litter, mounted his horse and galloped away in a cloud of dust and gun smoke. In his report of the affair to Madrid, Martínez Campos wrote: "I thought I was dealing with a stupid mulatto, a rude muleteer; but I found him transformed not only into a real general, capable of directing his movement with judgment and precision, but also into an athlete who, finding himself indisposed on a litter, assaulted by my troops, abandoned his bed, leaped upon a horse and outdistanced those pursuing him."[14]

Soon Maceo was again leading the rebels in Oriente against the Spaniards. On October 18, he completely defeated a Spanish army in the battle of Piloto. Thus with Maceo sound once more, the situation appeared promising in Oriente.

But in Camagüey and Las Villas the situation was rapidly deteriorating. In desperation, the House of Representatives removed Estrada Palma, who had assumed direction of military strategy, from direct command of the army. The House then asked Gómez to take over. It hoped that the Dominican General could revive the spirit of unity in the insurgent ranks and meet Martínez Campos's offensive with a unified revolutionary army. Unfortunately for the Cuban cause, Gómez let this opportunity to rebuild an effective Liberating Army pass by. He had become increasingly dismayed by the constant political intrigues, and he refused to accept the command offered to him. In his *Diary*, Gómez explained that he was refusing the post "so long as the political situation of the country was abnormal."[15] But this was precisely the situation that called for a man of Gómez's experience and leadership, and his refusal to take command only intensified the "abnormal" conditions.

While it is not difficult to understand Gómez's disgust over the constant internal bickering in the revolutionary movement and the repeated sabotage of his plan to invade the West, his decision was a serious blow to the cause to which he had already devoted almost a decade. His refusal to accept the command at this crucial point was, in the eyes of many Cuban revolutionaries, the final blow to the Ten Years' War.

In November, 1877, Estrada Palma was captured and imprisoned by the Spaniards. This was followed by the naming of General Vicente García as President of the Republic. Thus after a long history of rebellion against the chosen authorities of the revolutionary movement, García finally took over the helm. But the ship was already sinking. Many rebels were now thinking in terms of some kind of peace overture. Even Gómez was wavering. His advice to the government was that an uncompromising truce in the fighting should be obtained so that the rebels could gather together in assembly in order to decide whether they wished to have peace or continue fighting. In case they decided for a continuance, they must elect a government by democratic vote and form a united front. In that event, moreover, valuable time for reorganization would have been obtained by the truce period.

But while Gómez was offering his solution, rebel officers were already making separate peace agreements. By the middle of December, 1877, the government was ready to discuss terms with General Martínez Campos, and asked for neutralization of a part of the province of Camagüey in which the conference could be held. On February 5, 1878, a conference was held between the most important leaders of the government and the Spanish generals. At this conference, President Vicente García declared that continuance of the war would destroy the country, and he asked that peace be made. Martínez Campos answered that while his acts would have to be approved by the Cortes, he would consider terms proposed by the Cubans. The conference ended without having accomplished much, and at this point, the government, including President García and the House of Representatives, resigned. A *Comité del Centro* (Committee of the Central Department) was then formed to complete the negotiations. General Gómez was asked to join the *Comité*, but he refused to take part in the negotiations or the acts of the government on the ground that he was a foreigner.

On February 9, the *Comité del Centro* asked Martínez Campos for terms on which the Spanish would cease their fighting. The terms proposed by Martínez Campos were essentially "a general pardon" for the revolutionary leaders and men, the political equality of Cuba with Puerto Rico, liberation of the slaves and Asians in the insurrectionary forces, and liberty for all leaders who desired to leave the island. These terms were taken back to the insurgent leaders. They repudiated the implication of guilt in "a general pardon," and suggested "general amnesty." They asked also for a "status" for Cuba equal to that of the provinces of Spain.

Martínez Campos opposed granting a "general amnesty" on the ground that this would imply too great a recognition of belligerent rights. The phrase finally agreed upon as a compromise was "forgetting the past." As for the demand that Cuba be given the same status as the provinces of the Peninsula, Martínez Campos, after consulting his associate in command, pointed out that the province of Puerto Rico and the provinces of Spain possessed "substantially the same status." The insurgents accepted on this basis.[16]

On February 11, 1878, the Commissioners of the Cuban Republic met with Martínez Campos at Zanjón, a village in Camagüey province, and the conditions of capitulation embodied in the *Pacto del Zanjón* were accepted by both sides. The final peace terms included eight articles: (1) the establishment in Cuba of the political, organic, and administrative laws enjoyed by Puerto Rico; (2) no action to be taken against anyone for political offenses committed from 1868 to date; freedom for those who were under indictment or serving sentences within or outside the island, and amnesty to all deserters from the Spanish army; (3) freedom for slaves and Asians who were in the insurgent ranks; (4) no one who submitted to Spanish authority should be compelled to render any military service before peace was established over the whole territory; (5) every individual who wished to leave the island should be free to do so; (6) the capitulation of each force was to take place in uninhabited spots; (7) the insurgents of the other departments were to be offered free transportation within the Central Department; (8) the pact with the *Comité del Centro* was deemed to have been made with all the departments of the island which might accept the conditions.

The *Comité del Centro* specified February 28 as the date to effect the capitulation in Puerto Príncipe. Commissioners were sent to the different departments with instructions to join in the capitulation. An emissary was sent to New York to give the Cuban émigrés an account of the capitulation.

The majority of the generals of the Cuban revolution accepted the Pact of Zanjón and laid down their arms. This news was greeted with satisfaction in Spain. The Cortes, on hearing of the capitulation, voted a resolution of congratulations to the King and General Martínez Campos for their work in bringing the conflict to a close. In the island, all who had been loyal to Spain rejoiced, and a *Te Deum* was sung in the churches of Havana.

"The peace was a necessity imposed by necessity," wrote General Enrique Collazo. "Prolongation of the conflict would have been ruination of the country without hope of success. The conditions of the Spanish government were very bad . . . but our state was even worse." Nevertheless, there were many patriots who were grief-stricken and shocked by the capitulation. They did not minimize the war-weariness of the Cuban people after almost ten years of bitter fighting; they were aware of the hostility of the *hacendados*, particularly of the Occidental district, toward a renewal of the struggle, and of the refusal of the wealthy émigrés to send resources to the revolution. Nevertheless, these patriotic Cubans protested against the surrender of the two key demands of the revolution: independence for Cuba and emancipation of all Cuban slaves.[17]

It was Antonio Maceo who, more than any other Cuban patriot, rescued the revolution from the set-back it had received at Zanjón.

While the leaders of the Republic were negotiating the terms of surrender, Maceo was fighting the Spaniards in Oriente province with his tiny unit. Though usually outnumbered more than eight to one, he defeated the enemy in battle after battle, capturing rich war booty, and forced the Spaniards to retreat with large numbers of dead and wounded. On February 7–9, in the region of San Ulpiano, Maceo won a brilliant victory over the famous San Quintín battalion, which was almost completely destroyed.

Soon enough, Maceo learned through letters from Gómez that at the very moment he was winning victories for the revolution, a peace treaty had been signed at Zanjón. His immediate reaction, as reported by Félix Figueredo who was with Maceo, showed his keen grasp of the reasons behind the Spaniards' anxiety to end the war:

> Don't you understand, friend Figueredo, that when General Martínez Campos proposes or accepts a transaction, an agreement, it is because, with his experience of what this war is, he is convinced that they will never defeat us by means of arms? And this I say and maintain; doesn't General Gómez know it a thousand times better than we do?[18]

On February 18, the agents of the *Comité del Centro* gave Maceo a full account of all the events leading up to the Pact of Zanjón. They asked Maceo to join in the capitulation proceedings at Puerto Príncipe on the 29th. At the end of the report, the Negro revolutionist announced that he did not agree with the peace pact since it did not provide for independence and abolition of slavery. However, he would not take it upon himself to speak for the revolutionary movement in Oriente. Instead, he would call an assembly of the rebels of the province and abide by their democratic decision.

Soon after he rejected the efforts of the government commissioners to get him to accept the surrender, Maceo wrote to General Martínez Campos asking for a truce and requesting an immediate interview. Martínez Campos rejected the truce; he was not particularly anxious to meet with a Negro at close quarters. But he realized that he could not say he had ended the war until Maceo was forced to capitulate. *"This Maceo is the key to a real peace,"* he wrote on February 26.[19]

The interview was set for the middle of March at Baraguá, near Santiago de Cuba. On March 8, a week before the interview, Maceo camped in Baraguá. To present the strongest front possible at the time of his interview, Maceo invited the rebel chiefs who had not yet surrendered to gather with their units at Baraguá. Burying his ill feelings against Vicente García, he appealed to him to join him there.

Not all who were invited attended the gathering: the forces of Bayamo under Generals Modesto Díaz, Francisco Javier de Céspedes, and Luis Figueredo, had already surrendered. Vicente García, moreover, had encamped not far from Baraguá with his forces from Las Villas, and Maceo went to see him to get his co-operation. In their discussion, García explained that while he had participated in the peace negotiations, he now refused to accept the Pact of Zanjón. But he had his own idea of how to carry on the fight against Spain, which he was not prepared to reveal. He urged Maceo not to go through with the interview with Martínez Campos.

Maceo rejected this advice, and he was supported by the rebels who had come to Baraguá, consisting of 1,500 officers and soldiers. In a speech to these rebel commanders and their men, Maceo explained the process which had culminated in the Pact of Zanjón. He denounced the internal dissensions which had weakened the revolutionary struggle, criticized the wealthy Cuban exiles for having failed to provide funds for military supplies, and the *hacendados* for having sabotaged every effort to carry through an effective invasion of the West. These forces had been responsible for weakening the revolution, but this did not excuse those who had shamefully dealt with the enemy and signed a peace with Spain on a dishonorable basis. They had further degraded the Cuban people by requiring that the rest of the Republic in arms should be obliged to accept the shameful Pact. As for himself, he was determined "to save the Cuban Revolution from the claws of the intriguers and traitors, facing resolutely the Spanish monarchy and its representatives." But he could not speak for those who were at the meeting. Did they stand with him in this resolve?

The chief officers and soldiers of Oriente, 1,500 strong, unanimously endorsed Maceo's stand and resolved to follow him to the bitter end to achieve the independence of Cuba!

On the morning of March 15, 1878, the representatives of Spain, headed by General Martínez Campos, met with a small gathering of Negro and white Cuban officers, led by General Antonio Maceo. Martínez Campos began the interview with a lengthy discourse in which he emphasized that there had been enough war, that it was time to make peace, and time for Cuba "to unite with Spain in a march towards progress and civilization." He then requested General Polavieja to read the terms of the Pact of Zanjón. At this point, Maceo began talking. With measured words, putting into each phrase "dignified and expressive revolutionary firmness of a leader of a slave people," he told the representative of the Spanish monarchy that neither he nor his companions from Oriente were ready to accept the Pact of Zanjón which had been signed without consulting them. They still hoped that the island of Cuba and its people would achieve peace and happiness. But this would be impossible without liberty. He could not believe in the sincerity of the reforms that Martínez Campos had promised because these must be preceded by the immediate abolition of slavery.

"Gentlemen," said Martínez Campos after Maceo had finished, "I believed that you came to speak of peace. If you are not in agreement with any of the terms of the Pact, what is that you want?" "What we want is independence," quickly answered Dr. Félix Figueredo. Martínez Campos replied that he would never have come to the meeting if he had thought that Maceo and his companions would settle for nothing less than independence. It was beyond his power to promise that. Insofar as slavery was concerned, while he personally would like to see the institution abolished, there were opposing interests involved; hence the matter would have to be debated in the Spanish legislature. He could not compromise the government of Spain by an agreement in the field. What he could do, though, was to promise that the slaves who had fought in the revolutionary ranks would remain free.

General Calvar then replied for the Cubans, saying: "We cannot accept a peace without the indispensable provisions of independence and the abolition of slavery. Nor can we accept the Pact because it is dishonorable." Martínez Campos then asked Maceo directly: "That is to say, we are not in agreement." "No," replied Maceo. "We are not in agreement." "Then," asked Martínez Campos, "hostilities will again break out?" "Hostilities will again break out," Maceo replied emphatically. Martínez Campos then asked how much time the Cubans would need before the outbreak of hostilities. "For my part," answered Maceo, "I do not find it inconvenient that they break out right now." Finally, a truce of eight days was agreed upon by all present. "On the 23rd, hostilities break out," said Maceo, terminating the interview with these words.[20]

Thus ended the historic and dramatic meeting. The "Protest of Baraguá," as it was immediately called, was the symbol of the best that was in the Cuban Revolution; it was a great protest against those who had surrendered without achieving the main goals—independence and abolition of slavery—and it was a formal rejection of the Pact of Zanjón. It stirred the Cuban masses, Negro and white, who looked to the resistance movement led by Maceo with renewed hope. Juan Arnao put it well when he wrote: "General Maceo had saved the honor of the Cubans." The Spanish viewpoint is set forth by a Spanish historian who quotes a leading general as declaring: "The 'Protest of Baraguá' is the most arrogant act of the whole campaign since the cry of Yara."[21]

The "Protest of Baraguá" aroused international attention. On April 6, 1878, *La Verdad* of New York paid a tribute to Maceo's action in resurrecting the revolution: "The hero of the day is Maceo, and it appears it is up to him to raise Cuba again to the pinnacle of its glory." A month later, *La Verdad* published a message sent to Maceo by S. R. Scottron, the Negro Secretary of the American and Foreign Anti-Slavery Society (and also, it will be recalled, chairman of the Cuban Anti-Slavery Committee). He wrote:

> My Society has read with infinite pleasure your honorable and just demands in the recent conference with General Martínez Campos. You have demanded the immediate abolition of slavery as a price for your allegiance. Few men in the history of the world have had the good fortune of finding themselves in such an honorable position as that which you now occupy. And none have occupied one more noble. ... The friends of liberty in America as in Europe have their eyes anxiously fixed on you, hoping that perhaps you will save that noble Cuban army which successfully sustains the flag of liberty.

In England the Anti-Slavery Society of London cited the "Protest of Baraguá" in an appeal to the British government to apply pressure upon Spain for the fulfillment of its promise to emancipate all the slaves of Cuba, "a promise so many times repeated and so often violated."[22]

To give meaning to the "Protest of Baraguá," it was necessary to reorganize the whole resistance movement. All officers with the rank of Colonel and above who adhered to the "Protest of Baraguá" met, at Maceo's request, drew up a new constitution, formed a new government and dispensed new military commands. Although he was now the outstanding leader of the revolutionary movement, Maceo did not seek a position in the top leadership of the government and he became neither President nor Commander-in-Chief of the army. Instead, Manuel de Jesús Calvar was named President, and Vicente García, who had not even participated in the "Protest of Baraguá" was made General-in-Chief of the Liberating Army. Maceo accepted the post of Second-in-Command of the Army and Commander-in-Chief of the Military Department of Oriente. His decision was motivated by his desire to establish the strongest unity in the resistance movement. "To realize the formation of the new government," he wrote to General Julio Sanguily in New York, "I proposed that all the chiefs of this department should make friends with General García and that we should give him what he so much wanted to achieve by political means in order that all united they should help me to save our principles and the honor of our arms."[23]

The revolutionists faced almost insuperable odds. The long years of suffering and the consequent weariness had created demoralization in the ranks and a lack of will to fight. There were new surrenders by rebel commanders with their forces on the terms already granted. Martínez Campos's tactics of infiltrating the rebel ranks and persuading or bribing some of them to accept peace were producing results. With Maceo, however, the Spaniards were utterly unsuccessful. Cuban emissaries sent to persuade him to make peace were arrested by the Negro Commander. On one occasion the Spanish Military Commander of Barrancas de Cauto sent a messenger to Maceo with a letter offering large sums of money if the Negro leader would leave the island. When he had read the letter, Maceo asked the messenger brusquely: "Commander, do you know the contents of that document?" "No," replied the official, "I am only a messenger of my superior officer and am in absolute ignorance of its contents." "I am glad," said Maceo, "because it prevents me from having the pain of hanging you on that tree." With the approval of the provisional government, Maceo sent his answer by the same messenger. It stated that the author of the attempted bribe-letter was an "infamous coward."

On another occasion, when Maceo was offered a considerable sum of money if he would accept the Pact of Zanjón, he replied (March 18, 1878):

> Do you think that a man who is fighting for a principle and has a high regard for his honor and reputation can sell himself while there is still at least a chance of saving his principles by dying or trying to enforce them before he denigrates himself? Men like me fight only in the cause of liberty and will smash their guns rather than submit. I believe that the sentiments of General Martínez Campos are very noble, but we don't need anything else but the things for which we have to go on living. So on this account, it would be impossible for me to receive you with open arms after you have offended me so much.[24]

Led by Maceo, the rebels initiated an intense campaign of military action against the Spanish forces. At first, the Spaniards met these actions with passive resistance. General Martínez Campos instructed his soldiers not to fight and to answer all assaults with shouts of: *"Viva Cuba! Viva la paz! No hagáis fuego, pues somos hermanos."* (Long live Cuba! Long live peace! Don't shoot, since we are all brothers!)[25] But the Spaniards did not continue this peace strategy for long, and soon hurled all their soldiers against the rebel forces. Day by day, the rebel ranks were thinned by wounds and deaths, by constant Spanish pressure, and by a steady stream of desertions.

With all of Spain's forces concentrated against him and his followers, Maceo faced a hopeless situation unless he could obtain immediate aid and widen the scope of the battle. But now Maceo received the news that the official agents of the revolution in the United States had quit their jobs. The Cuban tobacco workers in Key West and Tampa had organized clubs and contributed funds for military supplies, and a demonstration had been held in the Masonic Hall of New York. But General Sanguily had met with only a cold response from the wealthy Cuban emigrants, and his expected supply expedition had failed to materialize.

The sombre situation which confronted the new revolutionary movement was clearly described by Dr. Félix Figueredo:

> The persecution directed by General Martínez Campos was so active that the provisional government and Maceo could not keep a fixed camp and could not rest except during the night hours.... Meanwhile, not a day passed without the arrival of unfavorable news for the revolution. The Cuban forces of Manzanillo and Bayamo, and those of the western border of Holguín, which Colonel Belisario G. de Peralta commanded, were dispersing amidst the most profound disorganization. What had already happened in Camagüey and western Las Villas was occurring in eastern Las Villas.... To complete this picture of dissolution, many *insurrectos* of clear intelligence, upon returning to their families and seeing themselves respected and well treated by the Spanish military chieftains, cooperated with the peace move by sending letters to their companions still in arms.[26]

On May 1, Figueredo noted in his diary that a return to peace was inevitable, and on May 3 he told of a plan offered to the government designed to save Maceo from the certain death that awaited him, and to prevent a forced and pathetic surrender. This plan proposed that Maceo be sent to foreign territories for the purpose of using his influence and reputation in securing supplies and reinforcements for the insurrection.

At first the idea received a negative response; the attitude was that all should go down or be saved. But finally the government decided that someone should be spared the dishonor of having to make any compromise. If sufficient aid could not be obtained, he could lead a new movement at some future date. General Mármol, another member of the government, argued that the revolution would almost certainly die without Maceo, but that there was no other choice than to send him for aid since it seemed likely to fail even if Maceo remained.

When Maceo was informed of this decision, he replied: "I will obey whatever order the government gives on condition that it promises, in the event that it has to leave the battle field, not to capitulate until my return or until I have made a report on this situation among the emigrants and on whatever hope they offer for the continuance of the fight."

Arrangements were made with the Spaniards for Maceo to depart. Meeting Martínez Campos, Maceo thanked him for his kind consideration for himself and his family, but added that he did not consider himself bound or restricted in his future conduct and he would try again. "As I am not compromised," he concluded, "I will do what I can to come back and then undertake my work anew."[27]

On May 10, 1878, a Spanish cruiser left Santiago de Cuba for Jamaica with Antonio Maceo aboard. On the following day, Henry C. Hall, the American Consul in Havana wrote to the State Department:

> The surrender of the Chief 'Maceo' is without doubt the most important event that has occurred since the capitulation of Maximo Gómez and others in February ultimo. . . . His force, according to the 'Diario' (de la Marina) of today, comprised four hundred men and upwards, and was admitted to be a very efficient corps, as was also Maceo himself considered a very efficient and energetic chief, frequently, and even recently it is said, successful in his encounters with the Spanish forces. His surrender is the more important as regards the pacification of the Island, as his force still remained a nucleus to which the many discontented spirits of the insurrection could rally.[28]

Hall was not entirely correct, for Maceo had not surrendered. Indeed, the Negro General left behind on Cuba a great symbol for the future: for it was Maceo's "Protest of Baraguá" that enabled all patriotic Cubans to say that the revolutionists had never surrendered, had never been defeated, and that only a temporary truce had been declared.

From Jamaica, Maceo went to New York where he began to

raise the desperately needed money for arms for the rebel government in Cuba. He had begun a report to President Calavar when he learned that the rebel government had accepted the Spanish peace terms on May 21. With the government he represented having ceased to exist, and no fighting force left in Cuba, Maceo halted his efforts in New York and returned to Jamaica.

The Ten Years' War was over—the war that José Martí so eloquently described as "that wonderful and sudden emergence of a people, apparently servile only a short time before, who made heroic feats a daily event, hunger a banquet, and the extraordinary, a commonplace."

> The war that has been by foreign observers compared to an epic, the upheaval of a whole country, the voluntary abandonment of wealth, the abolition of slavery in our first moment of freedom, the burning of our cities by our own hands, the erection of villages and factories in the wild forests, the dressing of our ladies of rank in the texture of the woods, the keeping at bay, in ten years of such a life, the powerful enemy, with a loss to him of 200,000 men, at the hands of a small army of patriots, with no help but nature! We had no Hessians and no Frenchmen, no Lafayette or Steuben, no monarchical rivals to help us; we had but one neighbor who confessedly "stretched the limits of his power, and acted against the will of the people" to help the foes of those who were fighting for the same Chart of Liberties on which he built his independence.[29] *

No accurate figures are available, but the cost in lives for the Cubans was about 50,000 dead; the Spaniards 208,000. (It is impossible to determine how many Cubans were killed by Spanish cruelty.) The cost in money amounted to $300,000,000. This sum was added to the Cuban debt, for Cuba was made to pay for the expenses of both sides.

In retrospect, it is clear that the inability to render the island

---

* Martí, of course, was referring to the shabby role played by the government of the United States, against the will of the American people, in helping the cause of Spain against the Cuban revolutionaries. This description of the Ten Years' War was written by Martí in 1889, in answer to an editorial in *The Manufacturer* of March 16, 1889, reprinted a few days later in the New York *Evening Post*, which said scornfully of the "native Cubans": "Their lack of manly force and of self-respect is demonstrated by the supineness with which they have so long submitted to Spanish oppression, and even their attempts at rebellion have been so pitifully ineffective that they have risen little above the dignity of farce." In his answer Martí tended to exaggerate the significance of the step taken against slavery by the Cuban Republic in the early days of the war.

useless to Spain (since the war was limited to the eastern portions), internal dissensions, the absence of substantial outside help, and the refusal of the government of the United States to recognize Cuban belligerency were key factors in the failure of the Ten Years' War. Fifteen years later, Martí said: "The Spaniard did not defeat us because of his courage, but because of our pettiness, only because of our pettiness." The war did, nevertheless, play an important role in the course of future events in Cuba. For those Cubans who feared the strength of Spanish arms, the long and determined stand of the rebels provided a sense of confidence. Proof of Cuban strength was the fact that the war could not be ended by force of arms but was brought to a close by a deal with dissident elements within the revolutionary ranks. Martínez Campos conceded that it was impossible to defeat the Cubans by armed might alone, and the Spanish historian Luis Morate in his work, *La Moral de la Derrota*, says concerning the Pact of Zanjón that it represented a victory of war-weariness and lack of resources, but "not a decisive victory of arms."[30]

From a practical military standpoint, the war was important too. It gave the Cubans training and experience in guerrilla fighting, and men like Gómez and Maceo became masters of this technique of battle. Moreover, mistakes made in the war could be studied so that they might be remedied in a future one. Indeed, in many ways, this decade of war served as the proving ground for the final revolution against Spanish absolutism. The same men who led the resistance in the Ten Years' War were also the leaders in 1895.

In reality, the Treaty of Zanjón must be considered as nothing more than a truce. The war had opened an abyss between the Spanish metropolis and its Cuban colony that could never again be closed.

chapter 22

THE LITTLE WAR

Shortly after the acceptance of the Pact of Zanjón, the leaders of the mediation movement took steps to organize their followers so that the promises made by Martínez Campos might be realized. Their preliminary organization was the *Comité Provincial Cubano*, which pledged itself to the legal fulfillment of the terms of the peace. The provisional organization soon gave way to a political party, *El Partido Liberal*, later called the Autonomist Party. The platform was drawn up at the first meeting of the party council, which took place in Havana, on August 3, 1878, even before such organizations in the island had been legalized. The program was built around three principles considered essential to the future of the island under Spanish rule:

1. POLITICAL: Civil rights and guaranties were to be extended to include freedom of speech, press, and assembly; Cubans and Spaniards to have equal opportunity to hold office; and civil and military authority to be separated.

2. ECONOMIC: Redistribution of the tax burden should be made; treaties of commerce should be drawn favoring Cuba, and treaties with the United States especially should be effected.

3. SOCIAL: Slaves were to be emancipated and no more Negroes were to be admitted to Cuba. However, no specific plan for emancipation of the slaves was drawn up and no time-table indicated.

On August 16, 1878, *El Partido Unión Constitucional* (the Constitutional Union Party) was organized by the conservative, pro-Spanish elements. The manifesto of the party stated: "Cuba is, and Cuba ought to continue forever to be a province of Spain. The Constitution of the monarchy is and ought to be for Cuba, as for every other province, the fundamental law." Within this framework, the party stood for the right of petition; for improvement in the methods of administration of the laws; for the enactment of special laws for Cuba, including protection for the various industries, the sugar planters, and the tobacco raisers; and for the removal of excessive import duties. It also sought a commercial treaty with the United States. On the social question, it stood for the abolition of slavery in accordance with the Moret Law, with modifications which seemed proper in the light of conditions in Cuba.[1]

Despite surface differences, the Liberal and Constitutional Union parties stood shoulder to shoulder in urging peace and order, promising that Cuba would receive more at the hand of Spain through co-operation than through unrest and revolution. This similarity of outlook stemmed logically from the social composition of the two parties. The base of the Constitutional Union Party, as the astute contemporary student of Cuban political affairs, the Negro Juan Gualberto Gómez* pointed out, was formed by

> individuals who had reached Cuba in an inferior position. The war had elevated them, had given them importance and put them in a position to influence public affairs. They had been active in the ranks of the Volunteers as "defenders of integrity"; they have become rich while the sons of the country were being ruined. . . . As was natural, they wished to keep on commanding after Zanjón, and fought to maintain their monopoly of governmental influence. . . . [They] were a true oligarchy formed by the overseas bureaucracy and commercial groups and directed by lawyers who defended the system of slavery, the basis of the fortunes of the great *hacendados* and their clients, the capitalists. . . . This was the Constitutional Union Party.

On the other hand, Gómez pointed out, the Liberal Party

> also formed an oligarchy, but it was formed in the main by those Creoles who had not taken part in the insurrection, and some of those revolutionary elements which contributed most to the Pact of Zanjón. It represented the true middle class of Cuba, distinguished lawyers, doctors, learned professional people, second-class *hacendados*, people of true property in the country. They felt the humiliation to which the old colonial regime condemned them, and were fighting to modify it. They wanted to have the same rights as the rest of the Spaniards.[2]

* Born in Cuba, Gómez had been sent to France as a youth by his parents to learn the trade of carriage-making. (In Cuba such opportunities for Negroes were few.) In Paris, Gómez assisted Francisco Vicente Aguilera in mobilizing support among the Cuban exiles for the Ten Years' War. After a stay in Mexico, he returned to Cuba following the Pact of Zanjón.

The liberals, in short, wanted the white Creoles to occupy a prominent place in Cuban society under Spanish rule, while the conservatives of the Constitutional Union Party sought to maintain their dominant position in the island. But on the question of Spanish domination and of white supremacy, both parties saw eye-to-eye.

There was a third political party projected under the leadership of Don Nicolás Azcárate, a distinguished lawyer and former member of the Reform Commission of 1866–67, who had just returned to Cuba from exile in Mexico, and Don Adolfo Márquez Sterling, a leading journalist. This party came out for free trade, free labor, the prompt and complete abolition of slavery, and universal suffrage. But in the absence of freedom of the press and assemblage, and in the face of Spanish hostility, this party could not be organized.

Although the Constitutional Union and Liberal parties, and especially the Liberal Party, represented the most substantial and influential elements among white Cubans, there were still many who expected nothing from Spain, rejected the idea of Cuba being assimilated as a Spanish province, whether autonomous or not (even if Spain were ready to grant this, which they doubted), and believed that independence by means of an armed victory over the oppressor was the only meaningful solution. As these Cuban patriots saw it, Zanjón was only a truce, not a surrender; the Cubans had stopped fighting not because they were tired, but because they needed to pause in order that they might take up the fight again with renewed strength and better weapons.

At first these views were not too popular in a country weary of so many years of bloodshed, but each passing month brought new adherents. It was soon demonstrated that the Pact of Zanjón was a cruel joke. The key provision—promising the same political concessions to Cuba as Puerto Rico then enjoyed—proved to be a hoax. Puerto Rico, it was revealed, was still legally in a state of siege. In 1874, the concessions made by the "Glorious Revolution" of 1868 had been suspended, and Puerto Rico enjoyed no other political right than representation in the Cortes. Again and again, Martínez Campos wrote his government, asking for fulfillment of the Pact of Zanjón as he understood it. But the Spanish government refused to budge.[3] Supported by the most reactionary elements in Cuba and by statesmen in Spain who considered all Cubans except the most reactionary groups in the island as disloyal, the government in Madrid continued to undermine the hopes that had surged with the capitulation at Zanjón. Even those who shunned a renewal of armed hostilities were forced to concede that it was obviously impossible to force Spain to listen in this critical moment to the plea for justice for Cuba. But beyond this they refused to go.

There were others, however, the best elements in Cuba, who raised the need for beginning again the task of liberating the island from the Spanish yoke.

The movement for a new rebellion was begun by a group of veterans of the Ten Years' War who had settled in New York after the Pact of Zanjón. The highest ranking officer of this group was Major General Calixto García. In 1874, after holding off the enemy for 100 days, García had shot himself under the chin so as not to fall into the hands of the Spaniards alive. The bullet was deflected and his life was saved, but he remained a prisoner until Zanjón, when he was released from a Spanish prison. He came to New York with his reputation unscathed, for he was one of the few leaders of the revolution who had not signed the Pact. He immediately reorganized the *Comité Revolucionario Cubano* (Revolutionary Cuban Committee) under his presidency. In October, 1878, General García issued a manifesto inviting all Cubans to unite in the fight against Spanish despotism, and urging all separatists on the island to organize in secret groups "to work by all means conducive to the achievement of independence, contriving and collecting financial resources and material for war."[4]

The response to this appeal was startling. An underground movement was organized in Cuba. Beginning in Oriente, it spread like wildfire to other parts of the island. Even in Havana, the conspiracy began to attract supporters. Many recruits came from the Negro population; they were eager to pick up the battle for independence and the complete abolition of slavery, and were encouraged to do so by some of the more radical leaders of the revolutionary movement. "Take your machetes in hand, and burn the cane," *La Independencia,* organ of the Revolutionary Committee in New York, urged the slaves on November 23, 1878.

One of the chief lessons learned from the Ten Years' War was that a merely regional movement could not successfully combat the overwhelming Spanish superiority in men and supplies. To be truly effective, a war had to be a simultaneous rebellion throughout the whole island. With this in mind, Colonel Pedro Martínez Freire prepared a detailed plan which was based on the idea of calling for a spontaneous uprising in all the provinces of the island. This revolt was planned to coincide with a complete seizure of the Spanish arsenals in Santiago de Cuba. According to Freire's plan, Calixto García and Antonio Maceo were to come to the island to assume supreme command immediately after the start of the rebellion.

This plan received the enthusiastic support of Calixto García, and he began to mobilize the revolutionary movement in the western part of the island from his base in New York. Freire sent emissaries from Santiago to discuss his plans with former rebel leaders: Francisco Carrillo, Emilio Núñez, and Serafín Sańchez in Las Villas; and in Havana, José Antonio Aguilera, José Martí, and Juan Gualberto Gómez.

Martí had returned to Cuba on September 3, 1878, from Guatemala, where he had been a professor at the Central Normal School. (He had resigned his professorship after an injustice done to its director, José María Izaguirre, a former teacher in Bayamo, Cuba, who had been forced into exile.) In conversations with associates in Havana, Martí immediately began to advance the position that Cuba must continue the struggle to obtain its independence, and to that end there was only one path to follow—armed revolt. In these discussions, he was soon supported by Juan Gualberto Gómez. Martí and Gómez met in the law office of don Nicolás Azcárate, and despite Azcárate's warning that they were pursuing a dangerous course, they formed a close friendship, united by the common desire to liberate their country. Together the Negro and white revolutionaries worked for independence: Gómez through political articles in *La Libertad*, a daily paper newly founded by Adolfo Márquez Sterling, and Martí in private conversations and public addresses. In one speech, Martí openly referred to Cuba as "Our Nation," and in another, April 19, 1879, at a banquet in honor of Márquez Sterling, sponsored by the Liberal Party, he stated his willingness to support the Liberals only if they would agree to work energetically for a radical solution of all of Cuba's problems. He made it clear that he believed independence, not autonomy, was the solution. Rights, he declared, were "to be taken, not requested; seized, not begged for."[5]

In Oriente province, José Maceo and Guillermo Moncada were making preparations for an uprising; in Las Villas, Emilio Núñez and Serafín Sánchez were preparing to join them; and in Havana and in other provinces, the revolutionary clubs were maintaining contact with these preparations. But the movement could not continue for long on such a smooth course. Spanish spies among the revolutionists easily learned of the project and sought to arouse the old divisive tendencies among the rebels. They shrewdly resurrected the old rumor that the Negroes were plotting a race war for the extermination of the whites. They pointed to the fact that Antonio Maceo was scheduled to lead the insurrection in Oriente, that other Negroes, José Maceo, Guillermo Moncada, Flor Crombet, Jesús Rabí, Cecilio González, and Serafín Sánchez, were among the most active conspirators, and that with Antonio Maceo at the head, these men were plotting to take over the direction of the newly projected revolution as the first step in the establishment of a Negro Republic.

The Spanish propaganda campaign was assisted by those Cubans still financially tied to the institution of slavery, and by the new political parties in Cuba which clung to reformism and wished to crush the budding revolutionary movement. The Liberals spread far and wide the charge that the new revolution was being planned solely by "4,000 Negroes who proclaim not only the flag of separation but also a war of the races." From Cuba, the Revolutionary Committee in New York received letters which emphasized: "A belief is circulating and being hotly discussed that the movement in Cuba is made up of people of color only, and is simply a prelude to a war of races."[6]

A number of Cuban exiles who occupied places of influence in the Revolutionary Committee, and who were themselves influenced by white supremacist ideology, reacted to these reports by calling for limiting the role of the Negroes in the revolution, and especially sought to prevent Antonio Maceo from assuming a commanding position. But General Calixto García and his followers discovered that no one commanded greater respect in Oriente than the Negro hero of the Ten Years' War, and Oriente, after all, was the seat of the real rebellious spirit in Cuba. On August 5, 1879, at a conference in Kingston, Jamaica, Maceo and García, as head of the Revolutionary Committee of New York, reached an understanding on the projected uprising. In the interview with García, Maceo was led to believe that he would be the commander of the Oriente district as well as the leader of an expedition to the island. Maceo immediately sent letters from Kingston to his friends in Oriente, advising them to make preparations for the approaching conflict: "The moment for returning to the field of battle has arrived. We must conquer what rightly belongs to us by armed might."[7]

On August 26, 1879, the revolt erupted in Cuba. What has historically come to be called *La Guerra Chiquita* (The Little War) began prematurely that day in Santiago de Cuba. As in the case of the Ten Years' War, the Spanish spy system forced the rebel leaders to begin hostilities prior to the fixed date, to prevent their being seized and imprisoned. When the Negro leaders, José Maceo and Rafael Maceo (brothers of Antonio), Guillermo Moncada, and Quintín Banderas raised the standard of revolt in Santiago, other declarations followed in the rest of Oriente and in the central part of the island. Las Villas responded under Brigadier Ramos, Emilio Núñez, Serafín Sánchez and Francisco Carrillo. These rebel leaders, Negro and white, were followed by hundreds of men, especially by large numbers of runaway slaves.

Calixto García and Antonio Maceo were waiting for the right moment to land in Cuba and assume leadership of the movement. Maceo, ready to depart for the island, sent a manifesto from Kingston to Santiago de Cuba calling on all Cubans to fight for liberty, and urging the Negro slaves to join the Liberating Army:

> You must remember at all times that your comrades who fought in the last war achieved their liberty because they embraced the Cuban flag which belongs to all Cubans alike. Get together again under the same flag, and you shall obtain freedom and your civil rights, and after that, you shall be able to make a common cause with those that today want to redeem you from the degraded situation in which you find yourselves now.[8]

In Havana the revolutionary clubs mobilized to give effective aid and to extend the revolutionary movement. A Central Committee was organized, with Martí as president, and steps were taken to collect contributions for the rebels in Las Villas and Oriente, and for the preparation of a similar uprising in the province of Havana.

From Havana American Consul Henry C. Hall informed the State Department that the Spanish authorities feared that "unless very promptly put down, it [the insurrection] may in some way be seconded by the slave population who, it is said, are becoming, day by day, less reconciled to their condition." On September 25, 1879, he wrote:

> It would appear that the government of Spain gives much importance to these movements, as according to the telegram published here, twenty thousand soldiers are to be sent out immediately, and the Governor General has been authorized to draw upon the Treasury of Spain for fifty thousand dollars a day; these prompt measures indicate a determination to put down the insurrectionary movement before it shall have assumed greater proportions.[9]

Alarmed by the growth of the revolutionary movement which had begun so vigorously, the Spanish government also retaliated by making wholesale arrests of all persons, particularly Negroes, who were under the slightest suspicion of sympathy with the rebellion. In Santiago alone, 350 Negroes were arrested, shipped to Havana, and thrown into the dungeon of Morro Castle, to await the sailing of ships that would transport them to the Ceuta penitentiary.

In the province of Havana, the revolutionary movement was crushed. Martí was deported under "surveillance" to Spain on September 25, 1879;* Aguilera and Gómez were arrested and shipped off to Ceuta; others were sent to the Isle of Pines; while still others who were involved succeeded in escaping to New York.

Thus Freire's carefully prepared plan could never be put into effect. Nevertheless, the revolutionary movement, frustrated in the Occidente region, was spreading all through the eastern portion of the island. Almost all of Oriente was in arms, and in the central part of the island, fighting was increasing. The rebels were awaiting the expeditions scheduled to arrive in Cuba with Calixto García and Antonio Maceo at the head. Maceo, they had learned, would lead the first expedition and assume leadership of the campaign.

* Captain General Ramón Blanco, who had heard Martí speak and use the expression "Our Country," regarded the Cuban patriot as "a dangerous madman" who should be promptly imprisoned. But, under pressure from Martí's friends, he promised him that he would not be brought to trial if he declared in the newspapers his adherence to Spain. "Tell the General that Martí is not the kind of man that can be bought," Martí replied. (Jorge Mañach, *Martí: Apostle of Freedom*, New York, 1950, p. 162.)

But the Revolutionary Committee in New York decided not to let Antonio Maceo head the expedition to Cuba. Instead, it placed Brigadier General Gregorio Benítez in charge of the expedition. When Maceo asked why Benítez, who did not have the Negro General's following and prestige, was chosen, he was told it was due to racial prejudice. Calixto García put it bluntly to Maceo: "Comrade, I have decided upon the departure of Benítez ahead of you, because the Spaniards have said that this is a racial war and the Cuban whites fear that this may be true. In order not to create the impression that this propaganda has validity, I thought it best you should not go first." The Spaniards were shrieking that Maceo wished to achieve Negro domination of the island, and many Cubans were swallowing the Spanish propaganda. "However," García added, "you know that I am not capable of believing such a thing." Nevertheless, to give the lie to Spanish propaganda, Maceo would have to wait. It was only a question of time, however, before he would be given notice to leave for Cuba.[10]

Although García was justified in claiming that he himself did not believe the Spanish propaganda, it is unfortunate that he yielded to the pressure of those elements in the Revolutionary Committee who either believed it or used the propaganda to foster their own ambitions. Certainly García should have foreseen that the exclusion of Maceo from the leadership of the revolution would disillusion many on the island. Many Negroes now felt that the Cuban rebels did not really have the interests of the Negroes at heart, and were only using them to advance their own purposes. How much faith could they now have that the Republic they were fighting for would abolish slavery and grant the Negroes equality of rights as citizens?

Although justifiably bitter, Maceo refused to sever his connections with the revolutionary movement. In 1876 he had decided, after some hesitation, not to allow the racists in the revolutionary ranks to stop him from fighting for Cuban independence and the liberation of his people from slavery. Now in 1879 his decision was the same.

Realizing the serious effect it would have on the rebel cause, many Cuban patriots deplored the exclusion of Maceo, and none more so than José Martí. He was in New York City, having arrived from Spain on January 3, 1880, and immediately joined the Revolutionary Committee. Anxious to mobilize more adequate support for the insurrection in Cuba and to cement greater unity among the exiles, he suggested a public meeting. The Revolutionary Committee agreed, and, on January 24, before a Cuban audience that filled Steck Hall, Martí made his first speech in the United States. To the discomfort of the wealthy aristocratic émigrés, but to the delight of the Negro and white tobacco workers who filled the rear of the hall, Martí dealt with the Negro question as it affected the revolution in Cuba. He recalled the heroic contributions of the Negroes in the Ten Years' War, and pointed out that they were continuing to aid the cause of independence in the current insurrection in Cuba. Referring to the charge that the slaves were using the insurrection to wreak vengeance on the whites, he denied it as Spanish propaganda, but went on to declare boldly "that the sins of the slave fall wholly and exclusively on the master."* Finally, before leaving the subject to deal with other aspects of the revolution, Martí announced his faith in "the Negroes and mulattoes—for there is no reason to avoid such designations, as plain and natural as other nouns," and called for unity among all Cuban patriots regardless of race or color.[11]

Martí's words had an electrifying effect on many in the audience. But it was a little too late to unite the revolutionary movement, so seriously disrupted by the racial issue. On April 17, 1880, General García sailed from Jersey City with 27 expeditionaries and landed in Cuba on May 7. Maceo, however, was still waiting in Santo Domingo for word to depart for the island.

The Revolutionary Committee in New York hailed the news of García's landing as signifying inevitable triumph for the revolution. But the Committee was whistling in the dark to keep up the spirits of the exiles. The truth is that the situation for the *insurrectos* was growing worse from day to day. The prolonged delay in bringing Antonio Maceo to Cuba had a demoralizing effect on the rebellion. Brigadier Benítez, with whom the Revolutionary Committee had replaced Maceo, had been captured by the Spaniards shortly after

---

* As a child, Martí had seen acts of such inhumanity committed against Negro slaves in Cuba that he could never forget them. In manhood he wrote: "What man who has seen a Negro whipped does not ever after consider himself his debtor? I saw it, I saw it when I was a child, and my cheeks still burn with shame." (José Martí, *Fragmentos: Obras Completas de Martí*, edited by Gonzalo de Quesada y Miranda, La Habana, 1949, p. 34.)

his arrival. In the central towns, Emilio Núñez, Serafín Sánchez, and Francisco Carrillo were defending their areas as best they could against numerically superior Spanish forces. In Oriente, where the movement had initially made the greatest progress, the situation had seriously deteriorated. Harassed by the vigorous efforts of a powerful Spanish army, and constantly lacking provisions and support, General José Maceo, Brigadier Rafael Maceo, Guillermo Moncada, and other leaders surrendered on June 1, 1880. The surrender was arranged through the efforts of the Consuls of France and England in Guantánamo, on the condition that the rebels be given safe passage out of the island. But on the high seas, a Spanish warship seized all 76 Cubans and took them to Spanish prisons in Africa.

The revolution had suffered a grievous blow, but the revolutionaries still looked to Calixto García to lead the fighting, and hoped against hope for Antonio Maceo to land with an expedition. On both points they were bitterly disappointed. The courageous García, relentlessly pursued by the Spaniards from the day he landed, had not even been able to make contact with the scattered bands of *insurrectos*. With his expeditionaries decimated by pursuit, hunger and weariness, and he himself sick with fever, García wandered through the hills with only six ragged, barefoot companions. On August 3, 1880, García was forced to surrender to the enemy, and soon he was on the way to Spain to suffer again the discomforts of a Spanish prison.

And what of Maceo? When the Negro leader learned of the setbacks suffered by the *insurrectos* and the surrender of his two brothers and other leaders in Oriente, he decided to depart for Cuba even though he had few men and resources for the undertaking. He left Santo Domingo with 34 companions and a cargo of arms on a steamer, on June 28, 1880, ostensibly for New York. But the efficient Spanish intelligence service had learned all of the plans of the expedition through a member who was one of their spies. For the next two months, Maceo and his companions were closely followed by a Spanish warship and harassed at every point. An attempt (though not the first) was made to assassinate Maceo, but it was discovered in time.

While Maceo was en route to Jamaica, trying desperately to bring his expedition to Cuba, he learned of Calixto García's surrender and the almost total deterioration of the Little War. He realized that it was all over and that his expedition was now useless, even if it could evade the Spanish man-of-war and land in Cuba.

By September, 1880, there was only the valiant young Emilio Núñez left fighting. All the other chieftains had surrendered. Finally, his camp at Los Egidos completely surrounded by a concentration of Spanish troops, Núñez agreed to negotiate, on condition that General Blanco would allow him to request the necessary authority to do so from the Revolutionary Committee in New York. The answer came 20 days later in the form of an official authorization signed by three officials of the Revolutionary Committee, one of whom was Martí. With the authorization came a letter from Martí in which he advised Núñez, "as a revolutionist, as a man who admires your energy, and as an affectionate friend, not to remain futilely on the battlefield to which those whom you are defending are powerless to send aid." It was now necessary to concede defeat, and draw the obvious lessons from it so that the future struggle, an inevitable one, would be successful.[12]

With Núñez's surrender, the Little War was over. Captain General Blanco publicly proclaimed "the nefarious separatist flag again subdued." The New York Revolutionary Committee disbanded, and publication of *La Independencia* ceased.

Repeated failures thoroughly disheartened many Cuban revolutionaries. But those who still remained firm realized that the revolution of the future would have to profit by the lessons of past defeats. For one thing, there had to be a pause until the Cuban people, influenced by liberal propaganda that reform, not revolution, was the way out, learned through bitter experience under Spanish domination that the only real solution for Cuba was, as Martí put it, "a radical and solemn redemption imposed . . . by force." There had to be an end to internal dissension in the ranks of the revolutionaries, of racist propaganda and white supremacist ideology, of lack of co-ordination, shortage of adequate, well organized material, and the exclusion of leaders who commanded the respect of the Cuban masses, or else the revolution of the future would also end in confusion and defeat.

But this could only be the result of a long and patient process of preparation and organization. To this process, the remaining Cuban revolutionaries now dedicated their lives, convinced that the long Ten Years' War and the Little War had demonstrated that the Cubans were not resigned to remain forever ground beneath the heel of Spanish tyranny, and that the desire for independence, though temporarily crushed by war-weariness, was for many Cubans a passionate and unquenchable longing.

chapter 23

POLITICAL, ECONOMIC AND SOCIAL DEVELOPMENTS IN CUBA, 1878-1895

The end of the Little War was followed by an intensive campaign by the Liberal-Autonomist Party to convince the Cuban people that, in order to obtain concessions from Spain, it would be necessary to lay aside all revolutionary action and peacefully accept Spanish rule. In November, 1880, Manuel Surí, an official of the party, issued an appeal urging that nothing be permitted to destroy the peace of Cuba:

> Your sensitiveness, oh people! Your love of order and other civic virtues ennoble you, elevate you above all other people of the world, because you will be a firm immovable barrier to the designs of that monster, revolution, which brings only blood, tears, mourning, desolation, misery, and total extermination of all moral and material goods, which constitute our supreme, our only happiness.[1]

Between 1880 and 1895, with the exception of a brief flurry of fighting in 1885, no armed conflict in a revolutionary sense took place in Cuba. But the promise that this would result in the carrying out of long needed reforms proved to be an illusion.

Politically, very little happened between the end of the Ten Years' War and the outbreak of the Revolution in 1895 to make Cubans more satisfied with Spanish rule. The realization of the reforms promised at Zanjón was a fleeting goal forever sought but never reached.

On June 9, 1878, Spain proclaimed with much fanfare that Cuba was entitled to elect deputies to the Cortes. On the same day, the island was divided into six provinces. A decree of June 21 instituted a system of provincial and municipal government and was followed by the necessary electoral regulations.

In theory, a measure of constitutional reform had been instituted. But in practice, the situation had hardly changed. To begin with, the election of deputies to the Cortes was to be effected through electors so qualified that the propertied element in the island would have control. The Negro and poor white Cubans were deprived of any voice in the elections.

A further definition of laws regarding the elections was promulgated by the royal decree of December 27, 1892. But universal suffrage was not extended to Cuba; it was explained that the failure to do so was "solely owing to the great difficulty existing where the negro race is in the majority, or where it may exert a decisive influence in the elections." Still the electoral regulations were so drawn that most poorer white Cubans were also excluded from suffrage. Indeed, almost half of those enabled to vote were Spaniards in residence in the island.

In a major sense, regulations for election to the Cortes hardly mattered. The deputies representing Cuba were never allowed to decide any important issues brought up in the Cortes. Luis Estévez y Romero has demonstrated that only four of the 40 deputies representing Cuba in the Cortes represented Cuban constituencies.

The whole machinery of provincial and municipal government established in 1878 proved to be meaningful on paper only. The Captain General had the right to dismiss the provincial assemblies in the event of any difference over policies. Furthermore, the really significant matters—tariffs, taxes, complete control of financial issues—remained entirely under Spanish control.

On April 7, 1881, the Spanish Constitution of 1876 was promulgated in Cuba. All the public liberties and all the rights of citizenship enjoyed by Spaniards were thereby granted to Cuba, and instead of being governed by direct orders from the Crown, the island was to be ruled by laws enacted for it by the legislative body in Madrid. But here again, in practice, little real change took place. Cuba had no significant influence in the Cortes, and the exercise of the rights of citizenship, especially freedom of speech and press and the right of holding public meetings, was placed under the control of the Captain General. The possibility of criticizing Spanish institutions and policies was severely limited.

In short, the principal improvements in political and constitutional matters after Zanjón appeared in legal phraseology rather than in practice. Year after year, the Liberal-Autonomist leaders in the Cortes reiterated the principles to which they adhered: sovereignty of Spain, colonial representation in the Cortes, and representative government in Cuba. Year after year, they assured the Cubans that if prudence and patience could be made the guiding light, the cause of home rule would eventually be looked on with favor by the conservative Spaniards. But the Cortes repeatedly ignored the pleas of the Autonomist Party. In 1890, *El País*, the organ of the Autonomists, acknowledged failure: "After twelve years of painful struggle against the combined action of intrigue and violence . . . the Cuban people find themselves in worse condition than in 1878, their spirit hurt by disillusionment, their patience worn out by suffering.²

In 1886, the Autonomist leaders announced that unless their program was successful, no more candidates would be proposed for office. In 1891, this threat was carried out. But it made not the slightest difference. "There are no political reforms to make—they have been made," was the monotonous Spanish answer to all Cuban pleas.

In January, 1895, the constitutional reform promises of the Pact of Zanjón still remained unfulfilled.* Cubans who still believed in Spanish rule had demanded a constitutional system in place of the autocracy of the Captain General. They had received constitutional provisions, but in reality, the authority of the Captain General remained absolute. They had requested freedom of the press, the right of assembly and association, but they had obtained only constitutional phraseology which provided little freedom, and the enforcement of these rights was left to the discretion of the Captain General. Representation in the Cortes had been provided, but it was more legal than real. Local self-government had been proclaimed in words, but in actuality, none really existed. Cubans criticized their exclusion from public office, but the Spanish bureaucracy still dominated the political life of the colony.

Seventeen years of peaceful struggle to alter the nature of Span-

* A gesture toward political reform was made by the Cortes after the Revolution of 1895 had started in February of that year, but it was too little and too late.

ish political rule had added up to practically nothing. "Poor Cuba," wrote Estévez, "always hopeful and always deluded."[3]

Spain did fulfill one promise. The Moret Law of 1870 had promised that the government would present a law of indemnified emancipation of all slaves in Cuba as soon as deputies from that island were admitted to the Cortes. On November 5, 1879, with the Cubans seated in the legislature, the government, headed by Martínez Campos as Prime Minister, presented a project of abolition. The law, in its first article, abolished slavery in Cuba. However, this long promised measure of "immediate abolition" established an eight-year state of tutelage (*patronato*) for all slaves liberated as a result of the law. The preamble explained: "In this manner, the production of the Island will not be threatened, and fears of social upheaval will be allayed."[4]

But there was another explanation. Contrary to the promise of 1870, the new law provided no indemnity for slaveowners. Therefore the *patronato*, guaranteeing the continued labor of the Negroes for their masters, was substituted as a form of indemnity. In Puerto Rico, the government explained, indemnity was possible because there were only 31,000 slaves in 1873, whereas in Cuba there were still 200,000.

The abolitionists condemned the *patronato* as "harder servitude than slavery itself." It was a new word for slavery, said Rafael de Labra, and others described it as indemnification paid for by the sweat of the slaves. The provision in the law permitting the emancipated Negro to buy his way out of the *patronato* by paying the high price of $30 to $50 annually to the patron caused one abolitionist to comment: "A law of liberty . . . in which liberty costs more than it did before, I do not understand."[5]

The reformist deputies of Cuba in the Cortes, who spoke for the newly organized Liberal-Autonomist Party, said they would accept the law even without indemnity so long as the government made economic concessions, particularly free trade for Cuba. Cheap slave labor had formerly permitted Cuban products to penetrate freely the American tariff wall. But with the abolition of slavery, Cuba would lack the means of competing in the American market. To avoid a terrible crisis, Spain must declare free trade, and negotiate an advantageous treaty with the United States.

The Spanish government rejected this plea. The question of economic reforms had "nothing to do with the law of abolition." On January 30, 1880, the Cortes approved the abolition law by a large majority. Several Cuban deputies voted against the law because it did not attach economic concessions.

Not at all satisfied with the law, the abolitionists continued to champion the cause of the Negro, petitioning repeatedly for the abolition of the *patronato*. Actually, the system was disappearing under the impact of economic forces. The patrons were required under the law to furnish their wards with proper food and clothing and pay them monthly wages. But it proved more profitable for the masters to give the *patrocinados* their liberty, and to hire them to work as day laborers, thereby avoiding the necessity of maintaining them during slack seasons. In the first three years of the existence of the *patronato*, more than 70,000 slaves acquired liberty in this way.

This process continued. By September, 1886, there remained about 26,000 Negroes in a state of compulsory labor, and Labra predicted that "it can very well be that before six months all the Negroes will be free." On October 7, 1886, two years before the eight-year *patronato* was to terminate, a royal decree abolished slavery in Cuba.

The disappearance of slavery did not liquidate racism in Cuba. The Autonomist Party, like the Conservatives, believed in white supremacy. Negroes, both parties held, "constitute a depraved and inferior race which must be kept in its proper place in a white man's society." One of the chief problems now confronting Cuba, in the eyes of these parties, was to prevent domination of the island by "inferior races." Hence they applauded the refusal of the Spanish government to establish universal suffrage in Cuba on the ground that the Negro might dominate the elections.[6]

In the two decades following the Ten Years' War, the Cuban sugar industry underwent a revolutionary transformation. Competition from beet sugar steadily increased; by 1884, 53 percent of sugar produced in the world was the product of beets. European beet sugar had increased at such a phenomenally rapid rate that the Continent no longer needed to import sugar; on the contrary, it had a surplus. Consequently, the Cuban market depended more upon the United States than ever before. But the ability of the Americans to obtain beet sugar from Europe kept them from paying more for cane sugar.

By 1890, moreover, the American market for Cuban sugar came mainly to represent one company: the American Sugar Refining Co., the "Sugar Trust." By combining 19 refineries under the leadership of Henry O. Havemeyer, and supplying from 70 to 90 percent of the refined sugar consumed in the United States, the Sugar Trust became "to all intents and purposes the American market for Cuban sugar." Inevitably, the price of duty-paid raw sugar in New York came tumbling down: from 10 cents per pound in 1870 to 8.6 cents in 1882, 5.9 cents in 1884, and 3.2 cents in 1894.

All this had a profound effect on Cuban sugar production. To market sugar profitably in the face of sharply reducing prices, production had to become more efficient. Those mills which could not afford new machinery were lost by their owners and passed into the hands of men with capital. "Thus," wrote José S. Jorrín, "the small and middle-sized mills are absorbed, concentrating the wealth of the land into very few hands, and plunging into deep misery those who were before this wealthy landowners."[7]

Most of the less efficient plantations ceased to mill their cane; they became attached to *centrales* under contract, devoting themselves entirely to raising cane rather than grinding it. In the nine years after 1885, there was a decline from 1,400 to only 400 mills in operation.

Together with the accelerated decrease in the number of sugar mills and the rise of the "central system," there also emerged the *colono* system. Under it, the *colono* contracted to plant cane on a certain amount of the land, and to deliver the product to the *hacendado* or millowner. The latter made advances to the *colono* to cover his expenses during planting, cultivation and harvest, and deducted the advances in settling for the crop. This frequently placed the *colono* in a chronic state of debt to the millowner.

> Little by little [writes Ramiro Guerra] in the decade of the 1880's, the *Colonias de Caña*, the name by which came to be known the fields dedicated to producing the cane for the mills, increased year by year.

The farmers or cultivators dedicated to this new agricultural enterprise were designated currently by the name *colono*. By *colono* is understood from that time in Cuba a person dedicated to the production of sugar cane to be sold to the mills.[8]

By 1887, it was estimated that from 35 to 40 percent of Cuba's crop was gathered and manufactured under the *colono* system. Eventually the system included the *central*, which purchased the cane and owned most of the land on which it was grown, the agricultural operators who stood in the middle, and the thousands of wage workers who did the actual work of growing and delivering the cane.

Through such reorganization, the Cuban sugar industry managed to forge ahead in spite of declining prices. But there were other results as well. "It bound the interests of the population more inextricably with the fortunes of the sugar industry. It tied the Cuban market more closely to the concentrated demand of the American sugar trust. It brought American capital into the producing end of the sugar industry."[9]

As early as 1865, the Count of Pozos Dulces wrote that "the *hacendados* cannot keep their capital as it is passing into the hands of business men and industrialists."[10] This development was intensified during the Ten Years' War. One result of the war was the bankruptcy of many Spanish sugar interests and the beginnings of American holdings in sugar plantations. Many of the planters found the long insurrection with its attendant destruction of property and financial repercussions more than their slender resources could cope with. Estates became deeply indebted to the American shipping merchants who handled their sugar crops. Frequently the merchant took over the estate as a means of settlement. An outstanding example was the acquisition of the Soledad estate by the Atkins company of Boston. Atkins' correspondents in Cienfuegos, the Torriente Brothers, a Spanish firm, had advanced funds, supplied by Atkins, to many estates during the Ten Years' War, and they were in no position to liquidate their indebtedness to the Boston firm. One of the chief debtors of Torriente Brothers was the Sarría family. It was finally arranged that a joint mortgage of $750,000 should be placed on three of the Sarría estates. When the Atkins company foreclosed the mortgage in 1884, it became sole owners of Soledad, one of the four Sarría plantations. By 1893, Soledad comprised 12,000 acres of which 5,000 were planted to cane, with 23 miles of private railway. It employed 1,200 men in harvest time, and was one of the largest mills in the island.

A second new source of American investment in Cuba accrued from the naturalization in the United States of foreigners who owned property in the island. The war had proved to many Cubans that owners of destroyed American property received compensation, while destroyed property under Spanish registration received none. Consequently, at the close of the war, a number of influential Cuban residents quickly obtained American naturalization, which expanded America's economic stake in Cuba.

As we have seen, the rapid expansion of European beet sugar production closed the Continent as a market for Cuban sugar and made the United States the largest buyer. It also lowered the world price of raw sugar, which bankrupted many Cuban growers, and invited further foreclosure by American merchants who held the mortgages. Abolition of Cuban slavery in 1886 added to American investment in Cuba, for as the labor wage rate rose, more machinery was used in sugar processing, much of which was American made and owned. The McKinley Tariff of 1890 also accelerated this trend. It placed raw sugar on the free list and included reciprocity features which were used to secure a favorable commercial treaty for the United States with Spain. The result was a large expansion of Cuban-American commerce and a concomitant expansion of sugar production. Imports in the United States from the island rose from $53,801,591 in 1890 to $77,931,671 in 1892 and $78,766,506 in 1893. American exports to Cuba attained new highs, $17,953,570 in 1892, and $24,157,698 in 1893, as compared with $12,224,888 in 1891. Only four times in the decade prior to the enactment of the McKinley Tariff had the Cuban crop exceeded 600,000 tons. In 1891, however, the crop was 816,980 tons, and the following year it rose to the record of 976,960 tons. In 1894, the million-ton mark was passed for the first time in Cuban history.

American capital was attracted to the island by the promise of future gains, and investments increased in milling machinery, short railroad lines (used to carry sugar cane to the mills), and sugar plantations. One of the first to enter the field at this time was Henry O. Havemeyer, president of the American Sugar Refining Co. and head of the Sugar Trust. In 1892, he and two other Americans (one of whom was E. A. Atkins) bought the Trinidad Sugar Co., which was incorporated in New Jersey the same year. Two other sugar companies were incorporated in New Jersey in 1892, the Mapos Sugar Co. and the Victoria Co.; and in the same year, the El Triunfo estate of 1,533 acres was also purchased by Americans. In 1893, the Mapos Sugar Co. purchased an estate of 2,800 acres at Sancti Spíritus. It was soon valued at $300,000 and its capacity production reached 6,000 tons.

Among the other sugar plantations taken over by American investors in this period were the Tuinicú Cane Sugar Co., Hormiguero, Los Canos, and the Constance Sugar Co., one of the largest in Cuba, producing approximately 20,000 tons annually. In addition, innumerable properties belonged to Cubans who had secured American citizenship, greatly increasing America's economic interest in the island.

The same decade that witnessed American investment in sugar plantations saw a similar movement in other enterprises. Most important were iron mines, the largest of which, the Juraguá Iron Co., was sold in 1884 to the Bethlehem and Pennsylvania Steel companies. By 1895, the development had produced a little over 3,000,000 tons of iron ore, and in 1897, its property at Santiago de Cuba was valued at $2,400,000. Two other American-owned iron companies existed—the Ponopu Mining & Transportation Co. and the Sigua Iron Co.—but they were still in process of developing production in 1895. In addition, a small amount of American capital was invested in cattle ranches, fruit and tobacco plantations, and public utilities.

An exact total of American investment in Cuba by 1895 is difficult to secure since statistics were not well kept. Richard Olney, U.S. Secretary of State in 1895, estimated American investment at $50,000,000. Recent scholarly studies indicate that investment in sugar production amounted to from $10,000,000 to $30,000,000 and that about $10,000,000 was invested in manufacturing. About 50 percent of the capital in sugar production was owned by naturalized Americans.

Within a generation or even less, the large American sugar corporations were to take over the bulk of cane production in Cuba. Still, according to the National Congress of Cuban Historians of 1947: "By the beginning of the year 1895, Cuba had definitely been converted into an economic colony of the United States."[11] In commerce, the United States dominated the Cuban market. The statistics of sugar exported from Cuba for the year 1892 reveal this clearly:

SUGAR BAGS EXPORTED	
United Kingdom	0
Spain and the Canaries	328,521
United States	1,154,193
Canada	2,500
South and Central America	10
Total	1,485,224

Between 1887 and 1897, the United States bought nearly all of Cuba's major exports—sugar and tobacco—while Cuba purchased during the decade about one-fifteenth of America's exports. Since Cuba was now mainly a single-crop economy and depended entirely on the American market, the health of its economy was in American hands. By increasing the tobacco duties, the McKinley Tariff had ruined the American market for all but the finest Cuban tobacco. By its protection to American refiners—the Sugar Trust received two cents a pound protection against competition from Europe and elsewhere in its refined product—it compelled a large number of manufacturers of high-grade sugar in Cuba to close down.

When the world-wide depression began in 1893, the rate of American investment and the size of its commerce with Cuba declined. The next year, the Wilson-Gorman Tariff placed a 40 percent duty on raw sugar, thus removing the advantages which the Cuban producer had enjoyed over other foreign sugars in the American market. He was now confronted with serious competition from heavily subsidized European beet sugar at a time when the world market was glutted. The average price of sugar in New York in 1894 was approximately $3\frac{1}{4}$ cents a pound, the lowest on record.

To add to Cuba's woes, Spain retaliated against the Wilson-Gorman Tariff by returning to the system of discriminatory duties against American imports into Cuba, a system which had been temporarily rescinded after the McKinley Tariff. With the monopolistic position of the Spanish peninsular merchants re-established, the cost of living soared in Cuba. In January, 1895, an agreement was reached placing American goods on an equality with other foreign products, but by then most of the damage had been done.

The serious economic conditions that engulfed Cuba in the winter of 1894-95 stimulated widespread discussions in the island. One group insisted that annexation to the United States was the only solution for Cuba's difficulties. Spanish laws restricted trade unnecessarily, and Spain, concerned lest closer economic relations between the island and the United States would wean Cuba away from the mother country, would never fully relax its feudal-like grasp on the Cuban economy. One Cuban writer asked: "How much of the Cuban sugar is consumed by Spain?" He estimated that Spain used perhaps 300,000 tons, which left close to 500,000 tons of unsaleable sugar. "Would England buy any? No, she has colonies to supply her needs. Will France? Less. Germany?—Even less. Italy? Do not even think about it." Only the United States could supply the market and unless closer relations were formed with the North American Republic, there would be no one to buy Cuban sugar.[12]

Another group insisted, however, that the cause of the difficulty was the single-crop system and its total dependence on the American market and the commercial goodwill of the United States. Ways had to be found immediately to create new industries which would manufacture by-products of the one great crop, sugar. To place such great reliance on the U.S. market was dangerous. Moreover, it gave the United States a weapon to hold over Cuba, and anytime Washington wanted to raise duties on sugar, Cuba would enter an economic decline. The case of the McKinley Tariff of 1890 was cited to prove this point. Sugar had been placed on the free list, but the President was authorized to impose duties on any nation which levied "unjust or unreasonable" duties on American products. If Spain had refused to make a commercial treaty to permit the favorable entry of American farm and industrial products into Cuba, the United States would have discriminated against Cuban sugar and the island would have suffered economic chaos. Fortunately, this did not happen in this particular case, but it did indicate how dependent Cuba had become on American goodwill. Hence if Cuba did not develop industrially, at the end of a few years the island would be a vassal of the United States.

But the most important effect of the economic crisis in Cuba in the winter of 1894–95 was to bring into sharp focus all the long-standing political and economic grievances against Spain: burdensome taxation, an overwhelming Cuban debt, exclusion of Cubans from government positions, discriminatory economic practices, the arbitrary treatment of persons and property, and the lack of freedom of speech, press and the right to assemble. More and more Cubans began to see that the argument that Spain would grant all necessary concessions if only Cuba avoided the path of insurrection was wishful thinking. More and more Cubans listened eagerly to reports that the revolutionists in exile were ready "to unfurl the standard of rebellion."

Among those who listened most eagerly were the members of the Cuban labor movement.

A considerable part of the tobacco industry emigrated to Key West, Florida, at the outbreak of the Ten Years' War and drew with it the workers who had taken the lead in the early labor organizations in the island. Still there was some labor activity in Cuba, partly stimulated by the Paris Commune of 1871, whose history and principles were studied by Cuban workers. In 1872, an association of tobacco graders was formed in Havana, and three years later one of tobacco strippers. There is a report of a strike of tobacco harvesters in 1872. There is evidence, too, of the formation prior to 1877 of a union of typographers, one of the first organizations of labor to be formed outside of the tobacco industry.

With the end of the Ten Years' War, the labor movement began to move forward rapidly. The re-establishment of factory and workshop readings was a stimulating influence. Organizational activity was especially strong among the tobacco workers, but it was by no means confined to the tobacco industry or to Havana. Organizations of workers began to appear in the 1880's in the principal cities of the island among compositors, cab-drivers, push-cart vendors, carpenters and cabinetmakers, tailors, bricklayers, coopers, cobblers, bakers, and port workers.

A number of these organized workers engaged in strikes. One of the most interesting was a strike by the tailors of Havana in 1882 to resist a cut in wages. The employers tried to obtain workers from New York to break the strike, and did secure 17 non-union tailors. But the unions in New York co-operated with the Havana union to prevent skilled union labor from emigrating to Cuba, and this international labor solidarity helped the Havana tailors to win a partial victory.

Despite these displays of militancy, the Cuban labor movement was still largely influenced by Saturnino Martínez who conducted an educational crusade among the workers in La Razón, which appeared as a weekly from 1876 to 1884. Martínez now called upon the workers to avoid strikes, and urged them to seek a solution for their problems in the establishment of co-operatives. Due to his influence, many co-operative societies were formed, all of which failed. There was even an ambitious and never-realized project to establish a cigar factory, with a capital of 250,000 pesos, to be raised in six months by a weekly contribution of 50 centavos from 10,000 workers.

Under Martínez's reformist leadership, labor organizations diverted their energy and funds into avenues which distracted them from the struggles against the employers and the reactionary government. Consequently, the labor movement made little progress.

The challenge to Martínez's leadership came in 1885 from younger men preaching the ideology of the class struggle and socialism. Although these men were profoundly affected by the doctrines of Marx and Engels which reached Cuba through Spanish sources, they were also influenced by the anarchist ideology which, as we have seen, was an important aspect of the working class movement in Spain. Basically, the new groups in the Cuban labor movement were anarcho-syndicalists, believing in trade unionism and socialism, but rejecting political action as a weapon to be used by the working class in the class struggle.

Most prominent among the anarcho-syndicalist leaders was Enrique Roig y San Martín. The son of an army doctor, he was educated in the Colegio San Anacleto in Havana. From 1860 to 1882, he worked in sugar mills; starting as a laborer, he rose to the rank of manager. His twenty-odd years of association with the slaves and the contract and free laborers in the cane fields made him eager to understand the basic causes of the exploitation of labor. He studied the works of Marx and Engels and of Bakunin, and became an anarcho-syndicalist. In order to spread the doctrine among the workers, he took a position as a reader in a tobacco factory.

In 1887, Roig founded the daily newspaper, *El Productor*, dedicated to the "economic and social interests of the working class." "Our principal purpose," it declared, "is to try to unite the workers in a common aspiration and to imbue them with the sacred belief in their social regeneration. In order to accomplish this, we must energetically protest all oppression on the part of the so-called bourgeoisie or of the little bosses who have unfortunately enthroned themselves among us."[13] *El Productor* helped develop a socialist ideology among the Cuban workers. In 1887, the paper championed the cause of the Chicago anarcho-syndicalists who were being railroaded to death in the notorious Haymarket affair. The explosion of a bomb at a labor protest meeting against police violence in Haymarket Square, on May 3, 1886, led to the indictment for murder of seven militant labor figures. In a trial reeking with prejudice against the defendants, and in which nothing was presented to prove that the men had thrown the bomb, the seven were sentenced to death. One committed suicide and two had their death sentences commuted to life imprisonment. Four of the Haymarket martyrs were hanged. Roig, in *El Productor*, raised funds for the defense of the American labor martyrs.

El Productor was the official organ of the *Círculo de Trabajadores* (Workers' Club), founded in Havana in 1885 by Enrique Crecci and Maximino Fernández, associates of Roig. Here various workers' organizations met regularly to discuss united action. In 1890, the *Círculo de Trabajadores* issued a May Day Manifesto calling upon the Cuban workers to support the Paris Congress of International Socialists which had set May 1, 1890, as a day for an international demonstration for the eight-hour day. The directors of the *Círculo* were immediately imprisoned and tried for violating the Penal Code.* Defended by Dr. González Llorente, they were acquitted. A

---

* The Penal Code issued by Royal Decree on May 23, 1879, contained two articles which sought to restrict the right to strike. Article 268 provided that "those who disturb the public peace in order to create a prejudice against any individual shall be punished." Article 567 ruled that "those who conspire to increase or lower wages excessively, or to regulate working conditions, shall be punished. . . . The maximum penalty shall be imposed on the leaders and instigators of the con-

great demonstration in the principal streets of Havana greeted the release of the *Círculo* leaders.

Challenging Saturnino Martínez and his reformist ideas, Roig declared: "We don't want co-operativism, we demand social revolution." By the time of Roig's death in 1889, the Cuban workers had deserted Martínez and were actively behind the socialist and anarcho-syndicalist leadership. At the First National Workers' Congress held in Cuba in 1892, Martínez was finally repudiated by his former followers.

On January 16, 1892, the First National Workers' Congress met in Havana in response to a call issued by the *Círculo de Trabajadores*. A thousand delegates attended, chiefly from Havana, though there were representatives from Pinar del Río, Matanzas, Santa Clara, Cienfuegos, Puerto Príncipe, and Santiago de Cuba. The chief issues discussed were the eight-hour working day, equality of Negro and white workers, the necessity for political action, and support for Cuban independence. The Congress was dissolved by the authorities after five days of sessions for violating the Penal Code, and its leaders were arrested. But before adjourning, the Congress passed the following resolutions:

> The Congress recognizes that the working class cannot emancipate itself unless it adopts the ideas of revolutionary Socialism, and therefore urges Cuban workers to study and adopt its principles.
>
> The preceding statement can be no obstacle to the triumph of the aspirations for liberty of the Cuban people, because it would be absurd that the man who aspires to individual liberty should oppose the liberty to which the Cuban people aspire, although that liberty might only be relative and consist in freedom from the yoke of another people.[14]

Thus the First National Workers' Congress rejected the antipolitical position of the anarcho-syndicalists, came out for revolutionary socialism, and linked the struggle for socialism with the struggle for national independence.

A wave of repression against the labor movement that was to last for several years followed the disruption of the Workers' Congress.

---

spiracy." (Moisés Poblete Troncoso, "Labor Legislation in Cuba and Certain Central American Countries," *Monthly Labor Review*, vol. XXIX, September, 1929, p. 508.)

(On April 29, 1894, *The People,* organ of the Socialist Labor Party of the United States and edited by Daniel De Leon, carried the following notice: "Cuba. A Socialist paper recently started in the Spanish colony was promptly suppressed by order of the Captain General on the ground that it advocated mischievous theories.") But the stand taken by the Congress in favor of national independence indicated that the Cuban workers were ready to give full support to a revolutionary struggle for the liberation of the island. A new force had entered the battle for Cuban independence that was to add power and strength to the revolutionary movement.

chapter 24

REVOLUTIONARY ACTIVITY, 1884-1890

Morale was so low among most of the Cuban revolutionaries in exile after the disasters of the Little War, that all active plotting came to an end for several years. Still the idea of future action was not abandoned. In Key West, the large colony of Cuban tobacco workers never relinquished the idea of a new insurrectionary movement, and revolutionary activity was kept alive by the newspaper *El Yara*, published in Key West since 1875, and by the Order of the Sun, a secret political organization established after the end of the Ten Years' War. In New York, José Martí was devoting every moment he could spare from office work at Lyons & Co., from translations, from writing poetry and contributing articles to *La Opinión Nacional* of Caracas and *La América* of New York, to reviving the spirits of the Cuban exiles and reorganizing the dispersed revolutionary groups.

In March, 1884, Máximo Gómez, then in Honduras, sent Colonel Manuel Aguilera to the United States with a message "To the Revolutionary Centers." In this document Gómez submitted a plan of action to which any movement undertaken for the liberation of Cuba must adhere: an advance increase in revolutionary centers; creation of a Governing Board with which the Commander-in-Chief of the revolution could deal; full military powers for the Commander, and the raising beforehand of $200,000 to finance the movement. At the same time he sent his message, Gómez wrote to Maceo informing him of his decision. Maceo replied immediately, pledging his support to Gómez's leadership and expressing eagerness to join him.

Colonel Aguilera returned to Honduras with the news that the various centers of emigration, including the Independence Club of New York, had approved the program and conditions Gómez had proposed. He also reported that he had been advised that a wealthy

Cuban merchant in New York, Félix Govín, was ready to advance the $200,000 for the new revolutionary movement as soon as the General placed himself at the head. Gómez and Maceo decided to move to the United States as soon as possible. Maceo notified his friends in Key West, New York, Jamaica, Santo Domingo, and other places that he was joining a new revolutionary movement in company with Gómez: "Our enslaved Cuba demands that her sons fight for her freedom. . . . When Cuba is free and has a constituted government, I shall request that we fight for the independence of Puerto Rico also. I would not care to put up my sword leaving that portion of America in slavery."[1]

On August 2, 1844, Gómez and Maceo, with their families, set sail for the United States to join the new Cuban independence movement. They arrived in New York on October 1, after stops in New Orleans and Key West, and immediately began to hold conferences at the little hotel of Madame Griffon on Ninth Avenue, the headquarters of the Cuban revolutionists. During the discussion plans were completed for the overall operation of the movement, for the purchase of arms and ammunition, and the hiring of transportation for the proposed expedition.

But everything hinged on the availability of money. Gómez had received $3,000 from the president of Honduras to assist the struggle for the freedom of Cuba, and he and Maceo, welcomed enthusiastically in Key West, had collected $5,000 from the tobacco workers and other émigrés. (In New Orleans, the wealthy Cubans had refused to contribute anything to the cause, which led Gómez to comment that "rich Cubans are only patriots when their purses are squeezed."[2]) But this was only a drop in the bucket. One of the chief reasons Gómez and Maceo had agreed to come to New York to launch the new revolution was the promise of Félix Govín to give substantial financial backing.

Shortly after arriving in the Empire City, Gómez and Maceo suffered the first great blow to their hopes. When Govín was asked to make good his promise to advance $200,000, the wealthy Cuban replied that he was engaged in attempting to recover property in Cuba which had been confiscated, that his success depended upon good relations with the Spanish administration in Havana, and that he could not afford to do anything to jeopardize these relations.

Gómez wrote bitterly in his *Diary*: "I have suffered a blow here in New York which I had not expected . . . my deception has been very sad because only the poor Cubans are disposed to sacrifice."[3]

The second setback to the movement headed by Gómez and Maceo was the withdrawal of José Martí. In order to raise the funds which they had not been able to obtain in New York, Gómez decided to send various missions to different centers where Cubans could be appealed to for financial aid. At a conference with Maceo and Martí, Gómez designated both to go to Mexico and raise funds. Martí agreed to go, and began to tell Gómez what he would do immediately after his arrival in Mexico. Gómez, who had ordered a bath to be drawn, interrupted Martí and said brusquely: "Look, Martí, limit yourself to what the instructions say, and as for the rest, General Maceo will do what he thinks should be done." Gómez then retired to his bath. Maceo tried to smooth things over, remarking: " 'The Old Man' considers the Cuban War almost as though it is his exclusive property, and he does not permit anyone to interfere."[4] This remark only served to annoy Martí still further, for even before this incident he had been increasingly alarmed over Gómez's tendency to handle the revolutionary movement as though it was his "exclusive property," insisting that his orders be obeyed without question.

Two days after the incident, October 20, 1884, Martí sent a letter to Gómez announcing that he was withdrawing from the movement:

> One does not found a nation, General, with commands as issued in a military camp. . . . Are you trying to suffocate thought even before seeing yourself at the front of a grateful and enthusiastic people with all the appurtenances of a victory? The nation belongs to no one, but if it did, it belongs to the one who serves it with the greatest disinterestedness and intelligence—and this only in spirit. How, General, could I utilize the friends which I have, attract new ones, undertake missions, convince eminent men, and melt frozen wills with these fears and doubts in my soul? Consequently, I resign from all the active tasks which you have begun to place on my shoulder.[5]

Although he was unusually sensitive, what ultimately compelled Martí to this decision was his fear of creating a dictator before the Republic of Cuba was even born. Unlike Maceo who knew the need, from past experience, for strong authority in the revolutionary struggle and was inclined to overlook Gómez's dictatorial conduct,

Martí saw in Gómez's behavior an evil which had to be combatted before the revolutionary movement degenerated into a personal operation divorced from the mass of the people. Gómez himself attributed this feeling to Martí, when he wrote in his *Diary*: "There is no lack of those who, like José Martí, fear a dictatorship."[6]

At first many Cuban exiles criticized Martí for his sudden withdrawal from the movement, and some even accused him of deserting the revolution. But Martí soon convinced them that, while he could not work with Gómez, he was "and always would be, with the Nation." Moreover, it was "indispensable to the health of the homeland that someone expresses without vacillation or cowardice the essential principle of thought and method which I have believed to be in peril."[7]

Following Martí's withdrawal, Gómez and Maceo continued with the plans to raise funds for their expedition. Sufficient money came from the Cuban workers ($25,000) and industrialists ($30,000) in Key West to enable Gómez to purchase arms and ammunition and even to enlarge the scope of the invasion, so that simultaneous landings could take place in various parts of the island, to co-ordinate with the general activity of revolutionary groups in Cuba.

But there were new setbacks. Gómez had sent the arms and ammunition to friends in Santo Domingo where they would be stored until the time when the expeditions were ready to start for Cuba. These materials of war were confiscated by the authorities who had replaced the government that had been friendly to Gómez and the Cuban cause. With dissatisfaction and dissension rising among the emigrants and revolutionists, Gómez decided that the expeditions would leave one at a time instead of all at once as had been planned. Maceo would go first, and he would be followed by Rafael Rodríguez and then Emilio Núñez.

New money, of course, was needed, and it could only come from one place—Key West, which had already contributed more than its share. In October, 1885, Maceo went to Key West on a fund-raising mission for the expedition he was to lead. Dr. Eusebio Hernández, who was to go on the expedition as Maceo's assistant, accompanied the Negro leader to Key West, and he described the reaction of a mass meeting after he "presented General Antonio Maceo as the leader of the first expedition which we must organize with money from them."

The effect of these words on those emigrants was immense and extraordinary. . . . They all rose to their feet demonstrating with *vivas* and applause, leaping on the stage to embrace us and emptying their pockets for the director. Women and young girls donated their rings, earrings, watches, and whatever they had. Daughters, wives, and sweethearts were seen removing the pictures of their loved ones from their lockets. I could not continue my discourse; with music, and followed by that enormous audience we were accompanied to the lodging which they had reserved for us. This extraordinary enthusiasm lasted until midnight.

The following day a committee of young girls was named at our request to raffle the collection of jewelry. General Maceo added a tie pin from his personal belongings.

In a week's time we had gathered more than we had asked for, that is, nine thousand instead of eight thousand dollars. In that Patriotic week, Americans as well as Cubans, in fact all men who loved liberty in that free place, took part in the campaign.

A hundred pages would not be enough to describe the different features which adorn the rapid, simple and superbly delicate labor of the Patriotic week. Young girls escorted Maceo and me on our trips through the tobacco factories. Some of them, with Cuban flags wound around their bodies and their faces radiant with patriotism and beauty, preceded me on to the honored tribunal reserved for the reader of the factory. Maceo, the man of bronze, was deeply moved. Repeatedly he was forced to stand in acknowledgment of the delirious and overwhelming ovations produced by references to him in the vibrant speeches of some of the peasant women, admirers of the hero.[8]

On the day of Maceo's departure for New York, the factories and shops were closed so that the Cuban workers could go to the docks to see him off. The Negro revolutionary leader left Key West as he had arrived, to the accompaniment of cheers, flags, and music.

In New York, Maceo turned over $5,711 to J. M. Párraga, treasurer of the movement, and Colonel Fernando López de Queralta was assigned the task of purchasing arms and ammunition and arranging for their transportation to Colón, Panama. From Colón, Maceo planned to launch his expedition in February, 1886. Meanwhile, he went to Jamaica to work out the final plans of the Cuban invasion, and from Kingston, Maceo issued a proclamation "To My Comrades and Conquerors of Oriente."

Liberty is not begged for; it is conquered. I swore to free you or to perish with you, fighting for your rights; I am coming to fulfill that oath.

Seven years have proved the Pact of Zanjón to be dishonorable . . . The government of despotism and barbarism declared the extermination of the Cubans, and it reduced their spirit and killed revolutionary action. Since that ominous date, with my soul lacerated by the sad and unmerciful fate assigned to you, I have been working for your salvation. I am bringing you a war of justice and reason; come with me and you will be sons worthy of Cuba.[9]

But now a whole series of difficulties, mishaps, and frustrations, coupled with bitter conflicts among the revolutionary leaders, converted the promising efforts to launch an armed revolution in Cuba into a fiasco. For lack of the necessary papers to claim the shipment of arms, the war materials were not allowed to land in Panama and were returned to New York. When Maceo arranged for the arms to be reshipped to Jamaica from whence the revolutionists would sail for Cuba, Gómez issued a proclamation postponing the invasion on the ground that desertions from the revolutionary movement had adversely affected prospects of success. Then after Maceo, in a bitter dispute, forced Gómez to continue the movement, complete disaster befell the cause. On July 20, 1886, five months after Maceo was supposed to launch his expedition to Cuba, the ship *Morning Star* arrived in Kingston with the arms and ammunition. But, fearful of being arrested with his dangerous cargo, the captain of the *Morning Star* threw the entire shipment into the sea and returned to New York.

Thus for the second time, the war materials were lost. With this new loss, the hope of launching an invasion of Cuba all but vanished. To be sure, at a conference on August 17 of all the military and civil leaders present in Jamaica, the majority voted, over Maceo's objections, to make one more effort to get the revolution started. But relations among the revolutionists had become so strained by the repeated failures and disasters, that co-ordinated action was almost impossible. On August 3, 1886, after a dispute over finances relating to the expedition, in the course of which Maceo openly questioned Gómez's authoritarian conduct, his integrity, and his fitness as a commanding officer, Gómez broke off their friendship. "There remains only one thing in common between us," he informed the Negro leader coldly, "a sacred thing which I have made mine—the cause of our country."[10]

Although Maceo's proposal that all efforts to launch an armed revolution in Cuba be suspended temporarily had been rejected at the August 17 conference, events soon demonstrated that his advice had been sound. The Cuban emigrants were by now so thoroughly disheartened that no prospect existed of raising new funds. Moreover, the final abolition of slavery in Cuba on October 7, 1887, dealt the revolutionary movement a serious blow since it had depended to a great extent on the support of the Negro people in the island. Temporarily grateful to the Spanish authorities for the royal decree abolishing slavery, the Negroes could hardly be expected at this particular moment to rally to the revolutionary cause.

In December, 1886, Gómez, convinced that "the Cubans . . . do not want to hear a word about revolution" and that there was no hope for the cause he headed, announced the end of the rebel movement. He explained that the movement had failed through "unfortunate happenings and obstacles generally always unforeseen, which are never lacking in this kind of undertaking."[11]

This was only partially true. The failure was also due to a serious flaw in the organization of the revolutionary movement. The total leadership had been in the hands of the military chiefs, with civilians confined to the task of raising funds. The movement itself had started with the military chiefs, who then had called in the revolutionary émigrés. This gave it a dictatorial character from the very outset, for the civilians were expected to accept blindly the dictates of the chieftains, especially the supreme commander. Inevitably, as was illustrated by Martí's withdrawal, friction would arise between the two forces in the revolutionary movement, and, indeed, as in the dispute between Gómez and Maceo, among the military chieftains themselves. Under these circumstances, it is hardly surprising that the entire movement deteriorated.

Martí made an effort to overcome this serious weakness in the revolutionary movement. In the fall of 1887, he and other Cuban advocates of independence were holding meetings in New York discussing the bases for a future uprising. Guided by Martí, the Cuban exiles drew up a circular which set forth a program for united action. Five essential points were stressed "to inspire our words and acts."

1. To achieve a revolutionary solution which will win support in the country, it must be based on democratic procedures.
2. To proceed without delay to organize the military leaders outside the country and co-ordinate this work with that which is to be done within the country.
3. To unite the émigré centers in one magnificent democratic enterprise.
4. To prevent revolutionary sympathies in Cuba from being twisted and enslaved by the interests of one group, by the preponderance of one social class or by the unlimited authority of a military or a civil group, or of one race over another.
5. To prevent annexationist propaganda from weakening the revolutionary solution.[12]

The circular was sent to Generals Máximo Gómez, Antonio Maceo, Rafael Rodríguez, and Francisco Carrillo, asking their support for the program. Gómez replied briefly but affirmatively to the New York Committee—he refused to address Martí directly, still rankling from the former dispute—announcing that he was always ready to occupy "my place in the line of combat for the sake of Cuban independence." Maceo replied directly to Martí, and declared himself in full agreement with the basic concepts of the circular. As the key to successful revolutionary organization, Maceo stressed the need for unity of all Cubans. "For the sake of our enslaved country, which each day becomes more unfortunate, we must purge ourselves of the seeds of discord sown in our hearts by the enemies of our noble cause."[13]

Although nothing developed immediately from the circular, it represented an important stage in the emergence of a new concept in the organization of the revolutionary movement which was soon to be fully developed by Martí. This was the concept of a democratic organization of the war for independence, uniting civilian and military elements and all classes for the liberation of Cuba.

Up to now the revolutionists in exile had sought to transplant the revolution to Cuba from the outside through an invasion of the island. But in 1890, Antonio Maceo organized groups for revolutionary action inside Cuba, and hoped, with the aid of invading forces from outside, to gain victory for the cause of independence.

Using as a pretext his desire to attend personally to the business of selling the properties belonging to his mother, Maceo asked permission of Captain General Manuel Salamanca to return to Cuba. Salamanca felt that a tolerant approach would destroy revolutionary influence in the island. He had allowed Flor Crombet to return, and he now granted Maceo a safe conduct and guarantees for a visit to his native land. On January 29, 1890, Maceo set sail for Cuba from Haiti. He entered Cuba, he wrote, "under the guise of peace and concord, when what I wanted was war and the extermination of the colonial system."[14]

Once in Cuba, Maceo took immediate steps to revive the spirits of the revolutionists. A steady stream of former rebel leaders passed through his suite at the Hotel Inglaterra in Havana. He was also visited by many young Cubans anxious to participate in the revolutionary movement. Maceo spent a good deal of time as well with the Socialist leaders of the trade unions and with the leaders of the Negro community, especially Juan Gualberto Gómez. He quickly discovered that the abolition of slavery had not, as he had been led to believe, brought the Negro people closer to Spain. On the contrary, facing the problems of unemployment and exceedingly low wages when employed, the Negro population was seething with discontent.

Although Juan Gualberto Gómez and Maceo were wholly in agreement on the necessity of achieving complete racial equality in Cuba, Maceo disagreed with Gómez's plan for a separate organization of the Negroes and mulattoes in the revolutionary movement. Maceo believed that this would play into the hands of the enemies of the revolution, and he was convinced that the struggle for independence could only succeed through unity of Negro and white Cubans. Maceo convinced Gómez of the merit of his position, as well as the value of having Máximo Gómez as the commander-in-chief of the military in the revolution. In spite of his recent split with the Dominican, Maceo pointed out that the General had superior military capabilities which were suited to the type of warfare required in Cuba, and that, in addition, he was thoroughly opposed to racial discrimination.

While Spanish authorities were disturbed in general by Maceo's open revolutionary activities, they were especially upset by the fact that leading white Cubans looked up to the Negro revolutionist as a logical leader of the struggle to liberate the island.

> Known revolutionists from all over the Island went to see him publicly in Havana [Camilo Polavieja, who replaced Salamanca as Captain General, reported to Spain]. This has given a rebirth of hopes hardly to the pleasure of Spain. And the very sad spectacle has occurred wherein he has been visited and accompanied by a considerable number of representatives of Creole families, some very notable for their social position. And this has happened notwithstanding the fact that Maceo belongs to the colored race, which generally is the object of profound depreciation by the Creoles. It is because Maceo symbolizes the idea of hatred for Spain. The Creole youth in particular, who fill the salons and literary and scientific centers of the capital, have sought him out. None of these people concealed giving Maceo the *title of General*.[15]

After a round of parties and banquets in his honor in Havana and Pinar del Río, which actually served as meetings for the establishment of new centers of rebellion, Maceo went to Santiago de Cuba, where he was greeted as a national hero. At one banquet, on July 29, 1890, an incident occurred that was to be long remembered in Cuba. A young man named José J. Hernández expressed the hope, in the form of a question to Maceo, that Cuba would be annexed by the United States and become "one more star in the great American constellation." Maceo replied immediately: "Young man, I believe, although it seems impossible to me that this can be the only outcome, that in such a case I would be on the side of the Spaniards." He was unalterably opposed to annexation of Cuba to the United States. He was ready to lay down his life for only one cause—the independence of Cuba. Indeed, only independence could justify an armed rebellion.[16]

Plans for a rebellion had been worked out in Havana by Generals Maceo, Manuel Sanguily, Manuel Suárez and José M. Aguirre. The date for the uprising in the capital was set for October 10—the anniversary of the *Grito de Yara* which began the Ten Years' War. The rebels would try to take possession of all strategic locations in the city, and if they failed, they would withdraw to the countryside and continue the battle.

In Santiago de Cuba, Maceo organized the movement for an uprising in the eastern part of the island. This called for the capture of Santiago, and once this city was taken, it would serve as a beachhead for the landing of Máximo Gómez and other exiles who were to be previously informed. Revolutionary groups in nearly all the towns of the province of Oriente—Manzanillo, Guantánamo, Bayamo, Baracoa, Tunas, Jiguaní, etc.—would then rise up, and the Spaniards would be confronted with a full-fledged rebellion throughout the entire province.

Although the plans should have called for a simultaneous uprising in Havana and eastern Cuba, for reasons which are not clear the date for the revolt in Oriente was set for September 8, over a month earlier than in the West. At any rate, by the third week of August, 1890, the structure and organization of the revolution had been fully completed. Working with Maceo, the principal leader in Oriente, were General Guillermo Moncada and Flor Crombet and other tested veterans of previous revolutionary struggles. The revolutionary conspirators included men of letters, workers and peasants, Negro and white, and a large representation of Cuban youth.

But the wealthy owners of manganese mines, sugar plantations and mills, and other properties were opposed to armed warfare. They were afraid that a revolution would interfere with profitable production, and they were frightened by the prominent role of Maceo and other Negroes in the revolutionary movement. The fears of the wealthy Cubans were reflected in the attitude of the leaders of the Autonomist Party, mainly lawyers who represented the manganese mining and sugar interests. Thus Captain General Polavieja notified the Spanish government that "what mainly determined the conduct of the chiefs of the Autonomist Party was racial hatred. They did not want to give preponderance to the colored element which was so numerous in the province of Santiago de Cuba. And the majority of the whites were naturally fearful of the public aspirations of Maceo, of imposing a government of his race, creating a Republic similar to the Haitian government."[17]

That Maceo had never expressed such aspirations was beside the point. The Spanish authorities knew well how to use the "Haiti" scare to split the ranks of the white Cubans, and they employed this weapon to influence the leaders of the Autonomist Party against joining the revolutionary movement. It worked well with the Autonomists who were accustomed to equating Negro participation in any Cuban political movement with Negro domination. When this was added to their fears of losing profits from mining and sugar production, their rejection of the revolution was to be expected.

Despite the inability of the revolutionists to win over the wealthy interests in Oriente, they went ahead with their plans for an uprising. But every move they made was known to the Spaniards. Even before he had reached Cuba to replace Salamanca as Captain General, Polavieja had received a complete report from the Spanish army and police concerning Maceo's revolutionary plans. Much of this information came from left-wing members of the Autonomist Party who had been taken into the confidence of the rebels but were actually opposed to an armed uprising. Actually, however, so many people knew of the conspiracy, and the revolutionary movement was conducted with so little attempt to avoid publicity, that it would have been a miracle if the Spanish authorities had *not* become fully acquainted with the plans.

Captain General Polavieja arrived in Havana on August 24. Within 48 hours he ordered the civil governor of Santiago "to arrange for the immediate departure of don Antonio Maceo and his family for Kingston or some other foreign port." On the afternoon of August 29, a police detachment called upon Maceo and his wife at their hotel and notified them that they must leave the following day on an American ship bound for New York. The police then occupied the whole building to prevent Maceo from leaving.

News of Maceo's detention by the police quickly reached the revolutionists. While many, especially the young conspirators, were ready to go through with the plans for an immediate uprising, dissension arose in the revolutionary ranks. The more timid elements felt that with the Spanish government fully prepared for an uprising, the revolution was destined to fail. Their view prevailed, and the order was given "to dissolve the groups which had already formed in various places and to call a halt to the movement."[18]

On August 30, Maceo and his wife left Santiago de Cuba on a boat, bound for New York via Kingston. Within a few days, Flor Crombet and other leading conspirators were also deported from Cuba, and a large number of others who had been implicated in the conspiracy left voluntarily for fear of being imprisoned. But there were some who were not so fortunate and were sent to the prison of Guane, in the extreme western portion of Cuba.

In informing Spain of the failure of the revolutionary conspiracy, Captain General Polavieja paid tribute to the wealthy Cuban leaders of the Autonomist Party, spokesmen for the manganese mining and sugar interests. (Because of the importance of the manganese mining interests in the failure of the revolution, the whole insurrectionary movement led by Maceo in Cuba in 1890 is referred to under the title of *La Paz del Manganeso* [The Peace of Manganese].) It was their opposition to Maceo that had prevented the revolution from succeeding:

> It was my good fortune [wrote Polavieja] and no small matter, that the leaders of the Autonomist Party rejected him [Maceo]. The conspiracy was known by many in the Island, and especially in the Province of Santiago de Cuba, where business was paralyzed by the fears which it inspired. After I expelled Maceo and some of his followers, some radicals of said party went to the offices of the newspaper, *El País* [organ of the Autonomist Party], and asked its directors to attack me for my action. They were refused and were told that I had just performed a good service for Cuba.[19]

Thus Maceo's seven months of revolutionary activity inside Cuba ended in failure, just as had all the other movements of the decade. But none of these endeavors to liberate Cuba had been entirely in vain. From the experience of the Gómez-Maceo plan, the revolutionists had learned the necessity of developing greater democracy in the organization of the revolution, and the proper place to be occupied by the civilian and military groups. From Maceo's experiences in Cuba, the revolutionists learned that mass support for independence was mounting in the island and that the Spanish tactic of splitting the Cuban ranks by race prejudice was not as effective as it had been in the past. As Herminio Portell Vilá points out: "all these symptoms revealed that neither autonomy nor annexation represented Cuban aspirations so perfectly as independence, and that this was the tendency which Spain feared."[20]

The revolutionary activity of the years 1884–90 failed in their primary goal of achieving the independence of Cuba. But these activities had repercussions which were soon to be felt inside the island and in the various revolutionary centers outside of Cuba.

chapter 25

THE CUBAN REVOLUTIONARY PARTY

A superficial glance at the Cuban revolutionary movement at the opening of the year 1891 would lead to the conclusion that the efforts to free Cuba from Spanish tyranny were all but hopeless. Within Cuba itself, the organization of any attempt at liberation seemed impossible. Protected by a defensive armor of oppressive soldiers and police, and with a spy or agent within earshot of any group that expressed opposition to the regime, the Spanish oligarchy seemed to have the situation under complete control. Outside of Cuba, the revolutionary movement among the exiles had degenerated to the point where it offered only rhetorical forms of resistance. Many of the exiles seemed to rely more on the chance that some unforeseen event would cause the downfall of Spanish despotism than on the will and strength of an active national resistance.

Yet beneath the surface there were signs that were encouraging. The events of the year 1890 in Cuba had demonstrated that the majority of the Cuban people wanted the redemption of the island politically and economically through independence. They would give their unconditional support to any revolutionary movement which could show a capacity for effective action.

On January 5, 1892, such a movement came into being—*El Partido Revolucionario Cubano* (The Cuban Revolutionary Party). Its leading spirit, inspirer and organizer was José Martí.

The Cuban Revolutionary Party was organized after two full years of intensive preparation. In January, 1890, Martí helped Rafael Serra, a Cuban Negro exile, to found *La Liga* (The League) in New York City for the education and advancement of the Negro exiles. To Martí, the formation of the League represented an important development in the revolutionary movement. The League was a society for poor people, and the revolution in Cuba had to base itself on the poor. Martí had discovered that many rich Cubans, losing their interest in independence for fear of endangering their economic interests, were prepared to accept a compromise solution in the form of autonomy. Then again, the League was made up of Negroes, and in Cuba over one-third of the people were Negroes. The "fear of the Negro," as Martí himself termed it, had long been an obstacle to a revolutionary solution, and it was an issue that could not be ignored. It had to be met head-on. In a letter to Maceo in 1882, pointing to the errors of the past, Martí had emphasized that anyone who introduced racial prejudice into the revolutionary struggle was an enemy of Cuban independence:

> There can be no political solution of the Cuban problem without a social solution. And this solution can only be obtained with the love and mutual respect of the one race for the other. . . . For me the one who promotes hatred in Cuba or who tries to take advantage of that which exists is a criminal. And he who tries to suffocate the legitimate aspirations of a good and prudent race is a criminal.[1]

By involving the Negro exiles in the organization of the revolutionary movement through *La Liga,* the foundation would be laid for bringing the Negroes in Cuba behind the decisive struggle, and at the same time, the groundwork would be laid for racial equality and harmony in the Republic.

> That [he wrote to Serra] is the point from which we must start if we want to go where we must. For our goal is not so much a mere political change as a good, sound, just and equitable social system, without demagogic fawning or arrogance of authority. And let us never forget that the greater the suffering, the greater the right to justice, and that the prejudices of men and social inequalities cannot prevail over the equality which nature has created.[2]

The League was a training school for the revolution. Classes and lectures were held in the evening throughout the week, and Martí, besides procuring the meeting rooms, obtaining teachers, and helping to increase the membership, taught a class every Thursday night. He talked of the necessity to win total independence for Cuba and of rejecting all halfway reform measures. He instilled in his students a pride in being Cuban and emphasized the important place that the masses, Negro and white, had to occupy in the liberation movement and in the future republic. The new struggle for Cuba,

Martí pointed out, must not be a war of landed classes as in 1868, but a people's war. To achieve this, the Negro had to be treated "according to his qualities as a man" and the worker "as a brother with the consideration and rights which assure peace and happiness as a nation." His Negro working class pupils emerged from the *Maestro's* class with a sense of confidence in the ultimate victory of the revolutionary struggle and a clearer understanding of the part they should play in it.

Martí's work with the Cuban masses in the League became known throughout the émigré centers in the United States, and nowhere was it discussed with greater interest than among the tobacco workers of Tampa and Key West. A desire grew to hear first-hand from Martí the ideas he was developing in his classes at the League. On October 16, 1890, the Ignacio Agramonte Club of Tampa invited Martí to deliver the main address at a meeting at which the club was to raise funds for Cuban liberty. Martí eagerly accepted; here was an opportunity to reach in person the émigré tobacco workers who had for so long dedicated themselves to the work of independence, and to begin with them the creation of a new, effective liberation movement. To the tobacco workers of Tampa, on November 26 and 27, 1891, Martí made two of his greatest revolutionary orations: "By All and For the Good of All" and "The New Pines."

"For Cuba in torment, my first word," he began his speech of November 26 at the *Liceo Cubano*. He spoke of the war for Cuba's liberation as a war of necessity, and assured his audience that Cuba was waiting impatiently for the inevitable moment to arrive when an organized, strong, and united revolutionary movement would lead the way to independence. To achieve this movement, it was urgent for Cubans to discard all outworn prejudices and false fears: the fear of the encroachments of the military clique of veterans; fear of the Negro—"the generous Negro, the Negro brother"; fear of the Spaniard, an unnecessary fear because "we are fighting in Cuba for the liberty of man and there are many Spaniards who love liberty"; and finally, the fear of those who, influenced by the propaganda in the Yankee press, doubted that Cubans had the ability to maintain the liberty which the revolution would achieve. "Let the flames of truth spring forth and ignite souls and vibrate as lightning, and let it be followed by free honest men." Away with all fears and prejudices! The time had come for action!

> Now! To form our ranks! Countries are not created by wishful thinking in the depths of the soul. . . . Let us rise so that liberty does not run any risk in its hour of triumph through disorder or indolence or impatience in its preparation. Let us rise for the true Republic and with our passion for right and our habits of work, we will know how to maintain it. Let us place around the star in the new flag this formula of triumphant love: *With all, for the good of all.*[3]

On the following day, November 27, the 20th anniversary of the shooting of the medical students in Havana, Martí gave his second speech. It was not a lamentation for the dead; rather, Martí stressed that those deaths had given strength to the continued struggle for liberty. "Let others lament necessary death; I believe in it as the cushion and the leaven and the triumph of life." It was necessary now to sing "the hymn of life before the not-to-be-forgotten tomb." Out of the past failures and setbacks, a new vitality had emerged which would surely triumph.[4]

Two concrete actions resulted from the fervor Martí's speeches had aroused. One was the adoption of a set of resolutions, drafted by Martí, which set forth his concept of national unity, of democratic revolutionary activity, and of gathering all the revolutionary groups together in a common cause, using the already existing local organizations as a basis—all "for the foundation of a just Republic open to all, one in territory, in law, in work and in cordiality, established with the collaboration of all for the good of all." The resolutions met with enthusiastic approval in Tampa and were unanimously adopted. This action marked the beginning of a new revolutionary impulse which was to culminate in the formation of the Cuban Revolutionary Party. Indeed, the resolutions were to serve as the principles of the Party until a formal constitution and program were drawn up.

The other action taken at Tampa was the formation of the *Liga de Instrucción* (League for Instruction), modeled after *La Liga* in New York, through which the Negro exiles of Tampa would gain an education and prepare themselves for active participation in the liberation struggle. Before Martí left Tampa for New York, the League for Instruction had already recruited 30 members.

La Liga of New York was the first link in the revolutionary chain being forged under Martí's direction. Tampa was the second. The third was Key West. Invited by a group of tobacco workers, Martí arrived in Key West on December 25, 1891. On January 3, 1892, having recovered from an illness, he spoke at the San Carlos Club. The following day, he attended a function of the Club *Patria y Libertad* (Fatherland and Liberty), visited the tobacco factories where the Cuban cigar makers worked, and held meetings with them. At the urging of the tobacco workers, he spoke in all the factories.

On January 5, 1892, at a meeting of representatives of the political clubs of Key West and Tampa presided over by Martí, the organization of the Cuban Revolutionary Party was agreed upon. The resolutions drawn up by Martí at Tampa in November, 1891, were approved as the organization's temporary principles; and Martí was instructed to draft the *Bases* of the new movement, which would set forth the reasons, justifications, and political ideas of the Cuban Revolutionary Party.

In Tampa, Martí obtained approval of the plan for the Party. He then returned to New York, and on February 17, 1892, at Hardmann Hall, told the Cuban émigrés about his experiences in Tampa and Key West. His contacts with the Cuban masses in the shops and factories had filled him with extreme optimism for the future, and he ended on a confident note: "What I have to say before my voice is stilled and my heart ceases to beat in this world is that my country possesses all the qualities necessary for the winning and maintenance of liberty."[5]

In the *Bases* of the Cuban Revolutionary Party, Martí set forth the ideas which he had been developing for ten years as to the best way to realize Cuba's independence. After asserting that the Party was organized "in order to obtain, with the united forces of all men of good will, the absolute independence of the island of Cuba, and to foment and aid that of Puerto Rico," the *Bases* declared that the new movement did not have for its object "the indefinite prolongation of a war in Cuba," but rather the launching of "a generous and brief war, undertaken to insure the peace and the labor of the inhabitants of the island," and through "a war of republican spirit and method," to achieve the establishment of "a nation capable of assuring the lasting good fortune of her children and of fulfilling in the historical life of the Continent the difficult duties which her geographical situation assigns her." The *Bases* then spoke of establishing democratic processes, of freeing the island from dependence upon the outside world as much as possible, and of substituting "for the economic confusion from which it is dying a system of public fiscal administration which shall immediately open the country to the diverse activities of its inhabitants." Article eight of the *Bases* enumerated the following concrete objectives of the Party:

> (1) to unite in a continuous and common effort the action of all Cubans resident abroad; (2) to encourage sincere relations among the political and historical elements from within and outside the island, which can contribute to the rapid winning of the war and to the greater force and efficacy of the institutions afterwards to be founded; (3) to disseminate in Cuba the knowledge of the spirit and the methods of the Revolution, and to gather together the inhabitants of the island in a movement favorable to their victory, by means which will not place Cuban lives in unnecessary jeopardy; (4) to collect funds for the realization of its program, at the same time opening up continuous, numerous sources of money for the war; (5) to establish discreetly, with friendly peoples, relations which tend to accelerate, with the least possible blood and sacrifice, the end of the war and the foundation of the new Republic which is indispensable to the balance of power of the Americas.

As set forth in the Statutes, also drawn up by Martí, the Party itself was to be composed of clubs which included as members both Cubans and sympathizers who would agree to pay the dues assessed. Each club had a president who was a member of a Council of Presidents. These councils were the intermediaries between the individuals and the national headquarters. The head of the Party in the United States, with offices in New York, was a Delegate, and associated with him was a national Treasurer. Both were to be elected annually by the clubs.[6]

The new revolutionary movement initiated by the Cuban Revolutionary Party was thus not the personal property of any individual or group of individuals. It was based on the organizations of Cuban exiles and would function democratically.

In organizing the Cuban Revolutionary Party, Martí had brought together "as many elements of all kinds as could be recruited." This had been no easy accomplishment. Thousands of the Cuban exiles had been sharply divided between rival factions, and differed drastically about the nature of the revolution and the republic to follow. It was Martí's great contribution that he was able to build unity among so many conflicting interests. He accomplished this, moreover, without yielding to the prejudices of certain elements in the alliance. He refused to yield to those who insisted that he place the Negro in a subordinate position in the revolutionary movement. He likewise rejected the demand of wealthy exiles that the Socialist working class leaders be eliminated from the movement.

Martí was no Socialist. He honored Karl Marx for "the way he put himself at the side of the weak ones," and he wrote of him as the "titanic interpreter of the anger of the European worker," "the uniter of men of different nations, and an untiring organizer," and the "triumphant penetrator of the whys and whereofs of human misery and the destinies of men, a man ridden with the anguish to do good."* But he felt that Marx "went too fast," and he felt that it was possible for the working class to gain their demands without a revolutionary struggle. He wanted the workers "to find an outlet for indignation . . . but without seeing it explode and cause fright."[7]

Nevertheless, Martí recognized the valuable contribution the Socialist working class leaders could make to the Cuban Revolution, and he welcomed their assistance and sought their advice. They were, he explained, "a factor in the independence movement." Carlos Baliño and Diego Vicente Tejera, two of the most active Socialists among the Cuban workers in the United States, worked closely with Martí. Baliño was one of the signers of the Constitution of the Cuban Revolutionary Party. Little wonder *El Socialista* said that while Martí was not a Socialist, it could be said truthfully that "in him we see a brother."[8]

To spread the propaganda of the Cuban Revolutionary Party,

---

* In his dispatch to *La Nación* of Buenos Aires, March 29, 1883, Martí described the memorial meeting at Cooper Union in New York on the death of the founder of scientific socialism. He noted that "Men of all nations come to honor him. The multitude is made up of honorable workers, the sight of whom is comforting." He reported the resolutions adopted by the meeting "in which Karl Marx is called the most noble hero and the most powerful thinker of the world of the workers." (José Martí, *Obras Completas*, La Habana, 1946, vol. I, pp. 1516-18.)

Martí sought to found a newspaper in New York. On March 4, 1892, *Patria* (Fatherland) was launched, the expenses of the first issue being met by the tobacco workers. Although it did not declare itself to be the organ of the Revolutionary Party, *Patria*, in its first issue, published in full on page 1 the *Bases* "which this newspaper respects and upholds." *Patria*, edited by Sotero Figueroa, a Puerto Rican Negro, was to conduct continuous, unrelenting propaganda for the Party, and was generally recognized as its official organ.

The Revolutionary Party did not consider itself established until the majority of the emigrant clubs had accepted it. By the end of March, 1892, all of the clubs had ratified the *Bases* and Statutes, and on April 8, the clubs of the South, New York, and Philadelphia elected Martí as Delegate and Benjamín Guerra as Treasurer. Two days later, on the tenth, the Cuban Revolutionary Party and its network of representatives and local member councils were formally proclaimed in all the clubs in Key West, Tampa, New York, and other émigré centers.

Thus by April, 1892, the first stage of Martí's work was complete. The Cuban Revolutionary Party was an established organization; groups associated with the Party were active in all the centers of emigration, and through *Patria* its message was reaching thousands—in Cuba as well as outside the island.

It was now time to call in the military and co-ordinate the invading forces and the revolutionary movement in Cuba.

Contrary to previous procedures in the Cuban revolutionary movement, Martí had left the military leaders completely out of his plans until a strong revolutionary organization was formed. Once this was achieved, Martí turned to Máximo Gómez, the man with whom he had split in 1884 because he believed him to be guilty of dictatorial conduct. He knew that Gómez was the man who by experience and influence was most suited to head the military phase of the liberation struggle. Still, before offering Gómez the post of military chief, Martí polled the exile centers to determine if they favored the step. By mid-August, 1892, the result of the referendum was in. Martí was authorized to offer Gómez the post. This he did in person, on a visit to Gómez in Santo Domingo, September, 1892, inviting him "without fear of refusal, to undertake this new task although I have no other remuneration to offer you than the pleasure of sacrifice and the probable ingratitude of man." Like Martí, the old General put past differences aside. "From this moment you can count on my services," he told the Delegate.

Gómez was impressed by Martí's achievements in organizing and building the Cuban Revolutionary Party. "The triumph of the Cuban Revolution," he wrote in his *Diary*, "is a matter of concord and unification, and, in my opinion, the work that Martí has done up to now is quite consistent, for he is gradually obtaining the unification of the discordant elements." He referred to Martí as "an intelligent and persevering man, and a real defender of the liberty of his country."[9]

On January 3, 1893, General Máximo Gómez was formally appointed military chief of all the men in arms. But many Cubans wondered if Antonio Maceo was being left out. Actually, Martí had every intention of enlisting Maceo's services, and shortly after leaving Gómez, he had made a special point of visiting Maceo's mother in Kingston, Jamaica. Mariana Grajales, then 85 years of age, deeply stirred Martí with her stories of the Ten Years' War in which she had lost a husband and so many of her sons. In a letter to Maceo, Martí informed him of the visit and observed that Mariana Grajales was "one of the women who have most moved my heart."[10] Martí could not have chosen a more effective way of approaching Maceo.

On February 1, 1893, Martí offered Maceo a leading place in the new liberation movement, and promised to furnish and deliver the necessary war supplies. Although he was pleased at the idea of no longer having to acquire these materials himself, Maceo hesitated. He had settled in Costa Rica, where he had established a colony —primarily of Cubans with experience in farming—which had turned out to be a great success. A successful plantation owner now, it may have been that Maceo was reluctant to sacrifice his new career. But this is hardly likely, for he had always been ready at a moment's notice to answer a call to fight for Cuba's independence. More likely, his recent experience in Cuba had made him wary of any revolutionary plan known to many people.

But Martí did not rest until Maceo was recruited for the cause. He visited Maceo in Costa Rica in June, 1893, spending a week with the Negro revolutionary and his family. Like Gómez, Maceo was impressed by Martí's achievements and he finally agreed to join. Before he left, Martí again promised the needed resources and advised Maceo to settle his affairs and get his men ready. The order to move would come from General Gómez.

With Máximo Gómez, Antonio Maceo, Serafín Sánchez, and other military veterans of 1868 residing abroad recruited and given responsibility for arranging military plans, Martí took the next step to solidify the revolutionary movement. One of the great defects of previous revolutionary planning was the attempt to organize the effort entirely from the outside, without effective co-ordination with the revolutionary groups inside Cuba; or, as in the case of the movement led by Maceo in 1890, insufficient contact between the revolutionary forces within Cuba and those on the outside. In organizing the Cuban Revolutionary Party, Martí definitely had this problem in mind, and he took steps to remedy the defect. Thus, after the military chiefs residing abroad were recruited, contact was made with the local chieftains in Cuba. Local military leaders were designated for each province and district of the island: General Guillermo Moncada in Santiago de Cuba, General Bartolomé Masó in Manzanillo, General Julio Sanguily in Havana, Pedro E. Betancourt in Matanzas, Manuel García Ponce in Havana, and General Francisco Carrillo in Las Villas.

At the same time, steps were taken to co-ordinate the activities of the invading army with the inhabitants of the island upon whom they would have to depend. Juan Gualberto Gómez was appointed by Martí, with the approval of the Revolutionary Party, as the political co-ordinator within the island. His duty was to select leaders for each local district on the basis of their revolutionary experience and ability, in order to take advantage of the peculiar circumstances which might prevail in the local areas. As the chief civil co-ordinator of the island, Juan Gualberto Gómez was to be responsible for the development of a system of municipal sub-delegates whose duties were to superintend the local propaganda and organization. These local sub-delegates were also to see to the preparation of the men of arms in their localities, supplying them with clothes, shelter, horses, and other necessities, with the advice and approval of the military commanders. In addition, local civil sub-delegates had the duty of applying in their respective localities the following instructions of Martí relayed through Juan Gualberto Gómez:

> Arm the decided, convince the undecided, supply information to all good Cubans, so that none will be ignorant of events. See that each one has the munitions and indispensables for the initial moment. For those who are not able to acquire these, you are authorized to recruit funds and employ the measures which occur to your imagination and judgment as necessary to that end.
>
> The work must be local and cautious in each locality, while general in all the island: in order that the thread of the conspiracy may not be attacked unexpectedly.[11]

Thus José Martí demonstrated again and again that he could supply the organizational qualities so painfully lacking in the previous efforts. Under his leadership, the Cuban Revolutionary Party became the tightly-knit, efficient "brain" of the revolution. Until this "brain" was created, "the history of Cuban revolutionary separatism . . . had always been an interminable series of more or less glorious failures."[12] With the creation of the Cuban Revolutionary Party as the supreme co-ordinating body, under Martí's direction,* a successful revolution became possible for the first time since the end of the Ten Years' War.

But no matter how effectively it was organized, the Revolutionary Party needed funds to function and to acquire the military stores for the initial expeditions. Martí worked untiringly to raise contributions, visiting Philadelphia, Chicago, Key West, and Tampa. The response of the tobacco workers was consistent. At Martí's suggestion, they agreed to contribute one day's earnings each week—varying from 25 cents to $2.50 per man. In *Patria* of July 2, 1892, Martí paid tribute to the workers of Ocala, Florida, for their regular weekly contribution:

---

* Martí was re-elected annually Delegate of the Party. He made it clear that he did not regard this as a personal honor. "The Delegate," he wrote in *Patria* on April 19, 1893, "is an émigré like the others. . . . The person, we have put aside. Blessed be the fatherland." One might add the words which Martí applied to Wendell Phillips, the militant and courageous American abolitionist: "Great men, even those who are truly great because they cultivate the greatness that is in them, and use it for the benefit of others, are merely the instrument of great forces." (José Martí, *Obras Completas*, Habana, 1946, vol. I, p. 1084.)

When all the years spent in hope and despair by the Cuban émigrés are considered; when the constant and unending sacrifice of the exiles is remembered; when the constant pain of existence has taught the real value of money earned with one's own hands; when one knows that every cent taken from them is one less pleasure for their children, less medicine for the ill, less food on the family table —one cannot but read with profound respect the following words in a letter from Ocala: "From this date on we will contribute from our humble wages the insignificant sum of 25 cents a week for the revolution for the independence of our fatherland, Cuba."[13]

In one of his best known poems, Martí wrote:

> With the poor of the earth
> I wish to cast my lot. . . .[14]

As his work in preparing the Cuban revolution went forward, he turned more and more to the humble masses for aid. The wealthy Cubans were cold to appeals for financial contributions, whereas the working people were always ready to give more than was required of them. This came as no surprise to Martí. "Truth," he observed, "is better revealed to the poor and those who suffer." Throughout the history of Cuba's struggle for independence, he noted, it had been "the humble, the barefooted, the helpless" who had given their all for the cause. "The Cuban workers in the north, those heroes of misery, were, in the first war [1868–1878], a constant and effective support."[15]

It was to the self-sacrificing working people of Tampa, Key West, and Ocala that Martí entrusted the fate of the revolutionary movement. "They are the best and most sacred among us," he declared. Describing with pride a meeting of exiled Cuban workers, he asserted: "This is the working people, *the backbone of our coalition:* the shoulder-belt embroidered by a woman's hand in which the sword of Cuba is kept sheathed, the arsenal of redemption where men build and forgive and foresee and love."[16]

By March, 1893, Martí had succeeded in raising organizational expenses and providing a fund of $12,000. Then in April, 1893, an unauthorized insurrection, under the leadership of Manuel and Ricardo Sartorius, broke out in Holguín. With only 30 men involved, the Sartorius revolt was doomed to sudden failure. The inevitable debacle caused the whole revolutionary movement to lose face by demonstrating that the rebels had failed again. Enthusiasm for the Cuban Revolutionary Party, even though it was not involved in the frustrated uprising, waned, and contributions began to dwindle.

On the heels of this set-back came new unfavorable developments for the Revolutionary Party. In May, 1893, an extremely serious economic crisis hit the United States, and by the fall, thousands of shops and factories shut down while thousands more worked part time only. The tobacco industry of the South was so adversely affected that most firms closed their factories. Deprived of a means of livelihood, the Cuban tobacco workers found it impossible to keep up their regular contributions to the Revolutionary Party. Since the tobacco workers of Key West and Tampa had heretofore been "an inexhaustible source of funds for the Revolution," these unfavorable developments did not bode well for the liberation struggle.

In the winter of 1893–94, the tobacco factories of the Key reopened. But now a new crisis emerged. Taking advantage of the business depression, the employers cut wages to the bone. Eight hundred Cuban workers answered by calling a strike. Immediately Spanish agents in Key West approached the employers and offered to assist them to break the strike through the importation of strikebreakers from Cuba. They pointed out that not only would the strikebreakers meet the employers' need in this particular struggle, but they would saturate the labor market and "save the future . . . from importunities on the part of labor."

The Spanish strategy is understandable. The strongest units of the Cuban Revolutionary Party were centered in Key West. (Sixty-one clubs existed in the Key; 15 in Tampa.) A defeat of the strike "would definitely weaken the Party fabric," and deprive it of its most important source of funds.

The employers took up the Spanish proposition, even though as émigrés themselves it might have been expected they would have been somewhat embarrassed to unite with the Spaniards. But their class interests were paramount. A committee of employers went to Havana, conferred with the Captain General, published advertisements, and with the aid of the Spanish authorities, arranged for strikebreakers. In December, 1893, "the first group of Spanish replacements of the Cuban workers left Havana for Key West." When the strikebreakers arrived in Key West, they were met by a picket line of Cuban workers. But the police, armed with revolvers, escorted the strikebreakers to their temporary quarters; and several of the pickets were arrested. A delegation of city officials, headed by the Mayor, welcomed the strikebreakers to Key West.

The strikers sent an appeal to Martí for assistance. He was then in Tampa and made plans to leave for Key West. Meanwhile, he summoned Horatio S. Rubens, a young New York lawyer, to join him. Rubens persuaded Martí to return to New York and help the strikers from that city. He himself went to Key West and gathered information on the importation of the strikebreakers. Because they had been hired before they left Havana, he claimed that the law outlawing contract labor (passed by Congress in 1885) had been violated. Rubens succeeded in having the strikers who were in prison released, and armed with testimony and evidence of various kinds, he carried his case to the Treasury Department in Washington, whose officials had supervision over the Bureau of Immigration. A committee of Key West public officials also went to the capital to defend their action in behalf of the employers, especially the Seidenberg Cigar Co. The Treasury Department decided in favor of prosecuting the charges made by Rubens. Eventually warrants for deportation were issued for about 100 Spaniards, and after more delays over legal technicalities, the "imported Spaniards were returned to Cuba." With the aid of the Cuban Revolutionary Party, the strikers won a complete victory.

The fact that the Cuban employers had been so eager to cooperate with the Spanish authorities in breaking the strike proved how little they could be relied upon in the struggle for independence. As never before, Martí realized that the revolution had to base itself on the Cuban masses. He pointed out, moreover, that the anti-labor alliance of employers and public officials in Key West proved that "since Cubans had no security in the land of liberty, they ought more than ever to create a free land for themselves."[17]

With the strike over, the tobacco workers revived their weekly contributions to the patriot cause. The clubs throughout the country added their donations to the war funds. The Cuban Revolutionary Party had emerged from the setbacks and crises of 1893–94 with its forces intact and its morale unbroken.

It was time to begin the revolution.

chapter 26

THE MENACE OF AMERICAN IMPERIALISM

The conclusion reached by the Cuban Revolutionary Party that the time had come to start the revolution for the independence of Cuba was influenced not only by the effective organization, under Martí's leadership, of the revolutionary forces in and outside of Cuba. It was also affected by their growing fear that the imperialist forces in the United States would succeed in annexing Cuba before the revolution could liberate the island from Spain. They knew that there was in Cuba a small but economically powerful group which favored annexation. If the order for an uprising were not given soon, it was not impossible that the annexationists in the United States and their allies in Cuba would make some sort of arrangement with Spain by means of which independence would be frustrated.

No one knew better than Martí that the Cuban struggle for independence was increasingly menaced by expansionist forces in the United States and their agents in Washington. "I have lived in the monster and know it from the inside," he wrote in 1895.[1]

Except for short trips to Mexico, Central America, Santo Domingo, and Jamaica, always in the interest of Cuban independence, Martí lived in the United States during the last 15 years of his life, from 1881 to 1895. Most of these years were spent in New York or on visits to other cities, especially those in which there was an important colony of Cuban exiles. For nearly 15 years while he lived in the United States, Martí sent out regular dispatches to the important newspapers of Latin America: *La Opinión Nacional* of Caracas, *La Nación* of Buenos Aires, *El Partido Liberal* of Mexico, *La Opinión Pública* of Montevideo, and others. This steady stream of excellent articles, in superb Spanish, were read all over South

The Menace of American Imperialism · 333

America, and "made the United States known as it was never known before."[2]

Martí's newsletters covered every aspect of American life. There were descriptions of Coney Island in summer, commencement in a girls' school, agricultural exhibitions, the opening of the Brooklyn Bridge, the memorial meeting to honor Karl Marx, Christmas and New Year's in New York, the publication of new books, murder cases and trials, the Negro question, trade union and political conventions, election campaigns, labor strikes, the plight of the American Indian, and the conditions of European immigrants. He introduced to Spanish America in his fascinating biographical essays such writers and thinkers as Emerson, Whitman, Whittier, Longfellow, Mark Twain, Louisa May Alcott, George Bancroft, Washington Irving; such social reformers and popular crusaders as Wendell Phillips, Henry Ward Beecher, Peter Cooper, and Father McGlynn; and such political figures as Garfield, Grant, Blaine, Tilden, Cleveland, Benjamin Harrison, and many others. Many of these biographical essays are among his masterpieces: Emerson, whom he deeply admired because of his complete independence of mind; Whitman whom he regarded as a "natural" poet belonging to no school in contrast to "puny poets," and an exponent of "the poetry of liberty"; Henry Ward Beecher whose stand against slavery he applauded; Wendell Phillips, of whom he wrote, "The whole Universe took the form of a Negro slave in his eye," and "He was implacable and fiery, as are all tender men who love justice"; Peter Cooper of whom he said, "He puts in practice the human Gospel," and "He saw himself as the administrator of his wealth and not as its owner"; Mark Twain whose *A Connecticut Yankee in King Arthur's Court* he described as a "fight, cowboy style, with a lasso and gun" against oppression and poverty.

When Martí arrived in the United States in 1881, he was immediately attracted, even dazzled, by its democratic institutions, its creative power, and the opportunity it provided for every kind of individual initiative. To one coming from Cuba, Spain, and some of the Latin American republics with their feudal societies, social castes, and artificial inequalities, the North American democracy seemed indeed a Promised Land. "Finally," he exulted, "I am in a country where everybody appears his own master. Here we can be proud of the species."[3] Little by little, however, the bitter reality of many aspects of life in the United States cleared away the mist from his eyes. Martí had arrived in the midst of a radical transformation in economic and social life, and he was quick to realize that his concept of the United States as a land where social distinctions were being obliterated and where the poor had equal opportunities with the rich to enjoy the fruits of democracy was in need of revision.

The 1880's were characterized by the rapid growth of American industry, accompanied by a tremendous concentration of capital and the appearance of giant corporations. With the rise of industrial trusts and huge banking houses such as J. P. Morgan & Co., monopoly became the dominant feature of American capitalism. The age of the small manufacturer, the age of free competitive enterprise, was passing. It was being replaced by what was widely called in the 'eighties "The New Feudalism." Said President Grover Cleveland in a message to Congress on December 3, 1888: "As we view the achievements of aggregated capital, we discover the existence of trusts, combinations and monopolies, while the citizen is struggling far in the rear or is trampled to death beneath an iron heel. Corporations, which should be carefully restrained creatures of the law and servants of the people, are fast becoming the people's masters."

"There are too many millionaires and too many paupers," declared the Hartford *Courant* in 1883. All of America was a land of contrast, of poverty amidst enormous wealth. At one end of the scale was magnificence unstinted. The "robber barons" who made up the new plutocracy vied with each other in "conspicuous waste." At the other end of the scale, the workers, earning between 50 cents and one dollar for a working day from ten to 12 hours, lived in gnawing poverty, lacking the bare necessities of life.[4]

The masters of capital, of banking, industry and commerce, were also masters of political life. The pernicious influence of big business in all branches of government—executive, legislative, and judicial —reached such scandalous proportions in the 1880's that scarcely a week passed without some public disclosure of advantageous and lawless concessions granted to corporations, passed into law by bribed legislators, signed by corrupt executives, and approved by judges who were subservient tools of the corporate interests.

The 1880's were also years of great workers' struggles. In cities and towns, the armies of labor organized and gave expression to the pent-up bitterness of years of exploitation in a series of strikes that shook the nation to its foundations. Never before had the United States witnessed labor struggles of such vigor and scope.

Martí observed and reported these radical changes. His reports reflected a new view of the United States. As early as 1882, he wrote:

> We are here in the midst of an all-out struggle between capitalists and workers. To the former it is credit in the bank, creditors' demands, sellers' terms, balance sheets at the end of the year. To the worker it is the daily grind, immediate and pressing need, wives and children eating in the evening what the poor worker earned for them in the morning. And the rich capitalist forces the poor worker to work for the lowest wages.[5]

A year later, he described the poverty of the working class districts of New York:

> There in the humid streets where men and women are massed and move about without air and without space; there in tortuous and gloomy buildings, where the poorest and most miserable people live in stinking cells, laden with dusky, fetid air; there like young cornfields in the path of the locusts, the children of the poor die by the hundreds in the path of summer. Like the ogres in fairy-tales, the cholera sucks out the lives of the children. A boa would not leave them like the summer in New York leaves the children of the poor—corroded, deprived, emptied-out and skinny. Their eyes appear cavernous, their skulls the bald heads of old men, their hands, bundles of dried twigs. They drag themselves along like worms: they exhale in whimpers. And I say that this is a public crime, and that it is the duty of the state to put an end to unnecessary misery.[6]

Martí understood clearly the need of the working class to unite, and welcomed the rise of the "fighting union" of American workers whose strength, he predicted, "will be tremendous." "They are already in it," he reported in July, 1882. "The battle will be such as will stir and shake the Universe."

In this "battle," Martí made it clear he stood with the workers against their callous employers.

> The strike is on [he wrote in one of his dispatches], a strike of thousands of men, in New York and Brooklyn. . . .
>
> In their negotiations with the employees, the coach companies refuse to deal with the representatives appointed by the workers' association; the employees, in mass, abandon the stables, in demand, not of higher salary, nor seeking fewer hours, but because they are to be deprived of the right of association; the companies, which are nothing more than associations linked together in mutual defense against the workers, want each worker to stand alone, facing them with his two hands and his hunger, without organization or support. In this way the employer can lower wages with impunity; and with the butter that they remove from the bread in 3,000 homes, they purchase another horse for their coach, another seal-coat for their daughter who already has one, another black-nosed dog for their mistress![7]

Describing the great railroad strike on the Gould lines in 1885, Martí hailed the courage of the workers in refusing to give up their demand for the right to bargain collectively with the railroad king:

> Since they have already drawn their code of rights, which they have founded solidly on reason; since they see that their ailments openly stem from the insolence and contempt of organized capital, from its illegitimate combinations, from the system of unequal distribution of profits that keeps the worker in his perpetual state of destitution; since they do not find it just that the wages of railroad workers should amount to a crumb of bread and a cheap blanket, in order that giant dividends may be distributed among company heads and their favored . . . and, further, since the sacred passion of human dignity refuses to leave the veins of men any longer, and it swells and spurs them, the workers have stood on their feet, with an act of justice here and an act of violence there, and decided never to sit again unless on equal terms with the capital that hires them.[8]

Appalled by the unscrupulous amassing of riches and the political corruption he saw all about him, Martí wrote fiery dispatches condemning the "cult of wealth." As he saw it, the power of big business had succeeded in corrupting "the courts, the legislatures, the church and the press, and has succeeded in twenty-five years of partnership in creating in the freest democracy of the world the most unjust and shameful of oligarchies." Speaking for all "honest Cubans," he wrote eloquently in a letter to the New York *Evening Post*:

> They admire this nation, the greatest ever built by liberty, but they dislike the evil conditions that, like worms in the heart, have begun in this mighty republic their work of destruction. They have made of

the heroes of this country their own heroes, and look to the success of the American commonwealth as the crowning glory of mankind; but they cannot honestly believe that excessive individualism, reverence for wealth, and the protracted exultation of a terrible victory are preparing the United States to be the typical nation of liberty, where no opinion is to be based on greed, and no triumph or acquisition reached against charity and justice. We love the country of Lincoln as much as we fear the country of Cutting.[9] *

As he witnessed the transformation in the United States, Martí was aware that it posed a real danger to the economic and political independence of Latin America, especially to Cuba. By 1889, he no longer had any doubts on this score. "What is apparent," he wrote in that year, "is that the nature of the North American government is gradually changing in its fundamental reality. Under the traditional labels of Republican and Democrat, with no innovation other than the contingent circumstances of place and character, the republic is becoming plutocratic and imperialistic." American imperialism, he was convinced, was about to launch an offensive to engulf Latin America and would begin by swallowing Cuba.[10]

When this was written, James G. Blaine was Secretary of State and the real leader of the new Republican administration under President Benjamin Harrison. Even before he took office, reports began to appear in the press that Blaine favored the acquisition of Cuba to secure the United States a valuable source of sugar and a strategic outpost for defense. Hailing the stand of the Secretary of State, the expansionist elements looked forward to the extension of American economic and political influence abroad. "The day is not distant," Senator Randall Gibson prophesied, "when the dominion of the United States will be extended ... to every part of the American continent—British America, Mexico, Cuba, Central America, and the islands on our coast."[11]

In the winter of 1889–1890, the first International American Conference met in Washington. All the republics of Latin America, except Santo Domingo, sent delegates in response to a call issued by Secretary of State Blaine. Blaine spoke of the need "to cement

---

* Francis Cutting was one of the leaders of the war of aggression against Mexico in 1846. This is one of the most frequently quoted sentences of Martí dealing with the United States.

interests" among all nations in the western hemisphere, to "bring about peace," to "cultivate friendly commercial ties with all American countries," and to improve communications. But the expansionist press in the United States, praising Blaine's action in calling the conference, talked frankly of the real reasons for the gathering. Editorials headed "Manifest Destiny," "Ships to South America," "Now It Is Our Gulf," "Reciprocity, the First Step to American Penetration," appeared daily. "Americans," said the New York *Tribune*, "are obliged to reconquer their commercial supremacy . . . and to exercise a direct and general influence in the affairs of the American continent." Other papers predicted the conference would lead to the establishment of an American protectorate over the republics of Latin America.[12]

As Uruguay's Consul in the United States, Martí was in close contact with the delegates to the conference. He had followed Blaine's career with great care and had written about him many times in his dispatches to Latin America. At first his comments were full of praise for Blaine, especially for his role as Secretary of State in 1881, in helping to settle frontier disputes in Latin American countries, and Martí called him "a friend of South America." But by 1884, his opinion of Blaine had changed considerably, largely because of Blaine's part in the Peru-Chile dispute over claims on guano territory. Blaine was accused of trying to incite war between Chile and Peru in order to further his pecuniary interests. A Congressional investigation cleared him of this charge, but censured him for the "obvious impropriety" of his actions. Martí saw Blaine's conduct as that of a man who "does not feel shame to use strength when he has it," and who believed that "now is the occasion for the United States to stretch their hand, and set it down wherever it reaches." By the mid-1880's Blaine had come to represent for Martí all the evil and corruption in American politics, a man who was "purchasable, who true to his character, buys and sells in the market of men," a man who sought "under the pretext of treaties of commerce and peace, the wealth [from other nations] of which the economic eras of the Republican Party had begun to deprive the [North American] nation."[13]

Martí saw clearly the danger to the economic and political independence of Latin America, especially to Cuba, in Blaine's "covered game and . . . secret intention" to use the International American Conference to expand U.S. economic and political domination south of the border. He knew, too, that a number of Latin Americans at the conference failed to see this danger, and what was more important, that several Cubans were ready to raise the question of Cuban independence at the gathering in the hope of obtaining the direct assistance of the United States. This Martí unalterably opposed. "I don't want the principle established of putting our fortunes into a body where, because of its influence as a major country, the United States is to exercise the principal part," he wrote to his friend Gonzalo de Quesada. The participation of the United States in Cuba's struggle for independence was fraught with danger: "Once the United States is in Cuba, who will get her out?" The only road for Cuba to follow was to win independence on her own and hold firmly to her sovereignty during and after the revolution. This was the only way to achieve "the reality of independence."[14]

In his article, "The Pan American Conference," Martí ripped aside Blaine's supposedly benevolent purposes in calling the gathering, and exposed it as American imperialism. He favored, he pointed out, Pan-Americanism, but not a false and obsequious Pan-Americanism which would serve as a mask for U.S. imperialist policy. But this was precisely what the International American Conference was seeking to achieve. The idea of reciprocity, proposed by Blaine, appeared on the surface to be a liberal trade policy, but when one examined it closely, it became clear that it was a device for the United States to dump surplus products on the Latin American market, and dominate that market for North American economic interests.* All this would be the prelude to political control of Latin America.

* In December, 1884, President Chester A. Arthur transmitted to the Senate a reciprocity treaty with Spain respecting Cuba and Puerto Rico, which proposed reductions in duties on American imports of tobacco and the free admission of sugar. "If the Treaty stands three years," prophesied John B. Hamel of Philadelphia, ship broker and commission merchant, "it will be the commercial annexation of Cuba, without the political responsibility." Others, however, saw commercial annexation as the first step toward Cuba's ultimate incorporation in the Union. (John B. Hamel to Secretary of State Frederick T. Frelinghuysen, Dec. 4, 1884, Miscellaneous Letters to Dept. of State, National Archives; New York Tribune, Dec. 9, 1884; New York Times, Dec. 9, 1884.) Opposition to the Treaty prevented favorable action by the Senate.

Spanish America knew how to free itself from the tyranny of Spain; and now, after looking with judicious eyes upon the antecedents, causes and reasons for the invitation, we are urged to say, because it is the truth, that the hour has come for Spanish America to declare its second independence. . . .

The International Congress will be the roll call for honor, where it will be seen who defends the independence of Spainsh America."[15]

Martí's article helped to alert the Latin American nations and was largely responsible for the failure of the Conference to agree to any of Blaine's proposals.* But the U.S. imperialists were only temporarily checked. The Pan American Union was started in 1889 by Blaine for the purpose of expanding United States commerce.† Blaine's policy was incorporated in the McKinley Tariff of 1890 which, it will be recalled, provided for the admission of sugar, molasses, tea, coffee, and hides free of duty, but empowered the President to impose duties on these products if he decided that countries exporting these commodities to the United States had placed unreasonable duties on the products of this country. The threat of such imposition, it was believed, would prepare the way for opening foreign markets to the United States. The reciprocity features of the act were inserted largely as a result of Blaine's efforts.

The *Review of Reviews*, a leading expansionist journal, asserted that since, in many areas of production, manufacturing capacity was larger than home demand, businessmen of all parties widely

---

* In 1891 Martí again warned the Latin American nations of U.S. imperialist aims. The occasion was the International American Monetary Commission, called by Secretary of State James G. Blaine, which met in Washington, D.C. from January 7 to April 3, 1891. As the largest silver producer in the world, the United States sought to persuade the Latin American republics to adopt bimetallism and the equalization of gold and silver. This would help it in getting all other nations to adopt the same policy. But Martí, who was appointed Uruguay's delegate to the Congress, wrote a magnificent study of the origin and purpose of the conference, which proved that the great majority of the Latin American countries, lacking silver, had little to gain from the proposed plan. Opposing the efforts of the United States to dominate the Latin American countries, he wrote: "The hands of every nation must remain free for the untrammeled development of the country, in accordance with its distinctive nature and with its individual elements." Martí's report was adopted unanimously and thus frustrated the efforts of the American silver interests, backed by the State Department, to ride roughshod over the welfare of the Latin American countries. (*Minutes of the International Monetary Commission, January 7–April 3, 1891*, Washington, D.C., 1891, pp. 47–78.)

† For 50 years the Union was headed by the U.S. Secretary of State, and its personnel was almost 100 percent from this country. Latin Americans soon came to call the organization the "U.S. Ministry of Colonies."

approved of reciprocity. The United States, it predicted, was on the threshold of large-scale economic expansion into Latin America and would soon achieve "a dominating commercial influence under the magic name of 'reciprocity.'" But the *Age of Steel* correctly noted that economic and political domination would go hand-in-hand. Reciprocity would "annex territories and markets"; it would be a "mapmaker" which would extend the United States' commercial and political domain.

Against all this, of course, Martí had warned in his attack on the International American Conference. He viewed the McKinley Act of 1890 with growing alarm, fully aware that its aim, so far as Cuba was concerned, was to make Cuban sugar production completely dependent on the market in the United States and would strengthen the annexationist elements in the North American republic and Cuba. This was precisely what happened. Writing in the *Review of Reviews* for October, 1891, W. T. Stead, the British journalist, declared that the American reciprocity treaty with Spain, following passage of the McKinley Tariff, "made Cuba virtually a commercial possession of the United States." In 1892, the British Consul offered proof of this statement in a report to his government from Havana: "the British trade with Cuba has almost become a thing of the past, and under the present reciprocity treaty the United States of America practically supplies all the wants of the island and receives all its produce."[16]

In 1894, E. Sherman Gould wrote in an article in the *Engineering Magazine*: "Cuba is a country of practically two products (sugar and tobacco) and one market (the United States). Indeed, we may almost say that it is a country of one product, so greatly does sugar outweigh in value the tobacco production." Martí did not share the glee of American business interests in this report. He had long feared this development and frequently warned against it. He understood the precarious nature of a national wealth based on a single crop, especially when it became dependent on one market. "The manifold crops of diverse agricultural branches and their related industries," he wrote, "keep in balance the countries given exclusively to major crops: coffee, sugar-cane, etc. These crops have become, through the great exchange operations, true games of chance, and like magic bubbles, at times they are golden, at times made of soap." "This bad habit of devoting oneself to a single crop must be seen with fright," he wrote.[17]

Martí repeatedly warned the Cuban people and the other people of "our America"* against relying on one main product for export to one main country. Economic submission meant political servitude. In 1891, in one of his keenest forecasts, he wrote:

> Whoever says economic union, says political union. The people that buys, commands. The people that sells, obeys. Trade must be balanced if our freedom is to be safeguarded. The nation that wants to die sells to a single nation; the nation that wants to live sells to more than one. Too much influence by one country in the trade of another turns into political influence. . . . The first thing a nation does to dominate another is to separate it from the rest of the nations.[18]

In the 1890's as a result of the development of an industrial economy and the growth of industrial and financial monopolies, the United States entered fully into the path of imperialism. Two decades earlier, the United States had achieved a favorable balance of trade, and the list of exports contained increasingly larger amounts of textiles, machines, railroad equipment, and other manufactured goods. As the settlement of the continental limits of the country was completed, foreign exports became more important to absorb the growing supply of American factories. Shipowners saw in expansion an opportunity to revive the faltering American merchant marine. Investors and promoters were looking for new investments for their capital.

The ideological arguments for imperialism were not long in coming. The argument of Anglo-Saxon superiority as a justification for territorial expansion, used during the Mexican War and the drive for the annexation of Cuba in the 1850's, began again to be heard. In 1885, Josiah Strong argued that "it surely needs no prophetic eye to see the civilization of the *United States* is to be the civilization of America, and that the future of the continent is ours." After 1890, this theme was echoed by scores of spokesmen for imperialism in books and articles in newspapers and magazines, many of whom boasted that the American flag would soon "float

---

* Martí always used the expression "our America" to differentiate Spanish America from the United States, the "other America."

unchallenged, supreme, and alone, over the North American continent and its islands."[19]

The flag would open foreign markets for agricultural and industrial surpluses and for surplus capital. Blaine declared in August, 1890 that in many departments, manufactures had overrun the demands of the home market and that the United States had reached the point where one of its highest duties was to enlarge the area of its foreign trade. The great demand, said Blaine, was for expansion abroad. The *Iron Age* declared that Blaine's views with respect to the necessity for a wider market for manufactured goods "are irrepressible."[20]

The demand for foreign markets for surplus production and capital naturally increased during the business depression that began in 1893. As a result of the depression, said the *Iron Age* in 1894, "we have been reconnoitering in new territory and have been taking the first steps towards accomplishing our manifest destiny, the control of the world's markets by American manufacturers." Senator Albert Beveridge summed up the needs and aspirations of American industrialists and financiers when he proclaimed:

> American factories are making more than the American people can use. American soil is producing more than they consume. Fate has written our policy for us; the trade of the world must and shall be ours. And we shall get it as our mother, England, has told us how. We will establish trading posts throughout the world as distributing points for American products. We will cover the ocean with our merchant marine. We will build a navy to the measure of our greatness. Great colonies, governing themselves, flying our flag and trading with us, will grow about our posts of trade. Our institutions will follow our trade on the wings of commerce. And American law, American order, American civilization, and the American flag will plant themselves on shores hitherto bloody and benighted, by those agencies of God henceforth made beautiful and bright.[21]

It was useless to look to Europe for overproduction, said many of the expansionists. The problem of the "inevitable supply" could be solved by turning to Asia and Latin America. Cuba was pointed to as the ideal area in Latin America for economic expansion. "Cuba offers a most inviting field for American enterprise," wrote an economic adviser to big business. In an article entitled "Business

Opportunities in Cuba" which aroused widespread attention in business circles, Eduardo J. Chibás wrote:

> The wonderful natural resources of the island of Cuba offer an opening for the profitable investment of capital and for the extension of trade.... In 1887 the total of exports and imports of Cuba reached $127,784,000 which was 17 percent larger than the foreign commerce of Mexico for the same period, and more than twice as great as the foreign commerce of the five Central American republics combined. In South America, the foreign commerce of Cuba is excelled in extent only by that of Brazil and Argentina. It exceeds that of Chile and of Uruguay and also the aggregate of the six republics of Colombia, Venezuela, Bolivia, Peru, Ecuador and Paraguay.... Surely, in all the wealth of Cuba's resources there is some inducement for a more widespread interest in the Cuban trade than has yet been manifested by the enterprising business men of the United States.[22]

Beginning in 1890, Captain Alfred Mahan started his campaign for a navy adequate to support and justify "a vigorous foreign policy." Mahan argued that "whether they will or no, Americans must begin to look outward." An expanding foreign trade was vital to national prosperity. The growing production of the country necessitated control of foreign markets which, in turn made necessary a powerful navy, a strong merchant marine and secure bases and coaling stations from which they could operate. Strategically as well as tradewise, the Caribbean area was crucial; indeed, nothing less than American supremacy in the Caribbean would suffice.[23]

The emphasis on Caribbean bases naturally focused attention on Cuba. Not only would acquisition of the island offer the United States a strong naval station, but it would provide a market for surplus production and an area for the investment of capital. "There are extensive mines in Cuba now lying idle for want of capital," one newspaper commented, "and if the island were annexed to the United States, this field of production would be fully developed."[24] "Cuba," declared the Detroit *Free Press* on May 16, 1891, "would make one of the finest states in the Union, and if American wealth, enterprise and genius once invaded the superb island, it would become a veritable hive of industry in addition to being one of the most fertile gardens of the world. There is a strong party growing up in the island in favor of reciprocity with and annexation to the United States. We should act at once to make this possible." In an article entitled, "Why We Need Cuba," in *Forum Magazine* for July, 1891, General Thomas Jordan called for the "political incorporation" of Cuba into the United States to strengthen this country's military system and to provide a market for surplus production and capital. "All considerations urge us to this acquisition, without regard to European opinion or antagonism."[25] In November, 1891, *Munsey's Magazine* vigorously urged "the extinction of Spain's sovereignty in Cuba by a reasonable financial reimbursement" on the ground that the island was essential for the defenses of the United States and would serve admirably as an outlet for American surplus production. It said flatly: "It may be stated as almost certain that Cuba will be ours before long."[26]

From 1892 onward, the cry that "Cuba will be ours before long" increased in intensity in the expansionist press. In 1895, the *American Magazine of Civics* featured a symposium on the topic, "Ought We to Annex Cuba?" "It makes the water come to my mouth when I think of the state of Cuba as one in our family," wrote Frederick R. Coudert, a leading Wall Street figure. Another spokesman for Wall Street wrote: "Canada will come in time; Mexico will follow Texas and California, and drop into her niche under the stars and stripes, when we are ready. *But we want Cuba now.*"[27]

Martí watched the aggressiveness of emerging American imperialism with increasing apprehension. He saw it beginning to spread throughout the Americas and he felt certain that the economic expansionism of the United States would soon engulf Cuba. He noted the growing cult of sea power, and observed with concern how the expansionist forces were building up a strong navy and urging the acquisition of naval bases and coaling stations in the Caribbean. He heard the increasingly bold demands for the annexation of Cuba from the military men and the politicians, and while many businessmen were still passive about the idea of acquiring the island, he knew that important Wall Street groups were backing the demand.

Martí knew, too, that the demand for annexation would meet with a favorable response from wealthy elements in Cuba:

> There have always been Cubans, cautious men, proud enough to abominate Spanish domination, but timid enough not to expose their well-being in combatting it. This class of men, helped by those who

wished to enjoy the benefits of liberty without paying for them with their precious blood, vehemently favor the annexation of Cuba to the United States. All the timid ones; all the irresolute, all those attached to wealth, have marked temptation to support this solution which they believe will cost them little. Thus they appease their conscience as patriots and their fear of being real patriots.[28]

The economic depression in Cuba in 1894 which followed the depression of 1893 in the United States and the Wilson-Gorman Tariff of the following year, increased the strength of the annexationists in the island. By the end of 1894, Martí had concluded that it was essential, in order to achieve the independence of Cuba, to thwart the designs and ambitions of the imperialist forces in the United States and their Cuban allies. To accomplish this, it was necessary to begin the revolution. "We must act," he told his close friend, Gonzalo de Quesada, early in 1895. "Cuba must be free from Spain and the United States." In May, 1895, after the outbreak of the war for independence, he explained why it had been necessary to act. "The Cuban war," Martí wrote, "has broken out in America in time to prevent . . . the annexation of Cuba to the United States."[29]

chapter 27

THE SECOND WAR FOR INDEPENDENCE BEGINS

During the year 1894, Martí worked more untiringly than ever at bringing the struggle for Cuban independence to a focus. Month after month, he redoubled his efforts to procure the necessary funds and to tie all the Cubans in the United States together. His most trying problems, however, were, on the one hand, to keep the over-zealous members of the Revolutionary Party quiet while the "finishing touches were being applied" to the carefully guarded details by which the revolution would begin, and, on the other, to act before the Spanish officials could provoke an uprising, force the rebels to declare themselves prematurely, and nip the new movement in the bud. It was necessary, as Martí put it, to "fall on the Island before the Government could fall on the Revolution."[1]

On December 12, 1893, Martí had given the order to the rebels in Cuba to be ready for action by the end of February, 1894. This date passed and the invasion was still not ready. Gómez, as the military commander, would not give his approval. He was not satisfied with the conditions in the province of Camagüey, where support for the revolution was slight and reluctant.

The long delay continued. Martí was waiting for an order from Gómez, but the old general was still preoccupied with the situation in Camagüey province, where the sugar mill owners pleaded for time to finish their harvesting and grinding. They promised money for the invasion if their pleas were heeded. But Gómez, who had little respect for moneyed and propertied groups, finally tired of the game, and ordered the movement to be put in motion. In coming to this decision, Gómez said: "This situation will not change; the rich people will never enter the Revolution. We must force the situation—precipitate the events."[2] On September 30, 1894, he wrote to Maceo: "After the 15th of November at the latest, we must all be prepared to move immediately. None the less, if you are completely ready, this letter, which may very well be my last one from here, constitutes the order to move which you desire."[3]

Maceo, although recovering from a bullet wound inflicted by Spanish agents in Costa Rica who had been sent to assassinate him, was overjoyed and impatient to move. Martí, of course, shared his joy. "How can I paint my happiness," the Delegate wrote to Maceo after learning of Gómez's decision, "which is only clouded by the news that you are still not well."[4]

Satisfied with the preparations, Martí organized the Fernandina plan. This plan called for the embarkation of an expeditionary force from Fernandina, Florida. Three yachts, the *Amadis, Lagonda,* and *Baracoa,* were chosen because their speed was superior to the boats used by the Spaniards. Ostensibly the destination was to be Central America, with stops as follows: at a certain point in Florida to take on board Carlos Roloff and Serafín Sánchez with 800 men; in Costa Rica for Maceo, Flor Crombet, and 200 men; and in Santo Domingo for Máximo Gómez's group. All members of this force would go as agricultural workers with suitable tools, which actually would be implements of war. When at sea, of course, the announced destination would be changed from Central America to Cuba. If the captains and the crews of the vessels objected, they were to be confined until the end of the voyage.

By late December, 1894, everything was prepared for the simultaneous embarkation of the three expeditions. In Cuba, the revolutionary leaders were informed of the impending action, although Martí did not reveal the details of the expeditions, and they were ordered to prepare to support and protect the invasion. On December 25, Martí informed Maceo of the imminent departure of the ship designated for his group.

Then the revolutionary leaders suffered an enormous catastrophe. López de Queralta, a member of the expedition belonging to the group of Serafín Sánchez, carelessly revealed the plan to one of the captains who, in turn passed the information on to the shipowners. In short order, a Spanish official heard of the plan, protested to Washington, and on January 14, 1895, the federal government detained the three yachts and confiscated the materials of war.

It was a terrible blow. Nearly three years of work and some

$58,000 had been lost. But what Martí feared even more was the loss of prestige and confidence in the revolutionary leaders.

Yet the catastrophe had exactly the opposite effect. The scope of the ill-fated Fernandina expeditions, as it was now revealed, startled the revolutionists in Cuba and the exiles in the United States. Who would have thought it possible that Martí could have organized such a detailed undertaking with the limited resources at his command, and carried it out (until the last fatal moment) with such efficiency and secrecy? Enthusiasm for Martí's leadership grew in Cuba and abroad. "Those who had hitherto thought him a poet and a dreamer," recalls Horatio Rubens, "now were more impressed by the magnitude and promise of his plan than its temporary frustration."[5]

All this was heartening to Martí, who had become very despondent when he first heard of the debacle. Heartening, too, was the reaction of the military leaders to the news of the failure of the Fernandina plan. General Gómez informed Martí that he was ready to embark for Cuba by whatever means possible whenever the opportunity presented itself. Maceo reacted in a like manner, as did Serafín Sánchez and the other military chieftains.

The effort to launch the revolution continued without delay. The Revolutionary Party immediately undertook another fund-raising campaign. Martí called upon Key West and Tampa for funds, and $5,573 was raised by the tobacco workers. To this was added 2,000 pesos General Gómez borrowed from President Heureaux of Santo Domingo.

On January 29, 1895, Martí, General Mayía Rodríguez, representing the Commander-in-Chief, Máximo Gómez, and General Enrique Collazo, representing the organization of revolutionists in the island, signed the order for the war to begin. The order promised that "immediate aid of valuable material already acquired" would be sent, and that military forces in Cuba could count on continued and untiring help from abroad.

Juan Gualberto Gómez in Cuba then received the responsibility of setting a date for the uprising, subject to the final approval of a military committee composed of the principal military chieftains abroad. Two basic criteria were adopted to guide the fixing of the date: first, no less than four provinces must be ready for and favorable to the revolution; second, one province besides that of Oriente must be prepared for the landing of military officers from the outside.

After consultation with local leaders, Juan Gualberto Gómez decided that these two conditions were satisfied. The date of February 24, 1895, was agreed upon.

The insurrection began in Cuba on the scheduled day. On February 24, 1895, the *grito* or "cry" was sounded at Baire, a village about 50 miles from Santiago de Cuba. Unfortunately, on that same day, the uprising in the West was defeated by the Spanish authorities. Having learned of the plans for the insurrection, they captured General Julio Sanguily and Don José María Aguirre de Valdés, the supreme and assistant chieftains of the whole Western department, as they were leaving the city of Havana to lead the uprising in the West. Without leadership, the revolution collapsed in the Western provinces on the very day it was supposed to begin. Thus one of the two basic requirements for the beginning of the revolution—that no less than four provinces must be ready for and favorable to the revolution—was not fulfilled.

When the *Grito de Baire* was sounded, the supreme military figures had not yet appeared in Cuba. Máximo Gómez was still in Santo Domingo and Antonio Maceo in Costa Rica. It was imperative that they leave for Cuba as soon as possible. On February 27, Gómez wrote to Maceo: "The smoke of gunfire is visible in Cuba, and the blood of our comrades is being shed on its soil. We have no other choice but to leave from wherever and however we can." Maceo agreed. "I do not think we can afford to wait any longer," he wrote. "We are running a great danger. Once in Cuba, we can depend on the machete to open the breach."[6]

Martí was in Santo Domingo working out the details of the invasion with Gómez when the news of the revolt reached him. At once, he wrote to all the revolutionary clubs and to *Patria* outlining the true character of the war:

> Let the tenor of our words be, especially in public matters, not the useless clamor of fierce vengeance, which does not enter our hearts, but the honest weariness of an oppressed people who hope, through their emancipation from a government convicted of uselessness and

malevolence, for a government of their own which is capable and worthy. Let them see in us constructive Americanism and not empty bitterness. This is our war; this is the Republic we are creating.[7]

This theme was developed in the Manifesto of Montecristi (Santo Domingo), written by Martí and signed by the Delegate and Gómez, March 25, 1895. This historic document, entitled *El Partido Revolucionario Cubano a Cuba* (The Cuban Revolutionary Party to Cuba), opened:

> The revolution for independence, initiated at Yara after a glorious and bloody preparatory process, has now entered a new period of warfare in Cuba, by virtue of the orders issued and the resolutions adopted in Cuba and abroad by the Cuban Revolutionary Party, and as a result of the well balanced association in it of all the elements dedicated to the eradication of the evils and to the emancipation of our country, for the good of America and of the World; and the chosen representatives of the revolution—which as of today is ratified —fully recognize and abide by their duty—without usurping the tone and the declarations that pertain only to the majesty of the duly constituted Republic—of re-stating before the Country, which is not to be stained in blood without reason or without a fair expectation of victory, the precise aims, born of sound judgment and alien to the thirst for revenge, with which this inextinguishable war has been prepared and which will carry it to its logical victory, and which today leads into combat, assembled in a wise and soul-stirring democracy, all the elements that make up Cuban society.

Martí then outlined five points relative to the policy of the war: (1) that the war of independence would be a civilized one; (2) that the participation of the Negro people was necessary for victory, and that the charge that "the Negro race is a threat" was "wickedly made by the beneficiaries of the Spanish regime for the purpose of spreading fear of the revolution";* (3) that non-combatant Spaniards would never be the object of revenge, persecution, or extortion; (4) that private rural wealth which did not intentionally

---

* Martí pointed out that the "fear of the Negro" was a danger to be overcome in all of Latin America and not only in Cuba. In his essay, "Our America," January, 1891, he warned that "the hour is fast approaching" when the United States "might go so far as to lay hands on us." One of the weapons the expansionists of North America would use to conquer Latin America would be to stir up racial hatred of the Negro. In the same essay Martí emphasized the equal rights of all men, regardless of color—a theme constant throughout his writings: "Whoever foments and propagates antagonism and hate between races, sins against humanity." (José Martí, *Obras Completas*, La Habana, 1946, vol. II, p. 113.)

hamper the revolution would be respected, and (5) that the revolution would introduce a new economic life in Cuba.

What kind of a country would Cuba be, after the Revolution? Martí answered:

> A free country with employment available to all and located at the crossroads of the rich and industrial world, will replace, unhindered and with advantage, after a War inspired in the purest abnegation and carried on accordingly, the abashed country, where well-being can be obtained only in exchange for complicity, explicit or implied, with the tyranny of hungry foreigners who bleed and corrupt.[8]

Anxious to bring together in the revolutionary movement "as many elements of all kinds as could be recruited," Martí refrained from spelling out specifically in the Manifesto the full nature of the republic that would follow a triumph over Spain. But he did emphasize that it would be a country in which economic opportunities would exist for all, and not only for the privileged few.*

On March 25, the same day the Manifesto of Montecristi was issued, Antonio Maceo bid farewell to his wife. The Negro leader was bitter because Martí had removed him from command of the expedition from Costa Rica, placing it entirely in the hands of Flor Crombet, who had said he could organize the expedition with the $2,000 available while Maceo had insisted on a larger sum. In requesting his full co-operation, Martí appealed to Maceo's love of country. "Cuba is at war, General," he wrote. "When that is said,

---

* Although he did not write a single book on the subject, Martí did deal in many of his writings with different aspects of the republic that would follow victory over Spain. In general, he believed that the country should be organized on democratic foundations with equal rights for all, regardless of color. Poverty and the concentration of economic power in the hands of the few would be avoided through the social organization of diversified agriculture. It would be a country which would do business with every nation in the world, but free from economic domination by any one of them. Education would be free and available to all, for "an educated country will always be strong and free." "A country where only a few men are wealthy is not rich," Martí wrote. "A country where everyone has a portion is." If everyone had a share in its wealth, the country would maintain "a balance in social questions." Not only would poverty be avoided but also violent class struggles and labor disputes such as he had witnessed in the United States.

The above is only a brief presentation of Martí's views about the nature of the Cuban republic. For a more detailed study, see Antonio Martínez Bello, *Ideas Económicas y Sociales de Martí*, La Habana, 1940, though the author tends to exaggerate Martí's inclination to socialism; Jorge Mañach, *El Pensamiento Político y Social de Martí*, La Habana, 1941; and J. I. Jiménez-Grullón, *La Filosofía de José Martí*, Universidad Central de Las Villas, 1960.

Second War for Independence Begins • 353

the picture is changed." Martí's plea was effective. Swallowing his wounded pride, Maceo agreed to go along in a subordinate post. "The Nation above all," he explained to his wife. "Forward then for the sake of the native land, and for it, the glory of sacrificing everything."[9]

Crombet, Maceo, his brother José, and 20 other rebels left Costa Rica on the *Adirondack,* an American craft, ostensibly bound for New York. The Spanish Consul in Costa Rica was not fooled, however, and at his warning, the *Adirondack* was kept under a close watch by Spanish cruisers. On the night of March 29, the captain of the *Adirondack,* frightened by possible reprisals, broke his promise to land the insurgents in Cuba, and deposited them instead at Fortune Island in the archipelago of the Bahamas. Here they finally prevailed upon the American Vice-Consul Farrington to rent them his schooner, the *Honor,* and with three sailors as a crew, the 23 rebels sailed for Cuba on the afternoon of March 30. The following day, the schooner was hit by a bad storm, but the seasick rebels recovered sufficiently, on seeing the beacons of Duaba and Baracoa, to break out the weapons and ready the cargo for landing. The schooner was wrecked in the landing on the beach near the town of Baracoa. But the first expedition had succeeded in reaching Cuba. The rebels were greeted with joy by the farmers in the area, and the word spread immediately: *"Maceo is here! Viva Cuba Libre!"*[10]

Maceo knew that the presence of the rebels would soon be known to the Spaniards, and that they would be pursued by strong enemy forces. To avoid encirclement and destruction while trying to join the other rebel forces, Maceo led the expeditionaries through the mountains and forests toward the district of Guantánamo. Living on berries and drinking water from streams, the small group of rebels made their way up and down the hills, through tangled undergrowth and dense woods. During a skirmish with Spanish soldiers, General Flor Crombet was killed. Maceo then split the rebels into groups, and, with five followers, moved ahead.

Soon there were left only three of the six, and eight days later, after extreme hardships, these *insurrectos* stumbled into the camp of Brigadier Jesús Rabí. Of the original 23 invaders who had left Duaba 20 days before, only 13 were still alive, and most of these were prisoners of Spain.

On the very night that Maceo reached the rebel camp, at the point of exhaustion, he issued a general order to the forces of Oriente announcing that General Maceo had arrived and had assumed command of the entire province. The following day he ordered all rebel officers "to hang every emissary of the Spanish government, Peninsular or Cuban, whatever may be his rank, who presents himself in our camps with propositions of peace. This order must be carried out without hesitation of any kind or without attention to any contrary indications. Our motto is to triumph or to die."[11]

That same day, April 21, Maceo issued a proclamation to the people of Cuba urging all Cubans to rise in arms. The response to this call to arms was most gratifying. On April 30, Maceo wrote to his wife:

> I have 6,000 men, well-armed, and with much artillery. . . . By the 15th of the coming month, I will have 12,000 armed men, and much territory conquered. . . .
> Three days ago José [Maceo] told me of the arrival of Gómez, Martí, Borrero, Guerra and two others on the beaches between Guantánamo and Baracoa.[12]

On April 1, 1895, Gómez, Martí, Brigadier Francisco Borrero, Colonel Angel Guerra, César Salas, and Marcos del Rosario, left Montecristi, Santo Domingo, bound for Cuba. (Borrero, Guerra, and Salas were Cubans; Marcos del Rosario was a Dominican Negro.) Although many Cubans in the island and outside felt that he should remain abroad organizing reinforcements for the revolution among the exiles, Martí had decided to go to Cuba with Gómez. His decision was motivated, in part, by the charge of certain critics that he was a mere man of words and that he was afraid to go into battle himself. More important, he felt that a country would not accept "without scorn and indifference" being served "by one who preached the need of dying without beginning by risking his own life." He was convinced, too, that his presence was just as "useful" in Cuba as it was abroad.

All this Martí set down in a letter to Dr. Federico Henríquez y Carvajal of Santo Domingo on the eve of his departure for Cuba. He wrote that he would abide by whatever was deemed necessary to achieve victory. If commanded to stay in the war, he would stay, and if to leave those who were dying, he would "have the courage for that too." "Wherever my first duty lies, in Cuba or outside Cuba, there will I be. . . . I called up the war; my responsibility begins rather than ends with it. For me, the country will never be triumph, but agony and duty. . . . I shall arouse the world. But my one desire would be to stand beside the last tree, the last fighter, and die in silence. For me, the hour has come."[13]

Gómez, Martí, and their four companions arrived in Inagua with a supply of weapons on April 2, where they found the schooner they had contracted for waiting. But the captain and crew deserted, and the rebels were left stranded. Fortunately, a German freighter, the *Nordstrand*, carrying fruit on the way to Cap Haitien, stopped at Inagua. With the aid of the Haitian Consul and the payment of $1,000, they were able to get the captain to agree to take them as passengers and to put them off at sea in a small boat as he passed Cuba on the return voyage.

On April 10, after a voyage to Cape Haitien and back, the fruit ship sailed from Inagua. By the late afternoon, the rebels could see the peaks of the mountains of Cuba. In the evening, the *Nordstrand* stopped three miles off the coast. The night was dark and stormy, and the captain hesitated to send the six men out into the fury of the wind and sea. But Gómez commanded: "To land." Martí tells the rest in the diary he kept:

> They lower the boat. Raining hard as we push off. Set course wrong. Conflicting and confused opinion in boat. Another downpour. Rudder lost. We get on course. I take forward oar. Salas rows steadily. Paquito Borrero and the General help in the stern. We strap on our revolvers. Steer toward clearing. Moon comes up red behind a cloud. We land on a rock beach, La Playita. I last to leave boat, bailing out. Jump ashore. Great joy.[14]

The place where they set foot on Cuban soil was at the foot of Cajobabo. Gómez kissed the earth.

On February 24, 1895, the *grito* of the Cuban people had been raised at Baire. On March 29, Antonio Maceo and a band of his followers from Costa Rica had landed in eastern Cuba. On April 11, Máximo Gómez, accompanied by José Martí, made his landing. The chief veterans of 1868 and the ideological leader and moving spirit of the revolution were at last in Cuba.

No previous insurrectionary efforts had attained such magnitude in scope or such thorough integration in the planning stages as had the Revolution of 1895. The years of preparation, of frustrations and setbacks were over. The revolution was a fact, and the vision of a *Cuba Libre* could now become a reality.

During the days following the landing at Playitas, Martí felt that his life was reaching its fulfillment. On April 16, he was informed that Gómez as chief of staff, supported unanimously by the other officers, had named him Major General of the Liberating Army. "With an embrace," Martí rejoiced, "they brought my life up to the level of their veterans' glory." On May 2, at the request of its editors, Martí wrote an article for the New York *Herald* defining the purposes of the war in Cuba: "Cuba wishes to be free in order that here Man may fully realize his destiny, that everyone may work here, and that her hidden riches may be sold in the natural markets of America. . . . The Cubans ask no more of the world than the recognition of and respect for their sacrifices."[15]

At La Mejorana, near Santiago de Cuba, on May 4, Martí, Gómez and Maceo met to decide on the strategy to be followed in the war. Among the topics discussed was the question of civil versus military control of the revolution. Martí expressed himself strongly in favor of superiority for the civil over the military authority, and proposed calling a convention of all the civil and military leaders to form a civil government and to elect its officials. As on previous occasions, he maintained that complete military control would be a very bad precedent for a post-war independent republic. The war might end, he feared, with Spain expelled from the island but with a Cuban military dictatorship in control.

This time Gómez sided mainly with Martí. But Maceo took a strong stand for a military *Junta* until victory had been achieved. He felt that the weakness, dissension, petty rivalries and incompetence of the civil government during the Ten Years' War had interfered with the prosecution of the revolution and had ultimately contributed to the collapse of the rebellion. He argued that, in order to avoid this error in the new revolution, the war should be conducted under the control of a small group of the highest military leaders.

Second War for Independence Begins · 357

The question of civil versus military control of the war was not fully decided. But evidently Martí's viewpoint was more or less adopted, for agreement was reached among the three men that Gómez was to be commander-in-chief of the army, Maceo, military chief of Oriente, and Martí, supreme leader of the revolution abroad and in non-military matters.

On May 18, Martí wrote from Dos Ríos to Manuel Mercado, his friend in Mexico. The letter opened: "I am now, every day, in danger of giving my life for my country."[16] The letter was never finished. On May 19, the Spaniards attacked. Though ordered by Gómez to remain with the rear-guard, Martí rode forth to his first encounter with the Spaniards. As he rode through a pass, Spanish soldiers in ambush shot him down. His companion, Angel de la Guardia, tried to rescue his body, but failed. Gómez's attempts to retake Martí's body were equally futile. The Spaniards carried it away to Santiago de Cuba, where on May 27, 1895, José Martí was buried.

"He died," wrote Charles A. Dana of the New York *Sun*, a friend and admirer of Martí, "as such a man might wish to die, battling for liberty and democracy."

Máximo Gómez paid eloquent tribute to Martí:

> He knew how to seek in book and newspaper the best and brightest facts, putting them before the Cuban workers in the shops in order to instruct them particularly to love things about the Fatherland, so that the Cuban worker should find himself at home with the new society which was to come, in this way creating the Republic by the people and for the people. He preached that the school would be the panacea which would cure all the evils that were the consequence of a former life of exceptionally crude backwardness of privilege and obscurantism. Even as a child, he set himself against the power usurping the rights of his country, and for this he paid by having to wear a brace on his foot, since tyranny took special care to extinguish in Cuba every lamp which like "Plácido" could give out the slightest spark of light.* To sum up, Martí was always proud, a rebel against all tyranny and usurpation.[17]

---

* Gabriel de la Concepción Valdés, known as "Plácido," was a free Negro poet in Cuba, executed during the suppression of the slave conspiracy of 1844. (*See* vol. I, pp. 214–16.)

José Martí was a rare combination of man of ideas and man of action. "Ideas were for him weapons in the fight for a better world, in which freedom for Cuba was the first step," one student has correctly observed. He was a man of many talents: a lawyer, a poet, a master of the most exquisite Spanish prose, a great orator, a teacher in many universities in Latin America of language, literature and philosophy, a distinguished journalist, a diplomat, and the organizer of every detail of the Cuban revolution. His writings made him so admired and respected throughout Spanish-speaking America that Argentina, Uruguay and Paraguay made him their consular representative in the United States.

Martí's writings, collected and edited by Gonzalo de Quesada y Miranda, fill 70 volumes. Even this edition is incomplete since there still remains uncollected material scattered in South American newspapers. But in these 70 volumes there is abundant evidence of Martí's broad culture and his remarkable talents as a political thinker and organizer. It is indeed unfortunate that the bulk of these writings are still not available in English. The only collection of Martí's writings in English is *The America of José Martí,* published in New York in 1953. This contains selections from his series of studies of North American life, but does not include his important articles about social and economic conditions in the United States nor those in which Martí expressed his views on the relations of the United States with Latin America, including Cuban-American relations. There are also some selections from Martí's writings about Cuba and the diary of his last days. The translation of the rest of Martí's writings into English is long overdue.

Martí died at the early age of 42. But the example of his unswerving loyalty to the cause of Cuban independence and freedom continued to inspire the insurgents and helped carry them through their bitter and bloody struggles. "The Invading Hymn," written on November 15, 1895, by Enrique Loynaz del Castillo opened with the lines:

> The adored memory of Martí
> Presents Honor to our lives.[18]

Martí's ideas served as guides for future generations of Cuban patriots. As one Cuban scholar and revolutionary wrote in 1953 on the 100th anniversary of Martí's birth: "He was the guide of his time; he was also the forerunner of our own."[19]

On a pine board in the camp at Dos Ríos were the pages of Martí's last letter which, though never completed, set forth what "The Apostle" of free Cuba believed were the tasks then facing the Revolution. It was indispensable, Martí emphasized, to liberate Cuba from Spain. At the same time, it was necessary to take steps to prevent the United States from substituting its own domination of Cuba for that of Spain's, and thus facilitate its domination over all of Latin America.

> It is my duty—inasmuch as I realize it and have the spirit to fulfill it—to prevent, by the independence of Cuba, the United States from spreading over the West Indies and falling, with that added weight, upon other lands of our America. All I have done up to now, and shall do hereafter, is to that end. . . . I have lived inside the monster and know its insides—and my weapon is only the slingshot of David.[20]

A free and independent Cuba, Martí pointed out, must not serve as an auxiliary for the penetration of United States imperialism into Latin America. Those who led the Cuban people in their fight for freedom from Spain, and those who would build the structure of free Cuba after that struggle was won, had the responsibility of creating a nation that would be truly sovereign, of safeguarding Cuba's independence from economic domination by Wall Street and political domination by the United States State Department, and of thereby preventing Cuba from being used by the United States as a bridgehead for the conquest of the West Indies and Latin America.

Death cut short José Martí's inspired leadership for the fulfillment of this program. This was the task he left for the Cuban people.

REFERENCE NOTES

chapter 1 THE CUBAN ANNEXATIONS

1. Reprinted in Antonio Núñez Jiménez, *La Liberación de las Islas*, La Habana, 1959, p. 461.
2. José Antonio Saco, *Colección de Papeles*, Paris, 1859, vol. III, p. 174.
3. Ramiro Guerra y Sánchez, *Manual de la historia de Cuba, económica, social y política*, La Habana, 1938, pp. 434–35.
4. Herminio Portell Vilá, *Historia de Cuba, en sus relaciones con Los Estados Unidos y España*, La Habana, 1938–39, vol. II, p. 54. (Hereafter cited as Portell Vilá, *Cuba*.)
5. Herminio Portell Vilá, *Narciso López y Su Epoca*, La Habana, 1930, vol. I, pp. 190–93. (Herafter cited as Portell Vilá, *López*.)
6. Guerra, *op. cit.*, p. 409.
7. Quoted in Sergio Aguirre, *"Quince Objeciones A Narciso López,"* Habana, 1960, p. 17. Mimeographed copy in possession of author.
8. Raúl Cepero Bonilla, *Azúcar y Abolición; Apuntes para una historia critica de abolicionismo*, La Habana, 1948, p. 39.
9. Gaspar Betancourt Cisneros, *en su impugnación a Saco*, in José A. Saco, *"Contra la Anexión" de José Antonio Saco*, La Habana, 1928, vol. I, p. 184.
10. Cepero, *op. cit.*, pp. 40–41.
11. Hugh B. Soulsby, *The Right of Search and the Slave Trade in Anglo-American Relations, 1814–1862*, Baltimore, 1933, Chapter III.
12. Saco, *Contra la Anexión*, vol. I, pp. 37, 44–51, 71, 72, 133, 167; *Revista Cubana*, vol. VI, 1887, pp. 545–50.
13. *"unos cubanos,"* Habana, 1848, reprinted in Robert G. Caldwell, *The López Expedition to Cuba, 1848–1851*, Princeton, N.J., 1915, pp. 25–26.
14. *Contra la Anexión, Colección de Libros Cubanos*, compiled by Fernando Ortiz, Havana, 1928, vol. I, pp. 33–67.
15. Vidal Morales y Morales, *Iniciadores y Primeros Mártires de la Revolución Cubana*, Havana, 1931, vol. II, p. 25.
16. *La Verdad*, June 12, 1851; Gaspar Betancourt Cisneros, *Thoughts upon the Incorporation of Cuba into the American Confederation in contraposition to those published by Don José Antonio Saco*, La Verdad 1849, pp. 25–26; Cepero, *op. cit.*, p. 46; Conde de Alcoy, *en carta al Ministro de Estado de fecha*, 9 de Septiembre, 1849, *Boletin del Archivo Nacional*, vol. XVI, No. 4, p. 281.

chapter 2 THE INGLORIOUS ATTEMPT TO PURCHASE CUBA

1. Philip S. Foner, *History of the Labor Movement in the United States*, New York, 1947, vol. I, p. 278.
2. *The Works of Calhoun*, Edited by Richard K. Crallé, New York, 1857, p. 466.
3. Robert B. Letcher to John J. Crittenden, Jan. 28, 1859, John J. Crittenden Papers, Library of Congress.
4. John Bigelow, *Retrospections of an Active Life*, New York, 1909, vol. I, p. 280; Basil Rauch, *American Interests in Cuba, 1848-1855*, New York, 1948, p. 54; Memorandum, O'Sullivan to James Buchanan, July 6, 1847, James Buchanan Papers, Library of Congress.
5. New Orleans *Delta*, May 14, 1848; *De Bow's Review*, vol. V, 1848, p. 470.
6. *Congressional Globe*, 30th Cong., 1st Sess., Appendix, pp. 597, 608.
7. Campbell to Buchanan, May 18, 1848, Dept. of State, Consular Despatches, Havana, XXI, National Archives, Washington, D.C. (Hereafter cited as N.A.)
8. Milo M. Quaife, editor, *Diary of James Polk*, Chicago, 1910, vol. III, pp. 478-88; Portell Vilá, *López*, vol. I, pp. 239-40.
9. Manuel I. Mesa Rodríguez, "*La Conspiración de la Mina de la Rosa Cubana*," *Cuadernos de Historia Habanera*, número 44, p. 38. Copy in Archivo Nacional, Havana.
10. Pidal to Calderón, Madrid, Sept. 16, 1848, annexed to Calderón to Buchanan, Nov. 21, 1848, Dept. of State, Notes from Legations: Spain, XII, N.A.
11. Buchanan to Saunders, June 17, 1848, Dept. of State, Diplomatic Instructions, Spain, XIV, N.A.
12. Saunders to Buchanan, June 27, July 24, 1848, *ibid.*, XXXV, N.A.
13. *Diary of Polk, op. cit.*, vol. III, pp. 493-94.
14. Saunders to Buchanan, Nov. 17, Dec. 18, 1848, Dept. of State, Despatches, Spain, XXX, N.A.
15. Buchanan to John M. Clayton, April 17, 1849; Robert B. Campbell to John M. Clayton, June 13, 1850, John M. Clayton Papers, Library of Congress.
16. Clayton to Barringer, Aug. 2, 1849, Dept. of State, Diplomatic Instructions: Spain, XIV, N.A.; Herminio Portell Vilá, "*El Gobierno Polk y las Conspiraciones Cubanas de 1848*," *Universidad de la Habana*, vol. II, 1938, p. 129.

chapter 3 THE DEBATE OVER CUBA

1. New Orleans *Delta*, Jan. 3, 1853; Aug. 27, 1855; New Orleans *Courier*, Jan. 27, 1855; J. F. H. Claiborne, *Life and Correspondence of John A. Quitman*, New York, 1866, vol. II, p. 211; Chester Stanley Urban, "The Idea of Progress and Southern Imperialism: New Orleans and the Caribbean, 1845-1861," unpublished Ph.D. thesis, Northwestern University, 1943, pp. 45-54.
2. *Journal of Southern History*, vol. V, Aug. 1939, p. 373.

3. Letter of A. J. Donelson, July 8, 1848, in *"Correspondence addressed to Calhoun,"* edited by Chauncey S. Brooks and R. P. Brooks, *Annual Report of the American Historical Association for 1929*, Washington, 1930, p. 456.
4. *Cong. Globe*, 33rd Cong., 1st Sess., Part II, p. 1021; New Orleans *Delta*, Feb. 26, 1854; New Orleans *Courier*, July 1, Dec. 24, 1851; Charleston *Mercury*, April 6, 1855.
5. J. T. Pickett to John A. Quitman, March 20, 1854; J. McDonald to John A. Quitman, March 10, 1854, John A. Quitman Papers, Harvard University Library; New Orleans *Daily Delta*, Dec. 15, 1852.
6. New Orleans *Daily Delta*, May 31, 1856, June 12, 1857.
7. *De Bow's Review*, vol. XVII, Sept. 1854, pp. 280–84.
8. New Orleans *Daily Delta*, Aug. 3, 1852; New Orleans *Orleanian*, June, 14, 1857.
9. New Orleans *Daily Picayune*, July 19, 1853, Feb. 3, 1859; *De Bow's Review*, vol. XVII, July, 1854, p. 45; vol. XVII, Sept. 1854, pp. 280–84.
10. *De Bow's Review*, vol. XVII, Oct. 1854, p. 523; New Orleans *Daily Courier*, Sept. 6, 1851; Richmond *Enquirer*, March 17, 1854.
11. New York *Journal of Commerce*, Aug. 23, 1851; Boston *Atlas*, May 9, 1854; Washington *National Intelligencer*, Nov. 18, 1854; New York *Tribune*, Jan. 25, 1853.
12. Boston *Courier*, Oct. 27, 1852; New York *Journal of Commerce*, Aug. 23, 1851; Jan. 31, 1859; *Hunt's Merchants' Magazine*, vol. XL, May, 1859, p. 564.
13. New York *Tribune*, Dec. 28, 1852; Nowlan Fowler, "The Anti-Expansionist Argument in the United States Prior to the Civil War," unpublished Ph.D. thesis, University of Kentucky, 1955, pp. 566–70.
14. Reprinted in *Ohio State Journal* (Columbus), Aug. 21, 1851.
15. Raleigh (N. Car.) *Register*, Dec. 1, 1852; *New York Times*, May 3, 19, 1854; *Cong. Globe*, 32nd Cong., 2nd Sess., pp. 190, 225; Appendix, p. 60; 33rd Cong., 1st Sess., Appendix, p. 437; 37th Cong., 2nd Sess., pp. 430, 1061, 1342, 1347; Philip S. Foner, *Business and Slavery: The New York Merchants and the Irrepressible Conflict*, Chapel Hill, N. Car., 1941, pp. 34–40.

chapter 4 THE FILIBUSTERS: NARCISO LÓPEZ

1. José Martí, *Obras Completas*, La Habana, 1946, vol. I, pp. 442, 533, 834.
2. McClean to Buchanan, July 17, 1848, Consular Despatches, Havana, N.A.
3. Lewis Pinckney Jones, "Carolinians and Cubans: The Elliots and Gonzales, Their Work and Their Writings," unpublished Ph.D. thesis, University of North Carolina, 1952, p. 100; Claiborne, *op. cit.*, vol. II, pp. 53–55; O'Sullivan to Calhoun, Aug. 24, 1849, *Calhoun Correspondence, op. cit.*, vol. III, pp. 1202–03.
4. Malcom W. Means to Clayton, Aug. 10, Sept. 1849, Dept. of State, Special Agents, XVIII, N.A.
5. Guerra, *op. cit.*, p. 450.

6. Caldwell, *op. cit.*, p. 55; I. P. Hall to Clayton, Received at Washington, Oct. 20, 1849, Clayton Papers, Library of Congress.
7. Portell Vilá, *Cuba*, vol. I, pp. 427–30; O'Sullivan to Calhoun, Aug. 24, 1849, *Calhoun Correspondence, op. cit.*, vol. II, pp. 1202–03.
8. "Manifesto on Cuban Affairs Addressed to the People of the United States by Ambrosio José Gonzales, September 1st, 1852," New Orleans, 1853, p. 7.
9. New York *Herald*, Dec. 6, 1849; Washington *Republic*, Dec. 10, 1849.
10. James Hays McClendon, "John A. Quitman," unpublished Ph.D. thesis, University of Texas, June, 1949, pp. 110–30; 328–29; Aguirre, *op. cit.*, pp. 22–24; Claiborne, *op. cit.*, vol. II, pp. 57, 384–85. My emphasis.—P. S. F.
11. New Orleans Daily *Picayune*, May 26, 1850. Emphasis mine.—P. S. F.
12. Chester Stanley Urban, "New Orleans and the Cuban Question During the López Expeditions of 1849–1851: A Local Study in 'Manifest Destiny'," *Louisiana Historical Quarterly*, vol. XXII, Oct. 1939, p. 1122; L. M. Peréz, "López Expeditions to Cuba, 1850–51, Betrayal of the *Cleopatra*, 1851," *Publications of the Southern History Association*, vol. X, 1906, pp. 345–62.
13. Portell Vilá, *Cuba*, vol. I, pp. 431–34; Portell Vilá, *López*, vol. II, p. 191.
14. John L. O'Sullivan to Quitman, June 26, 1850; John A. Quitman Papers, Mississippi State Archives; John O'Sullivan to Jefferson Davis, Sept. 5, 1865, Jefferson Davis Papers, Duke University Library. See also Sheldon Howard Harris, "The Public Career of John Louis O'Sullivan," unpublished Ph.D. thesis, Columbia University, 1958, pp. 342–60.
15. Urban, thesis, *op. cit.*, pp. 251–52; New Orleans *Daily Picayune*, May 26, 1850.
16. New Orleans *Weekly Delta*, May 30, 1850; New Orleans *Daily Picayune*, June 9, 1850; Richmond *Enquirer*, April 11, 1851.
17. John Claiborne to Thomas Claiborne, New Orleans, June 14, 1850, Thomas Claiborne Papers, University of North Carolina Library.
18. New Orleans *Weekly Delta*, May 15, 23, 1851; Richmond *Enquirer*, April 11, 1851.
19. Rauch, *op. cit.*, pp. 153–54.
20. Caldwell, *op. cit.*, pp. 90–92.
21. Translated copy in Dept. of State, 4 July, 1851, in collection entitled "López Expeditions to Cuba, 1849–1851," N.A.
22. Diego Gonzáles, *Historia Documentada de los Movimientos Revolucionarios por la Independencia de Cuba de 1852 a 1867*, Havana, 1939, vol. I, pp. 31–32.
23. Quoted in Aguirre, *op. cit.*, p. 30.
24. New Orleans *Crescent*, Aug. 21, 1851; New York *Sun*, Aug. 22, 1851; New Orleans *Weekly Delta*, Aug. 25, 26, 1851; Millard Fillmore to Daniel Webster, Sept. 2, 1851, Daniel Webster Papers, Library of Congress.
25. 30 Federal Cases, 18, 267. McLean, Circuit Justice.
26. "*A Ministro de Estado, Habana, 31 de Marzo, 1851*," *Boletín del Archivo Nacional*, vol. XVI, Sept. 1917, pp. 390–92; Everett to Crampton and

to Compte de Sartigas, Dec. 1, 1852, *Senate Document 13*, 32nd Cong., 2nd Sess., pp. 16–22; New Orleans *Weekly Delta*, Jan. 23, 1853; New Orleans *Daily Picayune*, Sept. 8, 1853; Washington *Daily Union*, Oct. 26, 1853.
27. Quoted in Amos A. Ettinger, *The Mission to Spain of Pierre Soulé; 1853–1855*, New Haven, 1937, p. 75.
28. Philip S. Foner, *The Life and Writings of Frederick Douglass*, New York, 1950, vol. II, p. 160.
29. *Invasión de Vuelta-Abajo*, Havana, 1851, p. 27. Copy in Archivo Nacional, Havana.

chapter 5 FILIBUSTERS AND CAPITALISTS

1. Portell Vilá, *Cuba*, vol. I, pp. 470–71; vol. II, p. 81; *New York Times*, Oct. 22, 1852; Ferencz and Theresa Pulsky, *White, Red, and Black*, London, 1853, vol. I, pp. 147–48.
2. Roberts to Webster, Oct. 6, 1852, Dept. of State. Consular Despatches, Havana, XXV, N.A.
3. New Orleans *Daily True Delta*, Oct. 8, 12, 1852.
4. New Orleans *Weekly Delta*, Oct. 17, 1852; Francis V. R. Maceo to Quitman, New Orleans, Oct. 14, 1852, Quitman Papers, Harvard University.
5. Washington *Daily National Intelligencer*, Oct. 20, 21, 25, Nov. 17, 25, 29, 1852.
6. *Ibid.*, Nov. 29, 1852; New York *Evening Post*, Dec. 2, 1852.
7. John Bach McMaster, *History of the People of the United States*, New York and London, 1913, vol. VIII, pp. 180–81.
8. Claiborne, *op. cit.*, vol. II, p. 388; Portell Vilá, *Cuba*, vol. II, pp. 82–83.
9. Claiborne, *op. cit.*, vol. II, p. 195.
10. New York *Herald*, Aug. 6, 1853; Ettinger, *op. cit.*, pp. 171–76; Rauch, *op. cit.*, pp. 262–64, 269; Marcy to Soulé, Washington, July 23, 1853, Dept. of State, Diplomatic Instructions: Spain. XV, N.A.
11. McClendon, *op. cit.*, p. 336; Claiborne, *op. cit.*, vol. II, pp. 56, 296–97; Alexander M. Clayton to J. F. H. Claiborne, July 27, 1879, Claiborne Papers, University of North Carolina Library.
12. A. M. Clayton to Quitman, Nov. 10, 1853; William S. Langley to Quitman, Quitman Papers, Harvard University Library.
13. "Outline of a plan of Organization," (1853), Quitman Papers, *ibid.*
14. Felix Huston to Quitman, March 4, 10, 1854, *ibid.*

chapter 6 THE "AFRICANIZATION OF CUBA" SCARE

1. Arthur F. Smith, "Spain and the Problem of Slavery in Cuba, 1817–1873," unpublished Ph.D. thesis, University of Chicago, 1958, pp. 117–23, 133–36, 178.
2. John H. Latané, "The Diplomacy of the United States in Regard to Cuba," *Annual Report of the American Historical Association for the Year, 1897*, Washington, 1898, pp. 245–46.
3. Marques de Rizaiejo, *Cheste o todo un siglo 1809–1906, el Isabelino tradicionalista*, Madrid, 1935, pp. 176–79; Guerra, *op. cit.*, p. 504.

Reference Notes • 365

4. *Gaceta de La Habana*, May 3, 1854, attached to Robertson to Marcy, May 3, 1854, Consular Despatches, Havana, XXIX, N.A.
5. Robertson to Marcy, Nov. 23, 1855, Jan. 5, 27, March 20, April 15, 26, 1854, Consular Despatches, Havana, XXVI and XXVII; Edward Worrell to Marcy, March 12, May 31, 1854, *ibid.*, Matanzas, N.A.
6. *Gaceta de La Habana*, May 3, 1854, *op. cit.*
7. Juan Martinez to "My Dear Sir," Habana, May, 1854, translation in Consular Despatches, Havana, XXVII, N.A.
8. Robertson to Marcy, April 26, 1854, *ibid.* My emphasis. P. S. F.
9. Marcy to Charles W. Davis, March 15, 1854, State Dept. Special Missions, III, N.A.
10. Davis to Marcy, May 22, 1854, Consular Despatches, Havana, XXIX, N.A.
11. *La Verdad*, Sept. 20, Nov. 10, 20, 1853.
12. Washington *Daily Union*, April 25, 1854; New Orleans *Daily Picayune*, May 6, 1854, Aug. 18, 1855; *Democratic Review*, vol. XXXI, Nov.–Dec. 1852, p. 440; *De Bow's Review*, vol. XVII, 1854, p. 222.
13. Urban, thesis, *op. cit.*, pp. 501–08; New Orleans *Courier*, July 29, Aug. 23, 1854.
14. *Cong. Globe*, 33 Cong., 1st Sess., pp. 1021–24.
15. Frankfurt (Ky.) *Commonwealth*, May, 10, 1854; Washington *Daily Intelligencer*, May 18, 1854; New York *Evening Post*, Aug. 17, 1853.
16. *Cong. Globe*, 33 Cong. 1st Sess., pp. 601, 1300; New Orleans *Daily Picayune*, May 19, 1854.
17. The Spanish Foreign Secretary to Lord Howden, Oct. 27, 1854, *British and Foreign State Papers*, vol. XLV, p. 118; Portell Vilá, *Cuba*, vol. II, pp. 76–77.
18. C. Stanley Urban, "The Africanization of Cuba Scare, 1853–1855," *Hispanic American Historical Review*, vol. XXXVII, Feb. 1957, p. 29; Robert Russell, *North America, its Agriculture and Climate*, Edinburgh, 1857, pp. 240–42.

chapter 7 THE QUITMAN EXPEDITION

1. Alexander Walker to A. G. Haley, June 15, 1854, in Jefferson Davis Papers, Library of Congress.
2. "Scraps for letter to President on Cuban Affairs, 1854," Quitman Papers, Mississippi Department of Archives and History.
3. Mike Walsh to Quitman, Sept. 6, 1854; Judge Lesesne to Thrasher, May 26, 1854, Quitman Papers, Harvard University Library; A. Nelson to Quitman, June 4, 1854; F. C. Jones to Quitman, June 10, 1854; Thomas P. Farrar to Quitman, July 6, 1854, Quitman Papers, Mississippi Department of Archives and History.
4. James D. Richardson, editor, *Messages and Papers of the Presidents, 1789–1897*, Washington, D.C., 1896–1899, Vol. V, p. 272.
5. Stephens to W. W. Burwell, May 7, 1854, "Correspondence of Toombs, Stephens, and Cobb," edited by Ulrich B. Phillips, *Annual Report of the American Historical Association*, 1911, Washington, 1913, vol. II, p. 344. Emphasis Stephens'.

6. New Orleans *Daily Delta,* June 20–25, July 2, 1854; Document dated New Orleans, July 3, 1854; Quitman Papers, Harvard University Library.
7. Crittenden, *op. cit.,* vol. II, pp. 195–209; Rauch, *op. cit.,* pp. 287–88.
8. *De Bow's Review,* vol. XVII, Nov. 1854, pp. 519–25; Rauch, *op. cit.,* p. 291.
9. Alexander H. Stephens to Quitman, Feb. 24, 1855; H. Forno to Quitman, Feb. 6, 1855, Quitman Papers, Harvard University Library.
10. *Journal of Southern History,* vol. V, Aug. 1939, p. 381.
11. Julio Beltrán, *Conspiración de Ramon Pintó, Havana,* 1924, pp. 88–94; Smith, *op. cit.,* p. 154.
12. Claiborne, *op. cit.,* vol. II, pp. 209, 391–92.
13. New Orleans *Daily Picayune,* Aug. 18, 1855.

chapter 8 "MANIFESTO OF THE BRIGANDS"

1. Alexander Walker to Haley, June 16, 1854, in Jefferson Davis Papers, Library of Congress.
2. Robert Benson Leard, "Bonds of Destiny: The United States and Cuba, 1848–1861," unpublished Ph.D. thesis, University of California, 1953, p. 176; Robert Leslie Stephens, "The Diplomacy of William L. Marcy, Secretary of State, 1853–1857," unpublished Ph.D. thesis, University of Virginia, 1949, p. 160; Marcy to Soulé, July 23, 1853, State Dept., Instructions to Ministers, Spain, XV, N.A.
3. Richardson, *op. cit.,* vol. V, pp. 234–35.
4. Marcy to Soulé, April 3, 1854, State Dept., Diplomatic Instructions: Spain, XV, N.A.
5. A. Dudley Mann to Marcy, Aug. 24, 31, 1854, William L. Marcy Papers, Library of Congress.
6. Horatio J. Perry to Marcy, Sept. 6, 1854, *ibid.*
7. Marcy to Buchanan; to Mason, to Soulé, all Aug. 16, 1854, State Dept.: Instructions, Gt. Britain, LXVI, France, XV, Spain, XV, N.A.; Mann to Marcy, Oct. 2, 1854, Marcy Papers, Library of Congress.
8. Buchanan, Mason, and Soulé to Marcy, Oct. 18, 1854, State Dept. Diplomatic Despatches: Gt. Britain, LXVI; Soulé to Marcy, Oct. 20, 1854, *ibid.,* Spain, XXXIX, N.A.
9. Sidney Webster, "Mr. Marcy, the Cuban Question and the Ostend Manifesto," *Political Science Quarterly,* vol. VIII, March, 1893, p. 23; Leard, *op. cit.,* pp. 197–98
10. Marcy to Soulé, Nov. 13, 1854, State Dept., Instructions: Spain, XV, N.A.
11. Leard, *op. cit.,* pp. 199–200.
12. George Bancroft to Marcy, Apr. 17, 1855; Marcy to L. B. Shepard, April 15, 1855, Marcy Papers, Library of Congress.
13. Lewis Cass to Marcy, April 9, 1855, *ibid.*
14. Marcy to A. C. Dodge, Apr. —, 1855, *ibid.*
15. *Cf.* John H. Latané, "The Diplomacy of the United States in Regard to Cuba," *Annual Report, American Historical Association, 1897,* Washington, 1898, p. 250.
16. Dodge to Marcy, Aug. 26, 1855, State Dept., Diplomatic Despatches: Spain, XL, N.A.

chapter 9 LAST OF THE FILIBUSTERS

1. Guerra, *op. cit.*, pp. 543, 549–51.
2. William O. Scroggs, "William Walker's Designs on Cuba," *Mississippi Valley Historical Review*, vol. I, Sept. 1914, p. 201.
3. *Ibid.*, p. 202.
4. Richardson, *op. cit.*, vol. V, pp. 371–73.
5. Nodina to Marcy, translation, May 22, 1856; J. Y. de Osma to Marcy, translation, Sep. 8, 1856; Irisarri to Marcy, translation, May 19, 1856, State Dept., Notes from Central America; Notes from Peru, II, N.A.
6. Scroggs, *op. cit.*, pp. 207–08; William O. Scroggs, *Filibusters and Financiers*, New York, 1916, p. 270.
7. New Orleans *True Delta*, New Orleans *Daily Picayune*, May 31, 1875.

chapter 10 END OF THE ANNEXATIONIST ERA

1. New Orleans *Daily Delta*, Nov. 11, 1856.
2. Dodge to Marcy, Aug. 26, 1855, Diplomatic Despatches: Spain, XL, N.A.
3. Buchanan to Fallon, 14 Dec. 1857, J. B. Moore, editor, *The Works of James Buchanan*, Philadelphia, 1910, vol. X, p. 165.
4. Belmont to Buchanan, Nov. 22, 30, 1852, Jan. 7, 14, 28, March 5, April 4, Nov. 18, 1853, Sept. 25, 1854, Buchanan Papers, Library of Congress.
5. Richardson, *op. cit.*, vol. V, p. 511.
6. *Senate Report 351*, 35 Cong., 2nd Sess., 1859.
7. R. B. Letcher to John J. Crittenden, Jan. 20, 26, 1859, Crittenden Papers, Library of Congress.
8. *Cong. Globe*, 35 Cong., 2nd Sess., pp. 94, 1127.
9. *Ibid.*, 36th Cong., 1st Sess., p. 2456; Richardson, *op. cit.*, vol. V, p. 561.
10. Reinhard H. Luthin, *The First Lincoln Campaign*, Cambridge, Mass., 1944, pp. 17, 221.
11. Richardson, *op. cit.*, vol. V, p. 642.
12. Howard L. Perkins, editor, *Northern Editorials on Secession*, New York and London, 1942, vol. I, pp. 157, 160, 181, 194, 390.
13. John G. Nicolay and John Hay, editors, *Complete Works of Abraham Lincoln*, New York, 1905, vol. VI, pp. 93–94.
14. Paul M. Angle, editor, *New Letters and Papers of Lincoln*, Boston, 1930, p. 105.
15. New Orleans *Daily Picayune*, Aug. 18, 1855.

chapter 11 CUBA DURING THE AMERICAN CIVIL WAR

1. Cepero, *op. cit.*, p. 71; *Constitución de la Sociedad Democrática de los Amigos de América*, New York, 1864.
2. Philip S. Foner, *Abraham Lincoln: Selections from His Writings*, New York, 1944, pp. 71–72.
3. *El Siglo*, Dec. 4, 1863; Cepero, *op. cit.*, p. 82; Guerra, *op. cit.*, p. 561.
4. J. Carlyle Sitterson, *Sugar Country: The Cane Sugar Industry in the South, 1753–1950*, Lexington, Ky., 1953, p. 226; Walter Prichard,

"The Effects of the Civil War on the Louisiana Sugar Industry," *Journal of Southern History*, vol. V, Aug. 1939, pp. 316–20.
5. *El Siglo*, Oct. 12, 1864; Cepero, *op. cit.*, p. 83.
6. *El Siglo*, Aug. 23, 1863; Jan. 28, 1864; Cepero, *op. cit.*, p. 82.
7. Emeterio S. Santovenia, "*Pasión Cubana por Lincoln*," *La Revista Biblioteca Nacional*, Havana, Jan.–March, 1953, p. 61.
8. Emeterio S. Santovenia, *Lincoln*, Buenos Aires, 1948, p. 465; Emeterio S. Santovenia, *Lincoln in Martí: A Cuban View of Abraham Lincoln*, Chapel Hill, N. Car., 1953, p. 4; Santovenia, "*Pasión Cubana . . . ,*" *op. cit.*, pp. 64, 66.
9. Smith, *op. cit.*, p. 92.
10. Philip S. Foner, *The Life and Writings of Frederick Douglass*, New York, 1952, vol. III, p. 399.
11. Carlos Rafael Rodríguez quoted in Cepero, *op. cit.*, p. 77.

chapter 12 BIRTH OF CUBAN WORKING CLASS CONSCIOUSNESS

1. Karl Marx, *Capital*, New York, 1939, vol. I, p. 287.
2. Quoted in Gaspar Jorge, *El Tabaquero Cubano*, La Habana, 1946, p. 23.
3. The decree was published in *Gaceta oficial*, July 30, 1851.
4. Fernando Ortiz Fernández, *Cuban Counterpoint: Tobacco and Sugar*, New York, 1947, p. 123.
5. José Antonio Portuondo, '*La Aurora*' *y los Comienzo de la Prensa y de la Organización en Cuba*, La Habana, 1961, pp. 16–17.
6. *Ibid.*, pp. 36–37, 111–12; Charles Albert Page, "The Development of Organized Labor in Cuba," unpublished Ph.D. thesis, University of California, 1952, p. 19.
7. Portuondo, *op. cit.*, pp. 39–42.
8. Quoted in *ibid.*, pp. 45–47.
9. *Ibid.*, pp. 42–43.

chapter 13 HIGH HOPES FOR REFORM

1. Smith, *op. cit.*, pp. 192–93.
2. *Cuba desde 1850 á 1873. Colección de informes, memorias, proyectos, antecedentes sobre el gobierno de la isla de Cuba, relativas al citado período que ha reunido por comision del Gobierno D. Carlos de Sedano y Cuzat, ex-diputado a Cortes*, Imprenta Nacional, 1873, pp. 272–73, 277. Hereafter cited as Sedano, *Colección*.
3. *Información: Reformas de Cuba y Puerto Rico*, New York, 1867, Tomo I, p. 33. Hereafter cited as *Información*.
4. Sedano, *Colección*, pp. 266–67; José L. Franco, *Antonio Maceo: Apuntes para una historia de su vida*, La Habana, 1951, vol. I, p. 29.
5. *Senado, 1865–66*, Tomo I. No. 52, pp. 617–20; Smith, *op. cit.*, p. 203.
6. *Información*, Tomo I., pp. 3–8.
7. *Ibid.*, Tomo I, pp. 47–48; Franco, *op. cit.*, p. 31.
8. *Ibid.*, pp. 13, 117; Sedano, *Colección*, p. 117.

9. *Información*, Tomo I, pp. 73–75.
10. *Ibid.*, Tomo II, p. 214.
11. *Ibid.*, pp. 207–49, 265, 286–87.
12. Sedano, *Colección*, pp. 150–51.
13. *Información*, Tomo II, pp. 34–38.

chapter 14 FAILURE OF REFORM AND OUTBREAK OF THE TEN YEARS' WAR

1. Franco, *op. cit.*, vol. I, pp. 32, 34.
2. Guerra, *op. cit.*, p. 581.
3. Franco, *op. cit.*, vol. I, pp. 27–28, 35–36; Lawrence Richard Nichols, "The Bronze Titan: the Mulatto Hero of Cuban Independence, Antonio Maceo," unpublished Ph.D. thesis, Duke University, 1954, pp. 13–22.
4. Eladio Aguilera Rojas, *Francisco V. Aguilera y la Revolución de Cuba de 1868*, La Habana, 1913, vol. I, p. 12.
5. Emilio Moreau Bacardí, *Crónicas de Santiago de Cuba*, Santiago de Cuba, 1908–24, vol. III, p. 38; Franco, *op. cit.*, vol. I, p. 35.
6. Rafael M. Labra, *La república y las libertades de Ultramar*, Madrid, 1897, pp. 22–23; Smith, *op. cit.*, p. 266.
7. Jesus Colon, "Puerto Rico's Women Have Played a Patriotic Role," *The Worker*, March 11, 1956; José Pérez Moris, *Historia de la insurrección de Lares*, Barcelona, 1872, pp. 212–13.
8. García Castellanos, *Panorama histórico*, La Habana, 1934, p. 22.
9. Ramiro Guerra y Sánchez, *La Guerra de Diez Años*, La Habana, vol. I, pp. 50–54. (Hereafter cited as Guerra, *La Guerra*.)
10. *El Boletín de la Revolución, Cuba y Puerto Rico*, Nueva York, No. 5, Dec. 31, 1868; Cepero, *op. cit.*, p. 112.
11. José Martí "My Race," April, 1893, in *The America of José Martí: Selected Writings*, translated by Juan de Onís, New York, 1953, p. 311.
12. José Antonio Portuondo, *Bosquejo histórico de las letras Cubanas*, La Habana, 1960, p. 32.

chapter 15 THE TEN YEARS' WAR: THE EARLY PHASE, 1868–1869

1. Quoted in Félix Lizaso, *José Martí: Martyr of Cuban Independence*, translated by Esther E. Shuler, Albuquerque, New Mexico, 1953, p. 20.
2. Eugenio Vandama y Calderón, Coronel, *Colección de artículos sobre el instituto de Voluntarios de la Isla de Cuba*, Madrid, 1896–97, pp. 30–37; Hall to Hamilton Fish, Matanzas, June 3, 1869; Phillips to Fish, Santiago de Cuba, June 25, 1869, N.A.; House of Representatives, *Exec. Doc. No. 160*, 41st Cong., 2nd Sess., pp. 77, 100
3. Guerra, *La Guerra*, vol. I, pp. 181–88.
4. *Ibid.*, pp. 204–05.
5. Lizaso, *op. cit.*, p. 29.

6. *Ibid.*, pp. 25–27.
7. José Gutiérrez de la Concha, *La guerra de Cuba y su estado político y económico de 1871–1874*, Madrid, 1875, p. 107; Willard Albion Smith, "The European Powers and the Spanish Revolution, 1868–1875," unpublished Ph.D thesis, Harvard University, pp. 9–10.

chapter 16 THE TEN YEARS' WAR: THE WAR UNFOLDS, 1869–1870

1. Franco, *op. cit.*, vol. I, pp. 51–52; Nichols, *op. cit.*, pp. 80–81; James J. O'Kelly, *The Mambi Land*, Philadelphia, 1874, pp. 91–102.
2. Enrique de la Osa, "*Una Interpretación Materialista de la Guerra de los Diez Anos*," *Bohemia*, Oct. 8, 1961, pp. 54–57; Cepero, *op. cit.*, pp. 107, 124.
3. Eugenio Alonso y Santurjo, *Apuntes sobre los proyectos de la abolición de las esclavitud en las islas de Cuba y Puerto Rico*, Madrid, 1874, pp. 44–50.
4. Translation of decree in Hall to Washburne, Consular Despatches, Havana, N.A.
5. *Constitution of the Republic of Cuba, April 10, 1869, at Guaimaro, Provisional Capital of Republic*, New York City, Nov. 17, 1869; Willis Fletcher Johnson, *The History of Cuba*, New York, 1920, vol. III, pp. 163–64.
6. Antonio Zambrana, *La Republica de Cuba*, Habana, 1922, pp. 50–52; Plumb to Davis, Aug. 31, 1869, Consular Reports, Havana, N.A.
7. Antonio Pirala, *Anales de la guerra de Cuba*, Madrid, 1898, vol. I, p. 642; Cepero, *op. cit.*, pp. 129–30.
8. New York *Tribune*, March 8, 1870; Allan Nevins, *Hamilton Fish: The Inner History of the Grant Administration*, New York, 1957, p. 338.
9. A. E. Phillips to Hamilton Fish, Jan. 3, 1870, published in New York *Tribune*, Feb. 23, 1870.
10. *Ibid.*; Nevins, *op. cit.*, p. 338.
11. Reprinted in New York *Tribune*, March 20, 1870.

chapter 17 THE UNITED STATES AND THE INDEPENDENCE OF CUBA, 1868–1869

1. "*A México*" in *Los Poetas de La Guerra, Colección de Versos a la independencia de Cuba, con un prologo de José Martí*, Habana, 1941, pp. 32–33.
2. *Facts About Cuba. Published Under the Authority of the New York Cuban Junta*, New York, 1870, p. 28; Johnson, *op. cit.*, vol. III, pp. 222–24.
3. Carlos Manuel de Céspedes, *De Bayamo a San Lorenzo, Selección y Prologo de Andrés de Piedra-Bueno*, La Habana, 1944, pp. 161–62.
4. Foner, *The Life and Writings of Frederick Douglass*, vol. IV, p. 303.
5. *Cong. Globe*, 41st Cong., 1st Sess., Appendix, pp. 18–21, 26–30.
6. Jerónimo Becker y González, *La historia política y diplomática de España desde la independencia de Los Estados Unidos hasta nuestros*

días, 1776–1895, Madrid, 1897, p. 502; Hall to Davis, May 18, 1869, Consular Reports, Havana, N.A.
7. Hamilton Fish Diary, March 24, 1897, Library of Congress.
8. Nevins, op. cit., pp. 180–81.
9. José A. Lemus to Fish, Aug. 1869, Hamilton Fish Papers, Library of Congress; Gabriel Rodríguez, La España del Siglo XIX, Madrid, 1883, vol. III, pp. 283–85.
10. Hamilton Fish Diary, April 6, Oct. 25, 26, 1869.
11. Reprinted in Facts About Cuba, op. cit., p. 29.
12. Guerra, La Guerra, vol. I, pp. 356–59; The Nation, Sept. 30, 1869.
13. James Harrison Wilson, The Life of John A. Rawlins, New York, 1916, pp. 359–61, 500–02.
14. Isaac A. Gates to Hamilton Fish, Cresco, Iowa, June 14, 1869, Fish Papers, Library of Congress.
15. House Ex. Doc. 160, pp. 13–16.
16. Paul S. Forbes to Fish, July 10, 16, 20, 1869; D. E. Sickles to Fish, Aug. 16, 1869, Fish Papers, Library of Congress; House Ex. Doc. 160, p. 21.
17. Bancroft Davis to Fish, Aug. 22, 1869, Fish Papers, Library of Congress.
18. Hamilton Fish Diary, July 10, 1870.
19. Fish to George Bancroft, Sept. 4, 1869, Fish Papers, Library of Congress.
20. Becker, op. cit., p. 35; New York Tribune, Sept. 7–8, 1869; Antonio Núñez Jiménez, op. cit., pp. 466–67.
21. Charleston Courier, July 19, 1869.

chapter 18 THE UNITED STATES AND THE INDEPENDENCE OF CUBA, 1869–1870

1. Hamilton Fish Diary, Dec. 13, 1869.
2. Richardson, op. cit., vol. VIII, pp. 31–32.
3. Smith, op. cit., p. 306.
4. La Revolución, Jan. 8, 1870; New York Tribune, Jan. 8, 1870.
5. A. E. Phillips to Fish, Santiago de Cuba, Jan. 3, 1870, Consular Despatches, Santiago de Cuba, N.A.; New York Tribune, Jan. 8, 1870.
6. Nevins, op. cit., p. 338n.
7. Hamilton Fish Diary, May 31, 1870.
8. Richardson, op. cit., vol. VIII, pp. 64–69; Cong. Globe, 41st Cong., 2nd Sess., Appendix, pp. 500, 4438; New York Tribune, June 15, 1870.
9. Hamilton Fish Diary, June 17, July 10, 1870.
10. Ibid., Dec. 23, 1869; Nevins, op. cit., p. 345.
11. Congreso 1869, Tomo XIII, pp. 8768–71; Smith, op. cit., pp. 308, 318–19.
12. Nevins, op. cit., p. 345.
13. Congreso 1869, Tomo XIV, No. 311, pp. 8992, 8994, 9029.
14. Smith, op. cit., pp. 331–33; Charles Sumner, Works, Boston, 1880, vol. XIII, p. 23; Carlos Manuel de Céspedes, De Bayamo a San Lorenzo, op. cit., pp. 112–48; Antonio Gallenga, The Pearl of the Antilles, London, 1873, p. 114.

372 · A History of Cuba

chapter 19 THE TEN YEARS' WAR: THE MIDDLE PHASE: 1871-1875

1. José Martí, *Obras Completas*, La Habana, 1946, vol. I, pp. 34-41.
2. *Ibid.*, pp. 42-49.
3. Guerra, *La Guerra*, vol. II, pp. 23-25.
4. D. E. Sickles to Bancroft Davis, March 7, 1871, Bancroft Davis Papers, Library of Congress.
5. Máximo Gómez, *Diario de Campaña*, La Habana, 1940, p. 487; Franco, *op. cit.*, vol. I, pp. 60-61.
6. Gómez, *op. cit.*, p. 26; Cepero, *op. cit.*, p. 179.
7. The original letter, Céspedes to Colonel Antonio Maceo, April 16, 1872 is in the Archivo Nacional, and reprinted in part in Franco, *op. cit.*, vol. I, p. 64.
8. Fernando Figueredo Socarrás, *La revolución de Yara*, La Habana, 1902, pp. 20-22.
9. *Ibid.*, pp. 120-22; Franco, *op. cit.*, vol. I, p. 67.
10. Gómez, *op. cit.*, pp. 47-48.
11. Fernando Figueredo, quoted in *Los Poetas de La Guerra*, *op. cit.*, p. 54.
12. *Ibid.*, pp. 54-56.
13. Manuel Sanguily y Arizti, *Páginas de la historia*, Habana, 1929, vol. I, p. 128; Franco, *op. cit.*, vol. I, pp. 81-82.
14. Franco, *op. cit.*, vol. I, p. 87; Cepero, *op. cit.*, pp. 159-60; Ignacio Mora, *Diario durante la guerra de los diez años*, Habana, 1910, pp. 198-99.
15. Emilio Roig de Leuchsenring, *Máximo Gómez, el Libertador de Cuba y el primer Ciudadano de la República*, La Habana, 1959, pp. 20-21.
16. Cepero, *op. cit.*, pp. 127-28; Don José Ferrer de Couto, *Cuba May Become Independent*, New York, 1872, pp. 47-50.
17. Henry C. Hall to J. C. B. Davis, April 25, 1874, Consular Despatches, Havana, N.A.

chapter 20 THE UNITED STATES AND THE INDEPENDENCE OF CUBA, 1871-1875

1. *New York Times*, Dec. 23, 1871.
2. Fish to Sickles, April 26, 1872; Hamilton Fish Diary, Oct. 24, 1872.
3. Fish to Sickles, Oct. 29, 1872, *Foreign Relations*, 1872, Washington, 1872, Part II, pp. 581-84.
4. Richardson, *op. cit.*, vol. VIII, pp. 189-90.
5. Printed in *Slavery in Cuba: A Report of the Proceedings of the Meeting Held at Cooper Institute, New York City, December, 13, 1872*, New York, 1872, pp. 3-18, 34. (Copy in Columbia University Library.)
6. Nevins, *op. cit.*, p. 360.
7. *Ibid.*, M. Quesada, *Address of Cuba to the United States*, New York, 1873, p. 4.
8. Fish to Sickles, Oct. 1873, Hamilton Fish Papers; Hamilton Fish Diary, Oct. 30, 1873.

Reference Notes • 373

9. Fish to Edward Pierrepont, Nov. 14, 1873, *ibid.*
10. Fish to William Cullen Bryant; Emilio Roig de Leuchsenring, *Martí, Antiimperialist*, La Habana, 1961, p. 18.
11. Hamilton Fish Diary, Dec. 7, 1873.
12. *Foreign Relations*, 1875, Washington, 1875, Part II, pp. 1251–55.
13. M. Quesada, *Address of Cuba to the United States, op. cit.*, p. 8.
14. *Foreign Relations*, 1874, Washington, 1874, p. 862.
15. "Circular to the Government of America in Relation to the Cuban Question, Bogota, September 26, 1872," N.A.; Herminio Portell Vilá, *"Un esfuerzo panamericano en favor de la independencia de Cuba, 1872–1873," Boletín de Historia y Antigüedes*, Bogota, vol. XXVI, 1939, pp. 221–24.
16. Fish to Julius White, Minister to the Argentine Republic, Jan. 30, 1873; Julius White to Fish, May 12, 1873, enclosing C. Tejedón to Julio White, Buenos-Aires, May 10, 1873; Fish to Francis Thomas, June 1873, all in N.A.
17. Nevins, *op. cit.*, pp. 636–37.
18. Carlos M. de Céspedes to President Ulysses S. Grant, District of Bayamo, March 22, 1873, original in Fish Papers.
19. Loreta J. Velázquez to Hamilton Fish, July 1, 1875, *ibid.*

chapter 21 THE TEN YEARS' WAR: THE FINAL PHASE: 1875–1878

1. Enrique Collazo, *Desde Yara hasta el Zanjón*, Habana, 1893, p. 213.
2. Pirala, *op. cit.*, vol. III, p. 218; *La Independencia*, March 4, 1875; Emilio Roig de Leuchsenring, *Gómez, op. cit.*, p. 20.
3. Collazo, *op. cit.*, p. 213; Franco, *op. cit.*, vol. I, pp. 90–91.
4. Cepero, *op. cit.*, pp. 133–35.
5. Hamilton Fish Diary, Oct. 29, Nov. 5, 1875; Fish to Cushing, Nov. 5, 1875; Fish to Bancroft Davis, Nov. 10, 1875; Fish Papers.
6. Fish to Cushing, Jan. 15, 1876; *ibid.*; "Report of Senate Committee on Foreign Relations Relative to Affairs in Cuba," *Report 885*, 55 Cong., 2nd Sess., pp. 44–52, 160–62.
7. Franco, *op. cit.*, vol. I, pp. 107, 117.
8. Maceo to the President of the Republic, Baraguá, May 16, 1876, Biblioteca de la Sociedad Económica de Amigos del País, *Documentos manuscritos de interes*, Habana, 1885, vol. I, p. 44.
9. Maceo to Vicente García, July 5, 1877, Archivo Nacional; Gómez, *op. cit.*, pp. 102–03; Franco, *op. cit.*, vol. I, p. 109.
10. T. Ochando, *Martínez Campos en Cuba*, Madrid, 1878, pp. 37–52.
11. Fish to Henry C. Hall, Aug. 7, 1877, Fish Papers.
12. *The Present Condition of Affairs in Cuba. A report of a Special Committee of the Cuban League of the United States. Submitted and adopted by the Executive Committee of the Cuban League, August 23, 1877*, New York, 1877, p. 11.
13. Figueredo, *op. cit.*, p. 182; Gómez, *op. cit.*, p. 123.
14. Franco, *op. cit.*, vol. I, pp. 123–25.

15. Gómez, *op. cit.*, p. 125; Johnson, *op. cit.*, vol. III, p. 299.
16. Franco, *op. cit.*, vol. I, pp. 140–41; Gómez, *op. cit.*, pp. 136–37.
17. Collazo, *op. cit.*, p. 137; Cepero, *op. cit.*, p. 181.
18. Figueredo, *op. cit.*, p. 180; Franco, *op. cit.*, vol. I, p. 138.
19. Figueredo, *op. cit.*, pp. 191–93; Franco, *op. cit.*, vol. I, pp. 144–45. My emphasis, P. S. F.
20. Franco, *op. cit.*, vol. I, pp. 146, 150, 154–58; Figueredo, *op. cit.*, pp. 196–200.
21. Juan Arnao, *Páginas para la Historia de la Isla de Cuba*, Habana, 1900, p. 247; Franco, *op. cit.*, vol. I, p. 163.
22. *La Verdad*, April 6, May 4, 1878; Franco, *op. cit.*, vol I, pp. 161–62; House of Commons, April 15, 1878, Hansard, third series, vol. CCXXIV, p. 426.
23. Franco, *op. cit.*, vol. I, pp. 159, 166–67.
24. Figueredo, *op. cit.*, pp. 209–10; Franco, *op. cit.*, vol. I, pp. 164–65; *Papeles de Maceo*, La Habana, 1948, vol. II, p. 338.
25. Franco, *op. cit.*, vol. I, pp. 166–67; Figueredo, *op. cit.*, p. 258.
26. Figueredo, *op. cit.*, p. 259; Franco, *op. cit.*, vol. I, p. 270.
27. Franco, *op. cit.*, vol. I, pp. 172–74; Figueredo, *op. cit.*, p. 263.
28. Henry C. Hall to F. W. Seward, May 11, 1878, State Dept. Consular Despatches, Havana, N.A.
29. Martí, *Obras Completas*, *op. cit.*, pp. 675–76; New York *Evening Post*, March 25, 1869.
30. Quoted in Emilio Roig de Leuchsenring, *Cuba no debe su independencia a los Estados Unidos*, La Habana, 1950, p. 13.

chapter 22 THE LITTLE WAR

1. Luis Estévez y Romero, *Desde el Zanjón hasta Baire*, Habana, 1899, p. 41; Johnson, *op. cit.*, vol. III, pp. 306–07.
2. Quoted in Franco, *op. cit.*, vol. I, pp. 180–81.
3. Rafael Maria Merchán, *Cuba: Justificación de sus guerras de Independencia*, Habana, 1962, pp. 155–59.
4. Enrique Trujillo, *Apuntes históricos*, New York, 1896, p. 5.
5. Jorge Mañach, *Martí: Apostle of Freedom*, translated by Coley Taylor, New York, 1950, pp. 141–55; Lizaso, *op. cit.*, pp. 135–38.
6. Franco, *op. cit.*, vol. I, p. 208; Cepero, *op. cit.*, pp. 192–93.
7. Aguas Verdes, *Antonio Maceo: ideología política*, Habana, 1922, pp. 130–31.
8. Herminio C. Levya, *El movimiento insurreccional de 1879*, Habana, 1893, pp. 22–39; Proclamation, Kingston, Sept. 5, 1879, in *La Independencia*, Oct. 18, 1879.
9. Hall to Seward, Sept. 25, Nov. 14, 1879, State Dept., Consular Despatches, Havana, N.A.
10. Calixto García Iñiguez, *Mi diario*, Habana, 1928, p. 210.
11. Martí, *Obras Completas*, vol. I, pp. 672–97.
12. *Ibid.*, pp. 70–72; Franco, *op. cit.*, vol. I, pp. 229–36.

Reference Notes • 375

chapter 23 POLITICAL, ECONOMIC AND SOCIAL DEVELOPMENT OF CUBA, 1878–1895

1. *Boletín del Archivo Nacional*, vol. XXVI, pp. 79–82.
2. Quoted in Mañach, *op. cit.*, p. 261.
3. Estévez, *op. cit.*, p. 112.
4. Smith, *op. cit.*, p. 383; Hubert H. S. Aimes, "The Transition from Slave to Free Labor in Cuba," *Yale Review*, vol. XV, May, 1906, pp. 79–80.
5. Smith, *op. cit.*, p. 384; Aimes, *op. cit.*, p. 81.
6. Cepero, *op. cit.*, pp. 192–95.
7. Leland Hamilton Jenks, *Our Cuban Colony*, New York, 1928, pp. 28–30; Edward F. Atkins, *Sixty Years in Cuba*, Cambridge, 1926, p. 80.
8. Ramiro Guerra y Sánchez, *La industria azucarera de Cuba*, Habana, 1940, pp. 98–99.
9. Jenks, *op. cit.*, p. 33.
10. *El Siglo*, IV, No. 165, July 14, 1865.
11. A Núñez Jiménez, *op. cit.*, p. 469.
12. Richard D. Weigle, "The Sugar Interests and American Diplomacy in Hawaii and Cuba, 1893–1903," unpublished Ph.D thesis, Yale University, 1939, pp. 189–91; *La Lucha*, Dec. 20, 1894; *La Discusion*, Dec. 21, 1894.
13. Page, *op. cit.*, pp. 22–23; Felipe Zapata, *"Esquema y notas para una historia de la organización Obrera en Cuba,"* Unidad Gastronómica, Habana, 1948, p. 29.
14. Page, *op. cit.*, p. 31n; "The Labor Movement in the Republic," *Ultima Hora*, May 22, 1952.

chapter 24 REVOLUTIONARY ACTIVITY 1884–1890

1. Maceo to Máximo Gómez, May 1, 1884; Maceo to Anselmo Valdés, July 6, 1884, originals in Archivo Nacional; reprinted in Franco, *op. cit.*, vol. I, p. 293.
2. Gómez, *op. cit.*, p. 183.
3. *Ibid.*
4. Franco, *op. cit.*, vol. I, pp. 303–04.
5. Martí to Gómez, Oct. 20, 1884, original in Archivo Nacional; reprinted in Franco, *op. cit.*, vol. I, pp. 302–03.
6. Gómez, *op. cit.*, p. 183.
7. Mañach, *op. cit.*, pp. 231–32.
8. Eusebio Hernández, *Dos Conferencias*, Habana, no date, pp. 96–97; Franco, *op. cit.*, vol. I, pp. 321–22.
9. The original manuscript is in the Archivo Nacional; excerpts are in Franco, *op. cit.*, vol. I, pp. 324–25.
10. Gómez, *op. cit.*, pp. 220–22; Franco, *op. cit.*, vol. I, pp. 347–50.
11. Gómez, *op. cit.*, p. 223; Franco, *op. cit.*, vol. I, p. 361.
12. Franco, *op. cit.*, vol. I, pp. 359–60.
13. Gómez, *op. cit.*, pp. 230–31; Franco, *op. cit.*, vol. I, p. 361.
14. Franco, *op. cit.*, vol. I, pp. 366–68.

15. Juan Gualberto Gómez, *Los Preliminares de la revolución de 1895*, Habana, 1913, pp. 11–12; Camilio Polavieja, *Relación documentada de mi política en Cuba*, Madrid, 1898, p. 109.
16. Emilio Bacardí Moreau, *op. cit.*, vol. II, p. 82.
17. Manuel J. Granda, *La paz del manganeso*, Habana, 1939, pp. 53–60; Polavieja, *op. cit.*, p. 114; Franco, *op. cit.*, vol. I, p. 408.
18. Granda, *op. cit.*, p. 64.
19. Polavieja, *op. cit.*, p. 114; Franco, *op. cit.*, vol. I, p. 408.
20. Portell Vilá, *Cuba*, vol. II, p. 232.

chapter 25 THE CUBAN REVOLUTIONARY PARTY

1. Martí to Maceo, July 20, 1882, original in Archivo Nacional; reprinted in Franco, *op. cit.*, vol. I, pp. 256–57.
2. Martí, *Obras Completas*, vol. I, pp. 311, 493, 810, 859.
3. *Ibid.*, pp. 697–706.
4. Lizaso, *op. cit.*, p. 215; Mañach, *op. cit.*, pp. 275–76.
5. Martí, *Obras Completas*, vol. I, pp. 707–18.
6. *Ibid.*, pp. 299–30; *Patria*, New York, March 14, 1892, p. 1.
7. Martí, *Obras Completas*, vol. I, pp. 1516–18.
8. *Ultima Hora*, May 22, 1952; Carlos Rafael Rodríguez, *José Martí and Cuban Liberation*, New York, 1953, pp. 20–21.
9. Gómez, *op. cit.*, pp. 268–73.
10. José L. Franco, *Antonio Maceo: Apuntes para una historia de su vida*, La Habana, 1954, vol. II, pp. 23–24.
11. *Orden y mando del Partido Revolucionario Cubano a los sub-delegados en la Isla*, Santiago de Cuba, Nov. 17, 1893. Copy in Archivo Nacional.
12. Juan Arnao, *op. cit.*, p. 281.
13. Reprinted in Martí, *Obras Completas*, vol. I, p. 572.
14. Martí, *Versos Sencillos*, New York, 1891, p. 16.
15. Rodríguez, *op. cit.*, pp. 17–19.
16. *Ibid.* Emphasis mine. P. S. F.
17. Manuel Deleufeu, *Martí, Cayo Hueso y Tampa*, Cienfuegos, 1905, p. 27; Horatio S. Rubens, *Liberty, the Story of Cuba*, New York, 1922, p. 40.

chapter 26 THE MENACE OF AMERICAN IMPERIALISM

1. Letter to Manuel Mercado, May 18, 1895, *Obras Completas*, vol. I, pp. 271–73.
2. Sturgis E. Leavitt in preface to Manuel Pedro González, *José Martí: Epic Chronicler of the United States in the Eighties*, Chapel Hill, N. Car., 1953, p. viii.
3. Martí, *Obras Completas*, vol. I, p. 1292.
4. Philip S. Foner, *History of the Labor Movement in the United States*, New York, 1955, vol. II, pp. 13–24.
5. Martí, *Obras Completas*, vol. I, p. 1484.
6. Martí, *Obras Completas*, Habana, 1941, vol. XXXIX, pp. 188–89.
7. Martí, *Obras Completas*, vol. I, pp. 1486–87; vol. XXXVII, p. 70.
8. Martí, *Obras Completas*, vol. I, p. 1683.

Reference Notes • 377

9. Martí, *Obras Completas*, vol. XXXVI, p. 12; New York *Evening Post*, March 25, 1889.
10. Martí, *Obras Completas*, vol. XXXVII, p. 56.
11. *Cong. Record*, 50th Cong., 1st Sess., p. 7653.
12. David S. Muzzey, *James G. Blaine: A Political Idol of Other Days*, New York; 1934, p. 207; New York *Tribune*, Oct. 1, 1889; *New York Times*, Oct. 8, 1889; New York *Herald*, Oct. 8, 1889.
13. *House Report*, 4th Cong., 1st Sess., No. 1790, p. XII; Martí, *Obras Completas*, vol. XXXI, pp. 36–37 and vol. I, pp. 306, 1417, 1875.
14. Martí, *Obras Completas*, vol. I, pp. 390–92; Leuchsenring, *Martí Antiimperialista*, op. cit., p. 16.
15. Martí, *Obras Completas*, vol. II, pp. 129–30.
16. *Review of Reviews*, vol. III, April, 1891, p. 215; *Age of Steel*, vol. LXXXI, Feb. 20, 1892.
17. E. Sherman Gould, "Commercial Relations Between the United States and Cuba," *Engineering Magazine*, vol. VII, July 1894, pp. 500, 504; Martí, *Obras Completas*, vol. II, pp. 474, 476.
18. Martí, *Obras Completas*, 1946, vol. II, pp. 470–71.
19. Josiah Strong, *Our Country: Its Possible Future and Its Present Crisis*, New York, 1885, p. 167; *Munsey's Magazine*, vol. VI, Nov. 1891, p. 245.
20. *Our Day*, vol. VI, Sept. 1890, pp. 234–37; *Iron Age*, vol, XLVI, Sept. 4, 1890, p. 386.
21. *Iron Age*, vol. LIV, Aug. 1894, pp. 264–65; Claude G. Bowers, *Beveridge and the Progressive Era*, New York, 1932, p. 69; *Century Magazine*, vol. XXXI, Nov. 1885, p. 152; Gould, op. cit., p. 505.
22. Eduardo J. Chibás, "Business Opportunities in Cuba," *Engineering Magazine*, vol. IV, Nov. 1892, pp. 266–68.
23. Alfred T. Mahan, "The United States Looking Outward," *Atlantic Monthly*, vol. LXVI, Dec. 1890, pp. 800–02.
24. Atlanta *Constitution*, Nov. 30, 1888.
25. *Forum Magazine*, vol. XI, July, 1891, pp. 561–67.
26. *Munsey's Magazine*, vol. VI, Nov. 1891, pp. 244–45.
27. *The American Magazine of Civics*, vol. VII, 1895, pp. 561, 586.
28. Leuchsenring, *Martí, Antiimperialista*, op. cit., pp. 9, 13, 35–39.
29. Letter to Manuel Mercado, May 18, 1895, Martí, *Obras Completas*, vol. I, p. 271.

chapter 27 THE SECOND WAR OF INDEPENDENCE BEGINS

1. Rubens, op. cit., p. 70; Mañach, op. cit., p. 322.
2. Gómez, op. cit., p. 278.
3. Cabrera, *Epistolario*, pp. 128–29.
4. *Ibid.*, pp. 57–58; Franco, op. cit., vol. II, pp. 51–53.
5. Rubens, op. cit., p. 74.
6. Gómez to Maceo, Feb. 27, 1895; Maceo to Martí, Feb. 1895, Archivo Nacional.
7. Mañach, op. cit., p. 344.

8. Academia de la Historia de Cuba, *Facsimil del Original del Manifiesto de Montecristi, Firmado por Máximo Gómez y José Martí, el 25 de Marzo de 1895*, La Habana, 1961.
9. Cabrera, *Epistolario*, pp. 67–69, 73–74; Franco, *op. cit.*, vol. II, pp. 199–200.
10. Franco, *op. cit.*, vol. II, pp. 106–11; Manuel J. Granda, *Memorias Revolucionarias*, Habana, 1936, pp. 88–92.
11. Maceo to the Forces of Oriente, April 20, 1895; to the Army of Oriente, April 21, 1895, Archivo Nacional.
12. Franco, *op. cit.*, vol. II, p. 125; Cabrera, *Epistolario*, pp. 75–76.
13. Martí, *Obras Completas*, vol. I, pp. 247–49.
14. *The America of José Martí*, *op. cit.*, pp. 317–18.
15. Lizaso, *op. cit.*, pp. 247–48; Mañach, *op. cit.*, p. 350.
16. Martí, *Obras Completas*, vol. I, pp. 271, 285–93.
17. New York *Sun*, May 23, 1895; Emilio Roig de Leuchsenring, *Máximo Gómez*, *op. cit.*, pp. 38–39.
18. Franco, *op. cit.*, vol. II, p. 253n.
19. Carlos Rafael Rodríguez, *José Martí and Cuban Liberation*, p. 8; Juan Marinello, "José Martí and the U.S.A.," *Masses & Mainstream*, vol. VI, Oct. 1953, p. 41; Juan Marinello, *"El Pensamiento de Martí y nuestra Revolución Socialista,"* *Cuba Socialista*, Jan. 1962, pp. 16–37.
20. Letter to Manuel Mercado, May 18, 1895, Martí, *Obras Completas*, vol. I, pp. 271–73.

INDEX

Abolition of slavery, 127–28, 156–59, 276–77, 292–93, 311
Abolitionists, 10, 14–15, 32, 123–24, 130
Acosta, José Julián, 156, 158
African slave trade, 15, 75, 77–78, 106–07, 127, 134–35, 149, 150–51, 152–53
"Africanization of Cuba" scare, 74–85, 86, 87–88, 90–91, 100, 102, 105
Agramonte y Loynaz, Ignacio, 175, 185, 186, 190, 195, 230
Agüero, Joaquín de, 57–58, 59, 71
Aguilera, Francisco Vicente, 167, 170, 171, 232, 277n., 283
Aguilera, Manuel, 305–06
Alabama claims, 204–05
Aldama, Miguel, 10, 12, 107, 126, 152, 156, 167n., 177, 178, 180
Armenteros, Isidoro, 57, 58
Anarcho-syndicalists, 301–02
Annexation, arguments against, 36–40; arguments in favor, 30–36; reasons for defeat, 23–24; relation to slavery expansion, 34–36, 38–39
Annexationists, in Cuba, 9–19, 21–27, 40–41, 79–80, 82, 105–06, 193, 202, 299, 332, 345–46; in United States, 9, 11, 19–20, 36–40, 64, 84, 103–05, 123–24, 337–38
Asociación contra la trata, 134
Atkins, E. A., 295, 297
Autonomist party, 276, 291, 315, 316, 317
Azcárate, Don Nicolás de, 143, 278, 281
Bancroft, George, 103, 210
Beach, Moses Yale, 11, 21, 22, 23
Belmont, August, 117
Bélvis, Segundo Ruíz, 156, 158
Benítez, Gregorio, 284, 285–86
Benjamin, Judah P., 68–69, 83, 119
Betances, Dr. Ramón Emeterio, 169
Beveridge, Albert, 343
Black Warrior affair, 97–98, 102, 103
Blaine, James G., 337–40, 343
Blanco, Ramón, 283n., 287
Borrero, Brigadier Francisco, 354, 355
Boycott, of Cuban sugar, 241, 243
Breckenridge, John, 119
Buchanan, James, 22, 23, 24, 25, 26–29, 31, 101, 115, 116–21
Burriel, Juan, 244, 246
Cabrales, María, 188

Calderón de la Barca, Angel, 25, 26, 144–45, 150
Calhoun, John C., 20, 31, 43
Calvar, Manuel de Jesús, 170, 171, 231, 269, 270
Campbell, Judge John A., 90
Campbell, General Robert B., 24, 25, 29
Cañedo, Valentín, 68, 70
Canovas, Antonio del Castillo, 149, 151, 153
Carrillo, Francisco, 280, 282, 286, 312, 327
Casino Español, 181
Cass, Lewis, 15, 23, 31, 51, 104
Castañón, Gonzalo, 177
Castro, Alejandro de, 154, 160, 162
Castro, Rafael de, 24
Cavada, General Emilio, 175
Cavada, Federico, 175
Céspedes, Carlos Manuel de, 167–68, 169, 170, 171, 174, 179, 189, 190, 191, 194–95, 199–200, 228, 229–30, 232–33, 244n., 251, 255
Céspedes, Francisco Javier de, 171, 267
Céspedes, Pedro de, 244n.
Céspedes, Ricardo, 258
Cisneros, Gaspar Betancourt, 10, 11, 14, 15, 16, 18, 43, 44, 47, 82, 108
Cisneros, Salvador Betancourt, 167, 232–33, 254
Civil War, U.S., 131–35, 229
Claiborne, John F. H., 55, 70–71, 194
Clay, Henry, 62–63
Clayton, Alexander M., 45, 50, 72
Cleopatra fiasco, 55
Club de la Habana. See Havana Club.
Collazo, General Enrique, 253, 254, 255, 265–66, 349
Colombian plan for independence of Cuba, 247–51
Colón, Jesús, 169
Colonial Reform Commission, 169, 171
Colono system, 294–95
Colunje, Don Gil, 248–49
Comité del Centro, 264, 265, 266
Comité Revolucionario Cubano, 279
Compromise of 1850, 33, 39, 46, 48, 63, 67
Concha, General José de la, 11, 58, 59, 60, 62, 92, 105, 106–07, 183
Confederate states, 122

379

380 · Index

Consejo del Gobierno Cubano, El, 47
Conspiracy, of the Cuban Rose Mines, 13, 24–25, 42; of Francis Estrampes, 93n.; of Ramón Pintó, 92, 106; of Trinidad, 57–58; of Vuelta Abajo, 66
Constitution of Free Cuba, 193–94, 232
Constitutional Convention at Guáimaro, 193–94
Constitutional Union party, 276–77
Co-operatives, 143
Creoles, 13–14, 108, 127, 128, 133, 135, 152, 162, 163, 210, 314
Crescent City incident, 68–70
Creswell, John A., 204
Crimean War, 86, 92, 101
Crittenden, John J., 58
Crittenden, William L. S., 58, 59, 60, 61, 71
Crombet, Flor, 281, 315, 348, 352
Cuba, abolition of slavery, 292–93, 311; annexationists, 9–19, 21–27, 40–41, 79–80, 82, 105–06, 193, 202, 299, 332, 345–46; anti-annexationists, 9–10, 14, 15–18, 62–63; as area for U.S. expansion, 343–46; economic dependence on U.S., 296–300, 341–42; class structure, 277; coffee industry, 128–29; conditions, 289–90; conspiracies, 13, 24–25, 41, 42, 57–58, 66, 92; constitution, 193–94; debate over, 30–40; Declaration of Independence, 171–72; during U.S. Civil War, 130–35; economic crisis, 163, 299–300; economic developments, 293–98; education, 11, 125, 143; fear of Negro, 284, 293, 315–16, 351; idea of independence, 107–08; immigration, 77; independence and U.S., 199–223, 240–52, 257–58, 262, 274; labor movement, 136–48, 300–04; mining, 297; movement for independence (1868), 163–73; must be free from U.S., 345–46, 359; plans for emancipation of slaves, 148–49, 276–77; plans for rebellion (1890), 314–17; plans of U.S. to purchase, 20–29, 116–21; political parties, 276–77; political status under Spain, 289–92; railroads, 12; Reformist Party, 125–26; restrictions imposed by Spain, 12. *See also* Ten Years' War.
Cuban Anti-Slavery Committee, 270
Cuban bonds, 217–18, 257
Cuban Council of New York, 11, 44, 47

Cuban *Junta,* 178, 184, 205n., 207, 208, 211, 214–15, 224, 245
Cuban League of the United States, 262
Cuban National Workers' Congress, 303
Cuban Revolutionary Party, 318–31, 347–53
Cushing, Caleb, 247, 257
Dana, Charles A., 357
Davis, Bancroft, 227
Davis, Charles W., 81–82
Davis, Jefferson, 22, 43, 55
Declaration of Independence, Cuban, 171–72
De Leon, Daniel, 304
Díaz, Modesto, 175, 267
Dodge, August Caesar, 104, 116
Domínguez, Fermín Valdés, 254
Douglas, Stephen A., 23, 31, 67–68
Douglass, Frederick, 30, 64, 200
Dulce, Domingo, 125–26, 149, 152, 162, 169, 178, 179, 180, 181
Echeverría, José Antonio, 10, 126, 134, 135, 152, 157, 158
Election, in Cuba, of 1866, 152; in U.S., of 1852, 70; of 1854, 93, 101; of 1860, 120–21
Emancipados, 77, 105
Emancipation, in West Indies, 31; plans for in Cuba, 134–35, 148–49, 156–59
Emancipation Proclamation, 130, 131, 132–33, 229
Estévez Romero, Luis, 290, 292
Estrada Palma, 255, 257, 261, 263
Estrampes, Francisco, 93n.
Expansion of slavery, 34–36, 55
"Facultades Omnímodas," 163
Fallon, Christopher, 116–17
Fernandina plan, 348–49
Figueredo, Dr. Félix, 189, 266, 268, 272
Figueredo, Fernando, 231, 233
Figueredo, Pedro, 164, 166
Filibuster expeditions, Round Island (1849), 42–47; Cárdenas (1850), 47–54; Bahía Honda (1851), 54–65; Quitman (1853–55), 70–74, 86–95, 96; Walker (1853, 1855–60), 108–14
Fillmore, Millard, 56, 57n., 61, 62, 63, 69–70
Fish, Hamilton, 201–02, 204–07, 208–19, 221–23, 240–41, 243, 245, 246, 247, 248, 249, 250–51, 257, 258, 262
Forbes, Paul S., 206, 207

Franco, José L., 152
"Freedom Anthem," 163–64
Free Soil party, 52
Free Soilers, 123–24
García, General Calixto, 186, 230–31, 233, 279, 280, 281, 282, 283, 284, 285, 286
García, Vicente, 234, 255, 260, 261, 263, 264, 267, 270
Goicuría, Domingo, 82, 92, 94–95, 108–13, 216–17
Gómez, Juan Gualberto, 277, 280, 283, 313, 327–28, 349–50
Gómez, Máximo, 175, 186, 227–28, 229–30, 231, 233, 234, 235, 236–37, 238, 252, 253–54, 256, 260–61, 262, 263–64, 273, 275, 305, 306, 307, 308, 310, 311, 312, 313, 315, 317, 325–26, 347–48, 349, 350, 351, 354, 355, 356, 357
González, Ambrosio J., 42, 43, 46, 47, 48, 49, 50, 53, 66, 67, 82
Grajales, Mariana, 165, 166, 188, 326
Grant, Ulysses S., 166, 199, 202–04, 208–11, 212–16, 217–19, 220–23, 240, 241, 243, 244, 246, 248, 257, 258
Great Britain, 10, 14, 31–32, 46, 62, 75–85, 105, 111, 270
Greeley, Horace, 36, 216
Grito de Baire, 350
Grito de Lares, 167
Grito de Yara, 171, 172, 314
Guerra y Sánchez, Ramiro, 13, 107, 131, 294–95
Guerrilla warfare, 185–89, 194–95, 203, 275
Hall, Henry C., 238–39, 273, 283
Haiti, 82, 114, 183, 188, 238, 315
Havana Club, 10, 11, 21, 22, 23, 24, 42, 46, 47, 92
Havemeyer, Henry O., 294, 296–97
Henderson, John, 47–48, 49, 51, 53
Henríquez y Carvajal, Dr. Federico, 354
Hernández, Dr. Eusebio, 308–09
Hernández, José Elías, 92, 114
"Hymn of Las Villas, The," 234–35
Imperialism, emergence in U.S., 124, 337–46
Independence, movement in 1868, 163–73; in 1895, 360–61; relation of Negroes to, 164–65
International American Conference, 337–40
International American Monetary Commission, 340*n*.

Irisarri, Minister, 110–11
Iznaga, José Aniceto, 11, 47
Jamaica, 16, 83, 188
Jordan, General Thomas, 184, 185, 195, 242*n*., 345
Jorrín, José Silverio, 134, 294
Junta Cubana, 44*n*., 70, 71, 72, 73, 82, 92, 93*n*., 94, 95, 96
Junta de Información de Ultramar, 151–61
Junta Pública Promovedora de los Intereses Políticos de Cuba, 47
Junta Revolucionaria de la isla de Cuba, 166, 171
Juárez, Benito, 198
Kansas-Nebraska act, 89–90, 93, 94, 101
Key West, 147, 256, 305, 306, 308–09, 322, 325, 328, 330, 349
La Aurora, 140–48
Labor movement, in Cuba, 136–48, 300–04
Labra, Rafael de, 292, 293
Lares, rebellion of, 169–70
Las Villas, invasion of, 234–35, 253–54, 260–61
Latin America, 198–99, 247–51, 351*n*.
La Verdad, 11, 14, 22, 44, 47, 269
Law, George, 67–68, 69, 70, 87–88, 109
Lee, Robert E., 43
Lersundi, Francisco, 146–47, 162, 169, 170, 176, 177
Letcher, Robert B., 119
Liberal-Autonomist party, 291, 293
Liberal party, 276–77, 280, 281, 288
La Liga, 318–20, 321, 322
Liga de Instrucción, 321
Lincoln, Abraham, 121, 122, 123, 130, 131, 133, 134, 337
Little War, The, 278–81
López, General Narciso, 10, 13, 24–26, 41–65, 67, 70, 71
Louisiana, 131–32, 183
McKinley tariff, 296, 298, 299, 340–41
McLean, Justice John, 61–62
McLean, Robert, 42
Maceo y Grajales, Antonio, 165–66, 178, 187–89, 230, 231, 233, 234, 235–36, 237, 255, 256–60, 261, 262–63, 266, 267–70, 271, 272, 273, 274, 275, 280, 306, 307, 308, 309, 310, 311, 312–17, 326–27, 347–48, 349, 350, 351, 352, 353, 354, 356, 357
Maceo, José, 262, 281, 282, 286, 353
Macías, Juan Manuel, 47, 208

Madan y Madan, Cristóbal, 10, 11, 18, 44, 47
"Manifest Destiny," 21, 30, 31, 37, 63, 124, 205
Manifesto of Montecristi, 351-52
"Manifesto to the American People," 67
Mann, A. Dudley, 99-100
Marcy, William L., 71, 81, 96-97, 99-100, 101-04
Mármol, General Donato Tamayo, 175, 178, 273
Martí, José, 41, 65, 125n., 134, 141n., 173, 179, 196n., 225-27, 245, 274, 280-81, 282, 283, 284-85, 287, 304, 307, 308, 311-12, 318-41, 345-46, 347-48, 349, 350, 351, 352, 353, 354, 356, 357, 358, 359
Martínez Campos y Antón, Arsenio, 261, 262-63, 264, 265, 266, 267, 268, 271, 272, 273, 275, 276, 278, 292
Martínez, Saturnino, 140-48, 300-03
Marx, Karl, 136, 301, 324, 333
Masó, Bartolomé, 167, 170-71, 327
Mason, John Y., 23, 101
Masonic lodges, 166, 167
Mendive, Rafael María de, 125n.
Mestre, José Manuel, 126, 152, 177
Mexican War, 20, 22, 31-32, 33, 43, 47, 48, 342
Mexico, 13, 20, 24, 25, 64, 164, 167, 198, 205, 257, 277n., 307
Moncada, Guillermo, 281, 282, 286, 315, 327
Monroe Doctrine, 110-11, 115, 257
Morales Lemus, José, 126, 134, 152, 155, 163, 166, 177, 178, 201, 202, 205n., 206, 208, 209, 214, 238
Moret Law, 220-23, 241, 277, 292
Mutual Aid societies, 138-39, 142-43
Narváez, General, 27
National Congress of Cuban Historians, 9, 211n., 298
Negroes, conditions in Cuba, 277n.; fear of in Cuba, 165, 237-38, 258-60, 281, 284, 315-16, 351; importance in revolutionary movement, 318-20, 321; in U.S., support Cuban independence, 241-43; relation to Cuban independence, 164; role in Cuban Revolutionary Party, 318-21; role in Little War, 279, 281, 282, 287; role in Ten Years' War, 242n., 285; role in U.S. Civil War, 131

Neutrality act, U.S., 44, 49-50, 56, 87, 88, 90
Nevins, Allan, 201, 216, 243
New Orleans, 53-54, 61
Nicaragua, 109-14
Núñez, Emilio, 280, 281, 282, 286, 287
O'Donnell, Leopoldo, 42, 150, 153
"Order of the Lone Star," 13, 67, 69, 70, 71, 73
Ortíz, Fernando, 138
Osorio, Francis Maceo, 170, 233
Ostend Manifesto, 99-104, 106
O'Sullivan, John L., 21, 22, 23, 24, 43, 45, 51-52, 53, 54-55, 114, 116
Pact of Zanjón, 265-66, 267, 268, 269, 271, 276, 277, 278, 279, 289, 291, 310
Palmerston, Lord, 75-76
Pan-American Union, 340
Panic, of 1857, 138; of 1873, 246; of 1893, 298, 330, 343-44, 346
Paris Commune, 300
Partido Incondicional Español, 126
Partido Reformista, 125, 163
Pastor, Luis, 156
Paz del Manganeso, La, 314-17
Peninsulares, 13-14, 107, 134, 154, 163, 165
Peru, 110, 198, 211, 250, 338
Pezuela, Marquis Juan de la, 76-85, 87, 92, 102, 105
Phillips, Wendell, 216, 328n., 333
Pidal, Pedro J., 26, 27-28
Pierce, Franklin K., 68, 70, 71, 73, 76, 80, 86, 87, 88-89, 93-94, 96-105, 108, 110, 111
Pintó, Ramón, 92-93
Polavieja, Camilio, 314, 315, 316, 317
Política de atracción, 125-26
Polk, James K., 20, 21, 22, 23, 27, 29, 45
Polo, Don José Bernabé de, 240, 243, 246
Portell Vilá, Herminio, 10, 12-13, 41, 45, 46, 51, 52, 54, 85, 317
Pozos Dulces, Count of, 13, 66, 108, 126, 131, 132, 134, 152, 163, 295
Preston, William, 117, 120
Prim, Marshal, 177, 184, 196, 206, 207, 208, 218, 224
Protest of Baraguá, 267-70, 273
Puerto Rico, 151-52, 156-58, 169-70, 227, 243, 264-65, 278
Quesada, Manuel de, 175, 195, 243-44, 247
Quesada y Miranda, Gonzalo de, 358

Index • 383

Quitman, John A., 48, 49, 51, 53, 66, 70–74, 86–95, 96, 106, 107, 108, 124
Rabí, Brigadier Jesús, 281, 353
Rawlins, John A., 201, 204–05, 209, 210, 211, 212
Readings, in factories, 143–47
Reciprocity, 337–40
Reform, failure of, 162–64; movement in Cuba, 127, 128, 131–33, 148–65
Reformist party, 125, 131, 177
Reglamento de Libertos, 194
Republican party, U.S., 119–20, 242, 338
Republican Society of Cuba and Puerto Rico, 127–28, 163–64
Revolución Gloriosa, La, 168–69
Revolutionary Committee, 284, 285, 287
Roberts, López, 213, 224
Robertson, William H., 80
Rochdale plan, 143
Rodas, Antonio Caballero de, 181, 213, 227
Rodríguez, Carlos Rafael, 135
Rodríguez, Rafael, 312
Roig de Leuchsenring, Emilio, 238
Roig y San Martín, Enrique, 301–03
Roloff, General Carlos, 260, 348
Royal Economic Society, 137
Rubens, Horatio S., 331, 349
Saco, José Antonio, 9–10, 14, 15–18, 126, 127, 135, 152, 158, 160
Salamanca, Manuel, 313, 316
Salas, César, 354, 355
Sánchez, Limbano, 261
Sánchez, Serafín, 280, 281, 282, 286, 327, 348
Sanguily, General Julio, 270, 272, 327, 350
Sanguily, Manuel, 59, 235–36, 314
Santo Domingo, 33, 53, 82, 100, 164, 175, 188, 211, 212, 217, 254, 308, 348, 349, 351, 354, 356
Sartorius revolt, 329–30
Saunders, Romulus M., 23, 25, 26, 27–28
Schlessinger, Louis, 54–55
Scottron, Samuel R., 242, 269–70
Secession, of Southern states, 67, 121–22
Second War for Independence, 347–58
Sellén, Francisco, 141
Serra, Rafael, 318, 319
Serrano, Francisco, 107, 125, 149, 162, 169
Seward, William H., 31, 122, 144

Sherman, General William T., 167n.
Sickles, Daniel E., 207, 210, 222, 227, 240, 247
Siglistas, 126
Sigur, Laurence J., 49, 53, 56
Slave revolts, in Cuba, 10, 133; in U.S., 32
Slavery, in Cuba, abolition, 292–93, 311; as issue in Ten Years' War, 172–73, 190–95, 220–23, 228–30, 232–35, 241–43, 248–49, 253–54, 268–70, 274; decline, 129–30; dominates Cuban economy, 136; effect of Pezuela's decrees on, 76–85; number of slaves, 16, 19, 128, 192; proposals for abolition, 127–28, 156–59, 276–77; relation to annexationism, 14–17, 31–36, 38–39
Slidell, John, 83, 89, 118, 120, 121
Smith, Cotesworth Pinckney, 49, 53
Smith, William, 68, 69, 70
Socialists, 183n., 302–03, 313, 324
Sociedad Abolicionista, 153
Sociedad Democrática de los Amigos de América, 128n., 164
Sollers, August R., 103
Soulé, Pierre, 67, 71, 72, 96–104
Southern slave empire, 112–14
Spain, confident of U.S. government support, 222–23; Constitution of 1876, 290–91; despotic rule in Cuba, 34–35; economic restrictions in Cuba, 12; forces in, favoring war against Cuba, 182; "Glorious Revolution," 168–69; liberals in, 149–50, 208; monarchy re-established, 277; Narváez government, 153–54; new taxes on Cuba, 162; refuses to fulfill Pact of Zanjón, 278–79; rejects U.S. proposal to purchase Cuba, 26–28; resists British pressure on slavery, 46, 62, 75, 115; republic, 226–27, 250–51; revolution, 86; role of Soulé, 96–99; and slavery in Cuba, 220–23; Socialists, 183n.; threatens to emancipate slaves in Cuba, 19
Spanish Abolitionist Society, 221
Spanish bonds, 76, 97, 116–17
Spanish party, 183, 219
Spotorno, Juan B., 255–56
Stead, W. T., 341
Stephens, Alexander H., 89
Sterling, Don Adolfo Márquez, 28, 278
Strikes, in Cuba, 147, 300–01; in U.S., 330–31, 335–36

Sugar, 12, 128–30, 131–32, 241, 293–300
Sumner, Charles, 222
Surí, Manuel, 289
Tacón, Miguel, 9, 11
Tampa, 147, 256, 320–21, 322, 325, 328, 330, 349
Taylor, Zachary, 29, 56, 62, 63
Ten Years' War (1868–1878), and abolition of slavery, 172–73, 190–95, 220–23, 228–30, 232–35, 241–43, 248–49, 253–54, 268–70; collapse of Cuban cause, 261–64; early phase, 174–83; end of, 271–74; fear of Negro during, 237–38, 258–60; final phase, 252–75; guerrilla warfare, 185–89, 194–95, 203, 275; internal dissensions among Cubans, 231–34, 255–56, 258–61, 263; invasion of West, 228–31, 233–37, 254–56, 260; Latin American support for Cuba, 198–99; middle phase, 224–39; outbreak, 169–73; Pact of Zanjón, 265–71, 275; Protest of Baraguá, 267–70, 273; reasons for failure, 275; role of Negroes, 242n.; role of tobacco workers, 256, 272; role of wealthy Cubans, 256, 267–68, 272; role of U.S., 199–223, 240–52; significance for Cuba, 275; slaying of medical students, 225; terror against Cuban people, 195–96, 224–25; war unfolds, 184–97
Texas, annexation of as a guide for Cuba, 41, 47, 58, 63–64, 73, 86, 91
Thrasher, John S., 10, 88, 90
Tobacco workers, 136–37, 138–39, 140, 142, 147, 256, 272, 300, 308–09, 330–31, 366
Tolón, Miguel Teurbe, 44, 50, 71, 72
Unconditional Spanish party, 150
United States, and "Africanization of Cuba," 83–84; and African slave trade, 15; and annexation of Cuba, 19–29, 30–33, 62–63; Civil War, 130–35; conditions of workers, 334–35; and Cuban belligerency, 200–03; demand for invasion of Cuba, 79–82; denounced by Latin America, 110–11; economic interests of citizens in Cuba, 12; efforts to mediate in Ten Years' War, 248–50; emergence of imperialism, 337–46; growth of monopoly, 334–35; and independence of Cuba, 199–223, 240–52, 257–58, 262, 274; investments in Cuba by citizens, 295–97; plan to mediate war between Cuba and Spain, 206–10; plan to purchase Cuba 20–29, 86–87, 97–99, 100, 116–21; power of big business, 336–37; role in fastening slavery on Cuba, 105; support for Cuban independence, 200–03, 205–06, 211, 241–43, 244–45, 251–52, 274
Urban, Chester Stanley, 51, 85
Valdés, Gerónimo, 42
Valle, Antonio Hurtado de, 198, 233
Valmaseda, Count of, 176, 181, 196, 224, 227, 231, 254
Vanderbilt, Cornelius, 109
Villanueva Theatre, 179–80
Villaverde, Cirilo, 10, 47, 49
Virginius affair, 233, 244–47
Volunteer corps, 176–83, 195–96, 223–25, 240
Walker, Samuel R., 90–91
Walker, William, 108–14
Webster, Daniel, 63
Webster-Ashburton Treaty, 15n.
Westcott, James D., 22–23
Whitman, Walt, 333
Wilmot Proviso, 32
Wilson-Gorman tariff, 299
Worth, General William J., 24, 25, 42, 43
Young America, 67, 70, 93
Zenea, Juan Clemente, 224

www.ingramcontent.com/pod-product-compliance
Lightning Source LLC
Chambersburg PA
CBHW020938180426
43194CB00038B/223